Ethnic Groups of North, East, and Central Asia

Recent Titles in
Ethnic Groups of the World

Ethnic Groups of Africa and the Middle East: An Encyclopedia
John A. Shoup

Ethnic Groups of Europe: An Encyclopedia
Jeffrey E. Cole, Editor

Ethnic Groups of South Asia and the Pacific: An Encyclopedia
James B. Minahan

Ethnic Groups of the Americas: An Encyclopedia
James B. Minahan

Ethnic Groups of North, East, and Central Asia

AN ENCYCLOPEDIA

James B. Minahan

Ethnic Groups of the World

Santa Barbara, California • Denver, Colorado • Oxford, England

Library of Congress Cataloging-in-Publication Data

Minahan, James.
  Ethnic groups of North, East, and Central Asia : an encyclopedia / James B. Minahan.
    pages cm. — (Ethnic groups of the world)
  Includes bibliographical references and index.
  ISBN 978-1-61069-017-1 (hardback) — ISBN 978-1-61069-018-8 (ebook)
1. Ethnology—Asia, Central—Encyclopedias.   2. Ethnology—East Asia—
Encyclopedias.   3. Ethnology—Caucasus Region—Encyclopedias.   I. Title.
  DS328.3.M56   2014
  305.8009503—dc23   2013033993

ISBN: 978-1-61069-017-1
EISBN: 978-1-61069-018-8

18   17   16   15   14   1   2   3   4   5

This book is also available on the World Wide Web as an eBook.
Visit www.abc-clio.com for details.

ABC-CLIO, LLC
130 Cremona Drive, P.O. Box 1911
Santa Barbara, California 93116-1911

This book is printed on acid-free paper ∞

Manufactured in the United States of America

Contents

Preface

A clear understanding of ethnicity and the many ethnic groups that populate the continents of our increasingly connected world is crucial to the tolerance and acceptance needed to maintain world peace and prosperity. Intolerance and a lack of knowledge of other cultures and religions have greatly contributed to the violence and wars that continue to disrupt large parts of the world. The purpose of this handbook to the cultures and ethnic groups of North, East, and Central Asia is to provide readers with an up-to-date, accurate, and easy-to-understand guide to the many ethnic groups inhabiting the vast territories of Asia. This book and the others in the series make up an essential guide to the world at a time when ethnicity, ethnic relations, immigration, and regional conflicts are important factors in global relations. The diversity of the world's numerous ethnic groups, cultures, and religions not only is one of humanity's great strengths, but is also an area of contention and misunderstanding. Ethnicity is one of the most important elements of modern culture, and an understanding of different cultures is a fundamental part of understanding the world around us.

Ethnic Groups of North, East, and Central Asia: An Encyclopedia forms part of the Ethnic Groups of the World series, which includes most of the world's many ethnic groups and cultures. This volume on the peoples and ethnic groups of North, East, and Central Asia, like the other volumes in the series, includes short chapters on each of the important ethnic groups inhabiting this vast geographic region. The individual entries are dedicated to the ethnic groups that make up the populations of the countries of the region. The value of this volume, and of the series, is evident in the up-to-date information and the clear historical evolution of the region's many ethnic groups and cultures.

Ethnic reference books published in the last decade often address only the nations and their core populations, relegating the numerous minority ethnic groups to brief paragraphs or simply footnotes. The selection of the groups to include in this volume presented numerous obstacles, not the least of which was the application of a uniform set of criteria. The ethnic groups presented in this volume range from the core or national populations of each of the region's nation-states to the many small, often virtually unknown ethnic groups that are usually ignored in texts and reference books on that region. The cultures and ethnic groups presented in this book include those societies that developed from ancient ethnicities, isolated tribal groups, and the modern cultures that make up the population of this vast and important region. Some of the ethnic groups presented in the book developed relatively recently as distinct cultures, arising from adherence to distinct cultural or religious traditions or as the by-products of collapsing empires and states. The selection of the ethnic groups to be included in this volume required a set of criteria based on a common history, language, religion, geographic location, a shared culture, self-identification, or identification as a distinct group by neighboring peoples. In general, strict observance to information published by the region's national governments has been avoided as these publications are often determined by local political considerations and the diverse policies that govern ethnic policies in each of the regional countries. The difficulties of researching the ethnic diversity of the region were complicated by a general lack of consensus on what attributes a group must exhibit to be considered a distinct culture. For example, the 56 officially recognized ethnic groups of the People's Republic of China are included though many of these official groups include subgroups that are geographically, historically, and culturally quite distinct. Other countries count ethnic minorities by language use, religion, or geographic location, often including large ethnic populations that remain aware of their separate ethnicity, as part of the country's core population.

Ethnic Groups of North, East, and Central Asia: An Encyclopedia covers the evolution of the peoples of North, East, and Central Asia from the earliest periods of their recorded histories to the present day. Each ethnic survey includes information on the culture, language or languages, religion, and geographic distribution of each group. The ethnic groups of this vast and diverse region include many that are often misunderstood, ignored, or are virtually unknown outside their geographic homelands. They represent a fascinating kaleidoscope of the human geography of Northeastern Asia. The ethnic surveys highlight the historical, political, cultural, and religious development of each of the included ethnic groups and the relationships between the group and neighboring peoples and the national governments of the region.

Some of the cultures and ethnic groups presented in this book will be familiar as the core nationality of the nation-states of the region, but the majority of the surveys are devoted to ethnic groups that are less well known though their distinct histories, cultures, and languages form important elements in the national society of each of the regional nations. Since some of the group names will not be familiar to many readers, the group's official or preferred name along with alternate and historical names have been listed. The group names often represent a colonial or imposed name, often considered derogatory or representing a long history of abuse and oppression by the governing nationality.

Each of the ethnic surveys is divided into several parts: the official or preferred name of the group, plus alternate names; the major population concentrations and other areas with representative communities; the estimated population of the group; a brief outline of the group's linguistic and religious affiliations; and a history of the ethnic group up to the 19th century, the group's cultural traits and traditions, and a history of the group from the 19th century to the present. Each ethnic survey is accompanied by a suggested reading list, including reference books, Web sites, and individual articles. The population figures are the author's estimates for 2013 based on a large number of sources, both official and unofficial. The population figures are gleaned from the latest census figures, where available, government and unofficial estimates, and population figures published by the ethnic groups themselves. A number of national governments in the region do not enumerate the minority ethnic populations within their borders, which makes reliance on other, often less reliable, population estimates a necessity. Since each of the ethnic groups in the book has its own history of events, conflicts, and development, the greater part of each survey has been devoted to the historical evolution of the ethnic group with a historical development that encompasses the consolidation, evolution, and territorial dispersion of each of the ethnic groups from its earliest recorded history to the present day.

This volume presents both the historical core nationalities of the regional nations and the many ethnic groups that make up the remainder of the population of each country. The many ethnic groups of the region, having survived conquests, colonization, and often ethnic hostility, are increasingly demanding recognition of their distinct identities as part of our increasingly integrated world. This book is offered as a unique reference source for the ethnic renaissance that is spearheading one of the most widespread and most powerful political movements of the 21st century—the reemergence of ethnic, religious, and regional cultures as the basis of identity.

Introduction

Robert André LaFleur[1]
András Boros-Kazai

Multilayered Culture

Imagine a little doll, six inches high and clad in spectacular ornaments, with bright-colored clothing and highly gendered—in almost all cases *female*—rendering. Next to it stands another small figure, of the same height and arrayed in different ornaments and colors. Another female. As your gaze widens, you see more and more dolls, more and more ornaments, and many more colors. You have to take a step back until you can grasp the full range of 56 little figurines, each representing a distinctive—yet powerfully linked—place in a complex social world. The close-up picture will tell you the story of each doll. Only the step-back perspective will tell you how they happen to fit together.

This is not fiction. The dolls are part of an elaborate construction of ethnicity that is known as the 56 ethnic groups of the People's Republic of China. They are just a small glimpse into ways that the ethnicity plays out in today's Asian world, with ethnic groups adjoining and sometimes overlaying one another in what we might think of as a truly cavernous room—like a large reception hall in a government building. The ethnic groups are big, diverse, and truly *different.* The reception hall contains all of them under its roof. This is the image conveyed if you buy a set of the 56 figurines, walk to the fifth floor of the Shanghai Municipal Museum, or watch the annual New Year's Eve gala produced by CCTV, which has almost half a billion viewers for every late-January or early February show. The groups—each in dynamic movements and splendid dress—swirl and twirl through almost half of the four-hour television production. You might even remember the Beijing Olympic Games opening ceremonies in 2008. Again, the 56 ethnic groups had a prominent place, far beyond the 10 percent of the population that 55 of them occupy.

And it is 56—not 60 (as the cosmologists might prefer) or 70. There are 56 officially recognized ethnic groups in today's People's Republic of China. These classifications have become a standard that has dominated the discussion of ethnicity in China—and, in profound ways throughout the rest of East Asia—for the last 60 years. Fifty-six discrete ethnic units, like rugs in a vast open hall.

Think about the picture! This image of rugs in a great hall works well to clarify our mental picture of the dolls. Asian ethnic groups have all sorts of things that hold them together as independent self-defined entities—like the swirling one-of-a-kind designs on a Central Asian rug. First, imagine more than a hundred rugs spread neatly through the vast space. Got it? Now, imagine further a rousing event in the big hall. People come and go, assortments shuffle and shift, and great movements shake things up (dancing, festivities, and a few fistfights). At the end of the evening, the rugs have moved, overlapped, folded, and changed their appearances.

Now imagine 20 or more centuries of those events in that very same hall.

The rugs don't look quite so neatly organized anymore, and numerous changes have taken place that will alter their configurations. Even the rugs themselves have been replaced—updated to fit whatever customs or particular needs of the present are in place. No matter how often the custodians rearrange the rugs, they keep moving, shifting, changing place, and running up against other rugs.

Ethnicity is a lot like that.

* * * * * *

This book presents well-researched portraits of over 100 ethnic groups in Asia. It is a great credit to the author, James Minahan, that each entry reads with an accuracy and scholarly care that allows readers to grasp both key points about each group and a sense of their history, changing cultures, and social lives. One of the great advantages of encyclopedic works like this one is the manner in which readers can focus on individual elements—like the rugs in our imaginary hall or the individual figurines in the Chinese ethnic doll set—and get a sense of their weave, texture, thickness, color, and shape. Without this, we would have only generalities. This book will give you the specifics and provide you with ways of thinking about particular ethnic groups in Asia *and* the dynamics of their interactions.

This last idea also conveys a hidden challenge. Encyclopedic works contain a small disadvantage within their structures, because individual entries cannot, in themselves, show the dynamics of large-scale movements, patterned change, and historical upheaval. It cannot, in short, tell how the rugs came to be all heaped into piles upon the floor—in the manner of, say, 3,000 years of intermarriage, movement, and travel along all directions of the Silk Road, and seafaring will do.

The individual entries masterfully tell bits of that story from the perspective of each group. That is their job. It is the purpose of this introduction to make explicit some of the larger matters that are difficult to see through the lens of individual ethnic group entries. As the title of this volume is *Ethnic Groups of North, Central, and East Asia: An Encyclopedia*, let's think of this introduction as "Ethnicity in North, Central, and East Asia" . . . or even "Asian Ethnicities." It is as though we are supplementing the high-powered microscope used to create the individual entries and adding to our research a wide-angle lens camera. This well help readers see how entries as disparate as "Tajik" and "Ainu" can be discussed in a wider framework and how ethnicity has come to play a powerful role not only in contemporary nationalism throughout Asia, but in a burgeoning tourism industry as well.

Defining Terms—Asian Ethnic Groups

Let us begin with three keywords from our title—Asian, ethnic, and group. The basic terms are surprisingly challenging, and even the modifiers (North, Central, and East) are more complicated than they might seem at first glance. Let's spend a little bit of time unpacking them and see how they might fit together to make reading of the individual entries both more accessible and more useful. "Asian Ethnic Groups" is a powerful combination of words, and they will sustain us through all of the discussions in this book.

"Asian"

First, what do we mean by "Asia"? Europe and Asia blend together in complex ways, and the history of each has intersected at several points over the past 3,000 years. "Asia" is a considerable landmass and has no obvious borders. It is not like Africa, North America, or South America in that way. In our cartographic experiences from school, we can "picture" them, even if we must add on the linkages and appendages (such as Madagascar or the Falkland Islands) that complicate our mental sketches.

As any 13th-century Mongol schoolchild could tell us, Asia blends fairly seamlessly into Europe, and at least one conquering force—those very same Mongol—negotiated the land far better than they did when trying to put out to sea. While it is easy enough to picture "East Asia" and "Western Europe," there is a great deal of blending in-between, and the histories of empires, nation-states, and ethnic groups in what is sometimes called "Eastern Europe" and "Western Asia" (or even the Near East, in an earlier idiom) are uncertain.

That very uncertainty is what makes the topic both perplexing and fascinating. Asia, in short, is a large span of landmass; "Eurasia" is even bigger, and much more confusing (even the word—a portmanteau—speaks to uncertainty). The beauty of this volume is that it does not try to cut things too finely into pieces. To be manageable, of course, each encyclopedia in the Ethnic Groups of the World series has had to define a part of the world. These are large and span many historical and cultural patterns, however. This volume, covering North, Central, and Eastern Asia, has the enormous advantage of bringing Central and Northern Asia fully into a picture that has been dominated too much by the powerful (and often overpowering) cultural influence of Chinese civilization. By widening the picture—and even going beyond the 56 ethnic groups officially recognized by the People's Republic of China—this volume complicates the picture of Asian ethnicity in a way that will help every reader understand it more deeply.

"Ethnic"

The term *Asia* seems complicated, but *ethnic* is even more so. The greatest challenge in studying ethnicity lies in the very orientation of this volume. It is impossible to understand the units that make it up without careful study of individual groups. We cannot study themes and adequately understand what makes the groups sense their togetherness, their history, and the possibility of a shared future. On the other hand, no understanding of individual groups can provide us with the larger questions that make up this introduction. What we have all over the world, really, is bundles of overlapping ethnicities. There is, in short, more to our studies than analyzing the functioning of individual engine parts—smooth, separable systems working together in a powerful machine. This latter image is precisely what the People's Republic of China is trying to convey in its own presentation of ethnicity, and it is a powerful message (and by no means untrue). The problem is that ethnicity only seems to be clear and separable. To the extent that we perpetuate the "parts of the whole" rhetoric, we fail to underline just how much merging and assimilating and, frankly, fighting has gone into every aspect of ethnic discussion in Asia—and beyond.

This leads to our next problematic definition, "group."

"Group"

Let's use a quick example. Even delineating an ethnic group in a few short lines can be highly problematic. The following line is paraphrased from a widely circulated Chinese tourism text. Just the following single sentence presents several challenges.

> . . . the Bai people live near Lake Er in Yunnan Province, wear colorful clothing, and make toys of bamboo . . . [2]

Although it may seem innocuous, it is actually quite ideological and pointed. While none of the information is wrong, it creates a picture that essentializes (carves into an essence) the Bai people. It just sounds more objective than it is and creates a picture of Bai people as "like" these characterizations. Part of the problem with the sentence is the combination of happy images that seem to convey a life different from the toil and tussle in busy, haggling, urban centers. This distancing from the ordinary challenges of life happens in almost every characterization we can make when describing groups. This happens in almost every characterization we can make when describing groups. Even in the best writing about *individual ethnic groupings*, it is hard to convey dynamism and change, so we are left with the implication that such groups are like this or like that. Yet if we study the dynamism and change, we often learn only fragments of information about the groups themselves. We learn what makes them interact, but not as much about what makes them cohere.

There is no solution to this problem other than to turn one's gaze smaller and larger in sequence—to remember large themes that link the histories of groups and to study the particulars of individual groups (and individuals within them) as well. In short, the very idea of ethnic groupings creates a profoundly mixed-up jumble of subjectivities that are not told well if they seem too clear and clean—like the minority group dolls in native dress that can be purchased in department stores all over China.

This introduction and volume should be thought of as a variation on those paper dolls, in which the very same clearly articulated and perfectly dressed figures start blending together, fighting, resolving disputes, coming to power, losing, and intermarrying . . . over 3,000 years of history. Imagine the ethnic dolls with children and grandchildren of their own, living in cities of many millions, trying to get top-rate educations, worrying about global market forces, and concerned about health care in their old age. Now imagine many generations of intermarrying, moving, worrying, and change. That is Asia today. Ethnicity—it is supposed to be complicated, and the best way to read this volume is to move back-and-forth between the entries themselves, this introduction, and then other entries that complicate and further our picture of Asian ethnic groups.

Let's turn now to some of the themes and patterns that link large swaths of Asia throughout its history, and especially in the dynamics of the present day. Northern and Central Asia are related in challenging ways to a resurgent China and the rest of the East Asian world.

North and Central Asia

The three large bioenvironmental zones of Central and Northeastern Asia are the *tundra*, the *taiga*, and the *steppe*. These constitute a large portion of the region, with the mountainous areas and strings of desert oases making up a much smaller—although culturally more important—portion of Central and Northeastern Asia. The region is heavily landlocked, and even the coastal regions do not have ready access to the outside world. Scarcity—of resources, opportunities, and even people—is a determinate common factor throughout the region. Peoples settling here faced great difficulties if they wished to survive, and archaeological research tells us that a number of them, beyond more than 120 distinct *ethnie* surviving to this day, did not meet this challenge. They needed great inventiveness and readiness to adapt to their material circumstances. An entirely unique (one might say revolutionary) lifestyle, of *pastoral nomadism*, is perhaps the best example of such widespread and historically successful innovation.

What we can learn from this is that potentially nation-creating ethnic identity in Central and Northeastern Asia was based less on shared language and common history (often one of the most frequently cited factors of ethnicity), and more on circumstances and things tied to basic survival. On one level, this can be narrowed down to a few items provided by nature. For most of the inland regions, the crucial enablers in the struggle to survive were the horse and the various livestock (primarily camel and sheep) that provided livelihood for their cultivators. In the coastal or riverine areas, fish or sea mammals are similarly requisite sources of survival. In this sense, our search for primary distinction (identity) may justifiably lead us to refer to fish people along the maritime coasts, horse people on the vast grasslands, and reindeer people on the tundra. It may be tempting to say, therefore, that the development of ethnic identity in Central and Northeastern Asia was primarily based on environmental factors that determine lifestyle. After all, we know that Chinggis (Genghis) Khan claimed to rule not merely over the Mongol or the various Mongol *ethnie*, but rather "all of the people living under the felt tent."

Nonmaterial aspects of traditional life in Central and Northeastern Asia exhibit similar broadly applicable elements. Nature's power, in all of its manifestations, was ever present and ever felt. The incessant struggle for survival provided little opportunity for peoples of the region to indulge in contemplation about this harsh reality. Superhuman forces—wind, cold, rain, thunder, and frost—had to be feared, respected, and pacified. Their aid had to be sought and purchased for every undertaking. At the very least, every effort had to be made to avoid the supernatural anger. This is something that histories of more temperate climates do not usually consider—at least in their life-taking ferocity. It is one of the key differences between the worlds of Central and Northern Asia, on the one hand, and the more southerly climates that prevailed in much of China, Japan, Taiwan, the Philippines, and southern stretches in Korea. For guidance, one had to turn to the world beyond the living, the spirit world. Gifted and practiced men and women, the *shaman*, performed the crucial tasks of guiding and mediating the communication with this other world—the world that could bring great benefits or utter disaster. Rituals and practices aimed at achieving the requisite state of ecstasy bear considerable similarity among the region's peoples.

In looking for the roots of ethnic identity in Central and Northeastern Asia, we must turn to kinship, lineage, and, in the end, the notion of belonging. A common utterance that speaks to kinship, fictive kinship, and identification with locality addresses this:

> Me against my brother; me and my brother against the neighbor; me and my brother and our neighbor against the next village; me and my brother and our neighboring villages against outsiders.

The daily task of survival—from landing a sea mammal to tending a large flock of sheep—called for coordinated group effort. It was natural for every member of a family to participate, but greater tasks called for larger teams. This resulted in blood ties being extended through fictive kinship networks to work- and habitat-related connections, with eventual development of shared habits, customs, and language. The formation of clans and tribes was formalized by the (self-) naming and (self-) identification of these human communities—a major cultural development that would influence the history of Asia in profound ways.

Small groups tended to organize themselves along the lines of extended families. However, clans and tribes needed to be controlled, organized, and administered in new ways. Rulership in Central and Northeastern Asia tended to reflect the inhabitants' views of transcendental authority. Although there existed a concept of a supreme divinity (e.g., the sky-god Tengri), a number of other divine forces were also recognized and celebrated. Similarly, earthly rulership often included a modicum of specialization. A military leader was tasked with bringing success in wars, while another leader was often empowered with the administration of daily life in peacetime—with perhaps another to provide spiritual guidance.

Although this particular configuration of rulership was eliminated by the power gained by monotheist Islamic rulers after the 16th century, it is still indicative of the multidimensional nature of Central and Northeastern Asian rule during much of the last 3,000 years. It would parallel the history of Chinese civilization (which it bordered—from the central and northeastern perspective—to the east and the south) in some ways and diverge profoundly from it in others. Yet one stark reality should be noted. In the last 1,000 years of Chinese history, northern groups from outside of China proper have ruled large swaths of the Middle Kingdom for more than half of that time. In short, it is not an option to pretend that Chinese civilization can be viewed in isolation from its northern and central neighbors, no matter how often popular textbooks seem to imply that very notion.

* * * * * *

Today's Central and Northern Asia has a complex dynamic that has been shaped by the changing power—and financial—configurations of the former Soviet Union, today's Russia, and a growing power from the People's Republic of China. The first things to contemplate are the vast spaces between urban centers and trading networks. Unlike the major urban centers in Japan, Korea, and China—where large cities dot the most common thoroughfares along the Tokkaido, or Eastern Sea Route, the coastal line in China from Tianjin to Fuzhou, or even the links from the southern tip of the Korean peninsula to the mid-north—travel respites of any size are far more scarce in Central and Northern Asia.

The reasons for the urban and rural developments are as distinct as the differences in the geographic areas. To begin, it is often difficult to place the precise settlement date of a Mongolian city, and for practical reasons that are based in the nomadic history of the region. The modern cities are evolved from camps or towns consisting of tents or movable dwellings. Ulan Bator is just one example of a mobile city that created a seminomadic patterning of stasis and change, which makes it impossible to place an origin, as one can do for Kaifeng or Rome. It literally and figuratively moved up and down the river and has been, as city boosters might say, "a city on the move."

The underpinnings of this idea can tell us a great deal about life beyond the settled regions of China. To begin, the presence of constant agriculture (even in conditions in the north and northwest that were not particularly well suited to it) marks a great break in the growth of civilization and empire. The early Chinese historian Sima Qian wrote that little children in the far north and northwest grew up riding sheep, sitting up in their already formidable stirrups, and shooting rodents on the prairie, even at a tender age.[3] The contrast with the children of cultivated China—and, of course, this phrase has several connotations—is dramatic. Although Mongol, Manchu, and many groups that were prominent in earlier Asian history (e.g., the Xiongnu) could wreak havoc on the Chinese plains, they were not built for a lasting presence unless they found ways to accommodate the presence of a vastly larger and far more urban agricultural and commercial population.

In the north, even today, the distance between even small cities is often vast. Today, the Jeep, long-distance trucks, as well as several train routes figure in long journeys. Even the centers themselves are quite intriguing when we contemplate the history of these transportation nodes. Many began as Buddhist monastic sites and grew only slowly into communities with a presence beyond the Buddhist orders. Even in their early incarnations as small cities, they partook of what the French ethnographer Marcel Mauss described as a dynamic of travel and respite.[4] The centers provided places of rest and regeneration in the cold months, before pastoralists would take their herds to farther-flung destinations in the spring, summer, and autumn. This patterning of movement and reconnection is so much a part of Central and Northern Asian life that it must be considered as one of the great dynamics in its history.

The contrast with settled areas of China and Korea (and Japan, although no conqueror penetrated its shores until the 20th century) is enormous. Settled agricultural life, with its concomitant market centers and precise agricultural calendar, created a dynamic that led to great domination in all cases, except when northern (or central) groups organized into large conquering forces. The latter happened several times in the past 1,000 years of Chinese history (and that narrative takes up, arguably, more than half of that time). This is hardly insignificant, and these entries will help to show the ethnic persistence of some of these groups.

* * * * * *

The challenge for understanding Central and Northern China today lies in balancing the dynamic histories of these areas with a rapidly changing economic, political, and social climate. The central, northern, and northeastern areas of Asia have figured prominently in the larger East Asian historical narrative, but only for several centuries at a time. Today's areas are in the vice-lock of an aging (former) Soviet Union and a growing and increasingly aggressive People's Republic of China. This can be seen in several examples that would ordinarily be overlooked by analysts. Which "way" do the railroads run? Well, mostly they still run to Moscow, or at least its environs. On the other hand, which way do the trucks drive? To Beijing (or its environs)—and even on bumpy, problematic, and uneven roads. The earlier pull of the former Soviet Union still affects mining cities all over Northern Asia. The same pressure plays into all of the politics and economics of the Central Asian countries, which have always been an amalgamation of complex ethnic, religious, and economic entities.

There is nothing analytically simple about understanding this region. For example, Buddhism is a powerful force that is not tied—at least not in a direct sense—to environment or the modes of production. As in China, and the rest of Asia, it has a powerful place in the history of the region and affects everything from the written languages of the various central and northern regions to their traditions. Anthropologists describe complex levels of fictional kinship that can be extended very far into personal family networks or kept evasively distant, depending on the situation.

Finally, linguists have noted many of these dynamics for the past two millennia. Even the Ballad of Mulan is widely known to be of Turkic descent.[5] The entire history of East Asia has much more to do with the cultural dynamics of Central and Northern Asia than many current textbooks show. And, indeed, even the ethnic histories of Eastern Asia show a complex mixing of ethnicity, region, and circumstance than we ordinarily see in overviews of the region.

* * * * * *

We turn now to a consideration of East Asia and China's pivotal historical role within it.

East Asia

The work of survival dominates in the history of East Asian ethnic groups, as well. The intensity of concern tends to flow along a northwest–southeast trajectory, and one historian of climatic history has noted that rainfall can be configured from very small amounts—barely tolerant of agricultural life—in the far northwest to abundant and plentiful amounts of water in the far southeast.[6] These general patterns prevail throughout the rest of East Asia. As one moves southeast, the harsh environment of Central and Northeastern Asia is replaced by an environment far more conducive to agriculture.

It should never be forgotten, however, that the very same acclimation to farming and subsistence on plots of land—the very backbone of Chinese, Japanese, and much of Korean civilization—held one of the key weak points for agriculturalists in East Asia. The same harsh northern climates that forged a horse-riding, sheepherding society helped facilitate punitive moves against the seemingly indolent and isolated farmers to the south.

China as Center (of a Sort)

China dominates discussions of ethnicity in East Asia on profound levels that are sometimes difficult to sort out after many centuries, and even millennia, of movement and change. For Westerners, a good way to think about Chinese culture (the analogy is partial, but fruitful) is akin to Greek and Hellenistic culture. When Jean Jacques Rousseau read Plato in the 18th century, he was surely reading a Greek author. Just as much, though, he was reading part of his own heritage. It was no longer *only* Greek. It was Western civilization, too. In a very similar fashion, a young scholar in Tokugawa Japan in the 18th century might read Confucius, the historian Sima Qian, or the philosopher Wang Yangming. He, too, was reading foreign authors—but only in one sense, and by no means, the most important one. In a far more significant way, he was reading his own civilization's great works, for they were as much a part of Japanese life (perhaps even more so in neighboring Korea) as they were in China. It was bigger than China as a nation or empire. It was *East Asian* civilization, which was merely born in China. China seems dominant only if we cannot see the ways in which internal dynamics in Japan and Korea—and in many of the areas to the north and west—worked.

This analogy leads us directly to the largest countries in East Asia—China, Japan, and Korea. In each of them, a kind of cultural dominance (an overwhelming ethnicity) had the potential to destroy diversity and imprint itself as a kind of monoculture. Yet, just as Japan and Korea developed distinctive identities within a larger East Asian culture (while reading the classics from China), so, too, did China's, Japan's, and Korea's ethnic groups both adapt to and gain distinction from the overwhelming numbers of the majority.

Their sheer size should not be forgotten, though. The largest ethnic groups of China, Japan, and Korea so dominate their countries' histories that they need to be understood "up front" and not as mere appendages to an "equal" treatment of several hundred ethnic groups. It is not—let this be absolutely clear—because they are more important. It is simply that the way each nation-state has developed, and the way in which people have studied ethnicity, is profoundly shaped by three groups, each of which constitute 90 or more percent of their countries' ethnic definition. These are Han in China, Yamato in Japan, and the Korean ethnic group in Korea. Each has been associated with the very history of each civilization, and it is only in the study of ethnicity that we can begin to piece together how these groups themselves have dominated, assimilated, modified, and changed.

Han Ethnicity (China)

The Han ethnic group is by far the majority in today's China, with more than 90 percent of the population identified under that category. This has been true for much of Chinese history, but with somewhat less dominant numbers. Indeed, one reading of Chinese history in the past 3,000 years shows a profound and sometimes highly divisive back-and-forth between Han Chinese and what today have come to be called minority groups. The first outright possession of China proper by non-Han rulers occurred during the Yuan dynasty (1368–1644), when Mongolian leaders ruled from Beijing. At no point was non-Han occupation more dramatically shown than in the Qing dynasty (1644–1911), when a Manchu domination of the imperial machinery penetrated into Han social life to the point that Han men were forced to wear the queue as a sign of submission that enveloped the vast majority of the Chinese population.

The more common case in Chinese history has been for the Han ethnic group to dominate and to portray Chinese history as a history of the Han peoples. Courses on China throughout the world have been so heavily influenced by this pattern that it is sometimes difficult to see that the Han ethnicity, even though it forms an enormous majority, is still but one cog in the vast interplay of ethnic interchange that has made up Chinese history and culture for the past 3,000 years.

Han is Chinese, but Han is not China.

The Han ethnic majority played a sizable role in China's history, and the growth of the Chinese state over the subsequent 20 centuries is a story of ethnic movement to and from the Yellow River drainage area, where most of China's early history played out. It should never be forgotten that, from well before the Han dynasty (206 BCE–220 CE) onward, there is a continuous and never-ending engagement with territories and peoples of non-Han origin. It is one of the most dramatic themes of Chinese history, but it is underplayed in Chinese textbooks to such an extent that one might quite mistakenly assume Chinese history to be a record of the Han peoples.

This is an error that this book corrects through many dozens of examples of rich individual culture, growth, and decline.

To say that the other 55 ethnic groups (there were actually many hundreds) simply played a supporting role is nonsense. To be sure, they were integrated into a complex and growing Chinese state, and that has continued in one way or another up to the present. This integration is often interpreted as a simplistic kind of assimilation, and textbooks not infrequently speak of the way that outsiders almost invariably adapted to Chinese (predominantly Han) culture. Far more rarely do they speak of significant changes that worked in the other direction—with outsiders (from the perspective of the narrative) deeply influencing Han culture. The fact that this was so is indisputable, but it is often only tacitly acknowledged in history textbooks in the Chinese-speaking world. In fact, the cultural and linguistic blending was a constant in Chinese history, and it can be seen in two broad sets of movements.

The first came with pressures from the north, as peoples from northeastern and northwestern territories made incursions into China. Some of these, even as early as the Zhou period (ca. 1050–221 BCE), were military incursions that forced Han Chinese out of their home territories. Others were part of the almost continual diplomatic give-and-take between a centralized Chinese state and northern territorial groups. Intermarriage and various embassies played an enormous role in the cultural interactions between peoples.

The second major wave of interaction resulted from the combined influence of territorial expansion, on the one hand, and the Yellow River valley being occupied by northerners, forcing Han peoples ever southward, on the other. This process, which can be seen even in Confucius's *Analects*, accelerated in earnest in the first millennium of the Common Era. Large ethnic groups in the southeast were increasingly confronted by the growing commercial and governmental reach of the central state. Many dozens of ethnic groups in southwestern China also began a long process of acculturation at about this time. In short, the history of China is a history of ethnic adaptation and territorial expansion over 3,000 years in the regions between and beyond the Yellow and Yangtze Rivers.

Much of that adaptation came through marriage alliances. The way that such exchange takes place—generation after generation for over 3,000 years of written records—has everything to do with the history of ethnicity in China. The Han ethnic group came to dominate, in part, because of strategic intermarrying and the strength of sheer numbers. Over the course of many centuries, practices of exogamy (marrying beyond one's group) combined with patrilineal organization gave sizable advantages to the Han ethnicity. When Han men married women from other ethnic groups, the children would belong to the Han man's family line. Multiply that process by many thousands of cases and carry it over to 20 or more centuries, and the impact is profound. The Han ethnicity, already strong, co-opted and engaged other ethnic groups in a continual process that has affected all parties.

"Yamato" Japan

Although many ethnic groups have strong senses of identity that often contrast the in-group quite markedly with outer groups, there are historical and cultural reasons why the dominant Japanese ethnic group has prevailed. Japan's distinctive island setting and consistent interpretations of its cultural history have provided some of the background for these perceptions.

The chief reason for the distinctive role of Japan in early East Asian history is its location, an island complex distant from Korea by more than 100 miles, with even exploration of adjoining islands and ethnic groups occurring only quite recently in Japanese history. Unlike its East Asian neighbors, Korea and Vietnam, Japan was not occupied by foreign armies until the 20th century. Foreign influences penetrated Japan more conspicuously than they did in Korea. They did not seep across a shared border but came, rather, by ship.

Through it all, one powerful force of ethnic and national identity flowed as a cultural constant—the imperial family that has been linked to the Sun Goddess since the earliest decades of the Yamato state. To this day, the Japanese imperial line is spoken of as an unbroken succession of 125 emperors, all of whom—in a secret ritual last carried out in 1989—merged with the Sun Goddess to achieve a kind of imperial immortality that has been used for purposes both peaceful and profoundly warlike over the centuries. Although the Showa emperor renounced the divinity of the emperorship in 1945, it is significant that the ceremony was still carried out for the succession of his son in 1989. It is another small glimpse into early Yamato images of legitimacy and centrality in the political life of a formidable modern political system.

Today, even with a falling birth rate and an economy that has not recovered to its peaks in the 1970s and 1980s, Japan remains a central player on the world stage. Japan's ethnic homogeneity has figured in international politics during this time, and it is not infrequently heard in private conversations that Japan's strengths are due in large part to that very homogeneity. Such a view is troubling to many in Japan, but it remains a significant theme in Japanese expressions of national identity.

This is by no means a hidden issue, either. In 1986, Japanese Prime Minister Yasuhiro Nakasone made a statement that received worldwide attention:

So high is the level of education in our country that Japan is an intelligent society. Our average score is much higher than those of countries like the U.S. There are many [minorities] in America. In consequence the average score over there is exceedingly low.

Attempting to clarify these remarks when the situation proved challenging diplomatically, Nakasone continued:

> But there are things the Americans have not been able to do because of multiple nationalities there . . . On the contrary, things are easier in Japan because we are a monoracial society.[7]

This view, while certainly not universal, is common in Japan and is clearly an outgrowth of the dominance of Yamato ethnicity on the main island of Honshu and throughout Japanese history. Yet only the Japanese royal family could make anything resembling a coherent (yet still flawed) argument for a kind of Yamato ethnic pedigree. The history of Japan—much like that of Korea or China—shows an interplay between and among groups. Despite expressions of ethnic superiority in some circles, patterns are changing, and intermarriage is more common today than at any time in the documented past.

This is especially relevant to the two largest indigenous ethnic groups in Japanese society—the Ainu to the north, on the island of Hokkaido, and the Ryukyuan people in Okinawa prefecture. In both cases, assimilation and intermarriage has led to remarkable changes in the cultural makeup of the groups. These have not by any means been seamless or without conflict, and anti-Japanese resentment has been common among both groups.

Perhaps the most difficult ongoing situation of this nature in Japan today has occurred with a group that is not, strictly speaking, ethnically distinct. The Buraku people (Burakumin) have been stigmatized for centuries. They were originally perceived as an employment group that was considered to be outcaste because members worked in ritually "impure" occupations ranging from tanners and butchers to undertakers. Although the caste system was abolished in the early years of the Meiji era, discrimination has remained in employment, marriage, and even—although far less commonly today—real estate purchases.

All of these groups have higher profiles within and beyond Japan than they have had in the past. Yet each one has also been defined to a very large extent by its interactions over the decades and even centuries with Japan's Yamato culture. This is equally true of other groups in Japan today, many of which are even larger. These include significant numbers from China (including the Republic of China on Taiwan), Korea (mostly South Korea), Brazil, and the Philippines. Even so, the total foreign population does not exceed 2 percent, and all ethnic politics takes place under assumptions of overwhelmingly numerical superiority.

Korea, Class, and Ethnicity

Korea is a mountainous peninsula that has been the continual home for a remarkably distinct and largely endogamous ethnic group. Only 20 percent of the land is

suitable for cultivation, and the geographic dividers have played a far more prominent role in Korea's history than ethnic conflicts. The Korean people came from
the north—as far away as Siberia—and have distant roots in Manchuria and Altaic-
speaking tribes that were, in turn, linked to Mongolian, Turkic, and other North
Asian peoples. For two millennia, Korea served as a cultural conduit between China
and Japan and has played a significant role in its own right in the historical growth
of both of those civilizations. The peninsula was divided into a number of political units during its early history, but it was in the early modern era that the greatest
contrast with our usual conception of ethnicity can be seen.

Profound social and economic changes shaped life on the Korean peninsula
during the five centuries of the Yi, or Choson, dynasty (1392–1910). Not the least
of these was the structuring of economic success and prestige—for individuals
and families—according to the rules of an examination system that was borrowed
from China and adapted to Korean social and economic conditions. Although the
wholesale adoption of the examination system made Choson Korea seem like the
Chinese empires of its time, one fundamental difference with China still remained.

There were not just educational, and therefore economic, limitations to those
who could hope to succeed; there were also class barriers. Successful candidates in
the examinations were limited for the most part to the hereditary ruling class, which
came to be known as the *yangban*, a term meaning literally "the two groups"—
that is, the civil and military branches of government. By dominating the exams,
the *yangban* families were able to monopolize political leadership and high government office. They also came to own most of the land. As a result, social status, landownership, and political leadership were concentrated in the hands of the
yangban class. Again, with ethnic similarity, class distinctions were exacerbated.

Below the *yangban* was a relatively small and legally undefined class that has
been called the *chungin* or "middle people." These served as petty government
functionaries and performed various specialized roles in government. Although
absolutely essential in the whole operation of the government, they had little opportunity to rise to high-policy posts. This essentially hereditary group received new
recruits from among the large numbers of illegitimate offspring of the *yangban*. It
is telling that this dynamic—aristocratic extras being relegated to a lower status—
took place as a class, and not ethnic, process.

The vast bulk of the population was made up of commoners, or *yangmin*, who
were for the most part taxpaying *corvée*-serving occupiers of government lands or
semi-serfs on *yangban* holdings. The lowest class was called *ch'onmin* or "base
people." These were government or private slaves, workers in industries, and professional categories, such as butchers (originally despised because of the Buddhist
prohibition against the taking of animal life), actors, and *kisaeng* female entertainers comparable with the Japanese *geisha* of a later date. The *ch'onmin* came the
closest to being treated as though they were ethnically separate from other Koreans.

This was not, of course, the case, and it represented rather a particularly severe form of class differentiation based on occupation rather than ethnicity.

Dynamics of Ethnicity

To set all of this into motion, we will now examine two cultural theorists whose work has been enormously influential in the past 30 years. During that time, we have gone from thinking of ethnicity almost exclusively in terms of separable elements—not unlike the dolls, rugs, or engine parts of our examples—to a complex weave of similarity and difference. Homi Bhabha and Pierre Bourdieu give us new ways of approaching the dynamics of ethnicity, in Asia and beyond.

The first key idea can be seen in hints and passages in the earlier sections. In a nutshell, Homi Bhabha emphasizes that the truly influential and fascinating aspects of culture must be found in the intersections—the interstices—of actions, patterns of life, and ways of knowing. The study of how group identity came to be is important, to be sure, but the dynamics of understanding flow from the various cultural units bumping up against each other, like so many rugs on a vast hallway floor. Here is how Bhabha puts it. Note that he emphasizes that singularities (our rugs, our dolls, and our ethnicities) should not only be understood alone.

The move away from the singularities of "class" or "gender" as primary conceptual organizational categories, has resulted in an awareness of the subject positions—of race, gender, generation, institutional location, geopolitical locale, sexual orientation—that inhabit any claim to identity in the modern world. What is theoretically innovative, and politically crucial, is the need to think beyond narratives of originary and initial subjectivities and to focus on those moments or processes that are produced in the articulation of cultural differences. These "in-between" spaces provide the terrain for elaborating strategies of selfhood—singular or communal—that initiate new signs of identity, and innovative sites of collaboration, and contestation, in the act of defining the idea of society itself.

It is in the emergence of the interstices—the overlap and displacement of domains of difference—that the intersubjective and collective experiences of *nationness*, community interest, or cultural value are negotiated.[8]

These ideas are worth unpacking, pondering. They speak directly to the challenge we have before us in understanding the ethnic groups of Asia. While we surely must understand the details in the entries themselves, we must never forget that the most dynamic and persistent changes in Asian history took place when these entities connected—from ethnic groups such as the Mongol or Manchu to budding nations such as Korea, Japan, the Philippines, and even Taiwan (or the

Republic of China on Taiwan, in the increasingly fuzzy political language of the island). We surely can understand individual entities and must seek to do so. Yet, it is in the way they respond, crash into, and even displace others that we see in the flow of human history. As Bhabha maintains, that can be found only in the interstices—in the ways that the Han and Bai people, for example, clashed (and married), as well as the manner of conflict and redemption found between smaller groups themselves, from the Miao and Zhuang to the Achang and Bouyei.

Take note of Bhabha's use of the word *contestation*. We often think of definitions, when we read them, as the thing itself. Bhabha reminds us that definitions are always contested. In isolation, this is a challenging concept. It is less so when we give it a concrete meaning—we'll use baseball as an example. The Boston Red Sox and New York Yankees meet more than a dozen times a year. Fans in each city feel strongly about their teams. Ask a Yankees fan to describe the Red Sox. In fact, ask her or him to write a description of the team. Now, ask a Yankees fan to describe the Yankees, the home team.

You may see where this is going. If you do the reverse for the Red Sox fan, asking the person to describe both the Yankees *and* the hometown Red Sox, you will have a fairly stark set of renderings. Why is this so? Precisely because it is contested. The participants care deeply about how they are portrayed and do what they can to portray others in a manner that suits them. They are, to use Bhabha's images, in the center of things.

If we move to the interstices, we can start to sense ways in which the Red Sox and Yankees merge, cohere, and repel. What if we were to ask another observer, someone who rooted for, say, the St. Louis Cardinals, to describe the Yankees and the Red Sox? Surely, the person's answer would not be quite as jaded as those of the participants. But would it be right? Let's take it just one step further. Imagine that we engage a fine writer who is familiar with baseball, but not really a fan of any team at all—a matter more of other interests than lack of passion for the sport. The writer writes another account of the Red Sox and the Yankees. Is this one true, if only because she or he has the least interest in the subject?

Homi Bhabha, of course, would say no and quite emphatically. From his perspective, there is no outside objective position. We are all, and always, complex subjectivities. Even the outside observer views the teams from an angle. Some people consider this to be problematic, and rail against the postmodern assaults against our knowing. The spirit of this introduction is different. While we can, and should, strive for accurate factual accounts (and we *can* get many, even the vast majority, of details right), our overall accounts are going to be an outgrowth of our very humanity. This is always subjective (we have known this since Kant's day) and the real key to understanding a complex social world.

As Bhabha might say—if he had interest in American baseball—the keys to understanding lie in jamming together the various accounts. It is as though we imagined a complex geology of understanding, and the various versions were so many tectonic plates ramming up against each other and creating vast *new* mountain ranges of knowledge. We cannot ever know *the* Red Sox or Yankees. We can come to know so much, and in such a dynamic fashion, however, that we never again want to go back to the false pretenses of isolated portraits alone.

It is not difficult to see the same dynamic at work with ethnicity in Asia. Ask a 13th-century Mongol about northern groups charging through the continent, and you will have one picture. Ask a sedentary Han farmer in the Yellow River valley the same thing, and you will have quite another. Now ask a historian of China . . . from China . . . the same question. Finally, ask another historian of China . . . from, say, Britain, to do the same.

Ethnicity is multilayered and complex.

* * * * * *

There is one more dimension that we must add to this equation if we are to get the deepest benefit from this volume's entries. To do so, let's go back, briefly, to our baseball example. In the second decade of the 21st century, can we really assume that everyone in Boston is a Red Sox fan? We already know that there is no possibility that everyone in New York—however, we define the area—is a Yankees fan (there have almost always been two or even three teams in the city). How do we account for the Baltimore Orioles fans living in Brooklyn and the Minnesota Twins fans living in Boston? Does Boston speak through a single idiom?

Of course not.

Too many discussions of ethnicity seem to assert that this people or that people acts, works, or plays in a manner that can be shared by the entire group. There is a tiny shred of truth to this, of course. To the extent that a group (Boston Red Sox fans and the Tajik people) can be called a group at all, they have to share certain qualities. The purpose of individual descriptions is in outlining exactly those items. These, too, are subjective if we parse them enough, but it is clear to any reader that the Boston Red Sox play their home games in Fenway Park, broadcast to all of the New England states, and won the World Series in 2004 and 2009. Those who try to claim that we can know nothing without our subjectivities getting in the way have missed the point. We need precisely that kind of detailed information if we are to understand any complex group.

On the other hand, such information can take us only so far. Homi Bhabha might say, "Fine; memorize that . . . now put it into motion—dynamic motion." For that, we need to understand how the Yankees and Red Sox played their games (myriad contests throughout the past). We need to understand marriage alliances, feuds, and treaties between the Bai people and the Han. We need, in short, to understand the interstices, the contestation.

And to do *that*, we need to understand that individuals inhabit their ethnic and cultural realms. There is no such thing as a culture (or even an ethnicity) doing, acting, or contesting anything. Individuals do that and make individual (sometimes weird and idiosyncratic) choices while doing so. Sometimes they make terrible mistakes. Sometimes they strike out.

And sometimes they hit a home run. Individuals hit home runs. Teams don't hit them; they help create them in many ways and then benefit from them. Only individuals can hit them.

Pierre Bourdieu, our second cultural theorist, has never forgotten the individual. His angle is a bit different from Bhabha's, but it merges with it nicely. His conception of social action, while enormously complex and nuanced, can be summarized in a useful idea—there are no *rules* that *determine* how people act. To the extent that researchers have focused on the way the Zhuang people behave, for example, they have missed a much larger and more powerful point. People make individual choices within a vast set of correspondences and challenges. Every social action—from a marriage alliance between Han and Miao people to the complex People's Republic of China decision to emphasize ethnicity as a part of the history and culture of the state—is strategic. These choices can be individual or engage many layers of people and opinion. Choice is always a large part of the equation.

Although this may seem obvious, enormous misunderstandings have flowed from "over-reading" the stories of individual groups. A minority family, for example, that wants to see its younger generation thrive will often embrace ethnicity in one manner (e.g., accepting the criteria for minority representation in universities) even while acting in a much more ecumenical manner in others, such as business dealings. Ethnicity is not a thing that is worn in the same way in all contexts. They change in time and space, and nuanced interpretations—and actions—are the norm.

* * * * * *

If we pair the insights of Bhabha and Bourdieu, we can see a sophisticated weaving of two themes. On the one hand, we best understand concepts like ethnicity by focusing on the margins, the interstices, of ethnic categories. On the other hand, following Bourdieu, every action at those margins—in the end, every action at all—is a (complex) layered medley of choices in historically and culturally situated settings. What this means for our study of Asian ethnic groups is that we must balance the detailed knowledge we can gain from the formidable information in this book's encyclopedic entries with knowledge of process, change, and choice. A Mongol family choosing to marry a member of the Han elite today would not be the same—in terms of power, class, or motivation—as one performing the same cultural act (engaging to marry outside of one's ethnic group) during the Mongol-controlled Yuan dynasty (1279–1368).

Ethnicity is always in motion, and this book will help you to understand both the dynamics of movement *and* the key elements shared by ethnic groups in Northern, Central, and Eastern Asia.

Ethnicity in Motion

One way to think about ethnicity in motion is to consider how various ethnic groups have come together and dispersed in relation to large-scale events in recent history. A particularly useful example can be seen with the 2008 Olympic Games in China. Most people outside of China saw those games as, by far, the greatest opportunity that the Chinese state would have to promote tourism and celebrate its unity as a historic civilization and vibrant modern country. Of course, the success of the Olympic Games in 2008 did show off China to the world in a spectacular manner. Several perceptive viewers noted, however, that, in many ways, the 2010 Shanghai World Expo would be even bigger. By 2010, this perspective could clearly be seen. The Shanghai Expo in 2010 captivated the domestic tourism industry. It broke all records and helped to cement a narrative that (echoing the Olympic Opening Ceremonies) celebrated the ethnic diversity and cultural cohesion of the People's Republic of China. On top of that, it told a tale of "coherent diversity," as I like to think of the state's message, in a complex world. Chinese tourists from all provinces, and all of the 56 ethnic groups, flowed to the Expo.

It is the purpose of this volume to show the details of those groups, on the one hand, *and* the great interstices (caverns of contestation and disagreement) on the other hand. Even more, its purpose is to show the detail and dynamism of an Asian world that, while often dominated by the Chinese state, goes far beyond it in society, culture, economy, and, of course, history. This book brings together the vast sweep of Asian ethnic groups from Central and Northern Asia, through China, and on to nations much farther south and east. Through it all, it blends the details with larger patterns of change.

Notes

1. I would like to thank Yitian Liao, Beloit College class of 2011, for the work she did during a Sanger Summer Research Fellowship. Her distillation of information about a large number of ethnic groups provided me with excellent material from which to create both this essay and the seminar that resulted from it.

2. "Travel Guide to Yunnan Province" (Yunnan luxing shuju, 1996), 68.

3. Sima Qian, *Historical Records* (Beijing: Zhonghua Shuju, 1982), 110.

4. Marcel Mauss, *Seasonal Variations of the Eskimo: A Study in Social Morphology* [Translated by Ian Cunnison] (London: Routledge and Kegan Paul, 1979), 76–77.

5. Chen Sanping, *Multicultural China in the Early Middle Ages* (Philadelphia: University of Pennsylvania Press, 2012), 39–41.

6. Ray Huang, *China: A Macro History* (Armonk, NY: M.E. Sharpe Publishing, 1996), 25.

7. *Chicago Tribune*, September 28, 1986. Clarence Page.

8. Homi Bhabha, *The Location of Culture* (London and New York: Routledge Classics, 1994), 2.

Bibliography

Bhabha, Homi. *The Location of Culture*. London and New York: Routledge Classics, 1994.

Huang, Ray. *China: A Macro History*. Armonk NY: M.E. Sharpe Publishing, 1996.

Mauss, Marcel. *Seasonal Variations of the Eskimo: A Study in Social Morphology* [Translated by Ian Cunnison]. London: Routledge and Kegan Paul, 1979.

Qian, Sima. *Historical Records*. Beijing: Zhonghua Shuju, 1982.

Sanping, Chen. *Multicultural China in the Early Middle Ages*. Philadelphia: University of Pennsylvania Press, 2012.

A

Achang

The Achang, sometimes known as Ngac'ang, Mengsa, Echang, or Maingtha, are a small ethnic group living mostly in China's Yunnan Province with another Achang population across the border in Myanmar. The estimated 50,000 Achang live in a multicultural region among other ethnic groups, which has greatly influenced their culture and language. Their language is thought to belong to the Tibeto-Burman branch of the Sino-Tibetan languages, though many Achang also speak the languages of the neighboring peoples. Most Achang practice a complex religious system that includes rites and traditions of Theravada Buddhism, Taoism, shamanism, and ancestor veneration.

Many scholars believe that the Achang are the descendants of the early Qiang tribes, which originated in the border region between Sichuan and Gansu Provinces some 2,000 years ago. There are numerous accounts of the frequent conflicts between the Han Chinese and the Qiang that lasted until the last days of the Han dynasty. The constant wars and natural disasters forced some Qiang clans to move to the south around the beginning of the modern era. Traditionally, the Achang are believed to have lived in the upper reaches of the Nu River as early as the second century CE. Among the first inhabitants of the Yunnan highlands, the

Achang were known to be officials of the Chinese Tang dynasty as Xunchuan over a thousand years ago. Historically inhabiting the areas along the east bank of the Lancang River, during the 12th century, they began to migrate to the lands west of the river. By the 13th century, some clans had settled in the area now known as Longchuan, while other clans settled around modern Lianghe, areas lying at the southern end of the Gaoligong Mountains. The clans settled on small plains often surrounded by mountains, with typical Achang villages being located at the edge of a plain or at the foot of the mountains. Villages generally consisted of households that represented several patrilineal clans. Some Achang villages also included areas inhabited by peoples of the neighboring ethnic groups. In 1448, a Han Chinese army of the Ming dynasty conquered the region. Chinese soldiers left to garrison the region married Achang women resulting in the Achang division known as the Husa or Fusa, who consider themselves a distinct group. Until the 16th century, the Achang were considered a division of the Jingpo peoples, with a clear differentiation appearing at that time. A clear population of Achang who differed from the closely related Jingpo were acknowledged by the local Dai and Han Chinese feudal rulers in the region in the 17th century.

Centuries of contact between the small Achang clans and the neighboring Han,

Dai, and Jingpo ethnic groups have greatly influenced the Achang culture. The Achang are mostly farmers, engaged in wet-rice cultivation. The rice crop is normally separated into what the family will need for the coming year and the larger part that is mandatorily sold to the government at a price set by the state. Besides rice, the Achang also raise some cash crops such as sugarcane and tobacco. The Husa or Fusa division is famous for making various types of knives and swords. The manufacturing of ironware has been a prosperous activity since the 14th century. Achang society is patrilineal, with descent through the male line. The only marriage restriction is the tradition of marrying outside the patrilineal clan, with marriage to a non-Achang quite common. The basic social unit is the patriarchal family, which includes two or three generations as part of an extended family. Traditionally, the youngest son remains in the family home to care for the parents, then inheriting either the family house or other property while assuming responsibility for the parents. Female offspring receive a dowry but do not inherit unless they have no male siblings. In the regions of Fusa and Lasa, nearly all Achang follow Theravada Buddhism, while in other areas, they worship ancestor spirits and believe in shamans and magic. The Achang language, part of the Lolo-Burmese branch of the Tibeto-Burman languages, is closely related to the Burmese language, the predominant language in Myanmar. Many Achang in China speak Mandarin or Dai, which is spoken by the neighboring peoples. In Myanmar, many speak Burmese as a second language. The Achang language has a strong oral tradition though Mandarin or Burmese are used as literary languages.

During the rule of the Ming and Qing dynasties, the Achang were most often governed by local village leaders who reported to Dai or Han Chinese feudal rulers. The Achang village chiefs and their lineages had the power to collect taxes and tribute, enforce labor needs, and rule in a feudal manner over the Achang villages. Most Achang villages remained isolated until the mid-19th century when Han Chinese administrators of the Qing dynasty began to penetrate the highlands, bringing the Achang and other indigenous groups under closer Han Chinese rule. The local feudalism remained largely untouched until the Communist Revolution in China in 1949. A major program of land reform followed by collectivization threw the Achang economy into chaos. The Achang experienced much hardship during the Great Leap Forward, a government program that focused on the economy, industrialization, and the further collectivization of agricultural land and labor. The Cultural Revolution, from 1967 to 1977, brought even greater chaos to the Achang region as all religious symbols, artifacts, and traditional festivals were banned along with many symbolic and material aspects of Achang traditional culture. Thousands of Achang died during these decades, especially those who owned property prior to 1949 who were denounced as traitors and exploiters. Since the 1980s, the stringent restrictions on religion and belief systems have been relaxed, and many Achang have embraced their traditional religious beliefs. Tourism, encouraged by the Chinese state, has brought many changes to the

Achang villages in recent years. Traditional ceremonies, dances, and music have been revived as tourist attractions, allowing the Achang to recuperate their ancient cultural traditions.

Further Reading

Ethnic Groups. "The Achang Ethnic Minority." Accessed July 30, 2013. http://www.china.org.cn/e-groups/shaoshu/shao-2-achang.htm

Jiang, Liu. *History of the Culture of the Achang.* Kunming, China: Yunnan Nationalities Press, 2001.

Mitchell, Sam. *Ethnic Minorities in Yunnan.* Kunming, China: Yunnan Fine Arts Publishing House, 2004.

Olson, James S. *An Ethnohistorical Dictionary of China.* Westport, CT: Greenwood, 1998.

Aimaq

The Aimaq, sometimes known as Aimak, Aymaq, or Eimak, are a Persian people of the west central highlands of Afghanistan in the region north of Herat and in the adjacent Khorasan region of Iran. Population estimates range between 250,000 and two million, but the most reliable estimates are between 1.5 and 1.7 million, including more than 200,000 in Iran and some 7,000 in Tajikistan. *Aimaq*, originally a Mongol word for tribe or grazing territory, in the modern Persian language means "tribal people," and most Aimaq are nomadic or seminomadic, moving with their herds on a seasonal basis. The Aimaq language is a Persian dialect closely related to the Dari and Khorasani dialects spoken by the neighboring peoples of Afghanistan and Iran. The majority of the Aimaq are Sunni Muslim, with a minority adhering to Shi'a Islam.

From ancient times, the area now known as Afghanistan has been one of the great crossroads of Central Asia, both for trade and for conquerors. Long before international borders divided the region, the Aimaq homeland was considered part of the Khorasan region of successive Persian empires. The nomadic tribes of the plains of the eastern regions of Greater Khorasan traditionally moved with their herds on a seasonal basis from the grasslands north of Herat in present-day Afghanistan to the plains of Khorasan around Meshed in Iran. In the fourth century BCE, the Greeks

The Power of Tribal Traditions

The Aimaq, made up of 4 tribal groups and more than 250 subtribes, are one of the most traditional ethnic groups in Afghanistan. Their homeland is geographically distant from the centers of government, and therefore the Aimaq have retained their tribal structure. Tribal customs remain stronger than Afghan national sentiment, and tribal law vested in tribal and clan leaders usually prevails over government authority and at times even some Islamic strictures. Attempts to bring the Aimaq tribal leaders into the local administration have historically been resisted. To the present day, the tribal traditions continue to prevail over government or religious laws.

of Alexander the Great conquered the region, which later formed part of the Greek–Persian Bactrian state. At some unknown time in history, the Aimaq were probably settled oases dwellers driven into the plains by conquerors, where they adapted to the life of nomadic herdsmen divided into a number of small tribal groups. The small tribes, numbering up to 20 distinct groups, formed a loose confederation through alliances and marriage to protect themselves from the successive waves of invaders. Invading Muslim Arabs began the conversion of the Aimaq to Islam in the seventh century. The tribal territories were so remote that until the 11th century, the region remained a pagan enclave surrounded by Muslim principalities. In the 14th century, the Mongol hordes of Genghis Khan invaded the region, either slaughtering or absorbing the conquered peoples. The tribal groups encountered by the Mongols north of Herat were called *eimak*, the Mongol word for tribe or a tribal grazing land and were incorporated into the hordes of the Turkic–Mongol armies. Under Mongol rule for several centuries, the name *eimak* was extended to all the small nomadic Persian-speaking tribes in the region. Over time, the Mongol and Turkic peoples mixed with the tribal groups adding Turkic words and phrases to the Aimaq dialects and changing the physical characteristics of the tribal appearance. In 1717, the Ghilzai Afghans, part of the Pashtun people, conquered Khorasan, which became part of the Afghan Hotaki dynasty. The Aimaq nomads, though forced to pay tribute to the Afghan rulers, remained in their tribal territories moving their herds from the lowlands to the highlands each season. In 1747, the region became part of the Durrani Empire dominated by the Pashtun peoples of southern and eastern Afghanistan.

The name *Aimaq* is still used to designate the tribal peoples and to distinguish them from the settled population in the area, mostly Dari-speaking Persians, Tajik, Hazara, and Uzbek. The largest of the tribes are grouped into the Char Aimaq, meaning the Four Aimaq. The Jamshidi, the Aimaq-Hazara, the Firukuhi, and the Taimani formed the confederation as a defensive league in the 16th and 17th centuries, when chiefs coming from outside the tribal areas unified the tribes. Descendants of these founding chiefs are still influential in tribal affairs, though they have lost their traditional powers. Tribal traditions continue to dominate the culture, with tribal concepts of honor and shame being more important than Islamic or state laws. Disputes are most often settled by tribal rather than by government authorities. In sharp contrast to the practices of other Afghan groups, the Aimaq accord women a high status in the society. Women participate in group discussions, even when outsiders are present. Traditionally, an Aimaq girl was free to reject a groom chosen by her father. Bride service is still observed in the rural areas, with a prospective groom living in the compound of his future in-laws and serves for a specific period of time before the wedding takes place, and the husband and wife can begin their life together. In areas where the orthodox Muslim clergy is stronger, particularly in the urban areas, such traditional practices are dying out. The Aimaq language is actually a group of related dialects belonging to the

Persian branch of the southwestern Iranian languages. The dialects are very closely related to the Dari and Khorasani dialects of Persian, though they have more Turkic loanwords. In Afghanistan, the Aimaq are counted as ethnic Tajik and some refer to themselves as Tajik, though most continue to use local tribal names to identify themselves. In recent years, the chaos and upheavals in Afghanistan forced many to settle as farmers or carpet weavers as their herds were decimated or stolen. Some remain seminomadic in the areas of good grazing, but their herds are greatly reduced and poverty is widespread.

In the early 19th century, Russian and British explorers visited the region but mostly ignored the nomadic tribes around Herat. The rise of the Qajar dynasty in Persia resulted in the fall of western Khorasan to Persian rule, with a new international border dividing the traditional territory of the Aimaq tribes. Competition between Russia and the United Kingdom for influence in Afghanistan culminated in a series of wars known as the Anglo-Afghan wars. Though Afghanistan remained neutral during World War I, some Aimaq responded to the Turkish Sultan, the titular leader of all Muslims, and his call for *jihad* or holy war against the Allies and fought skirmishes with British troops. They mostly remained away from the often-painful political maneuverings. In 1919, a power struggle over succession to the throne brought another British intervention, but the country remained unstable. The Aimaq reestablished their traditional confederation for the defense of the tribal lands as various bandit and mercenary groups rampaged through the region. In 1929, a number of the Aimaq

tribes in northwest Afghanistan rebelled against their subjugation by the dominant Pashtun people. The rebellion failed, and the Aimaq rebels were severely punished, leaving a lasting hatred of the Pashtun. In the 1950s and 1960s, drought became a severe problem, resulting in the loss of many herds and the forced settlement of some of the tribal groups. In the 1970s and 1980s, even more Aimaq settled in small villages or in Herat and other cities, often relying on their traditional carpet weaving for survival. Despite the fact that carpet weaving is now the main source of income for most of the Aimaq tribes, Aimaq culture still measures wealth through the number of animals in the tribal herds.

Further Reading

Adamec, Ludwig W. *Historical Dictionary of Afghanistan.* Lanham, MD: Scarecrow Press, 2011.

Barfield, Thomas. *Afghanistan: A Cultural and Political History.* Princeton, NJ: Princeton University Press, 2010.

Steward, Rory. *The Places In Between.* Boston: Mariner Books, 2006.

World Directory of Minorities and Indigenous Peoples. "Aimaq." Accessed July 30, 2013. http://www.minorityrights.org/?lid=5452

Ainu

The Ainu, sometimes known as Aynu, Aino, or Ezo, are an indigenous people in the northern Japanese island of Hokkaido and in Sakhalin and the Kuril Islands in the Russian Federation. The Japanese government estimates the Ainu population at 25,000, including the official 109 Ainu living in Russia, but Ainu leaders estimated the population of the ethnic groups upward of 200,000. The Ainu language is considered a language isolate, unrelated to other known languages. Most of the Ainu continue to adhere to their traditional beliefs, though a large number have adopted the predominant Buddhism of Japan or Russian Orthodoxy in Russia.

The origins of the Ainu people are not known, though many scholars and researchers have put forth theories. They are believed to have evolved from a Paleolithic culture that constituted the first known inhabitation of the Japanese archipelago. Gradually, a hunter–gatherer culture evolved, the ancestors of both the contemporary Ainu and the Yamato or Japanese people. Before the Tungus invasion of the archipelago from the Asian mainland some 3,000–4,000 years ago, the ancestors of the Ainu probably inhabited the entire island chain, possibly as far south as Okinawa. During the Yayoi period of Iron Age culture that flourished in Japan from southern Kyushu to northern Honshu, the peoples of northern Honshu and the northernmost island in the archipelago, Hokkaido, developed as the ancestors of the Ainu. Although known as a warrior people, the Ainu culture and religion evolved in harmony with nature. Holding their lands in common, various nomadic clans lived by fishing, hunting, gathering, and trading. The Yamato or Japanese began to colonize the Ainu lands of northern Honshu between the 13th and 14th centuries CE. The Ainu retreated northward to escape the incursions of the more advanced Japanese. In 1456–1457, the first serious Ainu uprising against the Japanese conquest occurred. Led by the Ainu warrior

Koshimain, the Ainu attempted to hold their traditional lands in northern Honshu. Sporadic warfare with the advancing Japanese decimated the Ainu population of Honshu, with many refugees crossing the narrow Tsugaru Strait to Ainu-populated Hokkaido. The expanding Japanese moved across the strait in the 16th century and began to colonize the southwestern part of Hokkaido. The commercial development of the newly conquered Ainu lands in northern Honshu and southwestern Hokkaido during the Edo Era, beginning in 1603, resulted in the total annihilation of the Ainu populations in the southern islands of the archipelago. In Sakhalin, the Russians gained control of the Ainu regions through violence, which decimated the Ainu population and eliminated the huge fur-bearing herds. In 1669–1672, the Ainu national hero, Shakushian, led the desperate Ainu in war against the Japanese invaders of Hokkaido, only to again suffer defeat. Japanese expansion into Hokkaido continued with the Ainu population pushed into the mountainous interior. In 1789, another national hero, Kunashiri Menashi, led the Ainu warriors in a final battle against total Japanese domination. Even though the Menashi-Kunashir Rebellion ended in defeat, the Ainu established their ethnic identity for the first time as a unifying social and political structure above their traditional village level identity though they were brought under the complete authority of the Japanese state.

The Ainu, simply meaning "people" or "human" in the Ainu language, are the descendants of the original inhabitants of the Japanese archipelago. Physically, the Ainu are usually light skinned and short statured, with round eyes, wavy hair, and abundant body hair. Many scholars believe that the Ainu are more closely related to the Caucasian peoples or the Altaic and Uralic peoples of eastern Siberia than to the Japanese or other Oriental peoples. They are often referred to by the Japanese as *dojin*, a term that connotes uncleanliness or vulgarity. Though the official Japanese government estimate of the number of Ainu in the country is only about 25,000, the actual number of people of Ainu or partial Ainu ancestry is probably much higher. Societal and economic discrimination over hundreds of years made the Ainu hesitant to express or define themselves as other than Japanese. In 1994, the first Ainu was elected to the Japanese Diet. In recent years, the Ainu have begun to recover their traditional culture, though the majority now speak Japanese. Efforts are under way to save the Ainu language from extinction as now fewer than 100 people are still able to speak the language fluently. Traditional Ainu culture was very different from that of the Japanese to the south. The Ainu men never shaved so they had full beards and moustaches. Traditionally animists, the Ainu believe that everything in nature has a *kamuy* or spirit. Bears play an important part in the culture and are considered powerful spirits that can benefit the people. The bear is still considered a mythological creature that taught the early Ainu to hunt, fish, weave, and gather in the forests. The most important ceremony in the Ainu religion, the "Iyomate" or "KumaMatsuri," focused on the annual sacrifice of a sacred bear. Distinctive rhythmic music and dance characterized all Ainu ceremonies and celebrations, some of which have been

preserved partially to attract the growing number of tourists visiting Hokkaido. The Ainu language, though largely supplanted by Japanese, is considered an isolated language possibly related to the language spoken in Okinawa and the Ryukyu Islands south of the Japanese home islands. Without a written language, the Ainu developed as masters of oral narrative. Many of the Ainu dialects were mutually unintelligible; however, the classic Ainu language of the *yukar*, the classical Ainu epic stories, was understood by all Ainu groups. Since the 1980s, a concerted effort has been made to extend the use of Ainu and to preserve the language from extinction. In 1997, the Ainu language began to be taught in Hokkaido schools.

Until the 19th century, the Ainu population of Hokkaido outnumbered the Japanese inhabitants of the island. Without any negotiations, treaties, or other official arrangements, the Japanese government annexed the Ainu homeland and extended its authority over the Ainu people. Until 1868, the Japanese government officially classed all Ainu as "foreign" and treated the Ainu as illegal foreigners living in the Japanese Empire. In the 1870s, a plan for government-sponsored Japanese emigration to Hokkaido formed an integral part of the strategy for exploiting the island's rich natural resources. The surviving Ainu were confined on small territories similar to the reservations of the North American indigenous peoples. Violence, oppression, and epidemics decimated the Ainu populations. By 1880, there were an estimated 15,000 surviving Ainu in Hokkaido, less than 2,000 in Russian Sakhalin, and around 100 in the Kuril Islands. The Japanese

Ainu in northern Japan. (AP Photo)

government, in 1899, passed a new law, the Hokkaido Former Aborigine Protection Law, a discriminatory and brutal law recognizing the Ainu as former aborigines with the aim of the total assimilation of the Ainu into Japanese culture. At the same time, all Ainu lands were confiscated by the government for Japanese colonization, and the Ainu were granted Japanese citizenship, thus denying them the protection of indigenous people status. For most of the 20th century, the Japanese government repeatedly stated that there were no ethnic minorities living in the country. The Ainu population of Hokkaido is mostly employed as low-paid workers, as their traditional pursuits of fishing, hunting, and gathering are prohibited. Of the millions of salmon caught in the waters around Hokkaido each year, the Ainu are allowed to have only 400 for ceremonial purposes, but not one for sustenance. Though the Japanese government continued to deny the existence of the Ainu, they were officially recognized as the region's indigenous people by the United Nations in 1992. In 1997, the Japanese government finally recognized the Ainu as an indigenous people with new laws passed to protect their culture and language. In 2008, a nonbinding resolution was passed by the Japanese Diet calling on the government to finally recognize the Ainu as indigenous to Japan and urged the end to all discrimination against the Ainu ethnic group. The resolution recognized the Ainu as an indigenous people with a distinct language, religion, and culture and officially rescinded the hated 1899 law, which approved official discrimination and caused so much suffering among the Ainu.

Further Reading

Fitzhugh, William W. *Ainu: Spirit of a Northern People.* Seattle: University of Washington Press, 2001.

Johnson, D. W. *The Ainu and the Folklore.* Seattle: Amazon Digital Services, 2010.

Johnson, D. W. *The Ainu of Northeast Asia.* East Windsor, NJ: Idzat International, 1999.

Akha

The Akha, sometimes known as Aini, Akka, Edaw, Ekaw, Hani, Houni, Ikaw, Kaw, KhaKho, Kho, Ko, or Woni, are a highland people originally from the region straddling the border between China's Yunnan Province and Myanmar. Over the past centuries, Akha clans have migrated southeast into northern Thailand, Laos, and Vietnam. The estimated 500,000 Akha speak a language belonging to the Loloish (Yi) branch of the Tibeto-Burman language family. The majority of the Akha continue to adhere to their traditional folk religion, with growing numbers embracing Christianity or the Buddhism of the neighboring peoples.

According to Akha tradition, their ancestors originated in the Tibetan borderlands though many scholars believe that they originated further southeast in the region of present-day Yunnan and northern Myanmar. The Akha oral traditions recount their southward migrations across mountains and numerous rivers. The Akha are believed to be one of the peoples that formed part of the kingdom of Nanzhao, now in southern China. The kingdom began with the founding of a small kingdom in the area of Lake Erhai in 649 CE. In 737, with the support of the Chinese Tang dynasty, six small kingdoms were united to form the new Nanzhao state. In 750, the peoples of Nanzhao rebelled against Tang rule. A Tang army, sent to reestablish Han Chinese sovereignty, was defeated in 751. A second Tang army was dispatched in 754, but it was also defeated. The victorious peoples of Nanzhao quickly expanded their territory to include parts of present-day Myanmar, most of Yunnan, and into the northern districts of present-day Laos and Thailand. They later expanded north into Sichuan in China. The kingdom slowly declined from the ninth century, and civil disturbances ended the Nanzhao dynasty. Most of the Akha then came under the rule of the Bai kingdom known as Dali or Great Li, established in 937. The region came under Mongol rule in the 13th century, mostly included in the new Mongol Province of Yunnan. Stronger peoples ruled the Akha clans or drove many into the less accessible highlands. Migrations of non–Tibeto-Burman peoples set off waves of Akha migrations, which continued into the 20th century. Most of the migrant Akha settled in remote highland areas to live as subsistence farmers. The isolated Akha mostly resisted outside rule during the 16th and 17th centuries. Some scholars believe that the Akha once formed part of the Lolo people that ruled the Baoshan and Tengchong plain regions before the invasion of the troops of the Chinese Ming dynasty in Yunnan in 1644. The Chinese conquest of the northern Akha clans began new migrations to the south and east, which continued throughout the 18th century.

The Akha live according to a complex system of traditional beliefs and rules. They consider that every activity, move, and sometimes even thought should be measured and balanced according to want, need, the auspiciousness of a particular day, the disposition of the spirits, the traditional calendar, the ancestor's opinions, and even the position of the village's gates. The Akha live in villages interspersed with those of other ethnic groups in the highland regions of southwest China, eastern Myanmar, western Laos, northern Thailand, and northwestern Vietnam. Census data are often inadequate and unreliable so that population figures are often total population estimates ranging from 400,000 up to 2.3 million. In recent years, the Akha have begun to move to the lowland urban centers among the Tai-speaking valley populations. The staple food of the Akha diet is rice, cultivated mostly by the slash-and-burn traditional method. Since the early 20th century, cotton and opium poppies have become the principal cash crops. Until recently, most clothing was made from local cotton, dyed with indigo. Patterns of embroidery and appliqué adorning men's and women's jackets are distinctive of Akha subgroups. Another distinction is the women's headgear embellished with silver ornaments,

coins, beads, and monkey fur depending on the region and clan traditions. Descent among the Akha is patrilineal with each child being given a genealogical name, with the last syllable of the father's name typically taken as the first syllable of the child's name. In most Akha populations, polygyny is still permitted, and in general young people are free to choose their own spouses. Either spouse can initiate separation or divorce. Lacking a stratified system of social classes, Akha culture is egalitarian with the ties of patrilineal kinship and marriage alliance forming the fabric of society. Though Akha oral traditions tell of warriors and warfare, nonviolence is upheld in everyday life. The Akha language forms part of the Loloish branch of the Sino-Tibetan language group. Linguists consider Akha to be a dialect of the Hani language, particularly in China, where the Akha are often considered part of the official Hani ethnic group. Ancient religious traditions, including shamanism and ancestor veneration, are the belief system of the majority of the Akha, with growing numbers adopting Christianity or the Buddhism of the neighboring lowland peoples.

The dispersed Akha population was often mistreated and abused by more powerful neighboring peoples or representatives of the states and kingdoms that asserted power in the region beginning in the early 19th century. Christian missionaries began to penetrate the Akha highland villages in the 1840s and 1850s, often forcibly converting the villagers to Christianity. Abuses included the kidnapping of Akha children into orphanages and forced labor. The Akha villages established in the present-day Shan State of Myanmar became subjects of the Shan prince of Kentung by the 1860s and perhaps earlier. The continued migration of Akha clan groups extended Akha villages into northern Thailand around the turn of the 20th century. The economic development of the region reduced the territory available for new Akha settlements or migrations. Akha populations were often displaced by local government officials to less fertile regions, while their traditional territories were opened to logging or opium production. In China, they were considered part of the Hani ethnic group, though this is rejected by the Akha, who see themselves as a distinct nationality. The activities of Christian missionaries increased in the early decades of the 20th century, often with teaching the Akha that their traditions are evil or backward. Abuse by Christian missionaries and local government officials is often unpunished due to the continuing inaccessibility of most of the Akha regions. In the late 20th century, the introduction of capitalism and rapid modernization brought rapid change that threatened the traditions and culture of the Akha people. Such alternatives as ecotourism have helped some Akha villages to support themselves through staging tourist events and selling souvenirs, but the majority of the Akha live with daily insecurity and little outside help from regional governments or other organizations.

Further Reading

The Akha Heritage Foundation. Last modified June 30, 2011. http://www.akha.org

Goodman, Jim. *The Akha: Guardians of the Forest.* London: Teak House Publications, 1997.

Grunfeld, Frederic. *Wayfarers of the Thai Forest: The Akha.* New York: Time-Life, 1982.

Mitchell, Sam. *Ethnic Minorities in Yunnan.* Kunming, China: Yunnan Fine Arts Publishing House, 2004.

Altay

The Altay, sometimes known as Altay, Oirot, Teleut, Tele, Telengit, Mountain Kalmyk, White Kalmyk, or Black Tatar, are a Turkic people inhabiting the Altai Republic, the Altai Krai, and neighboring areas in southern Siberia on the borders of Kazakhstan, China, and Mongolia. The ancestry of the Altai includes both Mongol and Turkic strains. The Altai language, spoken in two dialectical groups, is a Turkic language of the northern group of Turkic languages. The majority of the estimated 75,000 Altay are officially Orthodox Christian though pre-Christian shamanism continues as a parallel belief system.

Little is known of the Altay people until the arrival of the Pazyryks, the near-mythical ancestors of the various groups of Altay in the Altai Mountains. Of mixed Caucasian and Mongoloid descent, the Pazyryks created an advanced society in the Altai highlands between 600 and 300 BCE. The Altay were first mentioned in historical records as western Mongol tribes and Turkic tribes of the Altai region in the fifth century CE. The nomadic tribal groups survived on hunting, trapping, and herding cattle, sheep, and goats. Between the sixth and eighth centuries, the Altai tribes formed from a gradual mixing of the ancient Turkic peoples of the Altai Mountains with

Uyghurs, Oghuz, Kipchak, and other nomadic Turkic groups. The expanding Mongol Empire spread into the Altai region in the 13th century. Under nominal Mongol rule for more than two centuries, the Altay absorbed many Mongol traits and traditions. Around 1399, an alliance of Western Mongol and Turkic peoples known as the Alliance of the Four Oirats was formed. The powerful tribal federation annexed the Altai region in the 16th century and eventually extended its influence far across Central Asia. The confederation, completely destroyed by the expanding Chinese in 1758, ceased to exist, and the ensuing war greatly reduced the Altay population. Slavic Cossacks, leading the Russian expansion to the east, penetrated the Altai region in the 1500s. By the late 16th century, the Russians regularly collected a fur tax from the northern Altai tribes. Control of the important fur trade allowed the Russians to extend their authority among the southern mountain tribes over the next century. In 1756, the southern Altay tribes accepted Russian protection against the advancing Chinese. The Russians established a civil government in the region,

collected taxes in the form of valuable furs, but generally allowed the tribal groups to govern themselves under their traditional rulers. Called Oirot or Oyrot by the Russians, the Altay quickly succumbed to European diseases and Russian vodka.

The Altay people, of mixed Turkic and Mongol background, encompass two cultural and linguistic divisions comprising several tribal and clan groups, broadly divided into northern and southern Altay. The distinctions between the two groups include physical differences, with the southern group physically resembling the Mongols, while the northern group more closely resembles the Turkic peoples. Under Tsarist rule, the Altay were considered to be many different ethnic groups, as they only consolidated as a distinct people in the early Soviet era. Prior to the 1920s, they did not see themselves as one ethnic group and did not have a common name for themselves. Over many centuries, the Altay have tenaciously clung to their traditional culture and their ancient way of life. As a result of Orthodox missionary activity, many Altay adopted Christianity though others retain

Burkhanism, the Altay Religion

Burkhanism, called Ak Jang, the White Faith in the Altay language, began when an Altay man and his daughter reported visions of a figure dressed in white riding a white horse. They called the figure Ak-Burkhan and believed that his appearance foretold the imminent arrival of the mythical national hero Oirat Khan. Believers claimed that Oirat Khan promised to liberate them from Russian domination and to restore the Altay to their pre-Russian greatness. The new faith spread rapidly through the Altay tribes in the early 1900s, often violently suppressed by mobs of Russian peasants. In recent years, the religion has been revived in the Altay region.

their shamanistic beliefs or adhere to Burkhanism, an early 20th-century religious movement combining shamanistic traditions with Christian and Buddhist beliefs. The Altay speak two dialects of the northern Turkic language group. The two dialects, often considered separate languages, are not mutually intelligible with the northern dialects more closely related to the language of the Uyghur and the southern dialects belonging to the Kipchak Turkic languages. The southern dialect forms the literary language.

Under Russian pressure, many of the nomadic Altay clans began to settle on permanent plots in the early 1800s. A Russian Orthodox missionary center was established, and a majority of the Altay was officially converted to Christianity, often under force. In the 1840s, a written form of the Altay language, based on the southern Teleut dialect and using the Russian Cyrillic alphabet, was created by the Russian missionaries. In 1904, a religious movement, a distinctly anti-Russian messianic belief, spread through the Altay tribes. Known as Ak Jang or Burkhanism, the religion focused on Oirat Khan, who promised to liberate the Altay and to restore them to their pre-Chinese and pre-Russian greatness. The creed espoused a nationalist foundation promising the liberation of the Altay. Increased Russian colonization, facilitated by the completion of the Trans-Siberian Railroad from European Russia, further aggravated growing ethnic tensions in the Altai region. In 1917, the Russian Revolution swept through the region. United for the first time, the Altay tribes organized to resist attempts by local Bolsheviks to take power. Allied to the anti-Bolshevik White

forces, the Altay participated in some of the fiercest battles of the Russian Civil War. In 1920, the Whites were defeated though the Altay held out against the advancing Soviet forces until 1922. Partly as a punishment for Altay support of the rival Whites, the new Soviet government designated the huge Altai Steppe region as a Russian settlement area and restricted the Altay to a newly created autonomous province known as Oirat after the largest of the Altay tribes. Forced to settle and to collectivize their herds, the Altay lapsed into apathy and began to quickly decline and to lose population. Alcohol became a major social problem as pressure increased for the Altay to embrace a universal Soviet culture. During the course of World War II, the Soviet authorities accused the Altay leadership of being pro-Japanese. A purge sent many Altay political and cultural figures to forced labor camps or to be liquidated. In 1948, the Soviet government banned the use of the word *Oirot* as counterrevolutionary and changed the name of the Altay territory from Oirot to Mountain Altai. Despite harsh Soviet rule, the Altay made great strides in education and health. A modest revival began in the late 1950s, and by the mid-1960s, the long decline began to reverse. The collapse of the Soviet Union in 1991 allowed the Altay region to be upgraded to the status of a member republic of the new Russian Federation.

Further Reading

Altai Republic: Official Portal. "Ethnic History of the Altai Republic" Accessed July 30, 2013. http://eng.altai-republic.ru/modules .php?op=modload&name=Sections&file= index&req =viewarticle&artid=40&page=1

Bainbridge, Margaret. *The Turkic Peoples of the World.* London: Routledge, 1993.

Icon Group International. *Altay: Webster's Timeline History, 1869–2007.* San Diego: Icon Group International, 2010.

Ottung, Robert W., Danielle N. Lussier, and Anna Partetskaya, eds. *The Republics and Regions of the Russian Federation: A Guide to Politics, Policies, and Leaders.* Armonk, NY: M. E. Sharpe, 2000.

Aynu

The Aynu, sometimes known as Änyu, Ainu, Eyni, Abdal, Ani, or Aini, are a Muslim people living along the edge of the Taklamakan Desert in the Tarim Basin in China's western Xinjiang region. The estimated 30,000—50,000 Aynu mostly speak the Uyghur language, usually with outsiders and with women, as only men are allowed to speak the Aynu language. The majority of the Aynu are Sunni Muslims, with a minority of Shi'a Muslims, mostly in the southern districts.

The origins of the Aynu are not known, though their legends and language point to the Persian-speaking region of Central Asia, possibly among the powerful Sogdian peoples. The ancestors of the Aynu may have fled or been driven from their homeland by war or by the movements of larger and more powerful ethnic groups, probably moving east along the fabled Silk Road in the fifth and sixth centuries CE until they reached the oasis region around the city of Kashgar. Their arrival in the region, heavily populated by the Turkic Uyghur people, may have been as penniless refugees who had to beg to survive. The Aynu came under the rule of the Uyghur, whose empire stretched from China into Central Asia in the eighth and ninth centuries. In their new homeland, they evolved a semi-nomadic way of life based on the herding of goats and sheep. Others took up fishing along the Kashgar and Yarkant Rivers or hunting in the oasis regions around the edge of the Taklamakan Desert. Gradually, their Persian language, influenced by the neighboring Turkic Uyghur languages, took on a Turkic form and grammar though the vocabulary remained Persian. Some scholars believe that the Aynu adopted the Sunni Islam of the Turkic peoples of the region in an effort to gain acceptance as inhabitants of the overwhelmingly Turkic region. Many of their pre-Islamic rituals and traditions were retained as folk traditions. Many of the impoverished Aynu took up the profession of circumcisers, as circumcision is an obligation for Muslim males. Conflicts with the Uyghur and the other Turkic peoples of the region pushed the Aynu into the least fertile region of the Tarim Basin, with their villages mostly in the fringe of the Taklamakan Desert. In the mid-18th century, the Manchu Qing dynasty of China established a military government to rule the region, incorporating many local people into the administration and military units stationed in the region.

The Aynu culture is based on a mixture of their traditional Persian culture and influences borrowed from the neighboring Uyghur and other Turkic peoples. Though the reasons are not clear, the majority of the Uyghur despise the Aynu, who are called Adbal, a derogatory term meaning beggar. Intermarriage between the Aynu and the Uyghur and the other Turkic peoples is uncommon, partly due to discrimination and partly due to Aynu traditions. Despite the animosity between the Aynu and the Uyghur, the Chinese government counts the Aynu as part of the Uyghur ethnic group. Efforts to win official government recognition as a distinct ethnic group have been rejected or simply ignored. The Aynu live in six counties in Xinjiang that form a long crescent along the eastern edge of the Taklamakan Desert. The Aynu population is not counted separately from the Uyghur, with estimates based on speakers of the Aynu language as low as 8,000 to estimates based on connections to the Aynu culture as high as 50,000. Most Aynu are herders of goats and sheep, fishermen, or hunters, though in recent years, some Aynu men have been forced to travel to the region's large cities to seek employment in construction and industry. The Aynu are Sunni Muslims, worshiping in a string of mosques in their villages in the Tarim Basin. Very few Aynu have ever studied Arabic, and even their religious leaders are unable to read the sacred book of the Muslims, the Koran. Many people describe the Aynu as a caste of circumcisers due to their past position as official circumcisers among the Muslim populations of the region. Many of their pre-Islamic traditions are still practiced, particularly the ceremony called *lomante*. Annually, Aynu men carry out the slaughter of hibernating bears and then retrieve their cubs. The bear cubs are raised by the villages though after a few years, they are strangled in a sacred ceremony. The Aynu believe that the bears are spirits or godlike creatures. Many Aynu villages are adorned with tall poles like totem poles, carved with the images of bears and other spirits that protect the village.

In the 19th century, the Aynu, seeking acceptance from their Muslim neighbors, joined an Uyghur Rebellion in 1864 against Chinese rule. By the end of the 1800s, the Chinese held only a few strongholds in the region. Through diplomatic manipulations, the Chinese government gained Russian government support for the division of Central Asia into Chinese and Russian spheres. The Qing dynasty created the province of Xinjiang, the new frontier, and replaced the local political system with a Chinese administration. The former name Huijiang or Muslimland was banned, and the Muslim peoples were subjected to a policy of assimilation. The Chinese Revolution, in 1911–1912, ended the Qing dynasty, which was replaced by a republican government. The rallying cry of Muslim brotherhood persuaded the Aynu to support the Kumul Rebellion in the 1930s against the Chinese government. Promised equality and acceptance, the Aynu supported the Uyghur efforts to separate Xinjiang from Chinese control in the years before World War II. In 1949, China became a communist state, with the various ethnic groups given official recognition that allowed greater cultural and religious freedom. The Aynu applied for ethnic status, but due to the mixed nature of their language and culture, they were arbitrarily added to the large Uyghur ethnic group. The historic animosity between the Aynu and the Uyghur continues to the present, making relationships within the official ethnic group difficult for the minority Aynu people.

Further Reading

Johanson, Lars. *Discoveries on the Turkic Linguistic Map*. Stockholm, Sweden: Swedish Research Institute in Istanbul, 2001, 21–22.

Matras, Yaron, and Peter Bakker, eds. *The Mixed Language Debate: Theoretical and*

Empirical Advances. Berlin, Germany: Mouton De Gruyter, 2003.

Safran, William. *Nationalism and Ethnoregional Identities in China.* London: Routledge, 1998.

Starr, S. Frederick. *Xinjiang: China's Muslim Borderland.* Armonk, NY: M.E. Sharpe, 2004.

Azeri

The Azeri, sometimes known as Azerbaijanis or Azerbaijani Turks, are a Turkic people living principally in the Republic of Azerbaijan in the southern Caucasus region and in the Azerbaijan region of northwestern Iran. Outside their traditional homeland in Azerbaijan and Iran, there are large Azeri populations in Russia, Turkey, Georgia, the United States, Central Asia, and various parts of Europe. The Azeri population is estimated to number between 27 and 35 million, as the Iranian government does not publish exact figures for ethnic origins. The Azeri language, spoken in both Azerbaijan and Iranian Azerbaijan, is a Turkish language belonging to the Western Oghuz language group. The Azeri are primarily Shi'a Muslims with smaller numbers of Sunni Muslims, Christians, and Baha'is. Decades of rule by the officially atheist Soviet government resulted in an unknown number of Azeri with no religious affiliation, often describing themselves as cultural Muslims. The Azeri language, spoken in a number of dialects, forms part of the Oghuz branch of the Turkish languages and can be understood by speakers of other Turkic languages. The two major dialect groups, known as Azerbaijani North and Azerbaijani South, mostly follow the international border though the main differences are in pronunciation and basic grammatical structure. The language is written in a modified Latin alphabet in Azerbaijan and in the Perso-Arabic script in Iran. The language served as a lingua franca throughout much of the Caucasus region, eastern Turkey, and northwestern Iran from the 16th to the early 20th century.

The Azeri homeland has been inhabited since ancient times as documented by Stone Age remains found in many parts of the region. Historically, the region's earliest known inhabitants were Caucasian peoples living in organized villages, using copper implements, and engaging in irrigated agriculture. Situated at the southern edge of the Caucasus Mountains, the region was often overrun by invaders moving through the mountain passes between Europe and Asia. The Medes are believed to have settled among the Caucasian peoples in the eighth century BCE. The region often formed part of successive Persian empires and is traditionally the birthplace of Zoroaster, the originator of Persia's pre-Islamic religion. The ruler of the region officially adopted the Christian religion in the fourth century CE. The Caucasian population remained mostly Christian until the eighth century. Persian rule of the Azeri homeland ended with their defeat by the invading Muslim Arabs in 164 CE. The Azeri Caucasians remained under Muslim rule, with many adopting the new religion, until migrating Seljuk Turks overran the region in the 11th century. A Seljuk state ruled the region until the invasion of the Mongols in 1225. For centuries, the Azeri culture reflected the geography of their homeland as a frontier district at the confluence of the competing Persian and Turkish empires. The Persian Safavid dynasty brought all of the Azeri territories under Persian rule by 1551. The Shi'a sect of Islam, imposed as the official religion of Safavid Persia, became the predominant belief system among the formerly Sunni Muslim Azeri. Wars between Safavid Persia and the Sunni Muslim Ottoman Empire marked Azeri history for several centuries. As Safavid power waned in the 18th century, the Turkish Ottoman Empire and the expanding Russian Empire vied for power in the region.

The Jafari sect of Shi'a Islam remains the focus of Azeri religious beliefs although in northern Azerbaijan, the Republic of Azerbaijan, religious belief has been tempered by decades of Soviet atheism and modern Western influences. A minority of the Azeri, particularly along the international border between Azerbaijan and Iran that divides their ancient homeland and around Lake Urmia, adheres to Sunni Islam. Unlike other Muslim societies, religion is not a key identifying factor as Azeri identity is based more on culture and ethnicity than on religion. Fire, sacred to the pre-Islamic Zoroastrian religion, remains a powerful cultural symbol with Azerbaijan often called the Land of Fire. Azeri culture developed through a fusion of Persian and Turkish influences, including the Turkic dialect brought to the region by invaders from Central Asia. In modern Azerbaijan, but not in Southern or Iranian Azerbaijan, Western influences on the culture are strong. The cultural elements of music, art, folk dances, cuisine, architecture, and particularly the traditions associated with Novruz Bayram, the ancient Azeri New Year celebrations, remain important parts of modern Azeri identity. Azeri culture typically combines elements of East and West, particularly in the cuisine, architecture, music, and entertainment. Uzeyir Hajibeyov, in the early 20th century, led the movement to merge traditional Azeri culture, particularly music, with European influences. He was the first composer of an opera in the Islamic world, and the anthem he composed for the first republic was readopted following independence in 1991. Cinema, dance, music, and folk art such as carpet weaving, jewelry making, and metal engraving remain important cultural elements in both Azerbaijan and Iranian Azerbaijan. The growing prosperity in Azerbaijan derived from the expanding oil production has supported not only the revival of Azeri traditional culture but also the elements of a Western consumer society. Southern Azerbaijan, under the Iranian Islamic government, remains much less developed and culturally conservative.

By the early 19th century, most of the region was under the control of autonomous khanates. The expanding Russian Empire annexed the northern khanates piecemeal from a weakened Persia between 1805 and 1813. The Treaty of Gulistan, in 1813, recognized Russian control of northern Azerbaijan and divided the Azeri homeland into Russian and Persian spheres at the Araz (Araks) River, which now forms the border between Azerbaijan and Iran. The two halves of the Azeri nation developed in separate ways at a time when national self-consciousness was not strong enough to resist imposed cultural and political influences. In the late 19th century,

The Muslim World's First Opera

The opera *Leyli and Majnum*, by Uzeyir Hajibeyov, is considered the first opera to be written and performed in a Muslim territory. The first performance was in the Azeri capital, Baku, at the Taghiyev Theater on January 12, 1908. Based on a famous poem, the opera was very successful and is considered the foundation of a new genre combining both oriental and European musical forms. Now considered an important part of Azerbaijan's cultural heritage, the opera has been performed more than 20,000 times since its inception in 1908 and has been used as the basis for five motion pictures and several Azeri television programs.

nationalism developed in Russian Azerbaijan with the formation of specifically Azeri political parties, some espousing full independence. Large petroleum deposits were developed with the Baku oil fields producing more than 50 percent of the world supply of oil by the start of the 20th century. The Azeri oil fields were particularly important to the Russian war effort during World War I. The Russian Revolution and the collapse of the Russian Empire allowed the northern Azeri to declare their independence with a separate Azerbaijan Democratic Republic established in 1918. The new Soviet government of Russia, in desperate need of Baku's oil, launched an invasion of the new republic in 1920. The Soviet rulers effectively blockaded the new border between Soviet Azerbaijan and Iran, and all official contacts between the two halves of the Azeri nation were terminated. The southern Azeri closer ties to the Persians in religion and culture moderated the impact of nationalism, as did the threat of Russian aggression. Many southern Azeri held important posts in the Persian government, which tempered the social and

political demands during the 1920s and 1930s. Soviet rule brought modernization and development although religion and culture were suppressed in the name of Soviet brotherhood. The Azeri oil fields played a crucial role during World War II with hundreds of thousands of Azeri fighting as part of the Soviet forces. Approximately 680,000 Azeri, including more than 100,000 women, were conscripted and sent to fight the invading Fascist forces. An estimated 250,000 Azeri were killed in the fighting, and some 130 were named Heroes of the Soviet Union. Major General Azi Aslanov, the highest-ranking Azeri office in the Soviet military, was twice awarded the Hero of the Soviet Union. During the course of the war, the Soviet military occupied Iranian Azerbaijan, promising to leave the region within six months of the end of hostilities. Despite the promises, the Soviet troops remained after the end of the war to support a Soviet republic declared by Azeri communists of the Tudeh Party in alliance with local nationalist groups. In 1946, Western pressure and a new oil deal between the Soviets and the Iranian government ended the Soviet occupation, and the short-lived southern Azeri republic collapsed. The ban on contacts between the Soviet and Iranian Azeris became increasingly difficult to enforce as the use of radios became widespread in the region in the 1950s. Increased contact allowed the Soviet Azeri to lend covert aid to their kin in Iran. But despite the repression of the Shah's government, the southern Azeri prospered economically, dominated the bazaars across the country, and provided two-thirds of army officers and many of Iran's intellectuals, teachers, and writers. A relaxation of stringent Soviet controls and the modernization that swept Iran prior to the Islamic Revolution spurred a renewed interest in cross-border ties with cultural and family exchanges. In Soviet Azerbaijan, a religious reawakening accompanied the national resurgence. The fall of the Shah's government and imposition of a strict Islamic state in 1979 fueled opposition of the Islamic excesses and antigovernment rioting in many southern Azeri cities. In 1983, all Azeri political organizations in Iran were officially dissolved. In a massive crackdown, hundreds of Azeri religious and cultural leaders and members of banned organizations, including many Azeri women, were imprisoned. Of the many Azeri cultural and language publications that emerged in the wake of the 1979 revolution, by 1984, only one survived. The further relaxation of Soviet control in the 1980s allowed nationalist sentiment to spread quickly through Soviet Azerbaijan. Civil unrest and ethnic strife swept the region, particularly between the Azeri and the Armenians, who

formed a large minority within the Soviet Azeri republic. The rapid collapse of the Soviet Union resulted in the formation of an independent Azerbaijan Republic, which was quickly recognized by the countries of the West. The early years of independence were overshadowed by conflict with the neighboring Republic of Armenia and the Armenian populated Nagorno-Karabakh region in southwestern Azerbaijan. By the end of hostilities between the two newly independent republics in 1994, the Armenians controlled up to 16 percent of Azerbaijan, including the disputed Nagorno-Karabakh region. The conflict, involving ethnic and religious rivalries, resulted in the departure of many of Azerbaijan's Russian and Armenian minorities during the 1990s. Influences from independent Azerbaijan seeped into the southern Azerbaijan areas in Iran, resulting in widespread disturbances in 1999. Student demonstrations and cultural demands in Iranian Azerbaijan were the first important indications of discontent with the policies of the repressive and conservative religious leaders who control Iran. Many political, religious, and cultural leaders fled north to Azerbaijan, and the detention of Mahmud Ali Chehregani, a leading advocate of southern Azeri rights, became the focus of newspapers in the Azerbaijan Republic and international human rights groups. Religious influences from Iran resulted in the formation of conservative formations targeting religious minorities, Azerbaijan's traditionally liberated women, and calls for an Islamic government. But for the vast majority of the population of Azerbaijan, a more moderate form of Shi'a Islam supports the secular government and also the advances made by the society under the former Soviets and since independence in 1991. Closer ties to the European Union, Turkey, the United States, and other Western nations have supported the spread of a prosperous middle-class, Western-style equality for woman, particularly in the urban areas, and participation in many international organizations. The Azeri of Iran have suffered increasingly harsh treatment, particularly women demanding the rights past Islamic rulers promised. Sexual equality is one of the doctrines now considered as contrary to Islamic doctrine as interpreted by the Islamic government. The Azeri populations of Azerbaijan and Iran, though separated by political borders for some two centuries, retain strong cultural and linguistic ties, and some political groups continue to work for the unification of the two halves of the Azeri people in one sovereign republic.

Further Reading

Atabaki, Touraj. *Azerbaijan: Ethnicity and the Struggle for Power in Iran.* London: I. B. Tauris, 2000.

Azerbaijan Culture. "General Information on Azeri Culture." Accessed July 30, 2013. http://www.azerbaijan.az/_Culture/_General Info/_generalInfo_e.html

Bolukbasi, Suha. *Azerbaijan: A Political History.* London: I. B. Tauris, 2011.

Isgenderli, Anar. *Realities of Azerbaijan, 1917–1920.* Bloomington, IN: Xlibris, 2011.

B

Bai

The Bai, sometimes known as Baip, Bai Man, Baizu, Baini, Bo, Baipho, Baihuo, Sou, Minjia, or Miep jiax, are a Chinese ethnic group, one of the 56 officially recognized ethnic minorities in the People's Republic of China. The name *Bai*, meaning "white" in Chinese, was first applied by the Han Chinese due to the color of the white sheepskins that formed their traditional clothing. The estimated two million Bai are concentrated in China's Yunnan Province with smaller populations in neighboring areas of Guizhou and Hunan Provinces. The majority of the Bai now live in the Dali Baizu Autonomous Region of Yunnan. The Bai speak a language of the Sino-Tibetan language family though its classification remains undetermined. Though the majority of the Bai adhere to Buddhism, they also continue to revere their village gods; other clans have embraced Taoism, Islam, or Christianity.

Archaeological evidence indicates that the Erhai region of Yunnan was inhabited as early as 7000–3000 BCE. Stone tools from that period indicate a population with agricultural skills and small-scale farming operations, which supplemented their major occupations of fishing and hunting. Over time, the Bai have been considered a Tai people, even though their language belongs to the Tibeto-Burman language group. Physically, they took on many Chinese features through intermarriage and ethnic exchanges. The origins of the Bai are disputed by historians and ethnologists, with some scholars attributing their origins to the ancient Ji, Qiang, or Diqiang people, while others claim their separate identity developed toward the end of the third century BCE when their ancestors, living around Kunming and Erhai Lake, came into contact with the Han Chinese moving into the region from the north. According to Chinese historical archives, when the Qin troops unified China in 221 BCE, they conquered the southwestern kingdom of the Bo (Bai), taking many as slaves. Starting in 182 BCE, Han Chinese migration into the Bo territories of the present-day Sichuan-Yunnan border areas caused many Bo to migrate south into Yunnan. Gradually, the Bo peoples mixed with the Han Chinese to evolve as the Bai ethnic group. In 109 BCE, the Han dynasty dispatched imperial administrators and soldiers to the city of Dali on Erhai Lake, followed by a substantial number of Han colonists. Despite Chinese interference in the region, the Bai were able to maintain their independence, and in 729 CE, they formed the multiethnic Nanzhao state from a unification of six small Bai and Yi kingdoms. Initially encouraged by the Chinese to form a buffer state between Imperial China and Tibet, the new Nanzhao kingdom was soon seen as a greater threat than the Tibetans. Chinese troops invaded the region in 751 but were defeated only to return three years later but were again defeated. Nanzhao controlled the trade routes between China and India as well as maintained a monopoly on the sale of woven silk and cotton. The kingdom grew powerful and prosperous on trade and on the revenue from salt and gold mines. The Bai-dominated kingdom enjoyed a golden era of economic expansion and cultural renaissance. The kingdom expanded to the south and later turned north to conquer parts of Sichuan, including the largely Chinese city of Chengdu in 829. Over the next several years, the Bai-dominated kingdom reached its height, but by 873, Chinese attacks had driven the armies back into Yunnan. Buddhism spread to the kingdom in the ninth century. Slave rebellions and uprisings by non-Bai ethnic groups ended the Nanzhao kingdom, which was replaced by a smaller kingdom, known as Dali, in 902. The kingdom of Dali lasted for more than 300 years until its conquest by the invading Mongols in 1253. At its height, the Dali state controlled territory some three times as large as the present province of Yunnan. The historic province of Yunnan, including the territory of the former Nanzhao and Dali kingdoms, was created by the Mongol Yuan dynasty in 1274. Many Muslim soldiers, brought to the region by the Mongols, settled in the Bai territories. In order to strengthen their hold on the region, the Mongol Yuan dynasty offered former Bai chiefs official posts and granted their families hereditary privileges. Though most of the land was concentrated in the hands of the local aristocracy, the feudal land system began to give way to a landlord system.

The Chinese Ming dynasty took power in 1381 and ruled the region until it was overthrown by the Manchu in 1644. During this period, appointed court officials ruled the Bai territories as local chieftains were replaced with court officials. The political reforms weakened the political and economic privileges of the aristocratic families, freed many slaves, and gave peasants an incentive to farm the land. The subsequent Qing dynasty established by the Manchu appointed local officials and Bai chiefs as public administrators, in effect reestablishing the feudal privileges that led to the exploitation and oppression of many of the Bai during the 17th and 18th centuries. Over the centuries, the Bai created an advanced culture with scientific studies, agricultural wealth, and influences from other cultures blending into their unique culture. Inventions and advances in meteorology, astronomy, calendar development, architecture, the medical sciences, literature, music, and the arts were disseminated to other peoples through the important trade routes that connected China to the north to Burma and India. A wealth of literary works reflected their lifestyle, work, and struggles against nature and oppression. Religion played an important role in Bai life, with Buddhist monasteries and abbots holding huge amounts of land and other properties. The Bai peasants were often burdened by religious activities that required the sacrifice of cattle and other valuables.

Traditionally, Bai society is based on the nuclear, small extended family and the village, not the clan lineage. People living in the same village, no matter their family name, worshiped a common ancestor, usually the founder of the village. In the 17th-19th, and again in the early 20th centuries, probably due to Chinese influence, the practice of arranged marriage by parents became common. Children were often betrothed at infancy and wed in their late teens. Elderly parents usually lived with the youngest son, who later inherited the family home. Prior to the imposition of communism in 1949, Bai society consisted of a stratified system of classes including landlords, merchants, wealthy peasants living in towns or cities, artisans, peasants, and landless peasants. During the 1950s, 1960s, and most of the 1970s, the peasants were glorified, while the wealthy were abused and attacked. Since the beginning of the economic reforms in 1970s, there has been a reemergence of a more stratified socioeconomic society. The Bai language, sometimes known as Baip, is spoken in three major dialects corresponding to the three largest Bai-populated regions. The position of the Bai language within the Sino-Tibetan language family remains undetermined. Traditionally considered part of the Tibeto-Burman branch of the Sino-Tibetan languages, rival studies indicate that it may instead be an offshoot of Proto-Sinitic, along with Old Chinese. An estimated 60 percent of the modern Bai language has Chinese roots. The literary language was adapted to the Latin alphabet in 1957, with revisions updating the language instituted in 1993. Buddhism remained a strong social force until 1949. Since the early 1980s, the government of the People's Republic of China has relaxed its view of religion, allowing the Bai to rebuild many temples and revive many Buddhist and

Taoist associations even though religious rites and ceremonies are mostly practiced by the older generations. Though the Bai are traditionally Buddhist, they also continue to respect their village god, known as Benzhu, nature spirits, the revered rulers of the Nanzhao kingdom, and the heroes and heroines of Bai folklore. Throughout the region, there are villages of Muslims who usually refer to themselves as Bai Hui or Bai Muslim. Most claim that their ancestors were Hui people who fled to the region in the 1860s following the defeat of the Panthay Rebellion or that they are descendants of the Muslim soldiers stationed in the region following the Mongol conquest in the 13th century.

The stratified Bai society, in the 19th century, accorded town and village elders great respect. Women had a relatively equal status with men, even among the large peasant population. In 1874, a Hui Muslim, Du Wenxiu, united the peoples of Yunnan against the oppression of the Qing dynasty. The rebels established an autonomous Dali administration and adopted measures to promote agricultural and industrial production, reduce the high land taxes, and to eliminate discrimination by the Han Chinese against the various ethnic groups in the region. The rebellion lasted some 18 years before it was brutally crushed. The region was organized under the traditional Chinese civil service system of counties headed by a magistrate who was responsible for the administration of justice and the collection of taxes. Despite the existence of the government judicial system, the Bai preferred to solve problems among themselves or by referring the matter to the village elder. Both criminal and civil cases were most often settled this way, and punishments depended on the relationship of the parties involved. Beginning in the early 20th century, Christian missionaries made some converts in the region, but Bai Christians were regarded with suspicion and sometimes ostracized by their families or villages. The construction of the Burma Road, in 1937–1938, greatly increased foreign trade and brought increased missionary activity to the Bai territories. The events of World War II transformed Yunnan as many refugees from China's east coast and large industrial establishments were relocated to the relatively peaceful area. The extension of the Burma Road during World War II increased the importance of the region. The feudal landlord system continued to dominate the Bai territories with some 90 percent of the Bai working as farmers but holding only about 20 percent of the land. Many Bai families were peasant serfs working lands owned by landlords with neither land nor much personal freedom. By the mid-20th century, the Bai were rapidly assimilating into Han Chinese culture. The civil war in China, in the wake of World War II, ended with the communist victory and the imposition of a socialist system in Yunnan in 1949. As part of the communist minority system, the Dali Baizu Autonomous Region was established in Yunnan in 1956, encompassing about half of the ethnic Bai population. Communist minority policies encouraged the Bai to adopt an ethnic identification separate from that of the Han Chinese and to adopt ethnic markers based on their ancient history, including ethnic clothing, music, festivals, and language development. Prior to the communist revolution, the Bai most often referred to themselves as *Bai ni*, which

means "descendants of the Bai king." After the establishment of communist rule in Yunnan, the Bai were subjected to a nationality identification project in the 1950s and were identified as the Bai nationality, one of the officially recognized minority groups in the People's Republic of China. During the Cultural Revolution, 1967–1977, most Bai Buddhist temples were destroyed and religious practices were forbidden. Despite communist restrictions, the extended family and the village remained important units of both production and consumption. Unlike most other Chinese nationalities, women in Bai society are not treated as second-class citizens, and it is not considered a tragedy to have daughters and no sons. Among the ethnic groups living in Yunnan, the Bai are reputed to be one of the best educated and famous for their proud sense of self-respect and consciousness of their unique ethnic identity. Over many centuries, the Bai culture has absorbed much of the Han Chinese advances without losing their own identity.

Further Reading

Ethnic Groups. "The Bai ethnic minority." Accessed July 30, 2013. http://www.china.org.cn/e-groups/shaoshu/shao-2-bai.htm

Harrell, Stevan. *Cultural Encounters on China's Ethnic Frontiers.* Seattle: University of Washington Press, 2000.

McCarthy, Susan K. *Communist Multiculturalism: Ethnic Revival in Southwest China.* Seattle: University of Washington Press, 2009.

Mullaney, Thomas, and Benedict Anderson. *Coming to Terms with the Nation: Ethnic Classification in Modern China.* Berkeley, CA: University of California Press, 2011.

Baluchi

The Baluchi, sometimes known as Baloochis, Baloch, or Kur Galli, are a South Asian ethnic group whose homeland straddles the borders of Pakistan, Afghanistan, and Iran. The Baluchi homeland, often compared to a lunar landscape, is generally arid and lies outside the monsoon zone. Despite being rich in minerals, the region offers few ways to earn a sustainable income. Most Baluchis survive through government services, nomadic herding, and smuggling. Some work as fishermen or live in the small fertile regions as farmers engaged in dry land or irrigated agriculture. The largest part of their homeland forms the Baluchistan province of Pakistan. The Seistan and Baluchistan provinces of Iran have a Baluchi majority, but they have few ethnic or group rights. They are also spread across southern Afghanistan in the provinces of Nimruz, Helmand, and Kandahar. The Greater Baluchistan is home to an estimated 10–15 million Baluchis, including the 2.5–3 million Brahui, and, as defined by the many ethnic and nationalist groups active in the region, includes all the Baluchi-populated regions stretching from southeastern Iran into southern Afghanistan and central Pakistan. Except for small minorities of Shi'a Muslims, Baha'is, and Christians, the vast majority of the Baluchis are followers of Sunni Islam. Traditionally, the Baluchis include two distinct but culturally and historically related peoples, the Baluchis (Nharhui Baluchis, the formerly nomadic descendants of tribes that originated on the Iranian Plateau) and the Brahui (Brahui Baluchis, the traditionally settled population descended from the area's pre-Aryan Dravidian inhabitants). Cultural, social, and kinship relations unite the two Baluchi peoples and often cross international borders, but the harsh physical environment is reflected in the division into numerous, often antagonistic, tribal groups geographically grouped into Southern, Western, and Eastern Baluchis. The Baluchi language, known as Baluchi or Balochi, forms part of the northwestern Iranian language group. Many Baluchis speak Farsi, Sindhi, or Brahui as second languages with some people of Baluchi ancestry now speaking other languages such as Seraiki or Punjabi.

The region, broadly known as Maka from the port city now known as Makran, was known as an eastern territory of the early Persian empires. Some Baluchis trace their origins to Nimrod, the son of Cush, Noah's grandson. Others claim Arab or Persian ancestry. The early Baluchis devised many ingenious ways to survive in their harsh environment, including *qanats*, systems for providing water to the arid farmlands, and underground drainage tunnels that brought water from the highlands to water the gardens and palm groves on the plains. Baluchi traditions have it that they may have settled their present homeland at the beginning of the Islamic period in the seventh century, but recent genetic studies confirm their ties to the ancient peoples of the region. Many Baluchis believe that they are of Arab descent and trace their roots to the city of Aleppo in Syria. Dravidian peoples, dominant across the Indian subcontinent, were mostly driven into southern India by the Aryan invasions, which swept across the region from the Bampoor region (modern Bampur) of the Iranian

Plateau between 1700 and 1200 BCE. The Dravidians in the upland valleys in the arid northwest of the subcontinent escaped the onslaught as the Aryans mostly bypassed their valleys as they moved farther east, leaving only a few small nomadic Aryan tribes in the vast region. The interaction between the nomads and the settled Brahui Dravidians gradually merged their cultures into parts of the broad Baluchi population. The Brahui freely mixed with the surrounding Baluchi tribes, though they retained their own Dravidian language. In the seventh century, Muslim Arab invaders brought their Islamic religion to the settled Brahui valleys. Arab rule in Baluchistan reinforced the semi-independent tribal system that allowed local leaders to retain their autonomy while paying tribute to the Arab rulers as part of the Islamic social system. Other Baluchi tribes, driven from their homelands farther west by invading Seljuk Turks, moved into the arid regions in the 11th and 12th centuries forming new tribal groups. Refugees fleeing the Mongol invasion in the 13th century also moved east into the forbidding landscape to take up nomadic herding or to become fishermen on the shores of the Arabian Sea. The Mongol invasion of Baluchistan left a lasting impression on the region. The stories of the atrocities perpetrated by the Mongols, known later as the Mughals, are still well known and are passed down from generation to generation. Brahui-speaking tribes often recount their expulsion from the more fertile valleys due to the rampaging Mongol hordes. Frequent invasions and violent confrontations over the scarce resources of the region led to the development of a warrior

culture. Baluchi resistance to the various empires that attempted to extend their authority to the region generated legends of great warriors and a rejection of outsiders. The Brahui, with a long history of settled government, formed the dominant tribe; the powerful Brahui khans of Kalat ruled much of Baluchistan from the 17th century. The Mughal Empire to the east and Persia to the west often fought for control of the region and its important trade routes. The local tribal chiefs and the khans of Kalat retained their power, though often as vassals of more powerful neighbors. In the 18th century, as the power of the Mughals declined, the khans of Kalat extended their authority while maintaining the cooperation of the loose tribal organization. Cohesion between the settled Brahui and the mostly nomadic Baluchi tribes was preserved through a policy of parceling out a portion of all conquests among the tribal leaders. In the late 18th century, Nasir Khan I, known to the Brahui as Nasir the Great, became khan of Kalat. During his 44-year reign, local conflicts between tribal groups were halted, administration of the state was made more efficient, and strict attention to the precepts of Islamic law was enforced.

Baluchi culture is based on customs and traditions imposed by tribal laws. These historical traditions remain very important to Baluchi identity and have enabled them to retain their distinctive ancient cultural identity and a way of life that has changed little since the seventh century. Modern Baluchi culture remains stratified and has been characterized as feudal militarism based on an elaborate system of family, clan, and tribal ties. The Baluchis are deeply committed to their personal honor and continue to honor their ancient code of conduct, the *baluch-myar*. The code is an oral collection passed down from father to son and covers such subjects as hospitality, generosity, revenge taking, religious reverence, respect for religious and secular leaders, and conduct during war. Town and tribal leaders and elders often quote the Baluchi code when issuing verdicts over conflicts or other affairs at annual gatherings. The power of the traditional leaders has begun to wane as modernization spreads and many Baluchis leave their arid homeland to seek a better life outside Baluchistan. The largest urban Baluchi populations are in Quetta, the capital of Pakistani Baluchistan, and in Karachi, the largest Pakistani city in the neighboring region of Sind. The two groups that form part of the Baluchi people, the Baluchi and the Brahui, have lived in close proximity for many centuries and are often indistinguishable though the Brahui are regarded as a separate people due to the survival of their ancient Dravidian language. The Brahui language is related to the Dravidian languages spoken across southern India, but with a strong Baluchi admixture. Most Brahui are bilingual, speaking both their ancient language and the local Baluchi dialects. The Baluchi language is an Indo-Iranian language related to Farsi (Persian) and Kurdish. The language is spoken in various dialects and is divided into three broad groups—Eastern, Western, and Southern. In the 19th and early 20th centuries, Baluchi scholars used the Persian and Urdu scripts to transcribe oral Baluchi into a literary form, but since Pakistani independence and the rise of Baluchi identity, they have favored the

Nastaliq script, a Baluchi adaptation of the Arabic script. The majority of the Baluchis adhere to the Hanafi branch of Sunni Islam. Smaller groups include Shi'a Muslims, mostly located in the Baluchi areas of Iran and Afghanistan, and a Zikri Muslim minority in Pakistan Baluchistan. The estimated one million Zikris are followers of a sect founded in the 15th century in southern Baluchistan with most living in the Makran region and in Karachi. The Zikris believe in a messiah, Nur Pak, whose teachings they claim superseded those of the Prophet Mohammed. The Zikri beliefs, often considered heretical, have incited intermittent Sunni repression of the Zikri minority. Though ethnically related to the neighboring peoples, relations between the Baluchis and other peoples are a history of conflicts, often not only over the region's natural resources, but also due to the Baluchis' traditional rejection of outside influences.

Europeans first explored the Baluchistan region in 1810. European colonial rivalries played a crucial role in the European conquest of the area. The British occupied most of Baluchistan during the first Anglo-Afghan War in 1839, justifying the occupation as a way to prevent the Russians from gaining access to the Indian Ocean through the Baluchi ports. In 1846, the British authorities divided British Baluchistan into three distinct regions: the settled areas under direct British rule, the territory administered through the Khanate of Kalat, and the tribal zones under the rule of various Baluchi tribal chiefs. The British established the northern districts as the Protectorate of British Baluchistan in 1877. The southern districts, Kalat and the tribal states, known as the Baluchistan

States, remained semiautonomous countries tied to British India by treaties and resident British advisers. The border between British Baluchistan and neighboring Persian territory, settled by negotiated agreements in 1895–1896, left a substantial Baluchi population under Persian rule. Seeing the British as yet another in a long series of invaders, periodic uprisings were frequent and continued into the 20th century. During World War I, when many British troops were returned to Europe, a serious Baluchi uprising swept through British Baluchistan. In the 1930s, Baluchi leaders in British and Iranian Baluchistan first put forward demands for the unification of all Baluchi-populated territories. Frequent uprisings in Iranian Baluchistan were subdued when Reza Shah launched a series of pacification campaigns against the Baluchi tribes. By 1935, the Baluchis of Seistan and Baluchistan had been subdued. In the 1940s, rapid population growth pushed the ethnic Baluchi frontiers into sparsely populated southwestern Afghanistan. Prior to the independence of British India, in 1947, the British administration partitioned the subcontinent into predominately Hindu but secular India and Muslim Pakistan, forcing the many semiautonomous states and territories to choose between the two. The tribal leaders of British Baluchistan attached their territories to Pakistan, but the Baluchistan States, led by the Khanate of Kalat, refused to join either. On August 15, 1947, just one day after India and Pakistan were granted full independence, the khan of Kalat proclaimed the independence of the Baluchistan. In 1948, following intense pressure from the governments of Pakistan, Iran, Afghanistan, and Great Britain, the khan was forced to nullify the proclamation and accede to Muslim Pakistan. The Baluchi leadership, accustomed to indirect rule and substantial autonomy under the British administration, demanded the same from the new Pakistani government leading to tensions and conflicts between the Baluchistan Province and the central government. Local uprisings and violent conflicts continued to undermine Pakistani authority throughout the 1950s and 1960s. Following the secession of East Pakistan, now Bangladesh, in 1971, the government imposed a harsh administration and attempted to end the authority of the traditional leaders. In 1973, a widespread revolt broke out in Pakistani Baluchistan and soon spread to the Baluchi area of southeastern Iran. At its height in 1974, the rebellious Baluchis, numbering some 55,000, were faced with between 80,000 and 100,000 Pakistani and Iranian troops. The rebellion was finally crushed in 1977 as the victors razed whole villages, leaving more than 10,000 Baluchis dead and many more as refugees. Sporadic uprisings have continued in all the Baluchi-populated regions to the present. The divided Baluchi homeland remains among the poorest regions in all three countries. An influx of non-Baluchis into the region in recent years continues to spark unrest in the vast territory.

Further Reading

Axmann, Martin. *Back to the Future: The Khanate of Kalat and the Genesis of Baluch Nationalism, 1915–1955*. New York: Oxford University Press, 2012.

Scholz, Fred. *Nomadism and Colonialism: A Hundred Years of Baluchistan 1872–1972.* New York: Oxford University Press, 2002.

Titus, Paul, ed. *Marginality and Modernity: Ethnicity and Change in Post-Colonial Balochistan.* New York: Oxford University Press, 1997.

Biao

The Biao, sometimes known as Gang Bau, Kang Bau, Kang Pau, or Kang Beu, live mostly in the province of Guangdong and adjacent areas of Guangxi in southern China. The estimated 160,000 Biao speak the Biao language, a language that belongs to the Tai-Kadai language group, though its relationship to the other languages of the group is still being studied. The Biao continue to revere their traditional religious beliefs, often mixed with later Daoist and Buddhist teachings.

Archaeological finds show that the region was inhabited as early as the Neolithic Age. Artifacts found in the region indicate that the early inhabitants used stone tools, engaged in agriculture, livestock raising, fishing, and hunting. Many of the early inhabitants dwelt in caves. Around 2,000 years ago, they began to use bronze utensils, swords, and knives. The ancestors of the Biao developed close ties to the neighboring Han Chinese during the Qin and Han dynasties, from about 220 BCE to 220 CE. The Chinese government set up county governments and moved large number of ethnic Han Chinese to the region. The Han Chinese settlers introduced more advanced farming methods along with iron tools and weapons. By the seventh century, the Biao

farmers had achieved levels of production comparable to those of the central plains. Slaves were used for heavy labor, while free peasants and small farmers were subject to heavy taxation and were forced to render various services to the local rulers, including conscription into local militias and military units. Some of the Biao, when they lost their lands through natural disaster or other misfortunes, were then sold as slaves. Overrun by the invading Mongols in the mid-13th century, the Biao maintained their feudal society while paying tribute in grain to the Mongol Yuan dynasty in China twice a year. Following the overthrow of the Ming dynasty by Manchu invaders from the north in 1644, a number of Ming princes fled to the Biao region. For several years, Zhaoqing, the region's largest city, served as the capital of one of the pretenders to the Ming throne until the region came under definite Manchu rule. Under the authority of the Manchu Qing dynasty, beginning in the mid-17th century, the Biao region was divided into smaller administrative units responsible for collecting taxes and maintaining law and order. The units, known as *dong*, were mostly inhabited by families sharing the same surname.

The Biao culture displays both the traditional Tai influences and the borrowings resulting from centuries of contact with the neighboring Han Chinese. Officially, the People's Republic of China does not recognize the Biao as a separate nationality but has arbitrarily added the Biao to the Han ethnic group. Although they are classified as Han Chinese, the Biao consider themselves a distinctive ethnic group. Even prior to the 1940s, the agricultural economy of the Biao was comparatively advanced. Agricultural techniques, crop varieties, and farming tools were basically the same as those used by their Han Chinese neighbors. Oxen were the main draft animals, though horses were also used. The Biao are now mostly engaged in the cultivation of rice, sugarcane, fruits, rosin, and cassia bark. Horticulture and cash crops contribute greatly to the Biao economy. Traditionally, the Biao were known for their spinning, weaving, and dyeing, often using textiles as trade goods. Early marriage arranged by parents was a common practice before 1949. Brides did not live with their husbands but stayed with the bride's family until the first child was born. Intermarriage with the Han Chinese is permitted, but weddings are costly affairs that drain the wealth of a family. The Biao language, though known to form part of the large Tai-Kadai language group, is not clearly situated within the structure of the languages of the group. Many scholars believe that Biao forms part of the Kam-Sui group of Tai-Kadai languages, but the relationship is still being studied. The Chinese authorities are promoting the use of more Mandarin Chinese in schools in the Biao region. The majority of the Biao continue to practice their traditional shamanistic religion that revolves around reverence for the departed ancestors and the spirits that inhabit all living things and geographic assets. The teachings of Daoism and Buddhism are often mixed with their earlier customs in a unique Biao religious system.

In the 19th century, opium traded through the coastal region triggered the First Opium War between the United Kingdom and the Chinese Empire. The Chinese defeat began a period of foreign incursions and intervention. The port cities were also the major point of exit for laborers to Southeast Asia and to North America. Many impoverished Biao joined the exodus but were soon absorbed into the Han Chinese communities established overseas. Christian missionaries entered the region in the mid-19th century, bringing the first example of modern education. During the 1850s, the Taiping Rebellion, originally against foreign influence, became a civil war in southern China. Because of the long contact with the outside world, the province of Guangdong was a center of anti-Manchu and anti-imperialist activity. Many Biao joined their Han Chinese neighbors in activities deemed subversive, and many Biao villages were punished for the activity of the Biao activists. In the early 1920s, the region formed part of the territory held by the nationalist government of China, and the Biao were conscripted into the military to fight against the warlords holding power in many parts of the country and the growing power of the communists. The outbreak of World War II ended the fighting between government troops and the communist rebels, but the civil war resumed in 1945. The communists, victorious in 1949, forced the Biao into collectives and communes as employees of the communist state. Many of the old Bio traditions and customs, deemed antiquated or even subversive, were prohibited. The government began official recognition of many of the country's ethnic minorities, but despite petitions and demands, they rejected the Biao claim as a distinct ethnic group and arbitrarily added the Biao to the large

Han Chinese ethnic group. In recent years, despite government pressure to assimilate, the Biao have worked to save their distinct language and to recover their historic culture.

Further Reading

Brook, Timothy. *The Troubled Empire: China in the Yuan and Ming Dynasties.* Cambridge, MA: Belknap Press, 2010.

Diller, Anthony, Jerry Edmondson, and Yongsian Luo, eds. *The Tai-Kadai Languages.* London: Routledge, 2008.

Lewis, Mark Edward, and Timothy Brook, ed. *The Early Chinese Empires: Qin and Han.* Cambridge, MA: Belknap Press, 2010.

Blang

The Blang, sometimes known as Bulong or Bulang, are one of the 56 ethnic groups officially recognized by the People's Republic of China. They mostly live in China's southwestern Yunnan Province, with smaller communities in neighboring parts of Myanmar and Thailand. The estimated 95,000 Blang live primarily in Meng Hai County in southwestern Yunnan. The Blang speak a language of the Waic branch of the Mon-Khmer language group. Many also speak Dai and Wa, the language of the neighboring ethnic groups, along with Mandarin Chinese, the official language of China. The majority of the Blang are officially Theravada Buddhist, though most continue to revere their ancient animist beliefs and ancestor worship.

Historically, the Blang lived in small clan societies based on ancestral affiliations. Each clan possessed its own territory, and each member of the clan was responsible for assigned work and taking part in the harvesting of crops. According to ancient Chinese archives, an historic tribe called the Pu formed the earliest inhabitants of the Lancang and Nujiang River valleys. The Pu are believed to have been the ancestors of the modern Blang people. The name *Pu* remains in one of the Blang exports, the world famous Pu'er tea. Traditionally, the Blangs produced rice, maize, and beans, which formed the basis of their agriculture. Ancient Burmese and Chinese kingdoms often vied for control of the Blang homeland in the border region between the two often warring states. In 109 BCE, the Chinese emperor Wu sent an army south to establish Chinese control of the Yunnan region and to establish a trading route known as the "Southwest Barbarian Way" to connect China with Burma and India. The trade routes, often skirting Blang territory, brought new influences and advances to the Blang communities closer to the trading posts and towns. The Blang came under the nominal rule of the Bai rulers of Nanzhao kingdom that flourished in the region during the eighth and ninth centuries CE. The successor state to Nanzhao, known as the Dali kingdom, controlled a vast region that included all the Blang territories. Overrun by invading Mongols in the early 13th century, the Blang territories came under the rule of the Mongol-Chinese Yuan dynasty. The iron hoe was widely used by the Pu people, and the importance of this implement is demonstrated as it became the Blang tribute to the Yuan court. In the late 14th century, the Chinese Ming dynasty took control of the region, which was divided into counties under appointed magistrates who were also responsible for the affairs of the small ethnic groups like the Blang. From the end of the 15th century, the Burmese kingdom began to take an interest in the region, mounting an armed invasion in the early 16th century. The Blang, whose territory, known as Punam, was often overrun during the upheavals, retreated further into the jungled mountains. The Qing dynasty, established in northern China by the Manchu, finally took control of Yunnan in 1659. The new regime returned the region to a feudal administration, leaving the tribal peoples on the lower rungs of society.

The Blang are a highland people living typically between 1,500 (4,920 feet) and 2,300 (7,545 feet) meters. Mostly farmers, the Blang produce cash crops such as dry rice, cotton, sugarcane, and the famous Pu'er tea. Normally, Blang communities are made up of related families. They also raise livestock, which is kept on the ground floor of their two-story houses. The social structure is based on exogamous clans with some villages traditionally composed of 100 households or more representing up to a dozen different clans. The land farmed by the villagers is usually held in common, with each clan controlling a portion of the land. The Blang have a rich oral tradition that includes legends, folktales, poetry, stories, riddles, and ballads. Their oral tradition is the means of telling their history, imparting knowledge, and expressing their feelings. Music and dance are very popular, and most festivals are accompanied by dancing and musical events. Sword and stick dancing are popular in the mountain areas. The Blang are renowned for their hospitality. Older women chew betel nut, which stains the teeth black and is considered a mark of beauty. Dai influence on the Blang culture is evident in the music, dancing, and the Buddhist religion, brought to the Blang by Dai traders. The majority of the Blang adhere to Theravada Buddhism with many pre-Buddhist traditions and rites still practiced. A small community of Christians has existed since before missionary activity in the region was terminated by the communist regime in 1949. The Blang language, part of the Waic branch of the Mon-Khmer languages, is spoken in several dialects in China and Myanmar. Many Blang use Wa or Mandarin in their daily lives though most speak and understand their traditional Blang language.

In the early 19th century, development among the Blang was quite uneven. Dai influence on some communities changed religious and social customs. Other groups, in close contact with Han or other ethnic groups, often took on the cultural aspects of neighboring peoples. The export of their Pu'er tea, often called Red Tea, to China and Mongolia allowed many of the Blang villages to prosper. Tea remained an important part of the Blang culture, with special ways of refining the tender shoots and many ceremonies including tea as an integral part. Often exploited by landlords, feudal warlords, or neighboring peoples, the Blang continued their traditional method of escaping oppression by moving higher into the less accessible mountain regions. The construction of the Burma Road that connected Yunnan to Burma and the south, beginning in the 1930s, opened new markets for Blang products, particularly tea. During World War II, the region received many refugees, mostly Han Chinese, fleeing the fighting further north. In 1949, the

A man of the Blang ethnic group near Xishuangbanna in southern Yunnan. (Nicolas Marino/Aurora Photos/Corbis)

communists, victorious in the Chinese Civil War, took control of the region. The emphasis on the long-suffering peasants led to abuses of landowning Blang landlords or others prosperous from trade or artisans. In the early 1980s, the relative relaxation of stringent economic rules allowed the Blang to convert most of their fertile land to tea production, as demand for the Pu'er tea continues to grow.

Further Reading

Davis, Sara L. *Song and Silence: Ethnic Revival on China's Southwest Borders.* New York: Columbia University Press, 2005.

Ma Yin, ed. *China's Minority Nationalities.* Beijing: Foreign Language Press, 1989.

McCarthy, Susan K. *Communist Multiculturalism: Ethnic Revival in Southwest China.* Seattle: University of Washington Press, 2009.

People's Daily Online. "The Blang Ethnic Minority." Accessed July 30, 2013. http://english.people.com.cn/data/minorities/Blang.html

Bonan

The Bonan, sometimes known as Baonan, Bao'an, Baonuo, Paoan, Pao-an, or Paongan, are one of the People's Republic of China's officially recognized ethnic groups. The estimated 19,000 Bonan live in Gansu and Qinghai Provinces in northwestern China. Most of the Bonan live in the Jishishan Bonan, Dongxiang, and Salar Autonomous County located south of the Yellow River near Gansu's border with Qinghai. The religion of the Bonan recognized as a distinct ethnic group is Muslim, though there is a smaller group of Buddhist Bonan, numbering some 4,000, speaking the same language though they are officially classified as part of the Tu or Monguor ethnic group. The Bonan language forms part of the Mongolic languages, which is spoken by both groups.

The Bonan are believed to be the descendants of Muslim Mongol troops stationed in Qinghai during the Yuan dynasty in the 13th century. The soldiers were charged with protecting the region against the Tibetans. The name *Bonan* can be translated as meaning "I protect you." Over the centuries, they have mixed with other Mongol groups, Muslim Chinese or Hui, Tu, Han Chinese, and Tibetans to form the modern Bonan people. Traditionally, they wear clothing similar to that of the large Hui people of northern China. Historically, the Bonan were farmers and iron workers, making primarily knives for trade. Around 1585, they were recorded as living in the Tongren County of the Amdo region of Qinghai, north of the Tibetan region around the Rebong monastery. Historical records list them as Buddhists belonging to the Tibetan Lamaist form of the religion. Later, some of the Bonan Muslims moved north. Traditionally, some of the Muslim Bonan adopted the religion after conversion by the Hui Sufi master Ma Laichi in the 18th century. Often persecuted for their Muslim

faith, the Bonan formed a closed society. Bonan knives allowed them to prosper. Known for their beauty and durability, the knives formed an important part of the local economy, particularly in areas where farming or herding livestock was limited.

The Bonan are largely farmers, who augment their income by the fabrication of knives. One of the smallest of the officially recognized ethnic groups in China, the Bonan actually include two groups, the recognized group and the ethnically and linguistically related Bonan who adopted Lamaism and are now officially considered part of the Tu ethnic group even though they speak the Bonan language. The official concept of the Bonan ethnic group is considered artificial by many scholars and by many Bonan themselves. Both the Muslim Bonan and their Buddhist kin in Qinghai have historically spoken the Bonan language, a member of the Mongolic language family. The Buddhist Bonan of Qinghai speak a slightly different dialect, but the two dialects are mutually intelligible. The Bonan language is an oral language with Chinese characters used as the written language. In recent decades, the use of the Bonan language has been declining in favor of the Hezhou dialect of Mandarin Chinese spoken in Gansu. Modern Bonan is now more similar to spoken Tu or Dongxiang than it is to modern Mongolian. The Bonan share many cultural traditions with the Dongxiang and Hui Muslims. Their traditional clothing includes influences from the Tibetans, Hui, and Dongxiang. Married Bonan women usually wear a black veil, while unmarried women wear green veils. After centuries of relative isolation, many of the religious and cultural traditions and rites practiced by the Bonan are unique or have been lost in other areas.

Tensions between the Muslim and Buddhist peoples of the Gansu-Qinghai border region became a serious problem in the early 19th century. In 1862, religious friction led to persecution of the Muslim Bonan by their Buddhist neighbors, including the Lamaist Bonan. These disputes and a conflict over water rights caused the Muslim Bonan to migrate from east to western Gansu. Later, in the aftermath of the widespread Muslim rebellion known as the Dungan Rebellion (1862–1874), the Bonan moved farther east to their present homeland in the region known as Jishishan Bonan. Living among other Muslim peoples in Gansu, the Bonan prospered modestly by farming, herding livestock, and manufacturing their famous knives known as the Bonan knife. Their new homeland, though supported by plenty of water and lush grasslands, remained backward under the heavy burden of the region's feudal economic and social structure. Bonan and Hui landlords owned most of the land and forests, and the water mills, and monopolized the river transport system. Most of the Bonan were reduced to tenant farmers forced to rent lands, some rents being as high as 50 percent of their crop. During World War II, refugees fleeing the fighting in eastern China settled in the region, beginning a reform of the feudal system. In 1949, the communists, victorious in the Chinese Civil War, took control of the region. The new authorities punished the landlords and anyone owning land or businesses while glorifying the Bonan peasants. Land redistribution was later rescinded as all lands were collectivized.

Education became available and collective farms produced the area's food, while many Bonan continue to make the forged broadswords known as Bonan knives as a cottage industry. Since the 1980s, the production of the knives has increased as their value as souvenirs and collector's items increased with the relaxation of the stringent economic controls.

Further Reading

Akasov, Anna, Charles Burnett, and Ronit Yoeli-Tialim. *Islam and Tibetan Interactions along the Musk Routes.* Farnham, UK: Ashgate Publishing, 2010.

Ethnic Groups. "The Bonan Ethnic Minority." Accessed July 31, 2013. http://www.china.org.cn/e-groups/shaoshu/shao-2-bonan.htm

Ma Yin, ed. *China's Minority Nationalities.* Beijing: Foreign Language Press, 1989.

Olson, James S. *An Ethnohistorical Dictionary of China.* Westport, CT: Greenwood, 1998.

Bouyei

The Bouyei, sometimes known as Puyi, Glay, Buyei, Buyi, or Buxqyaix, are a southern Chinese ethnic group, one of the 56 officially recognized groups in the People's Republic of China. Numbering nearly three million, the Bouyei are officially a distinct ethnic group, but many Bouyei consider themselves to be Zhuang. The Bouyei homeland is the semitropical, high-altitude forests of Yunnan-Guizhou Plateau region of Guizhou Province, with smaller communities in Yunnan and Sichuan Provinces and a small population, known as the Lao Cai Bouyei, in Vietnam. The Bouyei speak a Tai-Kadai language belonging to the northern languages of the Tai branch. The majority of the Bouyei, perhaps as high as 80 percent, practice their traditional polytheist religion with a large and rapidly increasing Buddhist minority.

One of the most ancient peoples of China, the Bouyei are believed to have lived in the Guizhou region for more than 2,000 years. Studies of the language, place names, and geographic distribution of the Bouyei lead scholars to believe that they have a common ancestry with the closely related Zhuang people. For centuries, the ancient Chinese referred to the Yue (Zhuang-Bouyei) as the alien barbarians. The two groups began to separate around 700 CE, and by 900, they had separated into two distinct ethnic groups. By the time of the Tang dynasty, from 618 to 907, the Chinese administration had established an administrative system in the Bouyei territories. Local feudal lords were appointed prefectural governors, and the land was divided into feudal properties controlled by the aristocratic families. The system lasted for more than 1,000 years until the Manchu conquest of China in 1644. The Manchu dynasty, the Qing, forced ethnic minority officials to surrender their powers. The administration of the Bouyei region reverted to a feudal system with power held by local warlords. Feudal lords and local officials owned all the fertile lands, but did not own the serfs and peasants within their territories. The serfs and peasants suffered cruel treatment and exploitation though the owners of the land were no longer allowed to kill them at will. Each peasant household was allowed a piece of land to support the family, but

buying land was forbidden. Peasants and serfs were bound to the land they worked with many working for the aristocratic families, generation after generation. As exploitation and cruelty increased in the early 18th century, class conflicts intensified and resulted in many peasant uprisings. The most serious uprising, known as the Nanlong Uprising, began in 1797. Chinese reprisals and suppression of the Bouyei resulted in the emigration of many Bouyei to the south, with some settling in northern Vietnam.

Bouyei culture is based on their long history as agriculturalists in the Yunnan-Guizhou Plateau. They farm wet and dry rice, wheat, maize, millet, sorghum, buckwheat, potatoes, and beans. Cash crops are also raised, including cotton, tobacco, sugarcane, tung trees, coffee, tea, bananas, hemp, and cocoa. They also manufacture silk fabrics and other silk products. Though urbanization is advancing rapidly, most Bouyei continue to live in villages that often contain several clans. Most villages are located on the fertile plains or in the wide river valleys near the farmlands. Increasingly, the Bouyei are moving to the large urban centers to work in manufacturing and the service industries. Traditionally, a Bouyei woman indicated her interest in a particular man by throwing him a silk ball that she had embroidered. If he returned her interest, the couple spent time together and later became engaged to marry. In many areas, the Bouyei are heavily intermarried with the Han Chinese and have adopted the parentally arranged marriage tradition as part of the sinicization of Bouyei culture. The rich Bouyei culture has incorporated a medley of influences and philosophies taken from animism, polytheism, shamanism, occultism, Daoism, and Buddhism. Following the opening of the Chinese culture and economy in the 1980s, increasing prosperity and increased consumerism has resulted in many Bouyei, particularly the urban young, to embrace materialism while rejecting the traditional culture. The Bouyei not only have adopted many Han Chinese traditions and festivals but also have retained their ancient ceremonies such as Ox King's Day, when their oxen are honored for all their hard work for the past year. The traditional religious system of the Bouyei is a mixture of traditional animist beliefs and elements of Daoism. Many Bouyei have adopted Buddhism since the relaxation of controls on religion since the 1980s. In the past, they believed in a world of spirits and venerated their ancestors, with many of the ceremonies and rites forming part of their modern religious belief system. The Bouyei language, a northern Tai language of the Tai-Kadai language group, is spoken in three dialectical groups that pertain to the three major Bouyei population areas. Bouyei is partially intelligible to speakers of the dialects of the more numerous neighboring Zhuang ethnic group.

Well into the 19th century, many Bouyei worked as serfs or landless peasants on lands owned by wealthy Bouyei or Han Chinese gentry. Exploitation, abuses, and debt slavery were rife in many areas. Kin groups often joined together to buy and work land on a communal basis free of the landlords and big landowners. Local warlords often forcibly conscripted Bouyei youths into local militias that served to protect huge privately held lands. This feudal system of land tenure and landed aristocracy lasted until the Chinese Revolution of 1911 when rich landlords replaced the nobility as the dominant class. Little changed for the Bouyei peasants, who continued to work the rice paddies and fields of their landlords with little economic benefit to themselves or their village. Traditionally, the Bouyei kept chickens or pigs for their own consumption as both chicken and pork have symbolic attributes that go well beyond their value as subsistence. Pork signifies a good harvest, and various parts

The Longest Ballad

The Bouyei are renowned for their singing, especially their traditional ballads. During wedding festivities, scores of young men and women join together to celebrate by singing their antiphonal ballads. The ballads have been handed down from generation to generation, with many new stanzas added by each generation. In the Zhenning region of Guizhou Province, old women, charged with remembering the traditional songs, are often invited to sing the ballads as blessings. Accompanied by vertical bamboo flutes and copper drums, they can sing day and night for up to seven days without repeating the words of their ballads.

of the chicken symbolize good luck, accomplishment, or relaxation. The Bouyei territories experienced tremendous disruptions and changes with the various political transformations that swept through China in the early 20th century. Local warlords often defied the central government and ruled the area in a near-feudal manner in the 1920s and 1930s. The rise of communism brought a growing rivalry between the new philosophy and the governing nationalist Chinese. Differences were put aside during World War II, but in 1945, the conflict between the communists and the nationalists erupted in a civil war that engulfed all of mainland China. Fighting in the region devastated many Bouyei villages and towns before the communist victory in 1949. As a result of the implementation of communist ideals, the landlords and kinship groups were quickly replaced with large, state-run collectives and cooperatives that were worked by the Bouyei peasants while the former wealthier classes were often jailed and their properties taken by the new communist state. Despite continued abuses of workers and peasants, the production of rice and other grains increased as irrigation was introduced into the drier parts of the province. An increase in roads, education, and health care allowed many Bouyei to raise themselves out of abject poverty as part of the communist minority policies. During the Cultural Revolution, from 1967 to 1977, most of the historic Bouyei monuments, shrines, and religious structures were destroyed. Many Bouyei were sent to other areas as forced labor. Changes since 1979, particularly the relaxation of economic constraints, brought many new industries

to the region. By the mid-1980s, many Bouyei were enjoying a modest prosperity amid the new Chinese glorification of wealth and capitalist ideals. By 2010, the average yearly income for the Bouyei was roughly five times greater than that in 2000. In addition to increased manufacturing, improved agricultural output, and new laws on personal property, a rapidly growing tourist industry aided the prosperity of many Bouyei villages and towns. Bouyei traditional arts and crafts, particularly batik and silk products, experienced a rebirth after decades of officially sanctioned neglect. Bouyei ceremonies honoring their ancestors or the spirits they associate with various mountains, trees, rivers, lakes, thunder, and other natural forces have been revived not only as tourist attractions but also as part of the recovered cultural heritage of the Bouyei people.

Further Reading

Corrigan, Gina. *Guizhou Province.* Hong Kong: Airphoto International, 2002.

Newman, Jacqueline M., "Bouyei, Buyi, or Puyi: One People with Many Names," *Flavor and Fortune,* 16 (2009): 19–21. http://www.flavorandfortune.com/dataaccess/article.php?ID=90

Olson, James S. *An Ethnohistorical Dictionary of China.* Westport, CT: Greenwood, 1998.

Xiaoming, Xiao. *China's Ethnic Minorities.* Beijing: Foreign Languages Press, 2003.

Bukharan Jews

The Bukharan Jews, sometimes known as Bukharian Jews, Bukhari Jews, or Central Asian Jews, are a Jewish religious and cultural minority traditionally associated with their historic homeland in the Emirate of Bukhara, which now forms part of the republics of Uzbekistan and Tajikistan. The majority of the Bukharan Jews now live in Israel or the United States with probably fewer than 1,000 remaining in their ancestral homeland. Other Bukharan Jewish communities are in the European Union, Canada, Australia, and Russia. Many Bukharan Jews now speak Hebrew or English as their first language though about half of the estimated 150,000–200,000 Bukharan Jews are able to speak Bukhori or Judeo-Tajik, a dialect of Persian with a large admixture of Old Hebrew loanwords that is traditionally written in a Hebrew script. Modern Bukharan Jews have mostly adopted the religious practices of the Jewish majorities in Israel and the United States, though some traditional customs and practices have been retained.

The origins of the Bukharan Jews are unknown, though according to some ancient texts, Israelites began traveling to Central Asia as traders as early as the 10th century BCE. Bukharan Jews traditionally trace their ancestry to the Lost Tribes of Israel thought to have been exiled during the Assyrian captivity of Israel in the seventh century BCE. Another wave of Jews into Central Asia may have been the descendants of the Israelites who never returned from the Babylonian captivity in the sixth to fifth centuries BCE. The Bukharan Jews were effectively cut off from the rest of the Jewish world for more than 2,500 years. Somehow, they managed to survive and to preserve their distinct culture and religion against overwhelming odds. The establishment of the Silk Road linking Europe and the Far East allowed the Jews to prosper from the second century CE to the 16th century. However, they suffered periods of persecution, particularly during the Arab Muslim conquest of the region in the eighth century and the Mongol invasion in the 13th century. In the early 16th century, nomadic Uzbek tribes who established strict observance of Islamic laws overran

The Lost Tribe

There is a tradition among the Bukharan Jews that they descend from the tribes of Naphtali and Issachar, the lost tribes of Israel. Though there are written accounts of Jews traveling to Central Asia to work as traders that date as far back as the 10th century BCE, the existence of these Jewish groups was forgotten. The first chronicle to confirm the presence of Jewish inhabitants in Central Asia was written by Rabbi Shmuel bar Bisna, a Talmudic scholar, who traveled to Margiana, present-day Merv in Turkmenistan, at the beginning of the fourth century CE. Rabbi bar Bisna wrote in his journal that he feared that the wine and alcohol produced by the local Jewish people was not kosher.

the region. The Bukharan Jews suffered discrimination, many were forcibly converted to Islam, and the remainder was confined to ghettos in the larger towns and cities. They were forced to wear distinctive black and yellow clothing to distinguish themselves from Muslims. Around 1620, the first Jewish synagogue was constructed in the city of Bukhara during a period of relaxed Muslim rule. Discrimination and persecution returned in the 18th century when many Jewish centers and synagogues were closed, and most of the Jews were forcibly converted to Islam. By the mid-18th century, the remnant of the large Central Asian Jewish population lived mostly in Bukhara and had become known as Bukharan Jews. They had only three of the five books of the Torah, did not know the Hebrew language, and had replaced the ceremony of Bar Mitzvah with a local coming of age ceremony. In 1793, Rabbi Yosef Maimon (Rabbi Joseph Maman Maghribi), from Tetuan in Morocco, who later became a prominent scholar in Safed in Palestine, traveled to Bukhara and was amazed to find the small Jewish population nearly extinct, lacking knowledge and observance of the religious customs and laws of the Jewish people. He settled in the city, and under his tutelage, other Middle Eastern Jews came to settle in Bukhara, and the Bukharan Jews began to revive and expand their small community.

The culture of the Bukharan Jews, though transplanted from Central Asia to new homes in Israel, the United States, and elsewhere, retains its distinctive traditions of dress, cuisine, music, and worship. They are considered one of the most ancient of the ethnoreligious groups of Central Asia with a distinctive culture that has thrived in their new homes outside their traditional homeland. The Bukhori language, now modernized and standardized, remains the language of many Bukharan Jews. In Israel, the language is now written in the Hebrew script, while in the United States and Canada, a modified Latin script is often used. Some older Bukharan Jews know only the Russian Cyrillic alphabet that was forced on the language by the Soviet authorities in 1940. Isolated and forced to live in City Quarters or ghettos in their homeland, the relationships between the Bukharan Jews and their Muslim neighbors varied from relaxed tolerance to violent forced conversions, massacres, and expulsions. The new homelands of the Bukharan Jews, mostly in the Western world, have brought new challenges to preserve their ancient culture and to pass it on to the coming generations who have never known fear or persecution.

The Bukharan Jewish population increased in the 19th century, prompting the Muslim rulers to allow Jews to live outside the Jewish quarters. The destruction of the Jewish quarter of Meshed, Persia, and the forced conversion of the entire Jewish population of the city prompted a wave of Jewish immigration from other areas of the Muslim lands to the relative safety of the Emirate of Bukhara. The Bukharan Jews established a network of Jewish schools called *khomlo*, which often served as Jewish centers as the emir of Bukhara had forbidden the Jews to build new synagogues. The Russians conquered Central Asia in 1868, establishing the Emirate of Bukhara as a Russian protectorate. Russian intolerance and continuing oppression by the Muslim majority prompted a wave of immigration to the Land of Israel, then forming part of Turkish Palestine. They settled in Jerusalem in an area of the city that became known as the Bukharan Quarter. From 1876 to 1916, the Bukharan Jews were allowed to practice their religion, and many became successful in business or the entertainment fields. The upheavals of World War I and the Russian Revolution were far away until the imposition of Soviet rule, when religious oppression, confiscation of property, repression, and arrests forced thousands to flee to Palestine. The greatly reduced Bukharan Jewish community in Central Asia attempted to preserve their traditions while displaying loyalty to the Soviet government. Beginning in 1972, one of the largest emigrations began as most of the Bukharan Jews emigrated to Israel and the United States. In late 1980s and early 1990s, as Soviet emigration restrictions were removed, most of the remaining Bukharan Jews left for Israel or other countries in the west.

Further Reading

Cooper, Alanna E. *Bukharan Jews and the Dynamics of Global Judaism.* Bloomington: Indiana University Press, 2012.

Dymshits, Valery, and Tatjana Emelyanenko. *Facing West: Oriental Jews of Central Asia and the Caucasus.* Zwolle, Netherlands: B. V. Waanders Uitgeverji, 1998.

Goodman, Peter. "Bukharian Jews Find Homes on Long Island." *Newsday*, September 2004.

Ochildiev, David. *A History of the Bukharan Jews.* Moscow: Mir Collection Publishing House, 2005.

Buryat

The Buryat, sometimes known as Buriat, Byryat, Buriyad, Burgut, Buryat Mongols, or Northern Mongols, belong to the Central Asian branch of the North Asian Mongol peoples. Physically, the Buryat are Mongol, but they also display many Turkic and Tungus physical and cultural traits. The exact origins of the Buryat have not been clearly established, but most scholars believe that their ancestry includes Mongol, Turkic, Tungus, Samoyed, and other strains. The majority of the Buryat reside in the Buryat Republic, one of the member states of the Russian Federation, with other Buryat populations in the autonomous Russian okrugs of Aga Buryatia and Ust-Orda Buryatia, and in neighboring parts of Mongolia and China. The estimated 500,000 Buryat form the largest ethnic minority in Russian Siberia with most living around their sacred Lake Baikal in southern Siberia. The Buryat language, now taught in regional schools, forms a northern subgroup of the Mongolian languages. Most of the Buryat living west of Lake Baikal are now Russian Orthodox, while the Buryat of Transbaikalia, the region east of the lake, are mostly Buddhists, adhering to a local variety that combines Lamaism with traditional beliefs. A minority continues to practice shamanism and maintain the traditional belief in the spirit world.

The diverse peoples of the region around Lake Baikal are believed to have been absorbed by the peoples of a tribal federation that spread through Central Asia before the modern era. Following the disintegration of the federation, the tribes living around the huge freshwater lake began to form defensive formations that were the foundations of the later ethnic divisions. The origins of the Buryat can be traced back to the formation of the Karluk Turkic group east of Lake Baikal. The tribes of the region came under the loose control of the powerful Chinese empires until they threw off Chinese authority in 754 CE. Overwhelmed by successive waves of Mongol migrations from the south, the last of the Turkic tribes disappeared or was absorbed by Mongol invasion led by Genghis Khan in 1205. The various Buryat groups formed part of the great empire founded by the Mongols until the 14th century. By the 16th century, the Buryat tribes had formed a defensive confederation that incorporated many diverse tribal groups. Cossacks, the spearhead of Russian expansion, reached the Lake Baikal region in 1643. The Russians gradually took political and economic control of the region, bringing the last Buryat tribes

under their rule around 1700. Treaties between the Russian Empire and China in 1689 and 1727 effectively severed Buryat contacts with the other Mongol peoples to the south. The consolidation of the Buryat tribes into a distinct ethnic group occurred under Russian rule as the various tribal groups assimilated into a distinct Buryat culture. The Russian government allotted tribal territories to the four major Buryat tribes and opened the remainder of the large territory to Russian colonization. Throughout the 18th century, Russian colonists took the most fertile lands and displaced many of the Buryat living west of Lake Baikal.

Historically, the Buryat culture reflected their nomadic history as herders of cattle, horses, sheep, goats, and camels. The culture is organized through the paternal line with related clans grouped into villages that form part of tribal federations. Traditionally, the Buryat were divided into five large groups, but in the 20th century, the divisions eroded with the only modern division between those living west of Lake Baikal, known as the Irkutsk Buryat, and those east of the lake, the Transbaikal

The Old Believers

The Buryat, known for their love of learning and peace, took in many Old Believers beginning in the early 18th century. A violent religious schism within the Russian Orthodox Church in the late 17th century created a religious minority, the Old Believers, called *Raskolniki* or *Semeiskye*. The Old Believers suffered severe persecution in European Russia in the 18th and 19th centuries. Many Old Believers fled east to the new frontier districts around Lake Baikal, where they were welcomed by the peaceful Buryats, who aided the settlement of the refugees and taught them the ways of their new homeland.

Buryat. Buryat culture retains many of the customs and traits brought to the region by the Mongols, including their favorite sports—wrestling, archery, and horse racing—and the enormously long *uligers*, epic poems that preserve the oral history of the Buryat people. The traditional spiritualism of their shamanistic heritage coupled with the later influences of Buddhism has given the Buryat an innate sense peacefulness that supports the idea that avoiding conflict is far superior to engaging in it. The love of learning inherent in the Buddhist religion has served the Buryat well. The modern Buryat, particularly the urbanized Buryat in the republican capital at Ulan-Ude and in other cities and towns, have achieved a high level of education that has helped the Buryat to survive and has equipped many younger Buryat to work in regional industries.

The Tibetan form of Buddhism, Lamaism, spread through the Lake Baikal region in the 19th century, the gentle doctrine being adopted by a majority of the Buryat except in the more remote districts. The construction of the Trans-Siberian Railroad, which reached Irkutsk in 1898, brought a massive influx of land-hungry Russian peasants. This new invasion united the Buryat clans in opposition to religious and ethnic persecution and discriminatory Russian laws. Buryat life, which revolved around the 49 *datsan* in the region, remained vibrant and untouched by Russia's involvement in World War I until the Russian Revolution in 1917. The Buryat attempted to remain neutral during the ensuing Russian Civil War until the Bolshevik victory and the occupation of the region in 1920. A Buryat-Mongolian region was set under the Soviet minorities program in 1921 and was upgraded to the status of an autonomous republic in 1923. In 1925, a campaign against the Buddhist religion and the Buryat language was launched with libraries burned and temples forcibly closed. The collectivization of their herds further decimated the Buryat population. The Buryat rebelled against Soviet excesses in 1929 but were defeated with some 35,000 killed, including thousands of Buddhist monks, massacred on the orders of the Russian dictator, Joseph Stalin. The Soviet government encouraged Slavic migration to dilute the Buryat majority. By the end of World War II, the Buryat formed a minority in their ancient homeland. The collapse of the Soviet Union in 1991 began a process that allowed the Buryat Republic to become a member republic of the new Russian Federation. The revival of Buryat culture and the poor environmental state of their sacred Lake Baikal have been the major concerns of the strong cultural movement since the 1990s. Activists in the early 21st century have demanded the unification of three Buryat territories in Russia and a return to the former boundaries of the autonomous republic before it was partitioned on Stalin's orders in 1937.

Further Reading

Montgomery, Robert W. *Late Tsarist and Early Soviet Nationality and Cultural Policy: The Buryats and Their Language.* Lewiston, NY: Mellen Press, 2006.

Thomson, Peter. *Sacred Sea: A Journey to Lake Baikal.* New York: Oxford University Press, 2007.

Witczuk, Julia. *Siberia: In the Baikal Land of the Buryats.* Warsaw, Poland: Multico Oficyna Wydawnicza, 2001.

C

Chaunqing

The Chaunqing, sometimes known as Chu-anchun, Chuangqing, Pu, Shertu, Tunbao, or Old Han, are a people of mixed ancestry living primarily in the Anshun region of China's Guizhou Province. Neighboring peoples call the Chaunqing either *Da Jiao Ban*, meaning "big foot," or *Da Xiuzi*, meaning "big sleeves." The estimated 600,000–1,000,000 Chaunqing speak a regional dialect of Mandarin Chinese that incorporates many borrowings from the Hmu languages of their Miao ancestors. The majority of the Chaunqing are Buddhists, with about a third adhering to their traditional beliefs and a small Christian minority.

The origins of the Chaunqing people are traced back to the Han Chinese soldiers and forced laborers who were first sent into Guizhou in the eighth and ninth centuries CE. Around 1200, the colonization of Guizhou began with many other garrisons established. The soldiers established garrison towns using the slaves and forced laborers brought with them from Jiangxi Province. The local populations called the newcomers as *tunbao*, meaning "stone castle people," referring to the stone fortifications they built in the garrisons. Others called them *pu ren*, "garrison people," while the local Yi called them *sher-tu* or *sher-feizu*, meaning "white-skinned Han" or "snake-eating Han." The soldiers and

workers in the garrisons intermingled with the local Miao and Yi peoples though their offspring retained their Chinese language and many Chinese traditions; Miao and Yi cultural traditions were also adopted. The Chaunqing, their new name meaning "black-dressed people," clung to their distinct Chinese dialect over the centuries, distinguishing them from both the later Han Chinese settlers and the Miao and Yi populations. Chaunqing marriage customs and festivals also distinguished them from the surrounding populations. Over time, the Chaunqing evolved as a distinct ethnic group, with a part of the Chaunqing, those bands with fewer Chinese traits, separating to become the Tujia ethnic group. Invading Mongols overran the region in the 13th century, making it part of the territory of the newly established Mongol-dominated Yuan dynasty in China. In 1413, Guizhou was formally made a province, with new garrisons established to pacify the Miao and Yao people. The Chaunqing adopted Chinese-style agriculture from farmers moving into the province from Sichuan and Hunan. The feudal system of the region forced many Chaunqing to serve as tenant farmers under the control of Yi landlords. Many Chaunqing fought against the rebels during the Miao rebellions in 1735 and 1795–1806.

The Chaunqing, formerly known by a variety of different names, most alluding to their establishment in the region as garrison troops, evolved over the centuries through the fusion of the Han Chinese and the Miao and Yi peoples. The Chaunqing culture demonstrates what is essentially Han Chinese structure with many local traditions and customs. Over the centuries, the Chaunqing have maintained their distinctive dialect of Mandarin Chinese though often borrowing words and structures from the local languages. Despite their ties to the neighboring peoples, the Chaunqing celebrated their own festivals and maintained different marriage customs. The history of their Buddhist and Confucian beliefs, acknowledged if not practiced by the majority, is evidenced by the presence of ancient temples in their homeland, particularly the famous Wen Miao Confucian Temple built in 1368 and the Buddhist White Pagoda and the Tian Tai Shan Buddhist Temple built in 1616. Buddhism and Confucianism are closely intertwined with the Chaunqing culture. One of the most important Chaunqing festivals, called "Crossing the River," had its origins in the Buddhist tale of a woman who was banished by the King of

Hell to the lowest depths of his kingdom. When her children decided to rescue her, they left on a spring day, walking along the way their mother had taken. They broke through 24 barriers and finally encountered the King of Hell. When they saw their mother, miserable in a river of blood, they denounced the King of Hell for his cruelty, retrieved their mother, and spirited her back across the river into the human world. About 4 percent of the Chaunqing people are Roman Catholic, the result of early missionary activity in the region.

The Guizhou region remained in turmoil in the early 19th century. The non-Han minorities repeated rebelled against Chinese rule, often targeting the Chaunqing as part of the Han Chinese population. The Miao Rebellion of 1854–1873 brought chaos to the region, with many Chaunqing fleeing their villages to escape the violence. The long rebellion divided the Chaunqing, with some siding with the related Miao and others supporting the imperial government. In 1911, the Chinese Empire was overthrown and a republic

Official Status

The Chaunqing, though still not officially recognized by the Chinese government as an ethnic minority, have often been treated as such. When the family planning policy was still rigidly observed across China for the dominant Han Chinese, Chaunqing couples could have a second child, a privilege normally granted only to official ethnicities. Large protests, petitions, and pleas have not gained them the coveted recognition as an official ethnic minority, but the government of the People's Republic of China has now relented to the point of allowing the Chaunqing to change the Han nationality on their identity cards to that of the Chaunqing nationality.

created, though local warlords controlled most of Guizhou. A growing civil war between communist groups and the Chinese government brought renewed fighting to the region in the 1920s. In 1934–1935, the communist rebels took refuge in Guizhou during the famous "Long March." Though the local provincial military forces were not match for the growing communist forces, the government sent troops to the region that successfully drove the Red Army out of Guizhou and removed the local warlord. Provincial status was resumed under direct rule by the central government. The Japanese invasion of China and the events of World War II temporarily ended the Chinese civil war, but in 1945, the civil war resumed. A communist victory, in 1949, began a policy of officially recognizing minority ethnic groups in China. Official ethnic minority status allowed the ethnic group certain privileges that were unavailable to the general public. In the 1950s, the Chaunqing leaders made a formal application for full status as a minority ethnic group, but the new People's Republic government rejected it on the grounds that the Chaunqing were "originally members of the Han nationality." Despite the early rejection, the Chaunqing again applied for ethnic minority status in the 1970s, but again the application was rejected because of the Han Chinese ancestry, even though mixed with the local Miao and Yi people. Encouraged by the political thaw in the 1990s, the Chaunqing again attempted to win ethnic minority status, but their application was again rejected. They were added to a list of undetermined minorities in the country though officially they remained part of the majority Han

Chinese nationality. In the 21st century, many Chaunqing, despairing of separate ethnic minority status, seek to join their unrecognized ethnic group to that of the numerous Tujia people. Traditionally and culturally, the Tujia are closely related to the Chaunqing.

Further Reading

Chen, Jerome. *The Highlanders of Central China: A History 1895–1937*. Armonk, NY: M.E. Sharpe, 1992.

Herman, John E. *Amid the Clouds and Mist: China's Colonization of Guizhou, 1200–1700*. Cambridge, MA: Harvard University Asia Center, 2007.

Jenks, Robert Darrah. *Insurgency and Social Disorder in Guizhou: The Miao Rebellion 1854–1873*. Honolulu, HI: University of Hawaii Press, 1994.

Zhilong Zhang, "Minority Wants to Be Counted," *Global Times*, July 25, 2012, accessed July 30, 2013, http://www.global times.cn/content/723288.shtml

Chukchi

The Chukchi, sometimes known as Chukot, Chukchee, Chukcha, Luoravetlan, Luorawetlan, or Lygoraveltlat, are a Paleo-Asiatic people ethnically and culturally related to the Native American peoples. The estimated 16,000 Chukchi mostly live in the Chukotka Autonomous Okrug in the Far Eastern region of the Russian Federation opposite to the American state of Alaska. Many Chukchi now speak Russian, and about half are able to speak their traditional language, though the number is decreasing. The language, belonging to the Chukotko-Kamchatkan language group, is one of five Paleo-Siberian languages spoken by small ethnic groups in the Russian Far East that are related to the languages spoken by native Alaskans. Traditionally, the Chukchi practiced a form of shamanism, belief in spirits, both good and evil, though many now profess Russian Orthodoxy. Shamanistic and pre-Christian beliefs remain widespread.

Historically, the Chukot Peninsula formed the western extension of the land bridge that once connected Asia and North America. Beginning some 30,000 years ago, small groups of nomadic hunters began to migrate across the land bridge, following mammoths and other quarry. The bands that settled at the western end of the land bridge became the ancestors of the Chukchi and other indigenous peoples of northeastern Siberia. In prehistoric times, the Chukchi lived as nomadic hunter–gatherers but gradually divided into two groups, the Reindeer Chukchi or Chauchu and the Maritime Chukchi, known as Ankalyn. The Reindeer Chukchi engaged in nomadic herding in the inland tundra regions, while the Maritime Chukchi settled along the coast living primarily from hunting sea mammals. Cossacks who explored, established forts, and subjected the indigenous peoples to the rule of the Russian tsars spearheaded the Russian expansion into Siberia in the 16th century. The Cossacks explored the far northeastern coast of Siberia in the mid-1600s, eventually establishing a fort at Anadyrsk and attempting to exact tribute from the Chukchi. Realizing that the Chukchi could not easily be conquered by military means, the Russian authorities

Chukchi whale hunters in the Far East region of Siberia. (Andrew Stewart/Robert Harding Specialist Stock/Corbis)

changed tactics and offered the Chukchi a peace treaty that exempted them from paying the *yasak*, the hated tribute paid in valuable furs. Fearing competition by other European powers, the Russians explored the coasts and laid claim to Alaska across the Bering Strait. The Russians established several trading stations but mostly left the Chukchi, too warlike and with few furs, to their own way of life. Trade continued into the 19th century with little effort made to bring the Chukchi under direct Russian rule, though between 1763 and 1800, the Russian Empire formally annexed the Chukchi territories.

Culturally, the Chukchi are related to the Native American peoples of nearby Alaska though decades of Soviet rule have left a badly damaged environment and other problems. In the rural communities in the Russian Arctic, the average life span is under 50 years, with tuberculosis, alcoholism, parasitic infections, and high unemployment taking a terrible toll. Tribal divisions, important in the early history of the Chukchi, remain as traditional divisions and cultural groupings. Divided into the Reindeer and Maritime groups, the Chukchi are further divided into a number of regional dialectic and cultural groups. The Chukchi language is closely related to that of neighboring Paleo-Siberian peoples and to the Aleutian languages spoken by native Alaskans. A curious feature of the Chukchi language is a different system of pronunciation by men and women. The women's version lacks the "r" sound, which is traditionally regarded as unsuitable for females. Though many Chukchi now profess Orthodox Christianity, pre-Christian traditions remain widespread. Chukchi shamans, believed to be in touch with the spirit world, practice healing, divination, and sorcery. Local beliefs include invisible spirits that populate everything in the universe, and sacrifices to these spirits are important aspects of the Chukchi belief system. About 2 percent of the Chukchi are practicing Orthodox Christians though many others profess Christian beliefs. Shamanism survived as most religious services in Chukchi homes were with no visible religious hierarchy for the Soviet authorities to attack; Chukchi shamanism easily survived decades of oppression.

Ethnic Jokes

The Chukchi, despite their remote homeland in the far northeast corner of the Russian Federation, are the most commonly targeted for generic ethnic jokes in Russia. The jokes, making fun of the Chukchi, are similar to the Irish jokes in the United Kingdom, the Newfie jokes in Canada, or the Belgian jokes popular in France and the Netherlands. Example: A Chukchi man applies for membership in the Union of Soviet Writers. The examiners ask what Russian literature he is familiar with. "Have you read Pushkin?" to which he answers "No." "Have you read Dostoevsky?" but again the Chukchi answers "No." "Can you read at all?" the examiners ask. The Chukchi, offended, replies, "I not reader, I writer!"

The introduction of alcohol, firearms, and increasing Russian demands for valuable furs began to affect the Chukchi way of life in the early 19th century. The increased hunting of furbearing land and sea animals nearly caused the extinction of many species in the region. European diseases and alcoholism took a heavy toll on the small Chukchi population. Despite the enormous problems presented by the European presence, the seminomadic Chukchi resisted Russian domination and continued to function as a semi-independent entity well into the 1800s. Following the sale of Russian Alaska to the United States in 1867, the Russian government tightened its hold on Northeastern Asia in an effort to keep foreign, mostly American, whalers and traders at bay. The first Orthodox missionaries entered Chukchi territory in 1815 though the Chukchi majority did not accept conversion to Christianity. The missionaries established four Orthodox schools that introduced European education to many chief's sons. Virtually untouched by World War I, the Chukchi were dismayed as Russian civil government in the region collapsed and word of the Russian Revolution filtered into the region. Fighting between the rival Russian factions for control of the strategic region ended with the victory of the Reds in 1920. Soviet rule was quickly extended, and clumsy attempts to confiscate or collectivize the Chukchi reindeer herds, break the power of the shamans, and overcome growing Chukchi resistance led to much violence and oppression. The Chukchi were resettled on Soviet collectives, while many Chukchi leaders were killed or imprisoned. Ancient hunting and fishing grounds were declared as common ground and property of the Soviet state. By the 1930s, a vast chain of slave labor camps had been established in the region, mostly for dissidents and anti-Soviet groups from European Russia. In the 1950s, the Soviet authorities drove the Chukchi off their tundra and coasts into communal farms with prefabricated Soviet housing. By the 1980s, most Chukchi, affected by alcoholism, apathy, and unemployment, were living in poverty in the cultural wasteland of a totally Soviet Russian-language environment. The relaxation of Soviet rule and the final collapse of the Soviet Union in 1991 led to a vast exodus of the Russian colonists back to western Russia. The indigenous Chukchi were left behind to make the best of what was left of their traditional way of life. Most returned to reindeer herding, hunting, or fishing. Growing ties to Alaska, including deliveries of food aid and other goods by Alaskan groups, have allowed the Chukchi to reestablish ties to the indigenous peoples of North America as the Chukchi continue a long economic and demographic decline.

Further Reading

Gray, Patty A. *The Predicament of Chukotka's Indigenous Movement: Post-Soviet Activism in the Russian Far North*. Cambridge: Cambridge University Press, 2004.

Icon Group International. *Chukchi: Webster's Timeline History, 1605–2007*. San Diego: Icon Group International, 2010.

Kettula, Anna M. *Antler on the Sea: The Yupik and Chukchi of the Russian Far East*. Ithaca, NY: Cornell University Press, 2000.

Vahtre, Lauri, and Jüri Viikberg. The Red Book of the Peoples of the Russian Empire. "The Chukchis." Accessed July 31, 2013. http://www.eki.ee/books/redbook/chukchis.shtml

D

Dai

The Dai, sometimes known as Baiyi, Boyi, Chinese Shan, Pudai, Tai, Tai Lue, or Tai Mao, are a Tai people living in China's southwestern Yunnan Province and neighboring regions of Myanmar, Thailand, Vietnam, and Laos. Dai is the official Chinese designation for the group, which is known by other names, such as Shan, Tai, or Thai, outside China. The estimated 1.5–2 million Dai, about two-thirds living in China with the other third spread across the northern regions of Southeast Asia, speak various dialects of the Tai languages of the Zhuang-Dong group of Tai languages and often speak Mandarin Chinese or other regional languages as second languages. The majority of the Dai adhere to the Theravada Buddhist tradition with some of the more remote groups retaining their traditional animist beliefs.

Chinese archives from the first century BCE refer to the Dai as Shan or Dainyue, a numerous people that appear to have originated more than 3,000 years ago south of the Yangtze River in present-day central China. They gradually moved or were forced south by the expansion of the Han Chinese over many centuries. Eventually, most of the ethnic group now considered Dai settled along the fertile valleys of the Mekong River and its tributaries in southern China, with other groups following the rivers southwest and southeast into Myanmar, Thailand, Laos, and Vietnam. By 1000 CE, the Dai language emerged as the largest regional language as Buddhism spread and gained importance. The written Dai language is passed on in the form of scriptures written on the leaves of the Belye tree. In the 10th century CE, the Dai established a powerful regional kingdom in the west, Mong Mao, which was succeeded in the 11th century by the Kocambi kingdom. Between the 10th and 11th centuries, a second Dai kingdom, known as Yanaga or Xienrun, was established in the Xishuangbanna region in the south. The Dai were the dominant ethnic group in the Dehong Xishuangbanna regions now forming part of China's Yunnan Province. Around 1300, the Mongols invaded Mong Mao, accelerating the Dai migration to the south. In the 13th century, Venetian explorer Marco Polo visited the Dai kingdom. In the 14th century, the southwestern expansion of the Han Chinese moved into Yunnan, and the northern Dai soon came under Chinese rule. Between 1271 and 1368, the Dai territories mostly became subordinate to Yunnan Province of China. To control the restive ethnic groups in the region, hundreds of thousands of Han Chinese soldiers of the Ming dynasty remained in the region as military colonists. Recognizing the numbers and power of the Dai people, the Chinese established the *tusi* system, establishing the Dai as the local administration with authority over the other ethnic groups in the region. The Dai *tusi* leaders enjoyed absolute power within their domains so long as they obeyed the mandates of the Chinese imperial government and met the quotas of tribute, taxes, and forced labor. The Dai also owned all land, so that the Dai administrators were also the large landholders and landlords. The combination of powers created a feudal system in the territories controlled by the Dai. From the 13th to 18th centuries, the Lanna or Babai Xifu state, centered in northern Thailand, was a Dai-dominated state that controlled neighboring peoples such as the De'ang, Blang, Hani, Lahu, Achang, and Jingpo. In China, between the 14th and 19th centuries, the *tusi* system gradually weakened and was slowly replaced by the Han Chinese administrative system. For centuries, Dai interests focused on the struggle for power between them and the minority ethnic groups they controlled as well as between the Dai aristocracy and the Han Chinese. The number of Han Chinese in the region increased rapidly several times over the centuries following the first contact between the Dai and the Han in the first century CE. Han Chinese soldiers and colonists came to the region in the eighth century, during the war between the Chinese Tang dynasty and the Nanzhao kingdom of the Bai people; in the 13th century, when the Mongol hordes overran the Dali kingdom, which succeeded Nanzhao; and later during the wars of the Yuan dynasty with Burma and Babai Xifu to the south. Though Han colonization continued, the largest settlement was an army of more than 300,000 sent to the region by the Ming emperor to fight the Mongols in the early 14th century. By the late 18th century, the Dai feudal powers had been greatly reduced as the political system of interior China replaced it. Han Chinese took most of the administrative positions as Dai power waned. The centuries of Dai domination form the main themes of Yunnan history as well as the legacy of the region's ethnic relations.

The Dai ethnic group is closely related to the Thai and Lao people to the south, forming one of the most important of the Tai ethnic groups. Although officially recognized as a single ethnic group in the People's Republic of China, the Tai people included in the group actually form several distinct cultural and linguistic groups. The Dai are divided into three major regional groups that are further divided into dozens of subgroups based on geography and dialect. All the Dai groups and subgroups identify themselves as Tai, though the Chinese designation Dai is to differentiate between the Chinese Tai and the other Tai peoples. Traditionally, Dai culture was split between two classes, the aristocracy and the commoners, based on hereditary lineages. Within each class, there were several strata. It was nearly impossible to change the class into which an individual was born. Only the aristocrats were allowed to hold land or office, whereas the commoners were all considered serfs, engaging in different occupations in accordance with their social status. Following the communist victory in the Chinese Civil War in 1949, these historical class differences were abolished, and most of the Dai aristocracy was eliminated. The Dai language is divided into two major dialects corresponding to the historic centers of Dai culture, Dai Lü, also known as Xishuangbanna Dai, and Dai Nüa or Dehong Dai. The Dai dialects form part of the northwestern Tai branch of the Tai-Kadai language group that is spoken from Assam in northeastern India to Taiwan and eastern China. Most of the Dai or Tai peoples in Southeast Asia speak dialects belonging to the southwestern Thai branch of the language group. Dai literature has a long history and is rich in folktales and poetry. The spread of the official language, Mandarin Chinese, as a national language has eroded Dai literacy with responsibility for educating young Dai shifting from the village temples and schools to state educational systems whose primary language of instruction is Mandarin. To the Dai, poetry means talking and singing. Most Dai are Buddhists, adhering to the Theravada Buddhism school, though pre-Buddhist belief in spirits and other ancient rites have become part of the Buddhist tradition. Dai belief about death is a fusion of Buddhism and traditional spiritualism. Spirit offerings are also used as traditional cures as part of Dai medical practices.

Under the indirect authority of successive dynasties that continued extending their power into the territories to the south, the Han Chinese challenged Dai rule, imposed new taxes, and encouraged the minority peoples to assert their rights in the Dai-controlled lands. In 1800, the Dai, fearing the loss of their historic domination of the region, began a serious rebellion against Chinese rule. Chinese officers serving the Qing dynasty enlisted many of the minority ethnic groups to maintain control of Yunnan. Small waves of Dai refugees fled to the south, setting a pattern that persisted well into the 20th century.

Late in the 19th century, a number of Dai *tusi* landlords sold their lands to Han Chinese settlers, who then used Dai farmers as tenants and sharecroppers. The Dai feudal system faced constant challenges as the political system of the Chinese empire was gradually extended to Yunnan. By the early 20th century, Han Chinese settlers, using more advanced farming methods, were producing larger and more varied crops than the Dai, adding an economic element to the growing tensions in the region. The Chinese Revolution of 1911 brought rapid changes to the region, further eroding Dai authority in the region. The construction of the Burma Road to connect Yunnan to Burma and India to the south opened large markets for the agricultural products of Yunnan giving the Han Chinese an even greater advantage. World War II temporarily ended a growing civil war between the communists and the nationalists for control of China, but fighting resumed in 1945. A communist victory in 1949 was followed by the overthrow of the Dai aristocracy, who were persecuted as enemies of the state, and the glorification of the peasants, including the Dai commoners. Collectivization of the land brought new crops and methods to regional farming. The communist minority policy and the reforms of 1956 consolidated the five Dai languages into a standard language, rewrote Dai history to reflect communist ideology, and resulted in the confiscation of most remaining Dai properties. The Cultural Revolution, from 1967 to 1977, was particularly harsh in the region with most of the Dai monuments, shrines, and religious sites destroyed. The economic and social reforms that were adopted in China in 1979 allowed the Dai to begin to recover their long history and their ancient culture. New cash crops such as tea, sugarcane, rubber, and tropical fruits added to the growing prosperity in the region. The Chinese government's capitalist economist reforms allowed many of the former Dai landlord class to be liberated from reeducation and labor camps. The Chinese communist state, through state-run shops and cooperatives, dominated the Dai region from the 1950s into the 1980s. Since that time, the Dai have experienced a cultural and economic rebirth that is reflected in the region's growing importance as a tourist destination. As Buddhism once dominated both the religious and the political life of the Dai ethnic group, religion is playing an increasingly important role in the reculturation of the Dai people. Dai literature, particularly Dai poetry, is again allowed and is a popular element in many Dai ceremonies and celebrations. Ties to the small Dai ethnic groups in Thailand and Laos have aided the recuperation and reconstruction of temples and shrines. Monks from Buddhist temples in Thailand have supplied religious texts and icons. The ancient Dai epics, an important part of Dai poetry, long banned by the communist regime, are again being performed to large audiences. Since 2000, Dai community leaders in association with local social organizations have been working to preserve living knowledge of the traditional Dai (Tai) script by reviving temple educational programs. Due to the historic and modern settlement of the region by Han Chinese, the Dai and the other non-Han ethnic groups now form only 38 percent of the provincial population.

Further Reading

Heberer, Thomas. *China and Its National Minorities: Autonomy or Assimilation?* Amonk, NY: M.E. Sharpe, 1990.

West, Barbara A. *Encyclopedia of the Peoples of Asia and Oceania.* New York: Facts on File, 2008.

Xioming, Xiao. *China's Ethnic Minorities.* Beijing: Foreign Languages Press, 2003.

Daur

The Daur, sometimes known as Daghor, Dagur, Dawoer, Daguer, Dahur, Tahanerh, Takuanerb, or Tahuerh, are one of the officially recognized minority peoples of the People's Republic of China. The estimated 135,000 Daur are concentrated in the Morin Dawa Daur Autonomous Banner in the Hulin Buir region of Inner Mongolia and in neighboring districts of Heilongjiang Province. There is also a community of Daur living near Tacheng in Xinjiang, where their ancestors were removed during the Qing dynasty era and a smaller group in southern Kazakhstan. The Daur language is a Mongolic language related to the modern Mongolian dialects spoken in China's Inner Mongolia region and in Mongolia. The primary religious belief system of the Daur is a form of Tibetan or Mahayana Buddhism though a significant number retain their ancient shamanistic beliefs.

The Daurs are believed to be the descendants of the Khitan people who formed a powerful tribal confederation in the grasslands north of China in ancient times. Many scholars believe that the Daur can trace their ancestry to groups of Khitans who migrated from the lower Heilong River region to the western region of China during the reign of the Liao dynasty between 916 and 1125 CE. The history of the Khitans stretches back to the fourth century CE, when they dominated much of present-day Mongolia and Manchuria (northeastern China). From the fifth to eighth centuries, the Khitans were ruled by the steppe tribes to the west, the Turkic peoples, and then the Uyghur. The collapse of Uyghur power and the end of the Tang dynasty in China allowed the Khitan to establish the Liao dynasty in 907. The Liao formed a powerful state north of the Chinese plain with groups constantly migrating south and west to occupy territories formerly held by the Chinese Tang dynasty or the Uyghur. The Liao state was defeated by the ancestors of the Manchu in 1125 with many Khitan moving further west to establish the Kara Khitai state, which was later absorbed by the local Turkic and Iranian populations. The only survivors, later known as the Daur, living in the vast grasslands north of China, managed to retain much of their ancient culture and traditions. Until the 17th century, the Daur lived in the Amur River valley, but the expansion of Russian settlement in the region challenged the Chinese claim to the region. In 1643 and 1651, the Daur fought off Russian Cossack expeditions to the region. In 1682, the Russian government dispatched Russian Orthodox missionaries to work among the Daur and to convert them to Christianity. The Alarmed Manchu authorities of the Qing dynasty decided to relocate the Daur rather than allow them to fall under Russian influence. Forcibly driven from their lands, the Daur were resettled in widely scattered villages throughout northern Manchuria and the northeastern section of Inner Mongolia. Some were relocated farther west in northern Xinjiang. In their new regions, the Daur often faced hunger and hardship. Over time, they developed herds of horses and sheep that helped to sustain the population through the 18th century.

Daur culture is a Mongolian culture that retains a stratified hierarchic structure. Daur families sharing the same surname are grouped into *hala*, often encompassing two or three Daur towns. Each *hala* is divided into diverse *mokon* or clans that share the same towns and villages. When marriage between people of different clans is arranged, the husband continues to live with his wife's clan but without property rights. Marriages are normally arranged with the aid of a go-between, with spousal preference for matrilateral cross-cousin arrangements. In the past, many Daur were betrothed while still children, or even before birth. In spite of pressure from the Chinese government to assimilate Han Chinese social systems, most of the Daur continue to function within the traditional system of localized patrilineages known as *mokon*. Each Daur man is expected to maintain a lifelong interest in the children of his sisters, even to the point of protecting them or assisting them socially or economically. Though many Daur are officially Buddhists, the majority continue to practice a syncretic mixture of their indigenous religious beliefs, elements of Tibetan Buddhism, and ancestor veneration borrowed from the Han Chinese. The Daur view the world as a whole, with animals, plants, the moon, the sun, the stars, and the earth all imbued with spirits. They name every animal, tree, river, creek, meadow, mountain, hill, and valley, along with the days of the week, weeks, months, and seasons according to their spirit names. All of the creation is believed to have a spiritual essence, which aids the balance and solidarity of nature. The Daur, even those who have converted to Buddhism, revere a number of sky gods known as *tenger*. Daur shamans act as intermediaries between the physical and spiritual worlds and employ their special powers to influence the spirits. The majority of the Daur are farmers though a growing number work in manufacturing, particularly of chemical fertilizers and electronics. The Daur are often credited with the invention of field hockey, known to them as *beikuo*. This game was mentioned in *The History of the Liao Dynasty*, written more than 1,000 years ago. The Daur language is a Mongolic language spoken in four distinct dialects corresponding to the geographic distribution of the ethnic group. Because of the scattered Daur settlements, long association with other ethnic groups resulted in many Daur being bilingual, using Mandarin Chinese, Uyghur, Mongolian, or Kazakh as a second language. The Daur Mongol language has a significant Manchu influence, dating from the Qing dynasty between 1644 and 1911 when the Daur used the Manchu writing system.

In the 19th century, the Daur played an important role in the commerce between central China and the grasslands beyond the Great Wall. They traded furs, skins, and medicinal products for gold and items of daily use. They also sold the products of their fisheries and lumber mills. The Daur role as important middlemen in the trade between the interior Chinese provinces and the peoples of the northern grasslands continued until the Chinese Revolution of 1911, which ended the Qing dynasty's ban on Han Chinese settlements north of the Great Wall. The rapid increase in the Han Chinese population in the 1920s and 1930s quickly reduced the Daur monopoly on trade in the region. Before and during World War II, when the Japanese took control of Manchuria and later of Inner Mongolia, the Daur led the fight against the invaders. They first took up arms against the Japanese in 1931 in northern Manchuria. The communist victory in the Chinese Civil War that ended in 1949 brought rapid change to the Daur homeland. Collectivization and forced moves to permanent villages as part of new collectives or cooperatives ended the trade that had sustained many Daur for centuries. The economic reforms put in place in China since 1979 have allowed many Daur to prosper by logging, fishing, or opening stores in the growing urban areas. The end of the restrictions on religion has aided the Daur effort to recover their traditional cultural and religious traditions.

Further Reading

Humphrey, Caroline. *Shamans and Elders: Experience, Knowledge, and Power among the Daur Mongols.* New York: Oxford University Press, 1996.

Legerton, Colin. *Invisible China: A Journey through Ethnic Borderlands.* Chicago: Chicago Review Press, 2009.

McGrath, Charles. "A Chinese Hinterland, Fertile with Field Hockey," *New York Times*, August 22, 2008.

Schwarz, Henry G. *The Minorities of Northern China: A Survey*. Bellingham, WA: Western Washington University Press, 1984.

De'ang

The De'ang, sometimes known as Daeng, Dang, humai, Kunlois, Ang, Benglong, Benlong, Black Benlong, Palaung, Palong, Padaung, Pale, Palay, La'eng, Liang, Raang, Red Benlong, Rumai, or Ta'ang, are one of the 56 officially recognized ethnic groups of the People's Republic of China. The estimated 20,000 De'ang in China are part of a much larger ethnic group usually known as Palaung living in the northern districts of neighboring Myanmar. The language of the De'ang, known as Ta'ang, is a Palaung language of the Palaung-Riang group of Mon-Khmer languages. The majority of the De'ang are Theravada Buddhists with a minority continuing to follow traditional religious practices.

Traditionally, the De'ang are among the descendant ethnic group of the first settlers of the Dehong region of Yunnan, the Pu. Remains of ancient tea plantations, roads, towns, and villages that have been attributed to the Pu people have been found. Chinese records from 2,000 years ago register the Pu as the inhabitants of the area, leading most scholars to conclude that they were the ancestors of the other Mon-Khmer speaking in ancient China. Originally, the Pu are believed to have originated in eastern Tibet. Early migrants followed the Salween and Mekong Rivers south to settle the region later known as Dehong. By the eighth century CE, the De'ang and other Mon-Khmer peoples had come under loose Chinese rule before coming under the rule of the Nanzhao and Dali kingdoms of the Bai and Dai peoples. The De'ang have had close contact with the Tai-speaking Dai and other ethnic groups since the time of the Mongol conquest of the region in the 13th century. Once much more numerous in Yunnan, in the 12th century, they threw off the domination of the Dai people and formed one of the most powerful kingdoms in the region. In the 15th century, more powerful peoples, including the Han Chinese, moved into the region. The De'ang nobles were subjected to taxation and were forced to pay tribute. Many moved south into territory now forming part of Myanmar. During the rule of the Qing dynasty, from 1644 to 1911, the De'ang were known as the Benlong people. A long series of disputes and continuing migration out of Yunnan depleted the De'ang population, which numbered just a few thousand by the end of the 18th century.

The De'ang, like the larger related groups in Myanmar, are traditionally Theravada Buddhists. Religion historically formed an integral part of their culture. Prior to the communist takeover of China in 1949, most De'ang villages contained a Buddhist temple, and most families sent at least one son to become a monk. All the De'ang believed that it was their responsibility to support and to feed monks with donations of food and money. De'ang religious scripts and literature were written in the Dai alphabet, and all monks could read and write that language. The ban on religion under communist rule greatly affected De'ang culture, which was secularized, and references to Buddhism were forbidden. Since the 1980s, some temples have been reconstructed and operate with both personal and communal rituals. Young De'ang are again allowed to become monks, and Buddhism is again an important element in De'ang culture. Centuries of isolation from the larger Palaung population to the south has resulted in many cultural traits and rituals not practiced by their ethnic kin in Myanmar. Tea became the primary cash crop in the De'ang region in the 19th century and remains so to the present. De'ang society is made up of a web of intersecting patrilineal clans, each made up of 30–40 families. All recognize a common ancestor and related to one another through the principle of male descent. The De'ang speak their own dialect of the Ta'ang language, which is a group of related dialects sometimes known as Palaung. In China, the three divisions recognized within the De'ang-Palaung people, the Palé, Rumai, and Shwe, are grouped together in the ethnic group called Benlong until the name was changed to the self-identifying name De'ang in 1985.

In the 19th century, most De'ang paid tribute to Dai landlords while many working as peasant farmers or sharecroppers. Many of the De'ang worked on Dai-owned tea plantations or farmed communal lands owned by the De'ang villages. By the mid-19th century, private property arrangements began to appear in the De'ang territories. When large numbers of ethnic Han Chinese or Dai settlers moved into the region, many sold their land, and the alienation of the De'ang lands began. Most De'ang became tenant farmers, renting land from Han or Dai landlords. The events of World War II and the subsequent Chinese Civil War brought violence and chaos to the region until the communist victory in 1949. Glorifying the peasant, the new government seized many of the large landholdings, which were distributed to the De'ang farmers. Agrarian reforms, enacted in 1956, collectivized the private farms and properties, making the De'ang employees of the state on collective farms and cooperatives. The reforms led to the seizure of the Han and Dai properties, but made little difference to the De'ang, who were already working as sharecroppers or tenants. The reforms enacted by the government of the People's Republic of China, beginning in 1979, allowed capitalist activity and opened markets for De'ang products. De'ang craftsmen produce bamboo, silver, and cotton goods that they sell in Dai or Han Chinese markets as they have no local markets of their own. Buddhism, once an integral part of De'ang culture, is again flourishing with personal and communal events that have become important in the lives of the De'ang, marking marriages, births, deaths, and other important events.

Further Reading

Ethnic Groups. "The De'ang Ethnic Minority." Accessed July 31, 2013. http://www.china.org.cn/e-groups/shaoshu/shao-2-de%27ang.htm

Gall, Timothy L., and Jeneen Hobby. *Worldmark Encyclopedia of Cultures and Daily Life*. Farmington Hills, MI: Gale, 2009.

Ma Yin, ed. *China's Ethnic Minorities*. Beijing: Foreign Languages Press, 1989.

West, Barbara A. *Encyclopedia of the Peoples of Asia and Oceania*. New York: Facts on File, 2008.

Dekasegi

The Dekasegi, sometimes known as Latin American Japanese or *nikkeijin*, are a Japanese ethnic group made up of migrants from Latin America who migrated to Japan since the early 1990s. The estimated 350,000 Dekasegi in Japan are usually bilingual, speaking both Portuguese or Spanish and Japanese. There are a number of Dekasegi who are monolingual Portuguese or Spanish. The majority of the Dekasegi are Roman Catholic, with sizable minorities adhering to Buddhism and Shintoism, Protestant sects, or profess no religious beliefs.

Emigration from Japan was first recorded as early as the 12th century when a group of Japanese left their home islands to settle in the Philippines. Mass emigration began only during the Meiji Era, between 1868 and 1912. The end of the feudal era in Japan generated great hardship and poverty, particularly among the rural population. To relieve overcrowding and joblessness, the Japanese government began to encourage Japanese emigration to other countries. The United States and Australia, among other destinations, had adopted policies of excluding Orientals from the lists of acceptable immigrants on the basis that they would not integrate into society. Peru was the first Latin American country to establish formal diplomatic relations with the Empire of Japan in 1873. Peru was also the first country in South America to accept Japanese immigration in 1899. Several Latin American countries, particularly Brazil, suffered a shortage of labor following the abolition of slavery in the late 19th century. At first, these countries promoted emigration from Europe, particularly from Italy and Spain, but once the Europeans arrived in Latin America, they received very low wages, worked in poor conditions, including long hours and often abuses by their employers. Because of these deplorable conditions, the Italian government enacted the Prinetti Decree in 1902, which ended subsidized immigration to Brazil and other Latin American countries. A new labor shortage, particularly on the coffee plantations and ranches, resulted in renewed efforts to attract workers from other parts of the world. There were few jobs in Japan for the excess laborers, and opportunities for work in Latin America were plentiful. The Japanese government negotiated agreements with the major Latin American countries and took great pains to present the emigrants as other than manual labor by giving each a special certificate. After leaving Japanese shores, the immigrants were mostly forgotten. In 1908, the first Japanese immigrants began arriving in Brazil, where many became laborers on the country's important coffee plantations. The immigrants to Latin American, mostly from Okinawa, Gifu, Hiroshima, Kanagawa, and Osaka prefectures, arrived in Brazil, Peru, Argentina, Colombia, Mexico, and other Latin American countries under contract as laborers on farms, plantations, and other low-paid occupations. The vast majority of the Japanese immigrants planned to work for a few years, make enough money, then return home to Japan. However, the myth of getting rich quick proved elusive and difficult to achieve. The immigrants were paid very low salaries and worked long hours of exhausting work. The barrier of language, religion, clothing, dietary habits, lifestyles, and difference in climatic conditions resulted in an enormous cultural shock for the new immigrants. Many of the immigrants attempted to return to Japan but were prevented by employers requiring them to work out the terms of their contracts. During World War II, the Japanese community in Peru was mostly rounded up and shipped to detention camps in the United States. In Brazil, a policy of forced assimilation was adopted. In other countries, the migrants were also restricted and denied access to services and many professions. The first generation of immigrants, known as *issei*, meaning those born in Japan, usually maintained control of the immigrant Japanese communities in Latin America. The *Nisei*, those of the second generation, born in Latin America, and the *sansei*, three generations removed from their Japanese roots, began to assimilate into the cultures of the countries where they were born. By the 1960s, many of the second- and third-generation Latin American Japanese spoke no Japanese and considered themselves as Brazilian, Argentinian, Peruvian, and so on. For decades, the Japanese immigrant communities in Latin America were considered too alien to assimilate into the Latin cultures and often remained segregated and suffered discrimination. The Japanese diaspora has been unique because of the absence of new emigrants in the second half of the 20th century.

The Dekasegi community in Japan primarily comprises Brazilian-Japanese, Peruvian-Japanese, Argentine-Japanese, and Colombian-Japanese with smaller numbers from other Latin American nations. The term *Dekasegi* is used to refer to Latin Americans of Japanese descent who have migrated to Japan since the 1980s, taking advantage of Japanese citizenship offers, the *Nisei* visa, and immigration laws that encouraged people of Japanese descent to escape the economic instability in Latin America by immigrating to Japan. The original Japanese word *dekasegi* is roughly translated as "working away from home." It is often used in a derogatory manner and is much resented by those of Japanese descent born abroad, but have come to consider Japan as their permanent home. The Dekasegi resent the use of the word *dekasegi* when it is used to imply that they are *gajin* or foreigners. Japan's government until recently denied the existence of minorities in the country. The large number of Latin American Japanese in Japan faces many obstacles living in a country that is mostly homogeneous. Many of the Dekasegi are Roman Catholic, and many other speak only Portuguese or Spanish, creating additional challenges in the closed Japanese culture. Many Dekasegi consider themselves as Japan's abandoned people. Roman Catholicism, as a source of moral guidelines for living, often clashes with the Japanese ideal of religion, which mostly combines elements of Shinto and Buddhism and functions as the basis of mythology, traditions, and neighborhood activities. The language issue is particularly difficult as Japanese schools made little provision for students who speak little or no Japanese. Many of the Dekasegi, often considered foreigners despite their ethnic background, face racism and xenophobia. Many Japanese view the Dekasegi as the descendants of misfits or dropouts

Count Combat

Mitsuyo Maeda, a naturalized citizen of Brazil renamed Otávio Maeda, was a Japanese judo expert and prizefighter in the no-holds-barred competitions popular in the early 20th century. He was popularly known as "Count Combat," *Conde Koma* in the Spanish and Portuguese languages, a nickname he picked while fighting in Spain in 1908. One of the leading experts in the development of Jiu-Jitsu in Brazil, he was also a promoter of Japanese emigration to South America. During his long career, he won more than 2,000 professional bouts in South America, the United States, Mexico, Central America, Cuba, and Europe.

who left Japan seeking an easy life elsewhere. Other perceive the Dekasegi as objects of pity, descendants of people forced to emigrate by unfortunate circumstances such as their station or order of birth or a lack of opportunities in rural areas.

Lured back to Japan to take the jobs many Japanese rejected, the so-called three "K" jobs, *kitsui* (difficult), *kitanai* (dirty), or *kiken* (dangerous). During the 1980s and 1990s, Japan's economy continued to expand, and the need for imported labor drew in more and more people of Japanese descent from Latin America. In 1990, the Japanese government introduced a new ethnic-based immigration policy that encouraged the Japanese descendants overseas to come to Japan to fill the country need for foreign workers. The Japanese government welcomed the Dekasegi Japanese back and allowed many of those with a certain amount of Japanese blood to obtain citizenship. By 2000, there were more than 300,000 Dekasegi in Japan, with more than 220,000 from Brazil and smaller numbers from other South American countries. The majority of the returning Dekasegi took up work in factory towns where they worked

unskilled, low-paying jobs the local Japanese population did not want. Even though invited back to Japan by the Japanese government, they often found themselves very unwelcome in the local communities where they settled. They faced intense discrimination and found it difficult to integrate into Japanese culture. By 2010, with the Japanese economy stagnating, many Dekasegi found themselves unemployed, up to 70 percent in some areas. The factories that formerly welcomed them when labor was needed often shut down or transferred their economic activities overseas to cheaper labor markets. As a result, many Dekasegi communities suffered. The Japanese government began offering monetary incentives to those willing to leave Japan. Many are taking the government money and returning to countries that feel more like home.

Further Reading
Buerk, Roland. "From Brazil to Japan and Back Again." *BBC News*, May 1, 2009. http://news.bbc.co.uk/2/hi/business/8025089.stm

De Carvalho, Daniela. *Migrants and Identity in Japan and Brazil: The Nikkeijin.* London: Routledge, 2002.

Lie, John. *Multiethnic Japan.* Cambridge, MA: Harvard University Press, 2004.

Tsuda, Takeyuki. *Strangers in the Ethnic Homeland: Japanese Brazilian Return Migration in Transnational Perspective.* New York: Columbia University, 2003.

Derung

The Derung, sometimes known as Drung, Dulong, Dulonh, Dulongzu, Qiu, Tulung, or Tulong, are one of the smaller ethnic groups officially recognized by the People's Republic of China. The estimated 7,000 Derung mostly live in far northwest Yunnan, in the Gongshan Dulong-Nu Autonomous County along both sides of the Dulong River. The Derung language, formerly known as Qiuyu, is a dialect of the Nungish branch of the Tibeto-Burman language family. Traditionally animists, there are also Christian and Buddhist groups that form part of the Derung society.

The origins of the Derung are not known. The earliest mention of the ethnic group is in Chinese chronicles of the Tang dynasty (618–907 CE) when they were listed as a frontier people on the edge of the Nanzhao kingdom of the Bai and later were ruled by the Dali kingdom that succeeded the fall of Nanzhao. Archives from the Song dynasty, in the 10th century, mention the Derung as being largely ruled by Naxi landlords under the *tusi* system that allowed local chiefs and headmen a large measure of autonomy over their subject people in exchange for loyalty and tribute to the Chinese imperial government. Raids into Derung territory, particularly by the Tibetans seeking slaves, brought chaos to the region for hundreds of years. To make them unattractive to slavers, Derung women traditionally were subjected to facial tattooing with patterns that indicated their clan membership. Tattooing began at the onset of adulthood at the age of 12 or 13 years.

Derung culture has been based on their lifestyle as slash and burn agriculturalists for as long as they have appeared in Chinese records. Traditionally, the Derung raised corn, wheat, and beans and supplemented their diets with hunting, fishing, and gathering. Since the mid-20th century, they have been encouraged to cultivate rice paddies, with the surplus sold to the state at fixed prices. Traditionally, the Derung were organized into 15 patrilineal clans known as *nile*, with membership through the male line. A *nile* was divided into villages known as *ke'eng* with clan members living in multigenerational common longhouses. Members of a *ke'eng* believe in a common ancestor whose descendant, the *kashan*, is considered the headman with both administrative and ceremonial duties. Historically, the *ke'eng* were distinct political entities that sometimes allied temporarily in the face of a threat posed by outsiders. Derung women, unlike Han Chinese women, customarily have high status, participating in economic decisions, overseeing resource distribution, and participating in the yearly round of agricultural activities. The Derung language, known locally as Dulong or Trung, is a Nungish dialect of the Tibeto-Burman language family spoken in two major dialects known as Dulong and Nujiang. The language is closely related to that of the neighboring Nu people and shares with that language the same kinship terminologies as well as other cultural features. There is no written Derung language, and because of their small numbers, the government has made no attempt to develop a Derung script. The Derung religion is an eclectic fusion of traditional animist beliefs, shamanism, Buddhist teachings, and Christian rites. In the Derung beliefs, all animals, plants, minerals, the sun, moon, stars, and the earth are all endowed with spirits, which gives balance and solidarity to nature. Ancestor veneration, borrowed from the Han Chinese, is an important part of Derung ceremonies and traditions.

The Derung remained under the authority of Naxi landlords well into the late 19th century. Mostly serfs or sharecroppers, they often worked for the landlords some days of the week and farmed the common lands of the village the other days. Around the turn of the 20th century, the Derung region came under the political authority of a Tibetan monastery, which took over the role of both the feudal landlord and master of the Derung serfs. Some of the Derung were held in bondage by Lisu landowners who bought and sold them as slaves. Tattooing of women's faces continued as an effort to prevent abuses by landlords or attraction as slaves. Raids by Tibetan groups continued into the early 20th century. The communist government established in mainland China in 1949 greatly changed Derung life. Young women are no longer tattooed at puberty, and Derung families were forced to take a Han Chinese family name for government census purposes. Government plans included changing the economic structure of the Derung from slash and burn farming to irrigated rice farming in collectives or cooperatives with government-owned rice paddies. Their traditional clothing made of hand-loomed flax is now giving way to Han Chinese clothing under pressure from government agents. The reforms that swept China in the 1980s gave the Derung some relief from the stringent policies of Chinese Cultural Revolution of the 1970s, but many Derung worry that assimilation and the loss of their language and culture are inevitable despite more comprehensive policies that promote minority languages and cultures.

Further Reading

Olson, James S. *An Ethnohistorical Dictionary of China.* Westport, CT: Greenwood, 1998.

People's Daily Online. "The Drung Ethnic Minority." Accessed July 31, 2013. http://english.peopledaily.com.cn/data/minorities/Drung.html

West, Barbara A. *Encyclopedia of the Peoples of Asia and Oceania.* New York: Facts on File, 2008.

Xiaoming, Xiao. *China's Ethnic Minorities.* Beijing: Foreign Languages Press, 2003.

Dolgan

The Dolgan, sometimes known as Dolghan or Dulghan, are a Turkic people inhabiting the southern districts of the Taymyrsky Dolgano-Nenetsky District of the Krasnoyarsk Krai in north-central Siberia. The Dolgan form the largest of the non-Russian ethnic groups in the district. The estimated 8,000–10,000 Dolgan speak the Dolgan language, a northern Turkic language of the Siberian Turkic group. Most of the Dolgan, around 60 percent, are Orthodox Christian, though their traditional shamanistic beliefs still survive and are still practiced by some 35 percent.

The indigenous Siberian peoples lived in harmony with nature for thousands of years. Their nomadic way of life and small numbers allowed the tribal groups to survive and to flourish. Over time, the various groups developed territorial preferences where hunting and fishing were abundant. Reindeer herding became a major occupation following its introduction to the region by the Evenk people to the east. Russian explorers began to visit the region in the late 1500s, mostly mapping and surveying the vast territories of Siberia. In the 17th century, officials, tax collectors, traders, and Cossacks moved into the region leading to the near destruction of the traditional economy and way of life. The Russians demanded that the tribes pay taxes in the form of valuable furs. The tax collectors were often so demanding that many of the indigenous peoples were forced to abandon their herds or fishing grounds and devote themselves to procuring the furs demanded by the Russians. The Dolgan ethnic group formed only in the 18th century when groups of Evenk, Yakut, Enet, and other groups migrated northwest from the basins of the Lena and Olenyok Rivers to escape the ever-increasing demands of the fur tax. The migrants displaced the original Nganasan bands and took control of the hunting and fishing grounds. Many of the bands moved north with their herds of reindeer. Originally, the migrants survived as reindeer breeders, fishermen, and hunters in small isolated bands. Living as nomads in the tundra lands north of the Arctic Circle, the small bands traded and intermarried, and over time, the various groups adopted a common culture and a Turkic dialect heavily influenced by the Turkic language of the large Yakut ethnic group living mostly to the east. The various bands began calling themselves *dolghan* or *dulghan*, meaning "people living on the middle reaches of the river." Though the Dolgan language is basically a Turkic language closely related to Yakut, the traditional way of life of the Dolgan clans is closer culturally to that of their nomadic Evenk ancestors than to the pastoral Yakut. The Dolgan generally roamed the forest tundra belt in winter, moving out into the open tundra during the summer. The Dolgan winter camps were constructed on the border between the two seasonal zones. Because their reindeer would soon exhaust the food supply in the area of the camp, they would often move several times during the winter season along the edges of the tundra. As spring approached, the Dolgan winter camps broke up into small nomadic groups consisting of several related families.

The Dolgan culture developed as a distinct ethnic group in the 18th century during the migrations set in motion by the Russian invasion. According to Dolgan tradition and many Russian scholars, their ancestry includes 50–52 percent Tungus, 30–33 percent Yakut, 15 percent Russian, and 3–4 percent Samoyed. The Dolgan divide their small ethnic group into three tribal bands, the Dolgan, the Dongot, and the Edyan. Each of the tribes inhabits a different area of the Taimyr Peninsula. Traditionally, the Dolgan are patriarchal and patrilineal, like the Yakut and Evenk peoples; traditional Dolgan clan structures exhibit signs of a prehistoric matriarchal system. Historic traditions, such as

Dolgan reindeer herders move their camp of baloks. (Jacques Langevin/Sygma/Corbis)

electing a woman to supervise the daily routine of the camp, keeping the sacred fire burning, and caring for the group's sacred relics, are unique to the Dolgan. The nomadic people evolved a shamanistic belief system that included a belief in the spirits of all things in nature. The shamans guarded against evil spirits known as *abaasy* who were believed to cause illness as they entered a person's body and gradually devouring the soul. Other spirits, the benevolent *ayy*, were believed to dwell in odd-shaped stones or antlers that were preserved as group relics and were kept as a type of charm against the *abaasy*. Most of the shamanistic practices were nearly identical to those of the related Evenk. Many of the Dolgan traditions and customs revolved around their reindeer herds. The

Dolgan rode their reindeer, particularly while moving the herds over long distances. They also adopted the dogsled from the Nganasan and other Samoyed peoples. The Dolgan greatly revered traditional storytellers. They particularly favored tales about the animals that tell of the origins of the different clans. Missionary activity in the 19th century introduced Christianity with most Dolgan forcibly baptized. Over time, they adopted the Christian religion of the Russians though they retain many of their pre-Christian beliefs and customs. A small number profess no religious beliefs, the legacy of decades of Soviet atheism. In common with other indigenous peoples of Siberia, the Dolgan suffer from many social problems, particularly alcoholism, high unemployment, and abject poverty.

When the Russians moved north into the Taimyr Peninsula region in the early 19th century, they found different ethnic groups living together in the severe land. The unity of the various bands living together in one area created the formation of a totally new and unique ethnic community. At the end of the 19th century, a group of Russian colonists living along the Heta River adopted the way of life of the Dolgan reindeer herders and were gradually assimilated into the Dolgan ethnic group. The different languages and cultures became the primary foundation of the emerging Dolgan ethnic group. Russian officials again imposed a fur tax, often offering alcohol in trade. Other groups suffered fraud or were forced to give up their furs to traders or corrupt government officials. In the early 20th century, Russian exiles studied the culture and language of the Dolgan. Untouched by the World War in European Russia between 1914 and 1917 or the Russian Civil War that followed, the Dolgan were dismayed when Soviet cadres arrived in their homeland in 1920. Backed by troops, the Soviet officials forced the Dolgan to settle in permanent villages and collectives. The confiscation of their reindeer herds and their new status as herders but employees of the Soviet state led to conflicts and violence, most often brutally put down. The Soviet communes and collectives, worked by Dolgan under Russian supervision, continued the traditional pursuits of reindeer herding, fishing, and hunting, with new occupations such as dairy farming and market gardening introduced where the terrain and the weather permitted. In 1930, the Soviet authorities created the Taimyr National Okrug, sometimes called Dolgan-Nenets Autonomous Okrug, with the Dolgan forming the largest of the several Siberian ethnic groups included in the new territory. The following year, the Soviet officials abolished the old tribal councils, and new Soviet councils were formed. Under Soviet rule, many of the small bands in the region, mostly Evenk or Yakut, were added to the official Dolgan ethnic group. The loss of their traditional way of life, their tribal structures, and collectivization completely destroyed the Dolgan traditional economy. In 1935, the Russian city of Norilsk was built to exploit the mines and natural gas deposits in the Dolgan territory. Many of the western Dolgan were forced off their traditional lands or migrated to other territories to escape the massive industrial pollution and the damage to the environment and the animal populations of the region. Soviet policies of assimilation further damaged the Dolgan culture with Russian words and the Cyrillic alphabet becoming part of Dolgan life. By the 1980s, the social conditions in the Taimyr region were considered among the worst in the Soviet Union. Dominated by the industrial city of Norilsk and its large Russian population, the Siberian peoples were mostly ignored or pushed into the least productive parts of the peninsula. The small ethnic group survived the Soviet period and in 1991, with the collapse of the Soviet Union, began the difficult process of recovering their traditional culture and language. The social amenities accorded the large Russian population around the city, and industrial complex at Norilsk contributed nothing to the welfare of the people of the surrounding tundra. Apathy, alcoholism, and racial discrimination continue to be part of the daily lives of the struggling Dolgan people.

Further Reading

Balzer, Majorie Mandelstam. *Culture Incarnate: Native Anthropology from Russia.* Armonk, NY: M. E. Sharpe, 1995.

Nuttall, Mark, ed. *Encyclopedia of the Arctic.* London: Routledge, 2004.

Vahtre, Lauri, and Jüri Viikberg. The Red Book of the Peoples of the Russian Empire. "The Dolgans." Accessed July 31, 2013. http://www.eki.ee/books/redbook/dolgans.shtml

Ziker, John P. *Peoples of the Tundra: Northern Siberians in the Post-Communist Transition.* Long Grove, IL: Waveland Press, 2002.

Dong

The Dong, sometimes known as Kam, Gam, Tong, Tung, Tung-jen, and Tong-chia, are one of the 56 officially recognized ethnic groups of the People's Republic of China. Numbering nearly three million, the Dong are concentrated in the mountainous junction of three Chinese provinces, in eastern Guizhou, western Hunan, and northern Guangxi with small communities in Hubei and in northern Vietnam. The Dong represent the most northerly of the Ta-speaking peoples of China and Southeast Asia. The Dong language forms part of the Zhuang-Dong branch of the Tibeto-Burman language family.

The Dong are believed to descend from the ancient Rau or Lao peoples who inhabited much of southern China in ancient times. This group of peoples, speaking northern Tai languages, gradually divided into distinct ethnic groups. One group moved north along the coast to settle in the Guizhou-Hunan-Guangxi area, where they evolved as the ancestors of the Dong. Dong legends tell of a migration from the east, while other legends tell of groups migrating south from Guangxi or fleeing the east coast of China to escape locust swarms. Some scholars attribute their origins to the Baiyue tribes who lived in present-day Guangxi and Guangdong during the Qin and Han dynasties, from about 220 BCE to 220 CE. Archives from the Tang dynasty, 61–907 CE, mention the Dong, who called themselves Kam, as a feudal society dominated by an aristocratic, landholding class. During most of their history, the Dong were dominated by more powerful neighbors, with some held as slaves, while others worked as tenant farmers or share-croppers on lands controlled by other ethnic groups. Chinese records mention the Dong as an identifiable ethnic group during the 10th century. In the 13th century, pushed by the expansion of the Mongols to the north, the Dong began their southern migration, which eventually brought them to their present homeland in Guangxi, Guizhou, and Hunan Provinces. Han Chinese control of the region under the Ming and Qing dynasties, from the 14th century, was contested by the Dong with many rebellions against increasing Chinese authority. The history of the Guizhou region is marked by conflicts and tensions between the dominant Han Chinese and the Dong and other non-Chinese ethnic groups. During the Qing dynasty, from the mid-17th to early 20th centuries, agriculture developed rapidly in the Dong areas with irrigation greatly increasing rice production. Self-employed artisans lived in the Dong villages and towns, creating a tradition of arts and crafts that continues to the present. Market towns developed with important food and livestock markets in the bigger towns and county seats. Many of the feudal landowners also began to focus on cash crops on lands worked by Dong peasants.

The Dong, inhabiting 20 contiguous counties in southern China, are a Tai people speaking a number of local dialects. The Dong language is broadly divided into two major dialectal groups, northern and southern, that are mutually incomprehensible. The Dong language forms part of the large northern Tai language family known as the Zhuang-Dong group. Traditionally, it was only an oral language, and the Dong adopted the Chinese script for writing, though in 1958, the Chinese government commissioned researchers to produce a written language based on the Latin alphabet. The forests of their mountainous homeland are an important cultural and economic mainstay. Timber is produced for sale, while wood is the major material for Dong handicrafts and traditional utensils. The favored tree, the fir, holds symbolic significance in Dong society. When a child is born, the parents plant some fir saplings for the baby. When the child reaches 18 years of age, the mature fir trees are used to build houses for their children. For this reason, such fir trees are referred to as "18-year trees." Wood is also used in the construction of the famous Dong-covered bridges known as "wind and rain" bridges. The Dong language belongs to the Dong-Shui group of Zhuang-Dong languages. The language is divided into northern and southern dialectal groups, each with three regional dialects. Most Dong also speak Mandarin Chinese, as it has been used as the written language for centuries. The majority of the Dong practice a polytheistic religion with many gods overseen by the almighty Goddess Sasui, the Dong's protector. Each Dong village has a temple with a round stone altar some 4 feet in height and 10 feet in diameter, often surrounded by banana trees and brambles. On special occasions, the Dong bring chickens, ducks, sweetened fried flour, and other offerings to the altars of the goddess. A minority of the Dong, under the influence of their Han Chinese neighbors, have adopted Theravada Buddhism.

The large feudal landholdings worked by Dong peasants remained the norm in Dong territory in the 19th century. Following the Opium War of 1840–1842, the Dong were further impoverished by the exploitation of European commercial enterprises, adding to the burden of avaricious Qing dynasty officials, arrogant landlords, and debt slavery. The Dong often resisted the abuses of the landlords and the growing number of foreign commercial companies seeking wood and timber in their homeland but most remained mired in debt or tied to large estates as serfs. The coming of the Chinese Communist Party to their homeland in 1921 began a long series of incidents and a growing number of Dong cadres opposing the abuses of the near-feudal social system. During the Long March of the Communist Red Army in the mid-1930s, many Dong served as guides or supplied grain and food to the soldiers. In 1949, guerilla battalions organized by the Dong and other minority nationalities in the region fought with the People's Liberation Army to liberate the southern provinces from the Chinese government troops. The communist victory in 1949 was followed by the creation of autonomous Dong counties in the three regions of their homeland.

Agrarian reform ended the feudal system that had been in place for centuries allowing the Dong to advance in education and to take official positions in the autonomous counties. New schools across the region, teaching in the Dong language along with Mandarin Chinese, quickly raised the educational level and began to train a new generation of Dong cultural and political leaders. In addition to farming, many Dong are adept at wood working, carpentry, and building. Many younger Dong have left their home counties to live in urban areas where they have become traders or service industry workers. Despite recent advances, poverty and slow development of the economic resources of the region remain important social problems.

Further Reading

MacKerras, Colin. *China's Minorities: Integration and Modernization in the Twentieth Century.* Oxford: Oxford University Press, 1994.

Prayer Site for the Dong People of China. "General Information." Accessed July 30, 2013. http://www.dongteam.org/info.html

Rossi, Gail, and Paul Lau. *The Dong People of China: A Hidden Civilization.* Singapore: Hagley & Hoyle, 1991.

West, Barbara A. *Encyclopedia of the Peoples of Asia and Oceania.* New York: Facts on File, 2008.

Dongxiang

The Dongxiang, sometimes known as Tonghsiang, Tungsiang, Dongxiang Hui, or Mongolian Huihui, are one of the officially recognized ethnic groups of the People's Republic of China. Russians have historically referred to the Dongxiang as Shirongol Mongols. The Dongxiang call themselves Sarta, Sa'erta, Santa, or San-t'a. The name *Dongxiang* is the Chinese name for the ethnic group, meaning "people of eastern villages," which refers to the Dongxiang homeland east of the Han Chinese settlements. The estimated 625,000 Dongxiang are concentrated in north-central China, in the Gansu Province, with smaller communities in Xinjiang, Qinghai Province, and the Ningxia Hui region. The Dongxiang is a Mongolic language forming the Shirongolic branch of the Mongolic languages. The Dongxiang are mostly Sunni Muslims, unlike most of the other Mongol groups that are largely Tibetan Buddhists.

The origins of the Dongxiang are not known, though scholars speculate that the ethnic group, closely related to the Mongols of Mongolia, converted to Sunni Islam through close contact with the Central Asian peoples at the time of the great Mongol Empire in the 13th century. Others believe that they are the descendants of Mongol troops garrisoned in the Hezhou region of Gansu by Genghis Khan in the late 12th century. Another possibility is that they might be a fusion of many peoples over the centuries, including Mongol, Han Chinese, Hui Chinese, and Tibetan. Still others believe that the Dongxiang formed part of the ancient Chagatai Khanate, a powerful empire centered in present-day Xinjiang. Most Dongxiang believe that their ancestors converted to Islam and were driven from their homes by the Buddhist Mongols leading to a migration to what is now Minqin County in Gansu Province. The complex history of the ethnic group is evidenced by the family surnames that reflect Mongol, Han, Hui, and Tibetan origins. In the early years of the Ming dynasty that replaced the Mongol Yuan dynasty in China in 1368, the Mongol Dongxiang were offered an amnesty and were allowed to settle when they had been stationed during the waning years of the Mongol Empire. Over the centuries, the Dongxiang maintained their Muslim religion as an integral part of their unique culture. Borrowings from the Hui, the Chinese Muslims, and other ethnic groups further differentiated their culture from those of neighboring peoples. By the early 18th century, hundreds of mosques, religious schools, and Muslim shrines dotted the landscape of the Dongxiang homeland. Many of the Dongxiang were nomads herding large numbers of sheep, an animal that still plays an important part in the work and life of the Dongxiang people. Sheep are still considered a symbol of the Dongxiang national spirit. An independent people, the Dongxiang took up arms many times over the centuries to protect their freedom and their herds. Historically, the Dongxiang were religiously divided into three sects known as the Old, the New, and the Emerging sects. Relying on a "divide and rule" policy, the Hui and Han ruling classes often sowed dissension among the three sects leading to feuds and at times even violent clashes in the 18th and 19th centuries.

The Muslim Dongxiang continued to revere their religion and their history. At one time, there were 595 mosques and 79 other religious structures, one for around every 30 Dongxiang households. On a yearly basis, there were 34 different kinds of religious expenses to be paid by each household. Prior to the mid-20th century, the Dongxiang were considered a subgroup of the Muslim Hui people of China. Even today, the Dongxiang remain an extremely devout Muslim people. Historically, about two-thirds of the Dongxiang were Sunni Muslim, with about one-third Shi'a and a small group of Wahhabis. The Dongxiang language belongs to the Mongolic language family and is spoken in three mutually intelligible dialects. There is no written form of the language with Han Chinese script, the Arab alphabet of their religion, or the Uyghur script used to write in the language. Most Dongxiang live as farmers growing potatoes, barley, and yams and raising sheep. Many families also keep chickens as eggs are their primary trade commodity. As much of their territory is often short of rain, many Dongxiang suffer poverty and a lack of development and irrigation. The dry conditions have resulted in the area being largely ignored by China's development agencies with little in the way of agricultural or industrial development. One of the most traditional elements of the Dongxiang culture is the many folk songs, called "flowers" locally. In the past, they were sung by people to express their hope for a better future and to pour out their wrath against their oppressors. The "flowers" were ruthlessly stamped out during the long periods of oppression, but since the 1980s, they have been revived. The Dongxiang language, known as Santa or Shirongolic, forms a separate branch of the Mongolic language family. Knowledge of Arabic is widespread, as it is the language of their religion, with many often using Arabic script in informal writing. In recent years, an official Latin alphabet written form of Dongxiang has been developed but is not widely used.

In the 19th century, the Dongxiang often suffered from drought conditions with hunger and famine often close by. The introduction of potatoes helped to alleviate the extreme poverty and augmented a diet mostly based on grains and maize. Potato mash, used in the fabrication of vinegar noodles and liquor, became a prime trading product. By the early 20th century, the Dongxiang territories were among the poorest in northwestern China. Violence spread through the region when fighting erupted between the communists and government troops in the years before World War II. The Chinese Civil War resumed in 1945, ending with a communist victory in 1949. The communist minority policies resulted in the creation of the Dongxiang Autonomous County in Gansu in 1950. Cadres known as "Solidarity Committees" were created to eliminate disunity that still existed between the Dongxiang and neighboring ethnic groups. Trees and grass were planted on the barren hills to curb erosion that had plagued the region for centuries. Large tracts of hilly farmland were terraced, and irrigation programs were put in place. In 1954, the Dongxiang were recognized as a separate ethnic group rather than as a part of the larger Hui people. The Dongxiang became the target of political repression during the years of the Cultural Revolution in the 1960s and 1970s. Cadres of Red Guards defiled or destroyed

mosques and often forced Dongxiang religious and political leaders to eat pork, which is forbidden by the Koran. Their experiences during the horrible years of the Cultural Revolution greatly sharpened the Dongxiang sense of identity. Since the turn of the 21st century, the Chinese government has been more circumspect toward the Muslim peoples, fearing that the spread of fundamentalism could lead to ethnic and religious problems in the region.

Further Reading

Gladney, Dru C. *Muslim Chinese: Ethnic Nationalism in the People's Republic.* Cambridge, MA: Harvard University Asia Center, 1996.

Legerton, Colin, and Jacob Rawson. *Invisible China: A Journey through Ethnic Borderlands.* Chicago: Chicago Review Press, 2009.

Lipman, Jonathan Neaman. *Familiar Strangers: A History of Muslims in Northwest China.* Seattle, WA: University of Washington Press, 1998.

Yardley, Jim. "Deep in China, a Poor and Pious Muslim Enclave." *New York Times*, March 19, 2006. http://www.nytimes.com/2006/03/19/international/asia/19ethnic.html?pagewanted=all&_r=0

Dungan

The Dungan, sometimes known as Lao Huihui, Hui, Huizi, Huizu, Huai, Tonggans, or Chinese Muslims, are an ethnoreligious group living mostly in the Central Asian republics of Kyrgyzstan and Kazakhstan with smaller communities in Uzbekistan, Tajikistan, Russia, and Ukraine.

The descendants of refugees from China, the Dungan speak a Chinese dialect that incorporates borrowings from Arabic, Persian, Turkic languages, and Russian. The estimated 110,000 Dungan are officially Sunni Muslims and are closely related to the large Hui Muslim minority in China. Though they are called Dungan by neighboring peoples, members of this ethnic group call themselves Hui. The Central Asian peoples also call the Hui Muslims of China's western Xinxiang by the name *Dungan*. Though physically they resemble the other Chinese ethnic groups, the Dungan are distinguished by their traditional clothing, including turbans, and their Muslim religion.

The Islamic religion arrived in the Chinese Empire both by sea and overland, with small Muslim communities established in the seventh and eighth centuries CE. The early Arab, Persian, and Turkic Muslim settlers took Chinese wives and gradually adopted Chinese speech and culture. In the 11th century, the kingdom of the Tanguts, known as Hsi Hsia, in western China welcomed Muslims as traders, scholars, and soldiers. During the rule of the Mongol Yuan dynasty in the 13th century, a flood of Arabs, Persians, and Turks fleeing the Mongol conquest of their homelands settled in the remote region south of the Alashan Plateau region of the Gobi Desert. The Muslim refugees married Chinese, Uyghur, and Mongol woman and gradually assimilated. Eventually, the Muslims, collectively called Hui, took on the general appearance and many of the cultural characteristics of the dominant Han Chinese. In the 14th century, the Muslim population of the Alashan region began to expand by converting surrounding peoples. Far from the centers of Chinese power, the Muslims maintained a separate state ruled by Hui sultans, a source of irritation to successive Chinese dynasties. The Manchu conquest of China in 1644 gave the Hui a chance to throw off infidel rule. Invaded by Manchu troops in 1648, the Muslim Hui fought a long and violent campaign but were finally defeated by overwhelming Manchu military power. The Hui again rebelled against Han Chinese rule in 1785. The Manchu rulers, determined to eliminate the Muslim threat to their authority, loosed imperial troops on the Alashan region to carry out savage massacres, unprecedented in the East. Small numbers of Hui refugees escaped the onslaught by fleeing north to the Muslim regions of Central Asia.

The Dungan culture is a mixture of Hui, Chinese, and Turkic customs and traditions. The majority of the Dungan living in Kyrgyzstan and Kazakhstan are farmers, growing rice and vegetables. Some are involved in opium production, while others raise dairy cattle. Famous for their hospitality, the Dungan adhere to a yearly schedule of ceremonies and events to preserve their culture. The practice of marrying only within the Dungan ethnic group has helped them to preserve their unique culture, which includes many ancient traditions that have disappeared in modern China. The distinctive Dungan cuisine, much appreciated in Central Asia, resembles the cuisine of northwestern China but has adapted to the Turkic tastes of the region. The Dungan language, called the Hui language by the speakers, is similar to the

Mandarin Chinese dialect spoken in the Chinese provinces of Gansu and Shanxi, where many Hui Chinese still live. The language, though intelligible to Chinese speakers, contains many loanwords from Arabic, Persian, and Turkic. Since the 1950s, the Dungan language has been written in the Cyrillic alphabet. Most Dungan adhere to the Hanafi rite of Sunni Islam, with a small Hanbali rite minority. After decades of Soviet rule, many Dungan consider themselves cultural Muslims or simply nonreligious.

In the aftermath of the Manchu repression, the Hui homeland, an area larger than modern France, was devastated with many districts virtually depopulated. Refugees slowly returned to the region, but excess population from China's eastern provinces settled much of the land. Continued discrimination and oppression resulted in a renewed Hui uprising that began in Gansu Province in 1862, but rapidly spread to other Hui population centers in northwestern China. The uprising, known as the Dungan Revolt or the Hui Minorities War, lasted for 15 years and left up to 12 million dead. Three major groups of refugees fled to the Russian Empire over the Tian Shan Mountains during the exceptionally severe winter of 1877–1878. Another wave of refugees arrived in Russian Central Asia in the 1880s. Called Dungan by the Central Asian peoples, the Hui Muslims settled in separate towns and settlements seeking seclusion and the freedom to practice their religion and culture. Their Muslim religion, though shared with their Central Asian neighbors, retained many distinct elements that continued to separate the

Dungan from the surrounding populations. Over time, their Chinese dialect developed as a distinct language known as *Huihui hua* or Hui speech that served as one of the elements of ethnic identity. Isolated by poor relations between the communist governments of the Soviet Union and China, the Dungan retained many cultural traits that disappeared or were forcibly suppressed among the related Hui in China. A standardized language, based on a Gansu dialect rather than on the Beijing Mandarin standard in China, was used in schools in Dungan villages and towns. According to the Soviet statistics of the 1970s and 1980s, the Dungan maintained the use of their language much more successfully than other minority groups in the region. Over many decades, the Dungan developed a separate ethnic identity distinct from that of related Hui in culture, ethnic characteristics, and ethnic identity elements. The collapse of Soviet communism and the appearance of newly independent states in Central Asia in 1991 was a time of upheaval and insecurity for the Dungan communities. In the post-Soviet era, the Dungan adapted, learning the Turkic languages instead of Russian and becoming part of the multicultural societies in the region. In the early 21st century, cultural and religious ties to the Hui people of China have been renewed after decades of isolation.

Further Reading

Allès, Elisabeth. "The Chinese-Speaking Muslims (Dungans) of Central Asia: A Case of Multiple Identities in a Changing Context," *Asian Ethnicity* 6, No. 2 (June 2005): 121–134.

Kim, Hodong. *Holy War in China: The Muslim Rebellion and State in Chinese Central Asia, 1864–1877.* Palo Alto, CA: Stanford University Press, 2010.

Lipman, Jonathan Neaman. *Familiar Strangers: A History of Muslims in Northwest China.* Hong Kong: Hong Kong University Press, 1998.

Miller, Frederic P., Agnes F. Vandome, and John McBrewster, eds. *Dungan People.* Saarbrücken, Germany: Alphascript, 2011.

E

Ewenki

The Ewenki, sometimes known as Evenk, Evenki, Tungus, Tongus, Lamut, Owenk, Birar, or Manegry, are a Tungus people, one of the 56 officially recognized ethnic groups in the People's Republic of China. The Evenk of China make up about half the total number of Evenk with an ethnic population of about equal size in the Russian Federation, and smaller communities in Mongolia and Ukraine. Most Evenk inhabit the grasslands of China's Inner Mongolia region and neighboring Nehe County of Heilongjiang Province, formerly known as Manchuria. The estimated 34,000 Evenk in China speak the Evenki language, which forms the Evenki branch of the northern Tungusic language group. Most Evenk in China adhere to their traditional shamanism with a growing number embracing Tibetan Buddhism.

The origins of the Evenk in China is considered to be nomadic tribes in the Greater Khingan Range between the fifth and ninth centuries. Other ancestor tribes lived to the north, traveling over the vast distances between Lake Baikal and the Amur River. By 1600, the Evenk in territory claimed by Russia had adopted reindeer herding, while those in Chinese territory took up the horse breeding and *deel*, the traditional clothing, of the Mongols. The Solons, the ancestors of the Evenk in China, were originally nomads in the great valley of the Amur River. Closely related to the Duar ethnic group, they were also kin to the Khamnigan, another group of horse-breeding Evenk to the west of the Solon. The original home of the Evenk was probably in the Lake Baikal region of southern Siberia in the Neolithic era. From the Baikal region, they spread to the Amur River valley and other areas of Siberia. They were first recognized as a distinct ethnic group in the 14th century. In the 17th century, Cossacks serving the Russian Empire began to explore southern Siberia with contact made with many Evenk bands. The Cossacks imposed a fur tax on the Evenk tribes, often taking hostages to ensure that the tax would be paid. Contact with the Europeans and the constant demands for furs pushed many Evenk bands as far east as Sakhalin Island, while others scattered across a vast area of Siberia. Between 1635 and 1640, the various Evenk bands came under the domination of the Manchu, who took control of China to found the Qing dynasty in 1644. In the mid-17th century, as Cossacks and Russian troops invaded the Chinese territory of the Heilongjiang valley, officials of the Qing dynasty forcibly relocated large numbers of ethnic Evenk to the Nen River valley in Inner Mongolia, where they were politically integrated into the Mongol banner system. In 1732, the Evenk in the Buteha area of northern Manchuria were ordered, together with their families, to take up garrison duty as frontier guards in the Hulunbuir grass-lands. Their descendants make up the large majority of the modern Evenk in China.

Traditionally, Evenk culture was a mixture of pastoralists and hunter–gatherers. By the 19th century, they had divided into two major divisions based on different types of economic activity. Those in Russian Siberia lived mostly by hunting and reindeer herding, while the Solon and other small groups in Chinese territory became horse and cattle herders as well as some farming. The so-called Horse Evenk, sometimes called Sulun, Sulong, or Solon, officially known as Evenk or Ewenki since the 1930s, took on many of the cultural attributes and traditions of the neighboring Mongols. Migrations in the past resulted in population dispersion, which in turn led to great unevenness in the social development of the Evenk bands. The recognition of the Evenk as a distinct ethnic group in China in the mid-20th century allowed the Evenk to advance in education, farming, and, because of the coal found in their traditional lands, mining. Monogamy is the norm in Evenk society, though in the past, the bands practiced exogamy. Most Evenk are retaining their traditional shamanistic belief system while those in the pastoral areas are often Tibetan Buddhist. The Evenk language, usually known as Evenki, forms the northern branch of the Tungusic languages, which also include Manchu. In China, the Evenk language has been giving way as young Evenk learn Mandarin Chinese in school. Evenk is now considered an endangered language.

In the 19th century, other Evenk were driven out of Russian territory into China by pressure from the expanding Yakut people. The Manchu rulers of the Qing dynasty extracted tribute from the Evenk and often recruited Evenk men into the imperial army. The consolidation of the Evenk bands into a distinct ethnic group began under Manchu rule with many draftees from different bands were thrown together on frontier guard duty or in battalions used to suppress uprisings by other minority peoples. Following the overthrow of the Qing dynasty in 1911, many Evenk returned to their home regions but retained the pan-Evenk beliefs. Following the Japanese occupation of Manchuria in 1931, the Japanese exploited the Evenk and drafted many into the Japanese military forces. Some Evenk were used for bacteriological experiments while the spread of smallpox, typhoid, and venereal diseases decimated the people. A sharp population decline under Japanese rule left just a third of the 1931 Evenk population alive in 1945. The communist authority, following their takeover of mainland China in 1949, enacted reforms that aided the recovery of the Evenk population. By 1958, the Evenk were mostly employed on collectives and cooperatives, and efforts were made to raise their productivity and their cultural level. A series of economic measures since the 1980s, including the introduction of new breeds of cattle, the opening of grain and fodder farms, and improved veterinary services, have allowed the Evenk to prosper in the early 21st century.

Further Reading

Ethnic Groups. "The Ewenki Minority Group." Accessed July 31, 2013. http://www.china

.org.cn/e-groups/shaoshu/shao-2-ewenki .htm

Legerton, Colin. *Invisible China: A Journey through Ethnic Borderlands.* Chicago: Chicago Review Press, 2009.

Olson, James S. *An Ethnohistorical Dictionary of China.* Westport, CT: Greenwood, 1998.

West, Barbara A. *Encyclopedia of the Peoples of Asia and Oceania.* New York: Facts on File, 2008.

G

Gaoshan

The Gaoshan, sometimes known as Taiwanese Natives, Taiwanese Aborigines,
or Kaoshan, are the indigenous people of
the island of Taiwan off the east coast of
China. A small community, numbering
around 3,000, lives in Fujian Province in
the People's Republic of China. The estimated 512,000 Gaoshan speak Formosan
languages belonging to the Austronesian language family. The majority of the
Gaoshan identify themselves as Christians, perhaps as many as 70 percent, with
smaller groups who retain their traditional
animist beliefs and others who have adopted the Buddhist religion of the dominant Han Chinese.

The earliest evidence of human habita-
tion in Taiwan dates back more than 20,000
years, when the Taiwan Strait was often ex-
posed by lower sea levels as a land bridge
to the mainland. Around 5,000 years ago,
farming peoples from the mainland settled
in the island. These colonists, believed to
have been speakers of Austronesian languages, later dispersed from Taiwan to the
Philippines, Indonesia, Madagascar, Poly-
nesia, and Oceania. The Gaoshan are the
descendants of these early inhabitants of
Taiwan and mainland China. Over time,
the culture fragmented into tribes and territories, each with its own dialect and cultural traits. Around 2,000 years ago, iron
artifacts and other metals appeared in

Taiwan. At first, these are believed to
have come to the island as trade goods, but
by around 400 CE, wrought iron was being
produced locally. Distinct Iron Age cultures have been identified in different
parts of the island and the Fujian region
of the mainland. By the seventh century,
the Gaoshan had adopted settled farming
and livestock breeding to augment their
traditional occupations as hunters, gatherers, and fishermen. The Gaoshan of the
Taiwan plains entered feudal society at
about the same time as the Han Chinese
people of the mainland. Such concepts as
private landownership, land rental, hired
labor, and the division between peasants
and landlords became well established.
The arrival of Dutch merchants in 1624
began the European colonization of the island. Around the same time, Han Chinese
from Fujian and Guangdong of mainland
China began to cross the strait to settle
among the Plains tribes in the western
part of the island. The Spanish established
a settlement in the north but were driven
out by the Dutch in 1642. In 1662, Zheng
Chenggong, popularly known as Koxinga,
a Chinese military leader driven from the
mainland by the invading Manchu armies,
defeated the Dutch and took control of Taiwan. He used the island as a base for his
grand campaign against the Manchu Qing
dynasty in China. His son and successor,
Zheng Jing, established an independent
kingdom of Tungming in the southeast,

the first Chinese-ruled state to govern part of the island. During this period, continued Han Chinese migrations from the mainland began displacing many of the Gaoshan tribes, particularly in the fertile plains in the west of the island. Zheng Jing promoted immigration to Taiwan with the promise of free land and ownership of farms for peasants in exchange for compulsory military service. Following the death of Zheng Jing in 1681, the lack of an official successor created a chaotic situation that was taken advantage of by the Qing officials on the mainland. They dispatched a fleet that destroyed the Zheng fleet, and by 1683, the Qing had overthrown the Tungming kingdom. They incorporated Taiwan into Fujian Province, ending two decades of Zheng family rule. From that time, parts of Taiwan became increasingly integrated with China, while continuing immigration rapidly increased the Han Chinese population of the island. Qing officials categorized the Gaoshan tribes according to their attitude to Qing rule. The terms *raw* or *wild* were applied to the tribes that resisted Qing authority, while *cooked* or *tame* were applied to the tribes that accepted Qing rule through their payment of a head tax and the abandonment of traditional activities such as head-hunting. The epithet *cooked* was often considered synonymous with assimilation into Han Chinese culture. The terms *Pingpu*, meaning "Plains tribes," and *Gaoshan*, meaning "mountaineers" or "high mountain tribes," were used to differentiate between the assimilating Plains peoples and the tribes in the less accessible mountain areas.

The Gaoshan culture more closely resembles the cultures of the Philippines and parts of Indonesia than that of the dominant Han Chinese. The government of Taiwan recognizes 14 Gaoshan tribes: the Amis, Atayal, Bunun, Kavalan, Paiwan, Puyama, Rukai, Saisayat, Sakizaya, Seediq, Tao, Thao, Tsou, and Truku, with 11 tribes not officially recognized, the Babuza, Basay, Hoanya, Ketagalan, Luilang, Pazeh/Kaxabu, Papora, Qauqaut, Siraya, Taokas, and the Trobiawan. Traditionally, the family system is patriarchal and monogamous, though historically at least one of the tribal groups had a matriarchal system. The name *Gaoshan* means "mountaineer" in Chinese, referring to the mountainous terrain of eastern Taiwan, which is the homeland of most of the Gaoshan tribal groups. Over time, many of the tribal groups specialized in such areas as tanning hides, making fishing nets, weaving baskets, or making pottery, which were then traded for food and products that were not produced locally. The system broke down the tribal barriers and promoted the evolution of a similar culture throughout the region. The tribal groups, under greater pressure from Han Chinese settlers, are the most assimilated and their languages mostly extinct or endangered. In the mountainous west, the Gaoshan retain much of their traditional culture and languages. According to the government of the Republic of China, in Taiwan, there are 14 recognized tribes and 11 unrecognized tribes. With few exceptions, the recognized tribes are the highland peoples in the east of the island, and the unrecognized are generally Pingpu or lowland tribes that have lost their languages and are assimilating into Han Taiwanese culture. Many Gaoshan adopted Han Chinese family names, which helped them prosper and avoid the overt discrimination during the Qing and the later Japanese governmental periods. Han influences in Gaoshan culture are extensive, while Gaoshan influence on Taiwanese culture results in Han Taiwanese culture, demonstrating major cultural differences from other Han cultures. European missionaries, beginning in the 17th century, converted many of the tribal peoples to Christianity. Today an estimated 70 percent of the Gaoshan consider themselves Christian, mostly Taiwan Presbyterian Church or Roman Catholic. Confucian beliefs of Daoism and Buddhism were brought to the island with the Han migrants, with many of the Plains tribes adopting the religious system along with the Han culture. The Austronesian languages, known as the Formosan languages, are rapidly disappearing. Of the estimated 26 distinct Formosan languages, at least 10 are extinct, and another 4 or 5 are close to extinction with several others considered endangered. The Formosan languages form 9 of the 10 principal branches of the Austronesian language family, while the one remaining branch is made of around 1,200 Malayo-Polynesian languages found outside Taiwan, but are now considered to have their roots in ancient Taiwan.

Increasing Han Chinese immigration pushed most of the Gaoshan east into the mountains or led to the assimilation of the Plains tribes in the 19th century. The Qing dynasty, having been defeated in a war with Japan, ceded Taiwan to the Japanese Empire in 1895. The island produced rice and sugar for the Japanese market and served as a base for Japanese expansion into Southeast Asia and the Pacific during World War II. Some Gaoshan and Han Taiwanese resisted Japanese rule. By 1901–1902, most resistance in the western half of the island had been quelled, though Japanese patrols into the eastern districts often met armed resistance from the Gaoshan. Japanese rule was characterized by anthropological study of the indigenous peoples and attempts to mold the Gaoshan into loyal subjects of the Japanese emperor, often using military suppression. In 1945, the defeated Japanese surrendered Taiwan to the nationalist Chinese government, then engaged in a vicious civil war on the mainland with the increasingly powerful communists. In 1949, the nationalists were defeated and withdrew the government, known as the Republic of China, to Taiwan along with

Gaoshan Pop

In recent years, a number of Gaoshan singers have achieved fame throughout the Chinese world as pop stars, including A-mei, Difang, A-Lin, Pur-dur, Samingad, and Landy Wen. The triumph of these and other entertainers has given the indigenous Gaoshan both a sense of pride and a sense of modernity. The official theme song of the Atlanta Olympics in 1996, called Return to Innocence, included a traditional Gaoshan chant. Gaoshan pop has become so popular that in 2005, a full-time Gaoshan radio station, Ho-hi-yan, was launched to focus on Gaoshan artists and to serve the interests of the indigenous Gaoshan community.

a large civilian and military population. Thousands of refugees from the mainland arrived in Taiwan, making the Han population the largest portion of the island population. By the 1980s, the Gaoshan made up only about 2 percent of the Taiwanese population, though their cultural influence helped to differentiate Han Taiwanese culture from that of the Han Chinese culture of the mainland. These differences, plus the distinct island history, are often used to support demands for separate independence for Taiwan, which remains under the rule of the government of the Republic of China, whose authority is still restricted to Taiwan and a few small islands. Efforts have been under way for several years for the Pingpu peoples to gain official recognition from Taiwan's national government. In 2010, several tribes enlisted the aid of the United Nations in their quest for official recognition. Negotiators for the unrecognized Pingpu or Plains tribes and the Taiwan government are working to change the language of the law on tribal peoples, which now excludes all but the mountain people. A literal reading of the law on indigenous peoples has excluded the Plains tribes from gaining official recognition despite decades of negotiations and petitions.

Further Reading

Brown, Melissa J. *Is Taiwan Chinese? The Impact of Culture, Power, and Migration on Changing Identities*. Berkeley: University of California Press, 2004.

Cauquelin, Josiane. *Aborigines of Taiwan: The Puyama, from Headhunting to the Modern World*. London: Routledge, 2004.

Covell, Ralph. *Pentecost of the Hills in Taiwan: The Christian Faith among the Original Inhabitants*. Los Angeles: Hope Publishing, 1998.

Liu, Tao Tao. "The Last Huntsmen's Quest for Identity: Writing from the Margins in Taiwan." In Yeh Chuen-Rong, ed. *History, Culture and Ethnicity: Selected Papers from the International Conference on the Formosan Indigenous Peoples,* 427–430. Taipei: SMC Publishing, 2006.

Gelao

The Gelao, sometimes known as Gelo or Klau, form one of the 56 ethnic groups officially recognized by the People's Republic of China. The estimated 590,000 Gelao are concentrated in the western districts of China's Guizhou Province, with smaller communities in Guangxi, southeastern Yunnan, southern Sichuan, and northern Vietnam. The Gelao speak a Ge-Chi language belonging to the Tai-Kadai language family. The majority of the Gelao adhere to a mixed belief system that encompasses Daoism, Buddhism, and many of their ancient traditions and rites.

The Gelao are considered one of the earliest peoples to inhabit the region of southern China as part of the early Khitan or Liao peoples. Their earliest ancestors, known as the Xianbei, were nomadic tribes in the northern reaches of Manchuria, Inner Mongolia, and eastern Mongolia. They were mentioned in early Chinese chronicles as nomads north of the Chinese state of Yan in 699–623 BCE. They came under Chinese domination as guardians of the Chinese frontier in 93 CE. Gradually, some of the nomads moved south during the period of the Xianbei Empire between 141 and 181 BCE. In the south, they adopted the Tai culture and language, becoming the ancestors of many of the present-day Tai peoples through their successors, the Khitan people. More than 2,000 years ago, the ancestors of the Gelao settled in Guizhou. Then known as the Liao people, they formed part of a large Tai-speaking cluster of peoples across southern China. Between the third and fifth centuries CE, the Liao adopted a feudal system while spreading west into Sichuan and south in Guangxi and northern Vietnam. By the fifth century, the inhabitants were manufacturing metal spears, shields, fishing tools, and copper cooking utensils. They also learned to weave fine linen. The Liao people at first elected their kings, but later their leaders became hereditary. The Mongol conquest of the early 13th century brought the Gelao and the other Tai peoples under the Mongol Yuan dynasty in China. The overthrow of the Yuan dynasty by the Chinese Ming dynasty resulted in the differentiation of the various ethnic groups with the name *Gelao* first used. Under Mongol and Chinese rule, the Gelao were ruled by appointed chiefs, but by the advent of the Manchu conquest of China and the establishment of the Manchu Qing dynasty, the tribal chiefs lost their authority to civil servants dispatched by the Qing court. Due to the rugged terrain of their homeland, the Gelao separated into a number of regional groups speaking dialects that were not mutually intelligible. Many adopted the language of the Han Chinese for use as a lingua franca in the 17th and 18th centuries.

Gelao culture is one of the least known of the minority cultures in China. In the mountainous areas, they normally cultivated maize, while in the lowlands, they grew wheat, rice, millet, and sorghum as mainstays of their diet. Hot and sour dishes served with glutinous rice cakes are a favorite food of both the highland and lowland Gelao. Traditionally, marriage customs were based on the feudal rites, including arranged marriages, often during childhood. The Gelao language, which belongs to the Kadai branch of the Tai-Kadai languages and is spoken in a number of distinct dialects, including Green Gelao, Vandu or Red Gelao, Telue or White Gelao, A'ou, Mulao, and Qao, is now spoken by less than a quarter of the Gelao population. Mandarin Chinese, adopted as a means of communication among the speakers of the various dialects, is now the mother language of about three-quarters of the total population. A number of the dialects are near extinction or are considered endangered. Many of the Gelao also speak the languages of neighboring peoples such as the Miao, Yi, and Bouyei. Gelao folk literature, which usually glorifies the honesty, integrity, and bravery of the common Gelao people, often satirizes the upper classes. The Gelao religious beliefs are a mixture of Daoism, Buddhism, and their traditional animist beliefs such as ancestor veneration and a belief in spirits. At the annual Spring Festival, the Gelao offer a huge rice cake to their ancestors. Some communities also sacrifice chickens to bless the rice crop. Like some of the neighboring peoples, the Gelao celebrate the day of the Ox King Buddha, when their oxen are honored for the year of hard work.

In the 19th century, the majority of the Gelao groups lived in farming villages controlled by Gelao or Han Chinese landlords.

Usually, landlords and rich farmers controlled over half the lands even though they constituted only a small minority of the population. The Gelao, sharecroppers or small farmers, usually paid rent with a portion of their crops, sometimes over half. Gelao farmers also had to pay tributes to the landlords, which could be as high as the rent. In some areas, particularly in western Guizhou, Gelao farmers paid rent and tribute of maize, opium, soybeans, and peppers, but were also required to work as unpaid labor some 50–80 days each year. By the early 20th century, most Gelao groups were culturally indistinguishable from their Han Chinese neighbors. At the time of the Chinese Revolution that established a republic in 1919, scholars wrote that the Gelao were nearly extinct with many married into Han and Bouyei families. Without irrigation, the Gelao farmlands were often subject to drought with devastating consequences, such as hunger or even famine. To augment their incomes from farming, many Gelao established secondary incomes from cork production, bamboo weaving, and making straw sandals. The advent of World War II brought many changes as refugees and industries moved from the eastern provinces were established in the region. In 1949, the communist cadres, victorious in the Chinese Civil War, established their authority in the region. The common Gelao were welcomed as fellow sufferers, but the landlords and more prosperous peasants were punished or sent to reduction or labor camps. Officially recognized as a distinct ethnic minority known as Gelao or Gelo, the ethnic group made rapid strides in education and culture though the Han Chinese culture was stressed. The Cultural Revolution in the 1960s and 1970s again devastated the region with many of the few Gelao historical sites destroyed and many Gelao denounced as anticommunist or revisionist. Beginning in the early 1980s, as China's government relaxed its stringent controls, the Gelao began to revive as a distinct people though most now spoke Han Chinese as their primary language. Efforts to revive the culture, including the traditional festivals and ceremonies, has had limited success though many Gelao, who formerly claimed Han Chinese nationality to escape the excesses of the Cultural Revolution and the strict rules governing the ethnic minorities, are now reverting to their roots and claiming Gelao nationality.

Further Reading

Diller, Anthony, Jerry Edmondson, and Yongxian Luo. *The Tai-Kadai Languages.* London: Routledge, 2008.

Ethnic Groups. "The Gelo Ethnic Minority." Accessed July 31, 2013. http://www.china .org.cn/e-groups/shaoshu/shao-2-gelo.htm

West, Barbara A. *Encyclopedia of the Peoples of Asia and Oceania.* New York: Facts on File, 2008.

Xioming, Xiao. *China's Ethnic Minorities.* Beijing: Foreign Languages Press, 2003.

Gin

The Gin, sometimes known as Jing in Mandarin Chinese or Kinh in Vietnamese, are a small ethnic group forming one of the 56 officially recognized minority groups in the People's Republic of China. The estimated 23,000 Gin mostly live on the three small islands of Wanwei, Wutou, and Shanxin off the coast of the Guangxi Zhuang Autonomous Region in southern China near the border with Vietnam. Their language is a Vietnamese dialect mixed with Cantonese and Mandarin Chinese. The majority of the Gin adhere to Mahayana Buddhism and Daoism, often mixing their rites and ceremonies with beliefs handed down from generation to generation.

The Gin are the descendants of Vietnamese migrants who settled three small islands off the south China coast in the 16th century, when their area of Dai Viet formed part of the Chinese Empire under the Ming dynasty. The islands, sparsely inhabited at the time, gave the migrants a place to settle away from the heavily settled coastal region with its large Han Chinese and Zhuang populations. In the islands, the Gin took up fishing and farming, growing rice, sweet potatoes, taro, and fruits. During centuries of Chinese domination of Vietnam, the Vietnamese people were forced to send tribute to the Chinese emperor, including many young women and eunuch boys. Some scholars believe that the ancestors of the Gin moved north into China proper to escape the possibility of losing their children as slaves and tribute being sent to China. The Gin were brought under the rule of the Qing dynasty following the Manchu conquest of China in 1644. Under Manchu rule, their islands were added to a mainland prefecture that was under the authority of a court official. Tribute to the Manchu court from the islands was usually seashells, pearls, sea otters, and sea horses, prized for their medicinal value.

The Gin are an island people, though about a quarter of their population now live on the mainland among the Han Chinese and Zhuang. Over time, the Gin have become expert fishermen as there are more than 700 species of fish found in the waters around their islands. Some 200 of the species are of great economic value. Since the 1990s, the Gin islands have become favorite tourist destinations, bringing not only many outside influences but also prosperity. Many Gin now work in hotels and restaurants, sell souvenirs, or manage the many businesses that have opened because of the tourist boom. In the past, the Gin had great difficulty selling their fishing catch to the mainland because of a lack of transport links. Modernization of their islands has brought highways, hotels, restaurants, shops, banks, mobile telecommunications, and cybercafes to their once sleepy homeland. The majority of the Gin speak a dialect of Vietnamese that includes many borrowings from Chinese dialects and Zhuang. Most now also speak Mandarin Chinese, the most widely spoken language in China. Because they speak and understand Vietnamese, many Gin have been employed in the growing cross-border trade between China and Vietnam. Though their language is normally written using Hanzi, the Chinese script, they also maintain their own Zinan script, which was developed in Vietnam in the 13th century.

The Gin remained mostly poor fishermen and farmers in the 19th century. They maintained ties to Vietnam, which aided the maintenance of their historic language and culture. In 1884, France and China fought a war following the Qing dynasty's refusal to cede Vietnam to French rule. The French victory and the subsequent Treaty of Tientsin recognized French authority over Vietnam and Indochina and ended centuries of formal Chinese influence in Vietnam. The advent of French rule also brought an end to the close ties that the Gin had maintained with their Vietnamese kin. The imposition of communist rule in China brought new restrictions and official Chinese government recognition of the Gin as a distinct ethnic group in China. Vietnam's independence in 1954 allowed the Gin to reestablish some ties to northern Vietnam, but worsening relations between Vietnam and China again brought an end to relationships established to the region. A brief war between China and Vietnam in the late 1970s made the loyalty of the Gin in China suspect. For a time, they were under close official control. The economic reforms and political relaxation in the 1980s and 1990s allowed the Gin to prosper as people from the mainland flocked to the picturesque islands for holidays and weekends. Gin cultural performances, Gin cuisine, and their special festivals have all become part of the appeal of the region as a tourist destination.

Further Reading

Ethnic Groups. "The Jing Ethnic Minority." Accessed July 31, 2013. http://www.china.org.cn/e-groups/shaoshu/shao-2-jing.htm

Harrell, Stevan. *Cultural Encounters on China's Ethnic Frontiers.* Seattle: University of Washington Press, 2000.

Olson, James S. *An Ethnohistorical Dictionary of China.* Westport, CT: Greenwood, 1998.

Rossabi, Morris. *Governing China's Multiethnic Frontiers.* Seattle: University of Washington Press, 2005.

H

Hakka

The Hakka, sometimes known as Hak-ka, Hokka, Kejia, Kechia, or haak gaa, are a Chinese people located in southeastern China and the western districts of Taiwan. Of the estimated 80 million Hakka in Asia, some 45 million live in China or Taiwan while the remainder live mostly in Southeast Asia or other areas of Chinese immigration. The major Hakka populations are in Fujian, Guangdong, Sichuan, Jiangxi, and Henan, with smaller groups on Hainan Island and in Hong Kong. In other parts of Asia, there are sizable Hakka populations in Indonesia, Malaysia, East Timor, the Philippines, and Taiwan. Outside Asia, there are Hakka communities in East Africa, Europe, South America, Canada, and the United States. Taiwan, where Hakka is widely spoken, is an important center for the study of the language and culture. The majority of the Hakka are Buddhists of the Mahayana branch, often mixed with elements of Confucianism, Daoism, traditional animist, and shamanistic beliefs, and more recently Christianity.

The Hakka trace their ancestry back to the Yellow River region of the first unified Chinese kingdom, known as the Qin dynasty 221–207 BCE. The ancestors of the Hakka migrated southward several times fleeing social unrest, wars, upheavals, and invasions. Hakka migrations occurred at the end of the Tang dynasty in the 10th century CE and during the Northern Song dynasty in 1125. The last migration, in 1125, was the scene of a massive flood of refugees fleeing to the south following the capture of the Northern Song capital by the Jurchen people of Manchuria. A further migration was caused by the Mongol expansion and the establishment of the Mongol Yuan dynasty in 1271. The Hakka people often suffered persecution and discrimination by the Han Chinese who inhabited the territories they moved into. The name *Hakka* means "strangers" or "guest families," signaling their status as outsiders or internal migrants. During the reign of the Kangxi emperor of the Manchu-dominated Qing dynasty, from 1654 to 1722, the coastal regions of Fujian and Guangdong were evacuated by imperial degree for nearly a decade, due to the threat posed by the remnants of the Ming dynasty who fled to the island of Taiwan to escape the Manchu conquest of China. When the threat was finally eliminated, the emperor issued a new edict to repopulate the coastal regions, giving each family a monetary incentive. The newcomers were registered as guest families, reinforcing the distinctness of the Hakka settlers from the region's original Cantonese-speaking population. The Cantonese people were very protective of their own more fertile farmlands, forcing the guest families to settle on the fringes of the fertile plains or in the less accessible mountainous regions. Conflict between the two groups was often violent with Hakka used as a term of derision.

The Hakka, though proud of their culture and language, have never claimed to be a distinct ethnic group, but some do claim that they formed the original inhabitants of ancient China. Unlike other Chinese peoples, the Hakka never practiced foot binding. Because of their five large migrations and their pioneering spirit, the Hakka came to be known as the "Jews of Asia." Considered China's most mysterious minority, they are sometimes portrayed as a leadership caste, based on the fact that Sun Yat-sen, Deng Xiao Ping, and Lee Teng Hui were all of Hakka heritage. Differences in language and culture continue to define the Hakka population both in China and in other parts of the world.

Due to their agrarian lifestyle and conflict with neighboring peoples, the Hakka evolved a unique architecture based on defense and communal living. When the Hakka settled in areas with already large populations, there was often little agricultural land available to them. As a result, many Hakka men turned to careers in the military or public service so that traditionally the Hakka culture prized education and advancement. The conflicts also gave rise to a number of distinctive martial arts that are still performed as part of the Hakka culture. Religiously, the Hakka are almost identical to their Han Chinese neighbors, though ancestor veneration remains the primary form of religious expression.

Though they had inhabited the region for several hundred years, the Hakka population

A Hakka roundhouse in a walled village located in Fujian, China, 2011. (Ywjelle/Dreamstime.com)

of the southeastern provinces was still considered outsiders by the Cantonese population. A series of conflicts over land and water led to skirmishes and finally to open warfare between the Hakka and the Punti clans of the Cantonese between 1855 and 1867. The fighting was particularly fierce around the Pearl River delta. The war left more than a million dead and many more refugees fleeing as far away as the Taiwan, the United States, Southeast Asia, and the Philippines. Hostility between the Cantonese and the Hakka also erupted among the immigrant populations in the Malay Peninsula. A series of violent skirmishes between the Cantonese and Fujianese migrants and the Hakka became known as the Larut War, which was concluded by the signing of a peace treaty between the two groups in 1874. In the late 19th century, Hakka migrants began to settle in the British-controlled colony of Hong Kong, a migration that continued through the Cultural Revolution that convulsed mainland China from 1967 to 1977. Continuing migration to Taiwan was another outlet for those fleeing conflict, poverty, and discrimination though the Japanese takeover of the island in 1895 mostly ended migration from the mainland. Migrations to Indonesia began with miners in the Riau Islands and Belitung in the 18th century with a second group settling in the Kapuas River region of Borneo in the 19th century, the predecessors of the modern Hakka populations of Indonesia, Malaysia, and Singapore. Over time, the Hakka migrations reached Mauritius and Réunion in the Indian Ocean, Jamaica and Trinidad in the Caribbean, South Africa, Thailand, and the Americas, particularly Panama, Brazil, the United States, and Canada. The Hakka have had a significant influence, disproportionate to their actual population numbers, on the course of both Chinese and overseas Chinese history, particularly in the number of political, revolutionary, and military leaders of Hakka background. The Hakka continued to play prominent roles in the Taiping Rebellion against the Qing dynasty, and the later conflicts between factions in the Chinese Civil War, with Hakka soldiers fighting on both sides. Hakka influence continues to be felt in southern China, particularly in Guangdong Province, where the so-called Hakka Gang has consistently dominated the provincial government.

Further Reading

Constable, Nicole. *Guest People: Hakka Identity in China and Abroad.* Seattle: University of Washington Press, 2005.

Kiang, Clyde. *Hakka Search for a Homeland.* Pittsburgh: Allegheny Press, 1991.

Leong, Sow-Theng. *Migration and Ethnicity in Chinese History: Hakkas, Pengmin, and Their Neighbors.* Palo Alto, CA: Stanford University Press, 1997.

T'ing-yu, Hsieh. "Origins and Migrations of the Hakkas." Accessed December 6, 2008. http://weber.ucsd.edu/~dkjordan/chin/Hsieh HakkaHistory.html

Han

The Han, sometimes known as Han Chinese, Hanzú, or Hànrén, constitute the world's largest ethnic group, making up about 20 percent of the global population. The estimated 1.3 billion Han are concentrated in China, where they make up 92 percent of the total population, and in Taiwan, where they make up 94 percent of the population. The Han form the majority of the population in Hong Kong, Macau, and Singapore, where they make up 74 percent of the total population. Other large Han communities are in Indonesia, Thailand, Malaysia, the United States, Canada, Peru, Vietnam, Australia, Cambodia, the Philippines, Myanmar, Russia, Japan, Venezuela, South Africa, the United Kingdom, France, Spain, India, Laos, Brazil, Italy, New Zealand, the Netherlands, and Mauritius. Smaller groups of Han live in many other countries around the world. The Han speak the Chinese language, which is a group of related languages, some of which are not mutually intelligible. Though many Han are nonreligious, the majority adhere to a mixture of Chinese folk religion, Confucianism, Daoism, and Buddhism. There

are smaller communities of Christians, Tibetan Buddhists, and other religions.

The history of China, as taught in schools throughout the world, is in many ways the history of the Han people. The Han Chinese people trace their ancestry back to the Huaxia, their name for the initial confederation of tribes living along the Yellow River. During the period known as the Warring States, from about 475 to 220 BCE, the sense of Huaxia or Han identity developed. Though now used to identify their ancient past, initially Huaxia was used to define a civilized culture that was distinct and stood in regal contrast to what their ancestors perceived as the barbarian peoples around them. Traditionally, the Han believe that Chinese history began during the reign of the Yellow Emperor, the

A Han Chinese mother and son. (Corel)

legendary common ancestor of the Han. He remains a revered figure who is believed to have united the Huaxia. Though study of this period is difficult without written records, archaeological finds along the Yellow River show a succession of Neolithic cultures beginning with the Jiahu from about 7000 to 660 BCE, followed by the Yangshao culture between 5000 and 3000 BCE, and the Longshan from 3000 to 2000 BCE. Along the lower reaches of the Yellow River, there developed parallel cultures known as the Qingliangang from 5400 to 4000 BCE, the Dawenkou culture from 4300 to 2500 BCE, the lower Longshan culture from 2500 to 2000 BCE, and the Yuyeshi culture from approximately 1900 to 1500 BCE. During this period, the Han culture transformed from the late Neolithic to the early Bronze Age. The first dynasty to be chronicled in ancient historical archives was the Xia dynasty founded by Yu the Great around 2070 BCE. The Xia were overthrown by invaders from the east who founded the Shang dynasty in 1600 BCE. The earliest examples of Chinese writing date from this period with the development of written characters. Agricultural innovations during the Shang period led to significant population growth. The expansion of Han power incorporated non-Han peoples who were often assimilated over time. Over the next millennium, through conquest and colonization, the Han brought a large area under their control. The evolution of a truly centralized state greatly influenced all elements of Han culture. Extending their rule both north and south of their original homeland on the Yellow River, the Han culture became the dominant culture over a wide geographic area. Sinicization of the conquered populations extended Han influence far beyond the region actually inhabited by the Han and the assimilated peoples. During the latter years of the Zhou dynasty, around 250 BCE, royal relatives and military commanders were given territories to maintain Zhou authority over the vast territory in the empire. Many of these territories broke away as smaller states when the dynasty weakened. By the sixth century BCE, most of the small states had been annexed or were controlled by larger states during the historical period known as the Spring and Autumn Period. The development of a feudal system supported an educated class that produced the first great texts of ancient Chinese history and philosophy. The consolidation of the small states into several large states brought on the period known as the Warring States Period, which began around 475 BCE and concluded with the victory of the state of Qin that created a unified Chinese state under the Qin dynasty in 221 BCE. The development of a centralized empire set the pattern for Chinese governmental model that would dominate China for 2,000 years. The rule of the Qin dynasty fostered a process of great philosophical development known as the Hundred Schools of Thought. Among the most important elements that survive from this period are the teachings of Confucianism and the religious belief system known as Daoism or Taoism. The Qin dynasty unified the country economically and culturally by decreeing a standard in weights, measures, currency, and writing. The Qin dynasty was replaced by the Han dynasty in 206 BCE though the Han government continued many of the institutions created by the Qin. Under the Han, the arts and culture of the empire flourished, while the military expanded China's borders in all directions. The period of the Han dynasty, which lasted until 220 BCE, is considered one of the greatest periods in Han Chinese history, and the Han take their name for themselves from this dynasty. Though Han history mostly ignores the interactions with other ethnic groups, cultural and linguistic borrowings were a constant in Chinese history. Incursions by tribal peoples from the northeast and northwest, some as early as 1000 BCE, were sometimes military incursions that forced the expanding Han to abandon part of their colonized territories; others were part of the relationship between the centralized Chinese state and the northern tribal peoples. Intermarriage, diplomatic relations, and cultural interactions played an enormous role in the cultural interchanges between the Han and the tribal groups. In the 13th century, the Mongol tribes of the great grasslands northwest of China united and began a military expansion that eventually overwhelmed half the known world, including the great Chinese Empire. The Mongol conquerors of China established the Yuan dynasty in 1279, the first conquerors of the Han Chinese heart-

land. The Mongols divided Chinese society into four distinct classes, with themselves as the ruling classes and the Han relegated to the bottom two classes. The Mongols mandated that all Han Chinese men wear a long pigtail known as a queue as a sign of the Mongol domination of the much larger Han population. In 1368, a Han Chinese rebellion drove the Mongols back to the north and established the Han Chinese Ming dynasty. Han migration to the peripheral regions accelerated under Ming rule, particularly into the southern Yunnan region. In 1644, peasant rebels captured Beijing allowing the Manchu from the northeast to seize the capital and eventually to control the entire empire. The Manchu Qing dynasty prohibited further Han Chinese settlement of the northeastern region they designated as Manchuria, to which they could withdraw should they lose control of China. Russian encroachments and annexation of territory claimed by China forced the Qing to reverse its exclusion policy and to allow the consolidation of a demographic Han Chinese majority in Manchuria.

The Han Chinese are the descendants of one of the world's oldest and most complex cultures. The concept of patrilineal clans is

Lotus Feet

Lotus feet, sometimes called "bound feet," is the custom of applying painfully tight bindings on the feet of young girls to prevent further growth. The practice is believed to have begun among upper-class court entertainers in the early Tang dynasty in the 10th or 11th century CE. The fashion spread until all but the lowest classes practiced foot binding. Lotus feet were considered very attractive and was considered a way to show that a Han Chinese woman was worthy of a husband. Foot binding was primarily a Han Chinese practice with few of China's other nationalities adopting the practice.

deeply rooted in Han history and society. The continuity of a patrilineal extended family is a matter of prime importance in Han culture, having a great impact on attitudes and behavior in Han society to the present day. Another cultural element that has survived from the Han's remote past is the belief in divine will. Historically, the Han have accommodated religions of diverse belief systems and origins. The formation of three great religious traditions, Daoism (Taoism), Confucianism, and Buddhism, took place over a relatively short period of time between 200 BCE and 200 CE. Buddhism, though a religion with foreign origins, exerted the greatest influence, but most Han continue to pay homage to all three religions, thus avoiding religious conflicts. The official atheism of the communist government that took control of China in 1949 left a legacy of nonreligious families, but in recent decades as China modernized and eliminated many of the stringent controls, many people have again embraced religion as part of their newly allowed freedoms. The inclusive religious attitudes of many Han Chinese encompass the three major religions that are mutually complementary. Daoism focuses on man's relation to nature and the cosmos, Confucianism is centered on man's relation to society, and Buddhism on man's relation to the afterlife and beyond. Islam and Christianity, though embraced by a relatively small number of Han Chinese, never achieved a prominent position in the Chinese world. The Han language, usually called simply Chinese, is really a group of seven distinct dialects though the Chinese written script, developed more than 3,000 years ago, is compatible with all of them. In the 20th century, written Chinese, based on the Beijing

version of Mandarin, has been standardized and adopted as the official language of China. Beginning in the 1950s, following the communist victory in China's civil war, a simplified set of Chinese characters was adopted in mainland China and later in Singapore, while the Han Chinese peoples of Hong Kong, Macau, Taiwan, and other areas with large overseas Chinese population continue to use the traditional Chinese writing system. While there are significant differences between the two character sets, they are largely mutually intelligible.

In the 19th century, as European encroachments, a weakening Qing dynasty, and overpopulation plagued the empire, Han Chinese migrants left in large numbers for other parts of the world, including Southeast Asia, Australia, and North America. The Manchu-dominated Qing dynasty adopted a defensive stance toward European encroachments on its territory, even though the Chinese Empire engaged in an imperialistic expansion of its own in Xinjiang and Central Asia. The Han Chinese finally realized that their empire was not the center of the world and awoke to the significance of the expansion of the European powers in Asia. As the empire opened to foreign trade and even Christian missionary activity, opium produced in British India was forced on the country as part of trade agreements. The decade of the 1830s saw a rapid increase in the opium trade. An attempt to suppress the opium trade climaxed a series of trade and diplomatic crises resulting in the Opium Wars in 1839–1842 and 1856–1860. British victories in the Opium Wars marked the beginning of Western imperialism in the Chinese Empire. Unequal treaties, imposed by a number of European powers, curtailed China's national sovereignty and further weakened the Qing dynasty. The Sino-Japanese War of 1894–1895 led to further territorial losses. The humiliation of the Qing dynasty led to increasing Han Chinese unrest in the wake of the Taiping Rebellion, which ravaged China from 1850 to 1864, and other costly rebellions in several regions and among the non-Han minorities. These rebellions cost several million lives and had a devastating impact on the empire's fragile economy. The number of Han Chinese leaving the empire grew rapidly with millions seeking a better life overseas. The Boxer Rebellion, which broke out in 1898 and targeted the Westerners in Beijing, was finally put down in 1901 after causing an estimated 115,000 deaths. Mass disorders, calls for reform, and revolutionary activity accelerated until the Chinese Revolution of 1911 finally toppled the Manchu Qing dynasty. The Republic of China was proclaimed in 1912, but its inability to control the vast Han Chinese provinces resulted in the rise of warlords and local rulers wielding power in several areas. Revolutionary activity, aided by the new Soviet Union, attracted many Han Chinese in the 1920s and 1930s. Conflicts between the revolutionary groups and the government were put aside in the face of Japanese aggression during World War II, but the civil war erupted soon after the end of the war, culminating in a communist victory in 1949. Mao Zedong proclaimed the People's Republic of China. The new republic's Red Army captured all of China except Taiwan, where the old government fled, and went on to conquer Tibet in 1951. Mao encouraged population growth, and during his leadership of the country, the Han Chinese population almost doubled bringing the population of China close to more than 900 million by the late 1950s. Mao's Great Leap Forward, meant to modernize and industrialize China, resulted in an estimated 45 million deaths between 1958 and 1961, with most dying of starvation. In 1966, Mao launched the Cultural Revolution, leading to another major upheaval in China. Mao Zedong's death in 1976 brought an end to the excesses of the Cultural Revolution. By 1979, reformer within the Chinese Communist Party had won control with the introduction of economic and social reforms that permitted the majority Han Chinese of the country to recover much of their traditional cultural and religious customs. With a population of more than 1 billion, the vast majority ethnic Han Chinese, the government implemented a one-child policy that penalized Han Chinese parents who exceeded the one-child rule. The non-Han minorities were exempted from the one-child law, and a degree of flexibility was allowed in the poverty-stricken rural areas. The economic reforms of the 1980s and 1990s resulted in the rapid modernization and industrialization of the eastern half of the country with the growth of large wealthy and middle-class Han populations. The poorer western half of the country, with its restive national minorities and a large, mostly rural Han Chinese population, had raised a new division among the Han between the haves of the east and the have-nots of the west. The Han Chinese constitute the world's largest ethnic group though the monolithic view of the Han by most of the world overlooks the sharp regional, linguistic, economic, and historical differences that continue into the 21st century.

Chinese ethnolinguistic groups. (Used by permission of the University of Texas Libraries, The University of Texas at Austin)

Further Reading

Elliott, Mark, "Hushuo: The Northern Other and Han Ethnogenesis," *China Heritage Quarterly*, 19 (2009). http://www.chinaheritage quarterly.org/scholarship.php?searchterm=019_han_studies_elliott.inc&issue=019

Hall, David L. *Thinking from the Han: Self, Truth, and Transcendence in Chinese and Western Culture.* New York: State University of New York Press, 1997.

Lewis, Mark Edward, and Timothy Brook, ed. *The Early Chinese Empires: Qin and Han.* Cambridge, MA: Belknap Press, 2010.

Mair, Victor H., Sanping Chin, and Frances Wood. *Chinese Lives: The People Who Made a Civilization.* London: Thames & Hudson, 2013.

Hani

The Hani people, sometimes known as Hanhi, Haw, Haqniq, Hounis, Eoni, or Wonis, are an ethnic group living in the southern Chinese province of Yunnan, with smaller groups in Vietnam, Laos, and Myanmar. Forming one of the 56 officially recognized nationalities of the People's Republic of China, the total Hani population is estimated at 1.5 million. The Hani speak a language of the Loloish or Yi branch of the Tibeto-Burman languages that is related to the Akha, Yi, and Lahu languages also spoken in the region. The majority of the Hani adhere to their traditional animist religious beliefs with smaller numbers of Buddhists and Christians.

The origins of the Hani people are not precisely known, though their ancestors, known as the Qiang people, are believed to have migrated southward from the Qinghai–Tibet plateau region prior to the third century CE. Other scholars believe that the Hani are the descendants of the Heyis, a tribal people living south of the Dadu River in present-day Sichuan in the third century BCE. Hani legends state that they are descended from the related Yi people, having split the Yi as a separate tribal group more than 50 generations ago. According to ancient Chinese archives, some of the early Hani peoples had moved south, the area of the Mekong River between the fourth and eighth centuries CE. Local Hani chiefs paid tribute to the Chinese Tang dynasty and received official sanction to own most of the fertile land as landlords. The majority of the Hani lived as peasant farmers or share-croppers on large estates. Following the Mongol conquest of China in the early 13th century, the Mongol Yuan dynasty established a separate prefecture for the Hani and other ethnic minorities in Yunnan. The Ming dynasty, which overthrew Mongol rule in 1368, returned to the system of exercising authority through local chieftains and landowners, who were granted official government posts. During the Manchu-dominated Qing dynasty, from 1644 to 1911, court officials sent from the capital replaced the system of chiefs and landlords. The feudal landlord system that dominated during most of the recent Hani history led to harsh exploitation of the Hani peasants by the landlords who seized large tracts of fertile lands. In some areas, vestiges of primitive communal landownership continued with the majority of land held by the villages. Village members often owned paddy fields and tea plantations, and could claim and cultivate communal village land as well. However, private landownership gradually prevailed with landlords and rich peasants in possession of the most arable lands, the tea plantations, forests, and rice paddies. Poor Hani peasants were exploited in various ways, including debt slavery, and very high taxes and levies.

The Hani are ranked by the Chinese government's "quality of life index" as the lowest of the official minorities, scoring just 38.3 percent while the average for the minorities was 62.7 percent. The Hani also ranked last for life expectancy and infant morality. The Hani ethnic group is

A Hani woman holds her recently purchased chicken at a market in Yuanyang in southern Yunnan Province in China. (Erin Packard Photography/Dreamstime.com)

made up of more than a dozen closely related peoples who are officially included in the ethnic definition. The Hani dependence on the water buffalo is revealed by their most cherished legend. In the legend, the sky god, Abo-Momi, sent a buffalo to earth to teach man that grass and trees must be planted to enable crops to grow everywhere else. If man would do as the buffalo bid, then they would eat every second day. Unfortunately, the water buffalo was possessed of a very poor memory and told them instead that crops must be planted. He also told them to allow grass and trees to grow everywhere else, the opposite of the god's message. He told them that if they would follow his instructions, they would eat not every second day but twice a day every day. Naturally, man obeyed the water buffalo's instructions and planted crops everywhere but found that their lives did not improve at all. Abo-Momi was very displeased with the forgetful water buffalo and sent him back to earth to help the Hani to cultivate the soil. The water buffalo is still revered to the present among the Hani farmers. When a Hani man dies, his water buffalo is slaughtered and the carcass is buried with him so that the beast can guide him into the next world. The traditional animist beliefs of the Hani include a special adoration for the spirits of their ancestors with rituals regularly performed to appease the gods of heaven, the earth, the Dragon Tree, and their home village, as well as their family's patron gods and venerated ancestors. The Hani language, spoken in southern China, Vietnam, Laos, and Myanmar, is a Hanoid language of the Loloish or Yi branch of the Tibeto-Burman languages.

The language is spoken in two major dialectal groups, the Ha-Ya and the Hao-Bai. Ha-Ya is made up of five regional dialects, and Hao-Bai encompasses two distinct dialects. Together known as the Bi-Ka languages, they are now all considered dialects of Hani, since the speakers are officially classified as ethnic Hani by the Chinese government.

By the early 19th century, the social development of the Hani regional groups was very uneven with some areas more developed and prosperous while other areas remained among the poorest in China. Most of the Hani areas were in a sort of transition between a primitive economy of village communes and the feudal landlord economy that characterized most of 19th-century China. Unrest was often a problem among the Hani peasants burdened with exorbitant levies and taxes enforced by officials of the Chinese government through the local chiefs and landlords. In the early 20th century, many Hani joined groups seeking the overthrow of the hated Qing dynasty, many of which were later merged into the new Chinese communist party. Conflicts and violence between the communists and government troops erupted several times prior to World War II. At the end of the war, the conflict spread as the Chinese Civil War, with the communists victorious in 1949. Communist cadres marched into the Hani regions to overthrow the chiefs and landlords as part of the policy of uplifting the peasant classes as part of the communist land reform program that began in 1952. A number of autonomous counties were created in 1957, giving the Hani greater say in the administration of

their homeland though the decisions were made by communist officials. Many ancient terraced lands, abandoned over the centuries, that were reopened for use and other improvements, especially in education and agricultural productivity, aided the Hani to overcome their troubled past history. However, the Hani remain the poorest and least developed of the 56 official minority ethnic groups in the People's Republic of China.

Further Reading

Hansen, Mette Halskov. *Lessons in Being Chinese: Minority Education and Ethnic Identity in Southwest China.* Seattle: University of Washington Press, 1999.

MacKerras, Colin. *China's Minorities: Integration and Modernization in the Twentieth Century.* Oxford: Oxford University Press, 1994.

West, Barbara A. *Encyclopedia of the Peoples of Asia and Oceania.* New York: Facts on File, 2008.

Hazara

The Hazara, sometimes known as Hazarah, Hezareh, Hezare'I, Kewari, or Berberi, are a people of mixed Mongol and Turkic ancestry concentrated in the mountainous Hazarajat region around the city of Bamiyan in central Afghanistan with other large communities in the Parapamisus Mountains in western Afghanistan and in Khorasan Province south of Mashad in eastern Iran and around the city of Quetta in Pakistan. Smaller groups live in Tajikistan, the European Union, Australia, New Zealand, the United States, Canada, and Turkey.

Due to a lack of census statistics, estimates of the total Hazara population range from five million to more than eight million. Prior to the 19th century, the Hazara were estimated to make up around 67 percent of the total Afghan population, making them the largest Afghan ethnic group at that time. Since that time, oppression, violence, and massacres have decimated the Hazara, who now make an estimated 10–20 percent of Afghanistan's population. The Hazara language, Hazaragi, is a Persian language closely related to Dari Persian, one of the two official languages of Afghanistan, which many Hazara also speak. Hazaragi, though intelligible to speakers of other Persian dialects, uses many words and forms borrowed from the Turkic and Mongol languages. The majority of the Hazara are Shi'a Muslims, a religion they share with the Iranians to the west but not with their Sunni Muslim neighbors in Afghanistan and Pakistan. Smaller numbers adhere to Ismaili or Sunni Islam.

The origins of the Hazara have never been fully researched. Physically, the Hazara resemble the Mongol peoples, while their culture and language reflect both Mongol and Central Asian Turkic influences. Many Hazara believe that their ancestors who entered the region as part of the armies of Genghis Khan in the 13th century were Mongol soldiers and their slave women who settled to garrison the highlands in central Afghanistan following the 1221 siege of the city of Bamiyan. Other theories propose that the Hazara are the descendants of the ancient Kushans who are believed to have constructed the famous Buddhas of Bamiyan. Most scholars consider the Hazara as a people of mixed Mongol and Turkic background, which is supported by genetic research. Their physical appearance, closely resembling the Mongol peoples, has long distinguished them from the surrounding Persian and Turkic peoples. The first historical mention of the Hazara appeared in chronicles prepared under the rule of Babur, the first of the Mughal rulers of the Indian subcontinent and later by the court historians of Shah Abbas of the Persian Safavid dynasty in the 16th century CE. The Hazara developed a strong warrior tradition as invaders often overran their homeland from both east and west. In 1737, the Shi'a Muslim Persian ruler Nader Shah gained control of the Hazara region and supported the Shi'a Hazara against their Sunni neighbors. Considered heretics by the fundamentalist Sunnis, communal violence was endemic in the region. The Hazarajat was later annexed to the territories of the Pashtun ruler Ahmad Shah Durrani, at whose death, in 1773, the Pashtun-dominated Afghan Empire encompassed an area extending from eastern Iran into the Punjab and Kashmir regions of modern India and Pakistan. The rise of the Sunni Muslim Pashtun increased discrimination against the Shi'a Hazara, who were driven from the more fertile lowlands into the dry, barren highlands of the Hazarajat in the late 18th and early 19th centuries.

The Hazara are a distinctive people, set apart from their neighbors by religion, their mixed ancestry, and their independent character. Persecution and discrimination have shaped and defined the Hazara, particularly in the last two centuries. Hazara

The Bamiyan Buddhas

The Bamiyan Buddhas, the largest examples of standing Buddha carvings in the world, probably dating from the fourth or fifth century CE, were often used to represent the Hazara homeland in central Afghanistan. Carved into the sides of cliffs facing Bamiyan city, the two largest statues, standing 55 meters (180 feet) and 37 meters (121 feet) high, had survived invasions, wars, and natural catastrophes for more than 1,500 years. In 2001, the Taliban government of Afghanistan decreed that the ancient statues, listed among UNESCO's World Heritage Sites, were idolatrous and offensive to Muslims. The cultural treasures were demolished with antiaircraft artillery and explosives.

culture is unique in the region, with many distinctive traditions and customs, though it also shares influences with Persian, various Central Asian Turkic cultures, and the Mongol peoples. The name *Hazara* was originally a reference to a Mongol fighting unit of 1,000 men, but modern usage is usually interpreted to mean simply "mountain tribe." Traditionally, the Hazara preferred to marry only within their ethnic group, usually first cousins, and seldom mixed with outsiders. About a third of the Hazara are herders, still living semi-nomadic lives following their herds into the highlands while living in *yurts*, circular tent like dwellings made of horsehair felt. Others prosper as farmers or tradesmen though poverty and discrimination have forced some Afghan Hazara to leave their highlands for Kabul and other cities where they find work as day laborers. The Hazara's willingness to accept menial jobs has earned them a reputation as hardworking, but has also resulted in a low social status and increased discrimination. The Hazara language, known as Hazaragi, has a long oral tradition; though with greater

educational opportunities, there is a growing literature, including poetry and written accounts of traditional tales and stories. Traditionally, the Hazara have excelled at poetry, which is often memorized and used to teach children. Illiteracy remains high among the Hazara though in recent years efforts have been made to make education more readily available. Until the 1980s, most educated Hazara used Persian or Arabic as the literary language, but a movement to create a distinct Hazaragi literary language has gained momentum in recent years. Most Hazara belong to the Imani branch of Shi'a Islam, also known as Ithna Ashari or "Twelvers." Religious minorities include Ismaili or "Seveners," and Sunni Muslims, mostly among the western Hazara. The Imani have a particular reverence for the son-in-law of the prophet Mohammed. Historically, the Shi'a population in Afghanistan has been branded as heretical by the surrounding orthodox Sunni peoples. The Hazara probably converted to Shi'a Islam under Mongol rule in the 14th century or later in the 16th century under the influence of the Shi'a Persian

Safavid dynasty. Despite centuries of Islamic teaching, many Hazara continue to believe in a parallel spirit world such as the evil eye, superstitions about certain animals and dark nights, and the reality of ghosts.

European and Persian interest in the region culminated in the early 19th century. In 1809, the Afghan ruler signed an agreement with the British for aid against the encroaching Persians and Russians. The Hazara, seeking to avoid conflict, resisted both Afghan and British attempts to take control of their homeland, particularly during the first and second Anglo-Afghan wars in 1839–1842 and 1878–1879. During the reign of Abdur Rahman, from 1880 to 1901, the Hazara were declared "infidels" and could therefore be enslaved or killed with impunity. A *jihad*, a holy war, was declared and waged by government troops. Thousands of Hazara died in massacres instigated by Afghan government officials. A failed Hazara uprising in 1893 resulted in the wholesale killings or enslavement of entire districts, while other Hazara fled to Persian or British territory. Slavery in Afghanistan was officially outlawed in 1919, but the dominant Pashtun, until after World War II, kept some Hazara as slaves. Hardships, economic depredation, and religious persecution stimulated an activist movement in the 1960s and 1970s that concentrated on gaining political and cultural equality within the Afghan kingdom. The famed symbols of the Hazara, the enormous and ancient Buddhist statues carved into a mountainside at Bamiyan, though they predated the Hazara settlement of the region, became the symbol of the Hazara fight for equality.

The overthrow of the Afghan monarchy in 1973 was followed by a bloody coup in 1978, which ended with the installation of a communist government in the country. To support the shaky communist hold on Afghanistan, Soviet troops invaded the country in 1979, beginning a decade-long occupation that increasingly polarized Afghanistan's various ethnic groups that fought for or against the Soviet occupation and often fought each other. During the conflict, the Hazara managed to liberate most of their mountain homeland; during the 1980s, they secured an agreement with the Afghan government by which, in exchange for remaining neutral and not attacking government troops, they would be allowed to govern themselves in their highland communities. After 1982, interference and support for fundamentalist groups by the new Islamic government of Iran triggered fighting between Hazara groups that left thousands dead and wounded. The internal conflict, known as the Hazar–Afghan War by the Hazara, devastated the Hazarajat region and created tens of thousands of refugees. The Soviet forces withdrew from Afghanistan in 1989, leaving behind a country seriously divided among warring ethnic and religious groups. The thousands of Hazara refugees in Iran and Pakistan were unable to return to their homes due to the continuing violence and instability. The Taliban, a fundamentalist Sunni group made up mostly of ethnic Pashtun, appeared in 1994 and quickly overran about 90 percent of Afghanistan, including the Hazarajat. The Taliban zealots began enforcing a radical form of Sunni Islam, including beards for all men, almost total seclusion of women, and total bans on music, television, sports, and other entertainments. The Shi'a Hazara were particularly targeted as religious heretics. Taliban oppression drove thousands of Hazara to seek refuge in camps set up in Iran or Pakistan. A Taliban commander, Maulawi Mohammed Hanif, in 1995, announced that the Taliban policy was to exterminate the Hazara. Taliban sympathizers were encouraged to kill Hazara, as it was not considered a sin to kill a heretic. Massacres of Hazara occurred in several cities as they fell to the advancing Taliban forces. Hazara women, traditionally allowed a greater degree of social freedom than the women of the Sunni ethnic groups, were particularly adversely affected by the Taliban prohibitions on education, health care, or work for women. Traditional clothing worn by Hazara women, which included colorful red-and-green floral dresses, felt boots, and beaded headgear, that were deemed offensive to the Taliban were quickly banned in favor of the tent-like burka. The Taliban authorities, citing Islamic strictures against the depiction of human likenesses, dynamited the magnificent Buddhist statues at Bamiyan in March 2001. Widely condemned for their wanton destruction of the unique historical treasures, the Taliban retaliated by claiming that the statues were being used as superstitious talismans by the backward and antigovernment Hazara leadership. The Hazara, who considered the statues the heart of their mountainous homeland, mourned the destruction of the statues carved into a mountainside in the Hindu Kush Mountains. The terrorist attacks on the World Trade Center in New York in September 2001 began an international campaign against the Taliban and other groups practicing terrorism. Following weeks of bombings by the United States and its allies, the Taliban government collapsed. The overthrow of the Taliban government in 2001 ended many of the worst abuses but left the Hazarajat devastated. Their economy completely shattered, and many Hazara turned to the only crop that would grow in their ruined valleys, opium poppies. The Pashtun colonists settled in their midst as both spies and in a Taliban effort to dilute the Shi'a majority were mostly driven out of the Hazara districts. Despite centuries of persecution and the denial of their basic human rights, the Hazara have become leaders in the emerging democratic Afghanistan. Education, long denied them by successive governments, is especially important, and literacy rates are rapidly growing among both men and women. While Afghan women in many parts of the country are still struggling to overcome the legacy of the Taliban and to gain basic rights, Hazara women are achieving greater advances than their neighbors. Some 80 percent of eligible girls now attend school in Hazarajat as opposed to just 10 percent in the five Afghan provinces to the south. Many activists now focus on the plight of the estimated 650,000 Hazara living mostly around the large city of Quetta in Pakistan. In recent years, they have been targeted as both religious heretics and an ethnic minority. Sunni Muslim zealots have been blamed for a long series of suicide bombings, murders, arson, and attacks that have been largely ignored by the Pakistani government.

A family of the Hazara ethnic group gathers outside their cave house to warm themselves in the sun from below zero temperature in Bamiyan, Afghanistan, 2003. Bamiyan, about 60 miles west of the capital Kabul, was home to the glories of Afghan's rich history, of which a pair of towering, 1,500-year-old Buddhas was the crown. The Taliban dynamited the statues in 2001, calling them idols that offended their interpretation of Islam. (AP Photo/Amir Shah)

Further Reading

Hazara People International Network. Accessed July 30, 2013. http://www.hazarapeople.com/

Jawad, Nassim. *Afghanistan: A Nation of Minorities.* London: Minority Rights Group, 1992.

Monsutti, Alessandro. *War and Migration: Social Networks and Economic Strategies of the Hazaras of Afghanistan.* London: Routledge, 2005.

Mousavi, Sayed Askar. *The Hazaras of Afghanistan: A Historical, Cultural, Economic and Political Study.* Basingstoke, UK: Palgrave Macmillan, 1997.

Zabriskie, Phil, "Hazaras: Afghanistan's Outsiders," *National Geographic*, February 2008. http://ngm.nationalgeographic.com/2008/02/afghanistan-hazara/phil-zabriskie-text

Hezhe

The Hezhe, sometimes known as Nanai, Nani, Samagir, Sushen, Yupibu, or Hezhen, form one of the smallest of the 56 ethnic groups officially recognized by the People's Republic of China. The estimated 5,000 Hezhe form part of a Tungusic people who straddle the international border between China and Russia. The Hezhe language is a Tungusic language of the southern Nanai group of languages, though most in China now use Mandarin Chinese as their first language. Most of the Hezhe are followers of Tibetan Buddhism with many of their traditional shamanistic rituals and traditions now mixed with their Buddhist customs.

The ancestors of the Hezhe, known as the Sushi in Chinese chronicles, were mentioned as early as the second and first centuries BCE as nomadic people living in the regions around the Amur, Sungari, and Ussur Rivers. Like the other Tungusic peoples, the Sushi were often considered a vassal people of the Chinese Empire, sometimes paying taxes or tribute but not under the direct rule of the Chinese dynasties. The Hezhe trace their background to the nomadic Nuzhen people, a tribe of Tatar horsemen who ravaged the northern borders of the Chinese Empire under several different dynasties. The Nuzhen/Hezhe people first came under direct Chinese authority during the Tang dynasty in the seventh century CE when the Heilong Military Region was created in the area. The Hezhe soon came under the rule of the early Manchu state of Balhae, which was overrun by invading Khitan Mongols in 926. The southern clans of the Nanai/Hezhe remained closely tied to the neighboring Tungusic Manchu people, then known as Jurchen. In the 17th century, the Manchu moved south to conquer the Chinese Empire and to rule as the Qing dynasty. The Hezhe were incorporated into the Manchu military "eight banner" system along with the other related Tungusic peoples of the region. The Qing dynasty gave title and administrative power to the local Hezhe

chiefs, who in turn used their privileges to exploit the poorer Hezhe, thus creating a feudal society of rulers and peasants. Qing policies prohibited the settlement of ethnic Han Chinese in the huge region known as Manchuria, allowing the Manchu, Hezhe, and other Tungusic peoples of the region to maintain their distinct cultures and languages. Russian Cossacks led exploratory expeditions to the Amur region in the 1640s, but by the terms of the Treaty of Nerchinsk, signed by the Russian and Chinese empires in 1689, confirmed that the Sungar region and its Hezhe population belonged to China while their kinsmen, later known as Nanai, came under Russian rule. The Qing administrators attempted to impose their authority and to tax the Hezhe villages, but were successful only in those districts where Chinese farmers were settled alongside the Hezhe villages.

The Hezhe culture is a Tungusic culture related to that of the larger Manchu ethnic group in the region. The name *Hezhe* is taken from a name used by the inhabitants of the Sungari River basin, while in Russia they are known as Nanai, a name taken from their own word meaning people. Until the early 20th century, the widely dispersed Hezhe villages had no cultural or linguistic unity, usually calling themselves names taken from geography or mythology. The traditional culture is based on river fishing with the majority of the Hezhe village built along the banks of the Sungari River. Traditional clothing, made of sturgeon and deer skins, is no longer made, but the tradition of fishing continues to the present. The culture has a rich oral tradition with storytelling and singing their favorite pastimes. Readings of some of the longer epics can last for days, as stories of ancient heroes are narrated in speech alternating with songs. The Hezhe culture, nearly extinguished during World War II, experienced a resurgence in the late 1940s and continues to flourish to the present. The Hezhe retain much of their traditional shamanistic belief system with particular reverence for *Doonta*, the bear, and *Amba*, the tiger. They believe that their shamans have the power to expel evil spirits by means of offerings and prayers to the gods. The Hezhe continue to revere the spirits of the sun, the moon, the mountains, the water, and the trees. Idol poles, a form of totem poles, are now part of the folk culture but formerly adorned each Hezhe village. The adoption of Tibetan Buddhism resulted in a fusion of the two traditions, which is practiced by nearly all of the Hezhe in China. The Hezhe believe that every person has three souls, one that dies when the body dies, while the other two souls survive. One of the surviving souls will be reincarnated, while the other remains as a guiding spirit. The Hezhe language, also called Nanai in Russia, is considered an endangered language with young Hezhe normally using Mandarin Chinese as their first language. The dialect spoken in China, known as the Sungari dialect, is spoken mainly by older people though some efforts have been made to introduce it into school curriculums in the region.

As the Manchu dynasty in China began to weaken in the early 19th century, the Russians returned to the region. They traded with the local peoples and began to colonize the region just north of the Chinese border. The Amur and Ussur regions, long claimed as Chinese territory, was annexed to the expanding Russian Empire, again dividing the Hezhe/Nanai people. The Hezhe settlements in Chinese Manchuria, though traditionally isolated from the surrounding peoples, came under intense territorial pressure when Han Chinese settlement was finally allowed in Manchuria after 1878. Millions of ethnic Chinese flooded into the region, often displacing the Hezhe and other indigenous peoples and taking control of the best farmlands and fishing grounds. Many of the scattered Hezhe bands succumbed to pressure and assimilated into the neighboring Chinese or Manchu cultures in the first decades of the 20th century. In 1931, Japanese troops invaded and took control of Manchuria, setting off a long war with China. Japanese rule in the region was harsh and often brutal. A policy of deliberate genocide was adopted, with

Dancing King

Han Geng, the most famous ethnic Hezhe in China, is a Mandopop singer and a superstar in China. An actor, model, singer, and dancer, Han Geng is skilled in the traditional dances of all of China's 56 recognized ethnic groups, as well as traditional ballet and hip-hop. A former member of the South Korean boy band Super Junior, which debuted in 2005, he later returned to China to pursue a solo career. Han's dancing ability, along with his popularity in other entertainment fields, resulted in being dubbed "Dancing King" and "King of Popularity" in China. Known for his charity work, his fans, known as Gengfans, have also been active in various charities at his request.

the Hezhe herded into concentration camps. Inadequate food, the loss of their traditional hunting and fishing, and opium addiction took a heavy toll on the Hezhe people. According to later Chinese estimates, between 80 and 90 percent of the Hezhe perished under Japanese rule. Only some 300 Hezhe survived the camps and the brutal Japanese policies in 1945. The Chinese Civil War resumed at the end of the World War leading to a communist victory in 1949. The Chinese communists encouraged the cultures of ethnic minorities and helped to resettle the surviving Hezhe. Slowly, the ethnic group in China has recovered and has grown. In the 1960s and 1970s, farming was encouraged, and many Hezhe settled on collective farms. In the 21st century, the Hezhe form one of the officially recognized ethnic minorities, a status that allows them to produce more children than their Han Chinese neighbors and gives them other benefits that have aided the recovery of the small ethnic group.

Further Reading

Ethnic China. "The Hezhe." Accessed July 30, 2013. http://www.ethnic-china.com/Hezhe/hezheindex.htm

Hutton, Ronald. *Shamans: Siberian Spirituality and the Western Imagination.* London: Continuum, 2007.

Legerton, Colin. *Invisible China: A Journey through Ethnic Borderlands.* Chicago: Chicago Review Press, 2009.

Mackerras, Colin. *Ethnic Minorities in Modern China.* London: Routledge, 2011.

Hui

The Hui, sometimes known as Huais, Hweis, Hui-Hui, Panthay, T'ung-kan, Tonggans, Dungans, or Chinese Muslims, are a large ethnic group concentrated in China's northwestern provinces and the Central Plain. Outside China, there are Hui communities in Myanmar, Taiwan, Kazakhstan, Uzbekistan, Kyrgyzstan, Mongolia, and Thailand. The majority of the Hui in China inhabit the Ningxia Hui Autonomous Region. The estimated 10.6 million Hui mostly speak Mandarin Chinese, the most widely spoken language in China, along with other Chinese dialects. The Hui are overwhelmingly Sunni Muslim though culturally they are similar to the Han Chinese, with the exception of their religious practices.

The Muslim religion arrived in China both by sea and overland as Arab and

Hui men wearing traditional cloths, in Xining, Qinghai, China. The Hui are the most populous of China's Muslim peoples. (Hupeng/Dreamstime.com)

Family Names

The most common family names found among the Hui ethnic group are names often used by their Han Chinese neighbors, but the origins of the names, according to Hui sources, are Muslim. The most common Hui surname, Ma, is derived from Muhammad, as are the surnames Mu and Han. Other surnames are Ha, derived from Hasan, Hu derived from Hussein, Sai from Said, Sha from Shah, Zeng from Shams, and Cai, from Osman. A Hui legend states that four common surnames, Na, Su, La, and Ding, originated within the descendants of Nasruddin, called Nasulading in Chinese, who divided the ancestral name into four parts.

Persian traders and sailors traveled to China seeking riches and trade. There were established Muslim communities in various areas of China by the eighth and ninth centuries CE. In the 11th century, the kingdom of the Tanguts, known as Hsi Hsia, welcomed Muslim traders and scholars to western China. The name, *Hui* or *Hui-Hui*, first appeared in Chinese records of the Northern Song dynasty between 960 and 1127. During the early years of the Mongol expansion, in the 13th century, many Arabs, Turks, and Persians, fleeing the Mongol conquests of their homelands, settled in the remote region south of the Alashan Desert. The Muslim refugees took Han Chinese, Uyghur, and Mongol women as wives and gradually assimilated. As artisans, traders, scholars, and religious leaders, the Muslims spread to many parts of China as they slowly adopted Chinese traditions while retaining their Muslim religion. The Hui culture slowly consolidated from the time of the Yuan dynasty, in the 13th and 14th centuries, borrowing much of the Han Chinese culture in a mixture that included traditions, ceremonies, and rites from many parts of the Middle East, Central Asia, and Xinjiang. Intermarriage with Han Chinese slowly changed the distinct physical features to those of the dominant Han people. The Muslims of the Alashan region began to expand their borders in the 14th and 15th centuries, converting surrounding peoples to Islam. Only nominally under the rule of the Chinese Empire, the Alashan Muslims maintained a separate Muslim state ruled by a Hui sultan, a source of extreme irritation to successive Chinese dynasties. In the wake of the Manchu conquest of China in 1644, the Hui took the opportunity to attempt to throw off rule by the non-Muslim infidels. Manchu troops invaded the Alashan region in 1648 and, after a long and violent campaign, were finally able to conquer the rebellious Hui. Sporadic Hui rebellions continued over the next century, finally erupting in open rebellion in 1785. China's Manchu rulers, determined to finally eliminate the Hui threat to their authority, loosed imperial troops on the region to carry out savage massacres unprecedented in the east. The Hui homeland in the Alashan region, a territory larger than modern France, was left virtually depopulated. Hundreds of thousands of Hui fled into the desert or to other parts of China or into Southeast Asia. When the brutal

Manchu campaign finally ended, a remnant of the formerly large Hui population slowly consolidated in a corner of their devastated former homeland. The Manchu government resettled excess Han Chinese population from the eastern provinces in the former Hui region.

The Hui form the third largest ethnic group in China and the only Muslim ethnic group that is overwhelmingly Chinese speaking. The Hui are an ethnoreligious group, the descendants of Arab, Persian, and Turkic settlers who intermarried with the Han Chinese and gradually adopted Chinese speech and much of the Chinese culture. Though many Hui are now physically similar to the Han Chinese, the ethnic group has retained some Arab, Persian, and Central Asian features, and their unique culture has been shaped by both the Han Chinese influence and their position along the historic Silk Road trading routes. The modern Hui are distinguished by their dress, which includes Muslim restrictions for both men and women, such as turbans, and their Muslim religion. Traditionally veiled Hui women stayed at home to tend their children, but under the communist minority policies, Hui women were forced to renounce the veil and to leave their homes to do farmwork in the communes or production work in the factories. Despite efforts to homogenize the various Chinese peoples, the Hui's Muslim religion and related practices, such as refusing to eat pork or covering women's hair, continue to separate them from the majority Han Chinese population. Though many younger Hui are only nominally Muslim, they carry on the historic resistance of the Hui against assimilation into Han Chinese

culture. The Hui, unlike the other Muslim minorities in China, do not have their own language but usually speak the local variety of Chinese in their region. The spoken dialects of the Hui retain some Arab and Persian borrowings, particularly from the Arabic language of their religion. Arabic is often spoken as a second language by religious leaders and many educated Hui. Officially Sunni Muslim, there are actually several Muslim sects among the Hui. The older factions evolved from the need to adapt their Muslim religion to Han Chinese culture. In order to retain their religious purity and group identity, the Hui have historically remained socially segregated. Such Hui traditions, such as early and arranged marriages, veils for women, and polygamy have been outlawed in the People's Republic of China, and Hui women now officially have the same rights of divorce and inheritance as Hui men. According to Hui customs, women are forbidden to marry non-Hui, but Hui men may marry women of other ethnic groups who follow Islam or are willing to adopt Islamic practices. An estimated 90 percent of the Hui identify themselves as practicing Muslims.

During the mid-19th century, a series of upheavals and rebellions broke out against the excesses of the Qing dynasty. The Hui population of the southern province of Yunnan, many of them descendants of refugees from the 18th-century massacres in Ningxia, came into conflict with local Han Chinese populations in 1821 with several violent skirmishes. A rivalry between Han Chinese and Hui miners in central Yunnan resulted in severe clashes in 1855, which escalated into a massacre of Hui Muslims in and around the provincial capital at

Kunming. The massacre sparked a general Hui uprising that swept across the Yunnan region until it was finally defeated in 1873. Another Hui uprising broke out in northern China in Shanxi Province in 1862, quickly spreading to neighboring Gansu and to the Muslim Uyghur people of Xinjiang. The Muslim revolt, began as resistance to local discrimination and official persecution, left a lasting legacy among the Hui of distrust and hatred of the imperial government. The pacification of the Muslim rebels was delayed as the imperial army was occupied with the widespread Taiping rebellion in the eastern provinces, lacking the funds and troops to mount an expedition to the remote outer provinces until the 1870s. The rebellion, known as the Panthay Rebellion, raged in Yunnan from 1856 to 1873, leaving thousands of people dead and displaced. Excluded from government and certain professions, the Hui often lived as a despised minority, suspect due to their Islamic religion and their ties to the Muslim peoples to the west. Indiscriminate attacks by Han Chinese, along with a growing intolerance of the Muslim religion, provoked several serious Hui uprisings in various parts of China. The evolution of local Islamic movements at the end of the 19th century is closely linked to a great surge of social movements across China as the Manchu Qing dynasty began to falter. Antigovernment Western and Japanese influences further fanned the flames of Hui resentment and discontent. Crushing defeats by imperial troops in 1873 and again following a Hui uprising in 1895 dealt severe blows to the burgeoning Islamic movement in China. The overthrow of the Qing dynasty, known as

the Chinese Revolution of 1911, gave the Hui the opportunity to assert their Muslim identity. Led by local Muslim warlords, Hui rebels drove all the Chinese officials from Ningxia, the Hui heartland, and created an autonomous government headed by a sultan. Troops loyal to the new republic government entered the region and ended the rebellion, often by playing off one Hui warlord against the others. In the early 20th century, Ningxia became the political base of the powerful Ma clan of Ho-chou, a Hui clan that was wooed by the government as civil war with the growing communist movement spread across China. The weak Chinese government only nominally asserted authority in the Ningxia region in the turbulent 1920s and 1930s, though a separate Ningxia province was established in 1928 to give the Hui a degree of self-government and a reason to remain loyal to the central government. The Hui mobilized to protect themselves from rampaging warlords, communist cadres, and militias loyal to various political factions. Many young Hui joined a private militia recruited by the Ma clan in Ningxia. The central government gained control of Ningxia in 1936, but relaxed its former draconian restraints on the Muslim religion in order to win Hui support as the civil war escalated. Communist leaders also attempted to win Hui support, but the communist's emphatically antireligious stance alienated most Hui. A communist victory in the Chinese Civil War in 1949 brought active resistance from Hui religious and militia groups. One faction in the Alashan region attempted to create a secessionist Hui state known as the Chinese Islamic Republic in 1953, but the movement was quickly crushed. The Ningxia autonomous region, created as part of the communist minority policy in 1949, was dissolved, and the Hui became the only official minority without a designated homeland in China. In the 1950s, and particularly during the Cultural Revolution of 1967–1977, most Hui mosques were closed, religious leaders were paraded through towns and cities with pig heads tied around their necks, and many Hui women were forced to marry non-Hui. The end of the strident communist rule of the 1970s ushered in a new era of capitalist economic laws and greater self-government for the many minority peoples. A new law on religions, adopted in 1993, allowed the Hui to openly embrace their religion for the first time since the early 1960s. In the early 21st century, despite China's rapid economic development, Hui incomes remain less than the national average and considerably less than incomes in the favored southeastern provinces. The relationship between Islam and communism in China remains uneasy, with contradictory policies of allowing religious and ethnic practices while promoting assimilation and national unity.

In recent years, the central government, while balancing support for religious activity against efforts to retain the official atheism of the country, has emphasized the particular Chinese character of the Hui culture and religious practices. Many Chinese government officials fear that Islamic radicalism will infiltrate the country in spite of stringent government controls.

Further Reading

Gladney, Dru C. *Muslim Chinese: Ethnic Nationalism in the People's Republic of China.* Cambridge, MA: Harvard University Asia Center, 1996.

Legerton, Colin, and Jacob Rawson. *Invisible China: A Journey through Ethnic Borderlands.* Chicago: Chicago Review Press, 2009.

Lipman, Jonathan N. *Familiar Strangers: A History of Muslims in Northwest China.* Seattle: University of Washington Press, 1998.

"Muslims Clash with Chinese Police Who Destroyed Mosque." *Telegraph.* January 2, 2012. http://www.telegraph.co.uk/news/worldnews/asia/china/8988205/Muslims-clash-with-Chinese-police-who-destroyed-mosque.html

Itelmen

The Itelmen, sometimes known as Kamchadal, are a Siberian ethnic group, the original inhabitants of the Kamchatka Peninsula in northeastern Siberia. The Itelmen call themselves *itenme'n-itelmen*, which means "inhabitant of dry land" or a human being. The estimated 3,000–5,000 Itelmen live primarily in the valley of the Kamchatka River in the middle of the large peninsula and on the western coast. The Itelmen language forms the sole surviving representative of the Kamchatkan languages of the Chukotko-Kamchatkan language family. Most Itelmen continue to adhere to a polytheist religion based on shamanism and a belief in spirits. A minority have adopted Russian Orthodoxy or practice a combination of Christian traditions mixed with their pre-Christian shamanism.

The origins of the Itelmen are not known other than that they are the indigenous people of the Kamchatka Peninsula. They probably settled the peninsula some 6,000–7,000 years ago from the north Asian mainland. The earliest archaeological evidence of Itelmen presence on the peninsula is 5,200 years old. They lived as fishermen and fur hunters, often moving seasonally to fishing and hunting grounds in different parts of the peninsula. Many scholars believe that the ancient ancestors of the Itelmen had contact with the ancestors of the indigenous peoples of North America as the two continents were connected by a land bridge over the present Bering Strait. Russians, pushing east across Siberia, reached the Kamchatka Peninsula in the late 17th century. The first campaign against the estimated 15,000–50,000 Itelmen inhabiting the peninsula was carried out by Cossacks and Yukaghirs working for the Russians. The Itelmen were forced to pay a heavy tax in valuable furs. European diseases decimated the Itelmen population, which plummeted rapidly as death took whole villages. The name *Itelmen* was first used by Russian researchers visiting the region in the 1730s. By 1738, the Itelmen population had dropped to just 9,000 people. Russian colonial policies stressed assimilation of the indigenous peoples into the European Russian culture. Brutal colonial administrators, traders, and tax collectors often defrauded or stole from the Itelmen with compete impunity. When the fur tax was considered deficient, the tax collectors often confiscated boats, sledges, carvings, food, animals, or tools in lieu of furs. Often tribal members were held to ensure the payment of the hated *yurga*, the fur tax. Along with the burden of delivering furs to the conquerors, the Itelmen were also obliged to work as slave labor for the Russians. The surviving Itelmen resisted Russian rule in several uprisings in 1706, 1711, 1731, and a widespread rebellion by the entire Itelmen population in 1740s. The uprisings were brutally suppressed. In punishment, many Itelmen were deported and the tribes dispersed. By the early 1700s, the conversion of the Itelmen to Orthodox Christian became a priority. The Uspensk monastery was built on the peninsula, and from the 1740s, Christian Russian peasants were settled in the region. The Itelmen gradually resigned themselves to their colonial status. Following the example of the Russian colonists, they began to use iron tools, fishing nets, European clothing, and often intermarried. The Itelmen population continued to decline to just 6,000 in 1767, and only 3,000 following a severe smallpox epidemic in 1768–1769.

The Itelmen culture is one of the smallest and the most ancient of northeastern Siberia. Traditionally, the Itelmen were river fishermen and gatherers, with hunting and sea fishing as secondary occupations. The tribes lived in villages of extended families related by blood, sharing the same rivers and fishing grounds. All close relatives lived together in the same summer and winter dwellings. Each Itelmen community took its name from a particular part of the river they lived on. At the head of each community was a respected elder, whose dwelling served as a center of major decisions and community celebrations. So much intermarriage between the Itelmen and the Cossacks, beginning in the late 17th century, resulted in a new term, *Kamachal*, being used to denote those people of mixed Itelmen and Cossack background. Though the word is sometimes used for the entire group, both indigenous and mixed, the name *Itelmen* at some point became reserved only for the remaining speakers of the Itelmen language. The Itelmen

language, which belongs to the Kamchatkan branch of the Chukotko-Kamchatkan language family, is the only surviving language of the Kamchatkan branch. The language is severely endangered as most Itelmen are now monolingual in Russian. In recent years, there have been attempts to revive the language, and it is now taught in a number of schools in Kamchatka. The traditional belief system of the Itelmen is a polytheistic religion that recognizes many gods. The creative god is *Kutka* or *Kutga*, who is believed to have created all things though he is also blamed for misfortunes. The Itelmen also revere spirits known as *mitgh*, who dwell in the water and often take the form of a fish. The forest sprites, the *ushakhtchu*, are believed to resemble people. Gods or spirits are also believed to inhabit the high mountains, especially the regions with numerous volcanoes. The god or spirit called *billukai*, who inhabits the clouds, is responsible for thunder, lightning, and storms.

By 1820, the surviving Itelmen numbered only about 3,000, scattered in small villages among the Russian settlements. By 1870, the Itelmen were considered as extinct, having assimilated into Russian culture, using the Russian language, and at least nominally Russian Orthodox. By the turn of the 20th century, only about 58 percent of the people associated with the Itelmen ethnicity were able to speak or understand the Itelmen language. The Itelmen were mostly ignored and neglected as the resources of their homeland were exploited for the Tsarist government of Russia. In 1920, the communists, victorious in the Russian Civil War, took control of Kamchatka. The imposition of a Soviet regime did not improve the situation of the Itelmen. Unlike the other indigenous peoples, whose ethnic identity was initially supported by the Soviet authorities, the Itelmen were arbitrarily deprived of their ethnic nationality. In 1925, the Revolutionary Committee of Kamchatka decided not to consider the more assimilated indigenous groups of the southern districts of the peninsula as Itelmen, as they no longer spoke their traditional language and they mostly lived like the neighboring Russian peasants. These assimilated Itelmen and those of mixed Russian, and Itelmen ancestry were renamed Kamchadal. The decision greatly reduced the number of Itelmen, as from then on, only the inhabitants of the western coastline in the Tigilskiy District, numbering just over 800 people in 1930, had the name *Itelmen* stamped in their official documents. During the decades of Soviet rule, the assimilation of the remaining Itelmen speakers continued as official policy. Beginning in the 1950s, smaller villages in the Tigil region and the Kamchatka Valley were declared "nonviable," and their populations herded into larger collective villages where Russian speakers predominated. While the Itelmen mostly lost their language, they did not lose their ethnic awareness. The small number of people claiming Itelmen nationality actually increased between 1959 and 1979. The Soviet system finally collapsed in 1991, to be replaced by the Russian Federation. The removal of Soviet restrictions allowed the Itelmen to begin to recover their endangered culture and language. In the 2010 census, 3,193 people registered as ethnic Itelmen, which is considered by many scholars as only a small percentage of the population that is of Itelmen descent.

Further Reading

Bloch, Alexia, and Laurel Kendall. *The Museum at the End of the World: Encounters in the Russian Far East.* Philadelphia: University of Pennsylvania Press, 2004.

Forsyth, James. *A History of the Peoples of Siberia: Russia's North Asian Colony 1581–1990.* Cambridge: Cambridge University Press, 1994.

Sale, Richard, and Eugene Potapov. *The Scramble for the Arctic: Ownership, Exploitation and Conflict in the Far North.* London: Frances Lincoln Publishers, 2009.

Vahtre, Lauri, and Jüri Viikberg. The Red Book of the Peoples of the Russian Empire. "The Itelmens." Accessed July 31, 2013. http://www.eki.ee/books/redbook/itelmens.shtml

J

Japanese

The Japanese, sometimes known as Yamato, are the largest ethnic group of Japan, making up about 98.5 percent of the total population. The estimated 132 million Japanese include 127 million in Japan and large communities in Brazil, the United States, China, the Philippines, Canada, Peru, Australia, the United Kingdom, Thailand, Germany, Argentina, France, South Korea, Singapore, Taiwan, Micronesia, Mexico, Bolivia, and New Zealand with smaller communities in other parts of Asia, Europe, and the South Pacific. The Japanese language forms part of the Japonic or Japanese-Ryukyuan language family, which is often considered a language isolate as its relation to Korean or the Altaic languages is unclear and debated. Japanese religious traditions combine elements of Mahayana Buddhism and Shinto, Japan's indigenous religion.

The history of the Japanese people can be traced back to the Jomon period between 10,000 BCE and 300 BCE. Many scholars believe that migrants from Southeast Asia settled in the Japanese Archipelago during the Jomon period. A second wave of migration, from Northeastern Asia, is thought to have come to the islands during the Yayoi era, between 300 BCE and 300 CE. Others believe that the ancestors of the Japanese originated in Northeastern Asia, migrating to Japan

more than 30,000 years ago when the islands formed a long peninsula connected to the Asian mainland by a land bridge. The most widely held belief is that the Japanese are the descendants of the indigenous Jomon people and the later Yayoi immigrants. Though scholars are unable to agree to the origins of the Japanese, archeologists have found that Stone Age people inhabited the region during the Paleolithic period between 39,000 and 21,000 BCE. Some of the world's oldest known pottery pieces were created by the Jomon people in the Upper Paleolithic period in the 14th century BCE. The name *Jomon* comes from the word meaning "cord-impressed pattern," the characteristic markings found on the ancient pottery. Between 1200 and 1000 BCE, a primitive rice-growing culture spread through the islands. Around 400–300 BCE, the Yayoi migrants began to settle in the Japanese islands, absorbing or intermingling with the earlier Jomon people. The Yayoi introduced wet-rice cultivation and advanced bronze and iron technology. Better agricultural methods allowed the growth of a large population that spread over time and became the basis of the succeeding Kofun or Nara period of Japanese history from 300 to about 750 CE. The Kofun period saw the spread of the indigenous Shinto belief system that existed prior to the introduction of Buddhism. A local clan lord won control over much of the western part of the central island of Honshu and the northern parts of Kyushu to eventually evolve as the Imperial House of Japan. The first permanent capital was established at Nara in 710, which became a center of Japanese culture, religion, and Buddhist art. The current imperial family took power about 700, and would continue to rule to the present, most often with high prestige but little actual power. During the feudal period in Japan, political power in the islands was divided among several hundred small states, domains controlled by local *daimyo* or lords, each with a force of samurai warriors. From about 1185 to the middle 19th century, Japan was dominated by the rule of warlords or *shogun*. The emperor remained the titular head of the state but was mostly kept as a figurehead. The Kamakura period, from 1185 to 1333, was an era of governance by the Kamakura shogunate that saw Japan move into the medieval period, which lasted nearly 700 years. The emperor, the court, and the traditional elements of central government were allowed to continue but were largely relegated to ceremonial functions. Military, civil, and judicial concerns were overseen by the *bushi* or samurai class, the most powerful being acknowledged as the national ruler, the shogun. Zen was introduced at this time, and two attempted Mongol invasions of the islands were repulsed in 1274 and 1281. In 1333, the Kamakura shoguns were overthrown in a coup led by the emperor and his followers. The imperial house was restored to a position of influence, and a civilian government replaced the military rule of the

shoguns. Supported by a number of regional warlords, shogunate rule was again put in place in 1338, and the emperor was again only a figurehead. Rule by shoguns or warriors continued under different shogun clans until 1868. In the 14th and 15th centuries, conflicts between warlords and regional alliances resulted in near-constant warfare and the militarization of Japanese society. In 1600, the Edo period began following a war for supremacy won by Tokugawa Ieyasu, who established his capital at Edo, later renamed Tokyo. This era, also known as the Tokugawa period, was characterized by strict laws imposed to prevent Japan from lapsing back into anarchy or civil war, including laws to seclude the Japanese from contact with the outside world. Christianity, introduced first by Portuguese and Spanish missionaries in the 16th century, was suppressed, and many Japanese Christians were killed. Japanese society was divided into four strata or classes, the samurais, peasants, artisans, and merchants. The stable peace of the 17th and 18th centuries allowed rapid economic growth and the spread of literacy. The newly powerful merchant class dominated Japanese culture, with a great flowering of the arts, including *haiku* or Japanese poetry, novels, theater, and arts such as woodblock prints.

Modern Japanese culture is a mixture of the traditional culture that evolved over the millennia with influences from other parts of Asia, Europe, and North America. The evolution of the culture has been relatively rapid as the Japanese experienced a long period of relative isolation from the

The Burakumin, Japan's Outcasts

The name Burakumin means "hamlet people" or "village people," but is applied to a large group of outcasts at the bottom of the Japanese social order. Historically, the Burakumin have been the victims of severe discrimination and ostracism. The members of this caste were originally members of despised communities during the feudal era, mostly composed of those whose occupations were considered impure or tainted by death. Occupations such as executioners, undertakers, slaughterhouse workers, tanners, and butchers were all considered *kegare*, or defiled. Traditionally, the Burakumin lived in their own hamlets or ghettos in larger towns and villages.

outside world that ended with the arrival of "The Black Ships" and the Meiji restoration period. Such cultural elements as literature and music, originally reflecting the influence of China and India during the diffusion of Buddhism in Japan, mostly developed as a separate Japanese style during the isolation period. Since the reopening of Japan, in the 19th century, Western and Eastern literature and music have strongly affected each other and continue to do so to the present. Such ancient cultural values as painting, calligraphy, sculpture, woodblock prints, ikebana, and the performing arts have all retained much of their ancient traditions while adapting to the influences from other cultures. Other important cultural elements are architecture and gardens, which has the status of artwork in Japan. Japanese cuisine, once nearly unknown outside Japan, is now readily available around the world. The long feudal period under the rule of the samurai class left a legacy of well-ordered martial arts, including kenjutsu, kyudo, sojutsu, jujutsu, and sumo. Imported sports, including baseball

and football, are now important cultural icons as they are in most other parts of the world. Japanese popular culture not only reflects the attitudes and concerns of modern Japan but also provides a link to the past. Popular television programs, films, novels, video games, and music are often based on older artistic and literary forms. The Japanese language is not related to Chinese though it makes extensive use of Chinese characters, known as *kanji*, in its writing system, and much of its vocabulary is borrowed from the Chinese. Before the Japanese economic boom of the 1980s, the language was little known outside Japan, but since then, along with the spread of Japanese popular culture, the number of students has reached millions. Japanese religious beliefs have traditionally been a fusion of elements of Mahayana Buddhism and the indigenous system of Shinto. Shinto, a polytheistic belief system with no book of religious canon, is indigenous to Japan. Shinto was one of the traditional supports of the Japanese imperial family and was codified as the state religion in 1868. Mahayana Buddhism came to Japan from China and India in the sixth century and evolved into many different sects. The majority of the Japanese, between 84 and 96 percent, profess belief in both Shinto and Buddhism, both serving as a foundation for mythology, cultural traditions, and modern activities rather than as a single source of moral guidance. One facet of the Japanese culture that has remained static for centuries is Japanese disdain for the non-Japanese minorities living in the country and the Burakumin, a type of untouchable class that has been stigmatized for centuries. The large number of ethnic Japanese who have migrated to Japan in recent decades, mostly from Brazil and other parts of South America, often suffer discrimination and are treated as a non-Japanese minority.

The hereditary shogunate continued to regulate the entire economy, controlled religion, subordinated the traditional nobility, and maintained a uniform system of taxation, government spending, and bureaucracies. The Japanese rulers carefully avoided international involvements and wars. They also maintained a national judiciary and ruthlessly suppressed protests and criticisms. The Tokugawa shogunate, though often severe and arbitrary, brought the 19th-century Japan peace and prosperity. About 80 percent of the Japanese people were rice farmers, with rice production steadily increasing while the population remained stable, thus ensuring continued prosperity. In the growing cities, merchant guilds and artisans met the growing demand for goods and services. Commercialization of the Japanese economy grew rapidly, bringing more and more remote towns and villages into the national economy. Local shoguns, prohibited from engaging in farming or business, borrowed vast sums to sustain their families and retainers. Elaborate and expensive rituals occasioned even more borrowing that finally provoked a severe financial crisis from 1830 to 1843. Reforms were instituted, luxuries denounced, and measures were adopted to impede the rapid growth of business, but the reforms failed threatening the entire Tokugawa system. The national policy of isolation lasted for more than two centuries. In 1844, King William II of the Netherlands sent a message urging Japan to open itself to the outside world, which was rejected. On July 8, 1853, Commodore Matthew Perry of the United States, with a squadron of four warships, steamed into Yokohama Bay to show the power of his ship's cannon. These warships were known as the *kurofaun*, the Black Ships. Commander Perry returned the following year with seven ships and demanded that the shogun sign a treaty of peace and friendship to establish diplomatic relations between the Japanese Empire and the United States. Within five years, the Japanese government had signed similar treaties with most other Western countries. The treaties were forced on Japan while giving the Western nations control of tariffs and the right of extraterritoriality to all visiting foreigners. The treaties remained a sticking point in Japan's international relations until the early 20th century. Beginning in 1868, the Japanese adopted political, economic, and cultural reforms that resulted in the emergence of a unified and centralized modern state, the Empire of Japan. This period, known as the Meiji period, which lasted until 1945, was a time of rapid economic growth. Japan joined the Western nations in becoming an imperial power by colonizing Korea and Taiwan. The rise of a military clique that rapidly assumed control of the country led to escalating tensions with neighboring countries. In 1931, the Japanese began the conquest of Manchuria and China, in defiance of world opinion. Japan joined Germany, Italy, and the other Axis powers in a military alliance to offset the growing powers of the Western democracies in Asia. In December 1941, Japan launched multiple attacks on American, British, and Dutch territories. The Japanese attack on Pearl Harbor was planned to eliminate American naval power in the Pacific, thus allowing the Japanese military to conquer most the resource-rich areas of Southeast Asia. American military recovery in the Pacific resulted in a series of great naval battles that largely destroyed the Japanese fleet. American bombers raided the Japanese home islands, bringing destruction to the larger cities. The cult of the emperor demanded that all Japanese fight to the death to repel an anticipated Allied assault, but the nuclear attacks on Nagasaki and Hiroshima brought a rapid end to the Japanese willingness to continue the war. Japan surrendered in 1945, gave up its overseas territories, and was occupied by American troops. A demilitarized democracy was put into place that oversaw the reconstruction of Japan. After the democratization of Japan, American aid helped to restore much of the country's infrastructure. The American occupation turned Japan into a modern industrial state. Emperor Hirohito was allowed to retain his throne as a symbol of national unity. Japan regained full control of its government and economy in 1952 and, during the decades of the Cold War, became an important part of global alliances. Manufacturing, particularly in the automobile and electronics industries, turned Japan into one of the richest countries in the world by the 1970s. Despite the country's prosperity, Japanese culture retains many of the traditions and customs that have sustained the Japanese people for millennia, including social conformity and working for the common good. These characteristics served the Japanese well when the country was devastated by a massive earthquake and tsunami in 2011, including the largest nuclear meltdown since the 1986 Chernobyl disaster.

Further Reading

Brinckmann, Hans. *Japanese Society and Culture in Perspective.* Last modified January 15, 2010. http://www.habri.co.uk/

Davies, Roger J., and Osumu Ikeno. *The Japanese Mind: Understanding Contemporary Japanese Culture.* Clarendon, VT: Tuttle Publishing, 2002.

Morton, W. Scott, and J. Kenneth Olenik. *Japan: Its History and Culture.* New York: McGraw Hill, 2004.

Murray, David. *Japan.* New York: Amazon Digital Services, 2011.

Jingpo

The Jingpo, sometimes known as Jinghpaw, Jingpho, Singpho, Tsalva, Zaiwa, Lechi, Thienbaw, Singfo, Marips, Dashanhua, or Chingpaw, are a sizable ethnic group concentrated in southern China's

Yunnan Province, where they form one of the 56 official nationalities of the People's Republic of China, and in northern Myanmar, where they are known as Kachin. The estimated 135,000 Jingpo in China speak two distinct dialects of the Kachin language, which forms part of the Tibeto-Burman language family. While the larger Jingpo/Kachin population in neighboring parts of Myanmar are now largely Christian, the Jingpo in China are usually animists though some have adopted Buddhism and Daoism.

The ancestors of the Jingpo originated in the eastern part of the Tibetan Plateau. Around the eighth century CE, they migrated to south and east in the jungled regions of present-day Yunnan and northern Myanmar. The migrants settled in tribal groups often distinguished by their distinctive dialects, cultural traditions, and occupations. The numerous tribes never united under a central authority nor acknowledged the authority of the Chinese emperors or the Burman kings. Often warring among themselves, the tribal groups cooperated only when faced with an outside threat. The invasion of the Shans, a Tai people, in the 13th century eliminated many of the close ties between the Jingpo in Chinese territory and the Kachin groups to the southwest. Later in the 13th century, the tribes united to defeat the invading Mongol hordes. The Jingpo tribes were sustained by shifting agriculture, mostly hill rice production, supplemented by banditry, vendettas, and feud warfare. Petty chieftains with the support of their immediate patrilineal group held authority in most Jingpo

tribal areas. The Chinese, while pacifying the tribal groups of Yunnan, sent an expedition to occupy the region known as the Kachin Hills in 1766. To the dismay of the imperial government, the Chinese troops withdrew from the hills in disorder under ferocious Kachin attacks in 1770. The Chinese were able to gain control of only a small eastern region but continues to claim the northeastern part of Myanmar to the present. Over time, the Jingpo in China have gradually merged into two big tribal alliances, the Chashan and the Lima. They were headed by hereditary nobles called "shanguan." Freemen and slaves formed the bulk of the Jingpo population.

The Kachin tribes encompass a number of distinct tribal groups related by language and culture. While Kachin refers to the entire culture made up of a number of distinct tribal groups, the largest of the tribes, the Jingpaw, called Jingpo in China, are considered the only true Kachins. Historically free of Indian or Chinese cultural influences, the Jingpo never developed the caste or class distinctions of neighboring peoples and have retained their traditional tribal organizations to the present. The Kachin language forms a group of related dialects belonging to the Bodo-Naga-Kachin group of the Tibeto-Burman language family. The Jingpo of China speak at least five major dialects in addition to Jingpo proper: Zaiwa, Maru, Lashi, Nung (Rawang), and Lisu. A Latin alphabet was created and officially introduced in 1957. The Jingpo dialect serves as a lingua franca in a large area of both China and neighboring Myanmar. Most of the Jingpo have retained their traditional beliefs in China, while in Myanmar Christian influence is quite strong. The customs and rites of a form of animistic ancestor worship, often entailing animal sacrifice, remain the primary religious services of the Jingpo. Belief in spirits and witchcraft remains widespread as is the veneration of the ancestor of the Jingpo, Madai. For the Jingpo, all living creatures are believed to have souls, and rituals are carried out for protection from evil spirits in all activities, from planting of crops to warfare. As part of their culture, Jingpo men continue to wear turbans, white for youths and black for adults.

The British, seen as potential allies against the Burmans and Chinese, took control of the majority of the Kachin regions in 1886. The border between British and Chinese territory, though officially recognized by both governments, remained porous with tribesmen ignoring the invisible borderline. The Qing dynasty added the Jingpo area of Yunnan to the jurisdiction of prefectural and county offices set up to administer the region. Frequent conflicts arose between the fiercely independent Jingpo and the government officials and tax collectors. Under the influence of the Han Chinese and the neighboring Dai, the Jingpo adopted the use of iron tools, including the plough, and later learned advanced agricultural methods of rice production in paddy fields. This process was accompanied by a transition to a feudal system with Jingpo nobles appointed as administrators. By the middle of the 19th century, the economic progress in the region ended the historic slave system that had functioned for hundreds of years. In the rural areas, each Jingpo village was ruled by a tribal chief who assisted the "shanguan" in his administrative affairs. Though private property had taken root in the region, the less fertile lands remained the property of the village and could be used by any village member. Paddy fields were either privately owned or were worked by the same families through many generations. The nobles and chieftains, taking advantage of their positions, gradually gained control of most of the paddy fields, often taking the fields by force. By the time of the communist revolution in China in 1949–1950, the nobles, who made up about 1 percent of the population, and the chieftains and rich peasants, who made up about 2 percent, controlled between 20 and 30 percent of all the Jingpo lands. The communist cadres arrived in the region in the early 1950s. An autonomous region for the Jingpo was established in 1953, and they were recognized as one of the country's national minorities. Progress was rapid in education and economic expansion until the Cultural Revolution in the late 1960s and 1970s. Red Guard units moved into the region to destroy historic shrines, buildings, and other vestiges of the Jingpo culture. The end of the oppression and the economic opening of China in the 1980s allowed the Jingpo to establish cash crops such as tea and rice for export. The region, known as Jingpo Mountain, was connected to the rest of the province by an all-weather highway that further stimulated the economic prosperity of the Jingpo.

Further Reading

Leach, E.R. *Political Systems of Highland Burma: A Study of Kachin Social Structure.* Oxford: Oxford University Press, 2004.

Mulhaney, Thomas. *Coming to Terms with the Nation: Ethnic Classification in Modern China.* Berkeley: University of California Press, 2011.

Wang, Zhusheng. *The Jingpo: Kachin of the Yunnan Plateau.* Tempe: Arizona State University Press, 1997.

Xioming, Xiao. *China's Ethnic Minorities.* Beijing: Foreign Languages Press, 2003.

Jino

The Jino, sometimes known as Jinuo, are a small ethnic group forming one of the 56 officially recognized nationalities in the People's Republic of China. The estimated 22,000 Jino mostly live in Jinoluoke Township in the Xishuangbanna Autonomous Prefecture in China's Yunnan Province. The Jino language, part of the Tibeto-Burman language family, is still spoken along with Mandarin Chinese and often Dai spoken as second languages. Most of the Jino retain their traditional animism with a growing number embracing Buddhism.

The origins of the Jino are not well known though they believe that they migrated to their present homeland in Jinoluoke from places farther north. Historically, their society was organized as a matriarchal culture. Their name in their language means "descending from the uncle," which refers to the importance of the mother's brother in matriarchal societies. Jino legend tells of the first settler in the region, a widow by the name of Jiezhuo. She gave birth to seven boys and seven girls who later married each other. As the population of Jinoluoke grew, the big family was divided into two villages, groups or clans that could intermarry. Over time, the Jino population expanded, and more Jino villages were established but Citona, the patriarchal village, and Manfeng, the matriarchal village, remained the heart of Jino culture. Until the 1960s and 1970s, the Jino from all parts of Jinoluoke still went to offer sacrifices to their ancestors in the matriarchal and patriarchal villages. The conquest of the region by the Manchu in the mid-17th century began the replacement of the communal village with a feudal system of Jino chieftains organized as representatives of the imperial government. The Jino matriarchal system probably gave way to Han Chinese influence and converted to a patriarchal system some 300 years ago.

Traditionally, Jino society was organized into farmers, hunters, and gatherers. The Jino were renowned as hunters, using crossbows with poisoned arrows and later shotguns. They are also expert in the making and use of traps and nooses to catch wild game. They usually hunt in groups and divide the catch among the participants. While the men hunt, the women gather wild fruit and berries in the forest. Edible herbs are also gathered for soups and other dishes. Traditionally, the clan based on blood ties was the basis of Jino society, but modern Jino live in villages with people of many different clans. Primitive egalitarianism is still manifested in traditional Jino customs such as dividing the meat from hunting equally among all adults and children in the village. Monogamy is the norm in Jino culture, though prospective brides and grooms are permitted to have sex before marriage. Being animists, the Jino believe that all things on the earth have spirits or souls. Ancestral worship also continues to be an important part of their religious beliefs. Shamans are often still consulted to appease evil or troublemaking spirits through the use of animal sacrifices. The Jino language, spoken by as few as 10,000 Jino, is a Loloish or Yi language of the Tibeto-Burman language family. Linguists define Jino as a pair of Loloish languages spoken in Yunnan, the largest, Youle, spoken by about 10,000 people, and Buyuan, with some 1,000 speakers. The two dialects are not mutually intelligible. There is no written form of the language. Most Jino speak Mandarin Chinese and also one of the Tai languages of the neighboring peoples of Yunnan.

The life of the Jino remained static for most of the 19th century. Village elders made most of the day-to-day decisions while landlords made the economic decisions. Zhuoba, the village father, and Zhuose, the village mother, were the leaders of the communal villages being the oldest male and female in the village. Time-honored traditions included the blessings of the elders and the ritual slaughter of animals to ensure a good harvest. The elders also planted the first few seeds. The arrival of the communist revolution in China in the mid-20th century had a great influence on Jino culture. In 1954, teams of communist cadres sent by the new government of the People's Republic of China arrived for the first time in the mountainous Jinoluoke. The village elders, either won over or eliminated, cooperated in implementing reforms that put an end to many of their traditions and customs. In 1955, cooperative teams were organized to work the land more efficiently. Rice production in well-prepared paddy fields increased rapidly, helping to end the yearly cycle of hunger and poverty. By the early 1980s, there were 14 primary and middle schools in the Jino region where most people were formerly illiterate. The economic expansion has brought a modest revolution to the region. By the early 21st century, a string of trading stores offering all sorts of goods at moderate prices had replaced the traditional traveling merchants known for their high prices and cutthroat methods.

Further Reading

Davies, Sara L. M. *Song and Silence: Ethnic Revival on China's Southwest Borders.* New York: Columbia University Press, 2005.

People's Daily Online. "The Jingpo Ethnic Minority." Accessed July 31, 2013. http://english.people.com.cn/data/minorities/Jingpo.html.

West, Barbara A. *Encyclopedia of the Peoples of Asia and Oceania.* New York: Facts on File, 2008.

Xioming, Xiao. *China's Ethnic Minorities.* Beijing: Foreign Languages Press, 2003.

Juhuro

The Juhuro, sometimes known as Ivri, Yehudi, Judeo-Tat, Caucasian Jews, Caucasian Mountain Jews, or Mountain Jews, are an ancient ethnic group living in the Caspian Sea region of the southeastern Caucasus in Azerbaijan and neighboring parts of the Russian Federation. Juhuro is the name they use for their people, though many outsiders continue to call them Mountain Jews. The estimated 12,000–30,000 Juhuro in Azerbaijan live mostly in the eastern districts of the country. The city of Quba, particularly the suburb Qirmizi Qasaba, is home to Azerbaijan's largest Juhuro community and considered one of the largest Jewish communities remaining in the former Soviet Union. In successive censuses outside the Caucasus, there are large Juhuro communities in the Israel, estimated to number between 100,000 and 140,000, the United States, Canada, and in parts of the European Union. The Juhuro language, known as Juhuri, Juwuri, or Judaeo-Tat, is a Tat language belonging to the southwestern Iranian language group. The majority of the Juhuro adhere to their traditional Jewish faith though some are now nonreligious or nonpracticing.

The Juhuro are believed to have settled in the southern Caucasus in the fifth century CE from southwestern Persia, modern Iran. According to Juhuro traditions, their ancestors from ancient Israel migrated or were forced to migrate to ancient Persia as early as the eighth century BCE. Some scholars and historians believe that the Juhuro may be the descendants of Jewish military colonies settled on the eastern and northern slopes of the Caucasus by the Persian rulers as frontier guards against incursions by nomadic peoples from the steppe lands to the north. Others believe that the Juhuro are descended from the Turkic Khazars, many of whom adopted Judaism in the eighth century CE. In the fourth century CE, the ruler of the region known as Caucasian Albania adopted Christianity as the state religion, making the Juhuro a religious minority in a largely Christian state under loose Persian rule. The invasion of the region by Muslim Arabs in 642 drove many Juhuro to seek safety in the strong military tradition of their people. The Juhuro survived numerous historical threats by settling in extremely remote and mountainous regions. Juhuro strongholds in the high Caucasus became the centers of the Juhuro culture as most of the lowland population was forcibly converted to Islam. At the beginning of the

Azerbaijan's Jewish Town

The village of Qirmizi Qasaba (Qýrmýzý Qəsəbə), in the Quba district of Azerbaijan, is considered the only completely Jewish town outside of Israel. Qirmizi Qasaba, Red Town in English, was constructed in 1742 when the khan of Quba granted the Juhuro or Mountain Jews permission to establish a community across the river from the capital city of Quba. The village, guaranteed freedom from persecution, was originally known as Jewish Town until it was renamed Red Town under Soviet rule. The population, estimated at 18,000 in 1989, has dwindled to some 4,000 due to Jewish emigration to Israel, North America, and Europe.

11th century, the Oghuz Turks from Central Asia overran the region, followed by the second wave of conquerors, the Seljuk Turks. Many Juhuro migrated north as the mass migration of the Turkic peoples occupied much of the southern region. The Seljuk Turks became the rulers of a vast empire that tolerated religious minorities such as the Juhuro. By the 15th century, the Juhuro had adapted the Tat language to their own needs, including many borrowings from Hebrew. Most of the Juhuro adopted the highland Caucasian clothing. Elsewhere in the Jewish Diaspora, it was forbidden to own or till land, but in the Caucasus, the Juhuro were mostly farmers and gardeners cultivating grain, fruit, and grapes. Their traditional occupation in the lowlands had been rice growing, but in the highlands they produced wheat and barley, various fruits, and the Juhuro vineyards produced wine, an activity forbidden among the neighboring Muslim peoples. Raising silkworms and growing tobacco were also widespread. Though their traditions strictly limited meat consumption, they were well known as tanners. In the 1580s, during the wars between the Shi'a Muslim Persians and the Sunni Ottoman Empire, the districts along the Caspian Sea, including Baku, were occupied by Ottoman troops. Many Juhuro fled the occupation back to their mountain strongholds in the Caucasus Mountains. The Persians returned in 1603, but the majority of the Juhuro remained in the highlands rather than return to the coastal districts. The disintegration of the Persian Empire in 1747 resulted in the creation of a number of semi-independent khanates in the region.

Often threatened by local rulers or hostile tribes, the Juhuro developed a military tradition and were known as a warrior people. The Russian expansion into the Caucasus in the late 18th century brought a new threat to the Juhuro, the Russians' traditional anti-Semitism.

The Juhuro culture was formerly a rural culture of farmers cultivating grapes, rice, tobacco, and cereals. During the Soviet era, the Juhuro were forced to settle in Soviet communes and collectives, often living alongside other regional ethnic groups. Urbanization, beginning in the 1970s, has resulted in a large number of Juhuro living in towns and cities where the culture has adapted to an urban environment. A small number of Juhuro are still farmers, but the majority are now traders, tanners, rug-weavers, or leather workers. The tradition of welcoming guests and hospitality remains an important cultural element. In every Juhuro home, there is a special room or addition with the family's finest carpets set aside for guests. Juhuro hospitality is also reflected in the music and art of the people. Instruments such as the *tar*, a string instrument, and the *saz*, a longnecked flute, remain important parts of modern Juhuro music. Until the 20th century, the majority of the Juhuro were illiterate though they passed a rich oral tradition of stories and folklore from generation to generation. Since the 1930s, many of these tales, poems, and stories have been collected and published in the Tat and Juhuri languages. The majority of the Juhuro speak the Tat language adopted from the neighboring Tat people with many also able to speak Azeri or Russian. The Juhuri language is declining in the Caucasus though there is a large community that speaks Juhuri in Israel. Historically, the Juhuro practice a form of Judaism that is often considered pre-Talmudic in many ways. Many of the customs and traditions of other Jewish communities are now found in Juhuro religious practices, but the basics of the Jewish religion are faithfully followed.

The Russo-Persian wars between 1803 and 1828 confirmed Russian control of the Caucasus region. Russian treatment of the region's Jews was often brutal though the military tradition and horsemanship of the Juhuro warriors were admired by the Russian soldiers. Under Russian rule, the Juhuro resettled the lowlands though they continued to be called Juhuro or Mountain Jews. In the lowland villages and towns, as they had in the highlands, the Juhuro established *aouls*, separate districts or neighborhoods inhabited only by Juhuro. The first religious meeting house was built in Baku in 1832 and was reorganized as a synagogue in 1896. Other synagogues were built in Baku and its suburbs in the late 19th century, often by the growing number of Jews from other parts of Russia and Europe drawn to the booming oil industry in the region. Baku became an important part of the Jewish Zionist movement in the Russian Empire. Between 1899 and 1920, a period of war and revolution in the Russian Empire, the Juhuro community flourished despite the chaos and upheavals. Armenian Christians invaded the region in March 1918, often targeting the Juhuro along with the Muslim peoples of the region. In May 1918, during the Russian Revolution, nationalists declared the independence of Azerbaijan and created a democratic government. Periodicals were published by the Jewish communities in Yiddish, Hebrew, Juhuri, and Russian, and a number of Juhuro schools, social clubs, benevolent societies, and cultural organizations were created. Though many Juhuro lived in towns, Judaic restrictions ensured that they retained their own cuisine and that their faith was enshrined in their family and community life. The Soviet occupation of Azerbaijan in 1920 began a period of harsh repression for the Juhuro. Most cultural events, along with the use of the Hebrew language, were banned. In the early 1920s, several hundred Juhuro families left Soviet Azerbaijan and neighboring parts of Dagestan to settle in British Palestine, mostly in the new city of Tel-Aviv. Soviet restrictions ended immigration to Palestine, and after 1948, when Israel was established as an independent state, those restrictions remained in place. Better relations between Israel and the Soviet Union in the 1970s resulted in a lifting of the ban on immigration. Between 1972 and 1978, around 3,000 people, including many Juhuro, left Soviet Azerbaijan for Israel. Other Juhuro established thriving communities in large North American cities such as New York and Toronto. The collapse of the Soviet Union in 1991 allowed Azerbaijan to regain its independence, though efforts to assimilate the non-Azeri ethnic groups were continued. Since the fall of the Soviet government, the Juhuro population of Azerbaijan had declined due to immigration though the Juhuro population of Azerbaijan is not counted separately, and estimates range from a low of

12,000 to more than 30,000 Juhuro in the country.

Further Reading

Dymshits, Valery, and Tatjana Emelyanenko. *Facing West: Oriental Jews in Central Asia and the Caucasus.* Zwolle, Netherlands: B. V. Waanders Uitgeverji, 1998.

Matloff, Judith. "Dagestan's 'Mountain Jews' Flee Chaos." *Jewish Daily Forward.* September 3, 2012. http://forward.com/articles/162028/dagestans-mountain-jews-flee-chaos/?p=all

Mikdash-Shamailov, Liya, ed. *Mountain Jews: Customs and Daily Life in the Caucasus.* Lebanon, NH: University Press of New England, 2003.

RoutledgeCurzon. *The Mountain Jews: A Handbook (Peoples of the Caucasus Handbooks).* London: RoutledgeCurzon, 2002.

K

Karakalpak

The Karakalpak, sometimes known as Kara-Kalpak, Karakalpakian, Qaraqalpaq, Qorapalpog, Qoraqolpoqlar, Karaklobuk, Tudzit, or Tchorni, are a Central Asian people of mixed ancestry living in the Karakalpakstan region of western Uzbekistan just south of the Aral Sea. The Karakalpak include in their ancestry Oghuz and Kipchak Turks, Persians, Caucasians, and Mongols. The Karakalpak population is estimated at between 500,000 and 650,000, including communities elsewhere in Uzbekistan, Kazakhstan, Turkmenistan, Afghanistan, and Russia. Their name, Karakalpak, signifies "black cap" or "black hat," referring to their traditional black wool or felt hats. The Karakalpak, though their homeland now forms part of Uzbekistan, are more closely related to their neighbors to the north, the Kazakh, but unlike the Kazakh, they are physically more Turkic in appearance than Mongol. The Karakalpak language, belonging to the West Turkic or Kipchak languages, is sometimes classed as a dialect of Kazakh even though it developed as a separate literary language in the 1920s. The language is spoken by an estimated 96 percent of the Karakalpak as their first language with Russian often spoken as a second language. The Karakalpak are mostly Sunni Muslims of the Hanafi school, which promotes political conformity and strict adherence to Muslim law. There is a minority that adheres to the Sufi branch of Sunni Islam.

Caucasian peoples originally inhabited the region, which flourished from about 500 BCE to 500 CE as thriving agricultural area with an extensive irrigation system. In the seventh century, Oghuz Turks overran the region from their homeland in Mongolia. The invaders gradually absorbed the Caucasian as their Turkic language, and culture supplanted the Caucasian's original culture. Arab Muslims invaded the Aral Sea region in the eighth century. The Arabs converted the inhabitants to their new Islamic religion, often using force as persuasion. Seljuk Turks took control of the region accompanied by Karakalpak raiders who remained to settle the region. The Mongol hordes conquered the Aral Sea region in the 13th century. According to Karakalpak oral tradition, their ancestors, the Black Caps, split from the Mongol-Turkic Golden Horde as a separate people in the 15th century. Their division into often-antagonistic tribes facilitated their domination by Dzungar (Oirat), Bukharan Uzbek, and the neighboring Kazakh. In the late 15th or early 16th century, the Karakalpak may have formed a tribal confederation with the neighboring Kazakh of the Lesser Horde. The association would explain why the Karakalpak language, customs, and material culture are similar to those of the Kazakh. One group of

Karakalpak, known as Upper Karakalpak, settled along the Syr Darya River east of the Fergana Valley. The other group, known as the Lower Karakalpak, established settlements closer to the Aral Sea. In the late 16th century, the Karakalpak are mentioned in chronicles as a pastoral people in the valley of the Syr Darya east of the Aral Sea, subjects of the powerful Emirate of Bukhara. Between the 16th and 18th centuries, under pressure from the expanding Kazakh to the north and the Uzbek Bukharan forces to the east, many Karakalpak migrated southwest to settle the Amu Darya River basin south of the Aral Sea, a fertile region loosely ruled by the Uzbek khanate of Khiva. Russian explorers and Cossack soldiers encountered the Karakalpak while traveling through the Uzbek-dominated Muslim states of Central Asia in the late 17th century.

The Karakalpak culture is a Central Asian Turkic society that retains some customs and traditions from their Turkic, Mongol, and Caucasian ancestors. Unusually in the region, the status of women is more advanced than that in the rest of Uzbekistan, which is considered one of the few positive legacies of more than 70 years of Soviet rule. Even though the Karakalpak, who are considered the smallest of the Central Asian ethnic groups, have a well-developed sense of separate identity, their status as a separate ethnic group or as a subgroup of the Kazakh is still debated. In the past, large numbers of Karakalpak worked as fishermen in the Aral Sea, but Soviet disregard of the environment severely damaged the inland sea, which is now rapidly shrinking and no longer supports much marine life. The shrinking of the Aral Sea, formerly one of the world's four largest lakes, has been denounced as one of the planet's worst environmental catastrophes. Most Karakalpak are now herders or farmers with around a third of the population living in urban areas. Urbanization has reduced the formerly high birth rate, but large families remain the Karakalpak ideal. The Karakalpak language, which developed as a literary language under Soviet rule, is spoken in two major dialects, Northeastern Karakalpak and Southeastern Karakalpak, both of which include subdialects. Formerly written in the Cyrillic alphabet used by the Russians, since 1996, the language has been written in a modified Latin script. Many Karakalpak speak Russian or Uzbek as a second language. The Karakalpak Muslim religion has rebounded as the focus of community life following the collapse of the Soviet Union in 1991. Local traditions, many predating their conversion to Islam, continue to be practiced, particularly an altered mental state prompted by frenzied chanting and dancing. The legacy of Soviet atheism continues to be felt as only about 78 percent are practicing Muslims, some 19–20 percent claim they are nonreligious or nonpracticing Muslims, and about 3 percent espouse no religious belief. There is a small Christian community—the result of missionary work by evangelical Protestant sects—and portions of the Bible were translated into Karakalpak in 1996.

The Central Asian emirates and khanates repulsed early 19th-century Russian attempts to extend tsarist rule to the region; however, the Cossacks spearheaded a Russian invasion in the mid-19th century. Between 1865 and 1876, nearly all of the Central Asian states came under Russian domination. The Russian authorities annexed the western Karakalpak districts in 1873, leaving the eastern districts under the rule of the khanate of Khiva, which became a Russian protectorate. Except for the loss of favored grazing lands, the Karakalpak experienced little of direct Russian rule until World War I. In June 1916, the hard-pressed Russian forces, in desperate need of manpower, began to conscript Central Asians into labor battalions. Kalpak resistance to conscription provoked serious and violent incidents and Karakalpak participation in a widespread uprising in August 1916. Fearful of Russian reprisals, many Karakalpak fled their homes to shelter in the marshes in the Amu Darya delta. The Central Asian rebellion forced the tsarist government to withdraw badly needed troops from the front to confront the rebel forces. Confrontations between the Central Asian rebels and the Russian troops ended soon after the news of the Russian Revolution reached the area in February 1917. Several rival governments of differing ethnic makeup and political ideology attempted to take control of the Karakalpak homeland south of the Aral Sea. In 1918, the Russian Civil War spread from Europe into Central Asia, adding to the already chaotic situation. The Karakalpak generally favored the White forces over the Bolsheviks and their antireligious rhetoric, but in 1920, the victorious Bolsheviks occupied the region. The Soviet government dissolved the traditional territorial divisions and divided Central Asia along ethnic lines in 1924. A nominally autonomous Karakalpak region, created in 1925, was first transferred

to the authority of the Soviet Russian Federation in 1930 and, then in 1932, was made a subdivision of the Uzbek Soviet Socialist Republic, one of the member states of the Soviet Union. Under Soviet rule, in spite of the political confusion and the official repression of their Muslim religion, the Karakalpak made great strides in education, language development, and culture. They developed a strong sense of their separate ethnic identity and fostered a cultural revival that continued until the repression of the Stalinist era between the 1930s and the early 1950s. After Stalin's death in 1953, the Soviet authorities devoted the region around the Aral Sea to the development of cotton production to the exclusion of traditional agricultural and pastoral pursuits. The Amu Darya River, one of the major sources of water for the Aral Sea, was diverted for cotton irrigation in 1962. The river and the surrounding districts rapidly became heavily polluted with chemical fertilizers. Its major feeder rivers diverted, the Aral Sea began to shrink rapidly, an enormous ecological disaster that remained a closely guarded Soviet secret until the liberalization of Soviet life in the later 1980s. Revelations of the wide extent of the health problems caused by the massive use of chemical fertilizers in cotton production over decades both shocked the Karakalpak and galvanized activists working for remedies and the reversal of the massive Soviet disaster in their homeland. The disintegration of the Soviet Union in 1991 allowed Uzbekistan to become an independent state, including the Karakalpak Autonomous Republic as part of its national territory. The Karakalpak, with a sense of identity as strong as their more numerous neighbors, defied the Uzbek government and adopted the Latin alphabet, giving them access to Turkish newspapers and publications and continue to demand government action to clean up the most damaging aspects of the Aral Sea disaster. An estimated 66 percent of the Karakalpak have typhoid, hepatitis, or throat cancer due to the heavy pollution of their homeland. One out of every 10 Karakalpak babies dies before its first birthday, and some 85 percent of Karakalpak children suffer long-term medical problems.

Further Reading

Bissell, Tom. *Chasing the Sea: Lost among the Ghosts of Empire in Central Asia.* New York: Vintage, 2004.

Glanz, Michael. *Creeping Environmental Problems and Sustainable Development in the Aral Sea Basin.* Cambridge: Cambridge University Press, 2008.

Icon Group International. *Kara-Kalpak: Webster's Timeline History, 1924–2002.* San Diego: Icon Group International, 2009.

Richardson, David, and Sue. "The Karakalpak People." *The Karakalpak.* Last modified February 8, 2012. http://www.karakalpak.com/people.html

Kazakh

The Kazakh, sometimes known as Kazak or Qazak, are the most numerous of the Central Asian peoples with an estimated population of between 13.5 and 15 million. Most Kazakhs live in Kazakhstan, the largest of the Central Asian republics, though there are important Kazakh communities in the neighboring areas of China, Uzbekistan, Russia, Mongolia, Turkmenistan, Kyrgyzstan, and Turkey with smaller groups in Iran and Europe. Kazakhstan is more than twice the size of the other four Central Asian republics combined and is second only to the Russian Federation among the states of the former Soviet Union. The Kazakh language is a Turkic language belonging to the Kipchak or Western Turkic branch of the Turkic languages. Like their Central Asian neighbors, the Kazakh are overwhelmingly Muslim, most adhering to the Sunni branch of Islam.

The region now known as Kazakhstan or the Kazakh Steppe has been settled for tens of thousands of years and was most often dominated by nomadic peoples. Some studies suggest that the horse was first domesticated in the region, and apples were also developed and later spread to other areas. In the eighth century CE, Turkic tribes conquered the region and spread across the vast steppe lands. The various tribal groups formed a powerful federation that prospered on the trade that passed through their territory on the fabled Silk Road, the trading link between the Orient, Central Asia, the Middle East, and Europe. Arab Muslims invaded the region in the eighth century bringing with them their new Islamic religion though the majority retained their traditional spirit beliefs. Conversion to Islam began in the southern regions and slowly spread north. Mongols, extending the borders of their rapidly growing empire, invaded the region in the 13th century, destroying the sophisticated trading towns and the extensive irrigation system that provided for a large settled population. The Turkic survivors of the conquest scattered across the steppe lands to escape the ferocious Mongol conquerors. A division of the Mongol horse soldiers, known as the White Horde, began to settle the largely depopulated areas in 1456. The Mongols gradually absorbed the surviving Turkic peoples and adopted much of the Turkic culture and the Turkic language while retaining their traditional Mongol organization into *jüz* or hordes, large tribal groupings. The Mongol-Turkic state created in the region, known as the Kazakh Khanate, was established as a tribal confederation of the three powerful hordes. Islam was introduced to most of the Kazakh during the 15th century but was not fully assimilated into Kazakh culture until much later. Cossacks, leading the Russian expansion to the east, made contact with the nomadic Kazakh hordes in the early 16th century, beginning a long period of gradual encroachment on the Kazakh Steppe. The first organized Russian expedition reached Kazakh territory in 1715, during a time of chaos and war. The Kazakh, under attack by the expanding Oirat Confederation, viewed the Europeans as possible allies. Russian military power greatly impressed the Kazakh chiefs, and the three major Kazakh hordes or tribal federations accepted Russian protection between 1731 and 1742. Having gained a foothold in the region, the Russians slowly extended their influence until the tribal groups, the hordes, were finally abolished and the Kazakh brought under direct Russian rule.

Kazakh culture is a modern Central Asian culture based on the traditional pastoral history of the region. Because herding was central to the Kazakh's historical way of life, most of their traditions and customs relate in some way to livestock. Though the Kazakh are rapidly urbanizing and adopting new ways and technologies, traditional curses and blessings are related to animals, and good manners require that a person ask first about the health of a man's livestock before greeting him personally. The formerly nomadic Kazakh lived in a tentlike construction known as a yurt. The yurts were constructed over a flexible framework of willow then covered with varying thicknesses of horse or yak hair felt. Yurts and other historic references are now often used as decorative motifs in the burgeoning cities where the traditional culture has blended with influences from the West, as well as from Russia and China. The Kazakh population, divided into clans and regional groups, is still in the process of forming a united ethnic and national entity. Due to the departure of large numbers of Europeans from the region following the collapse of the Soviet Union in 1991, plus a very high birthrate has resulted in the percentage of ethnic Kazakh in the country expanding from just 40 percent in 1991 to nearly 65 percent in 2012.

The Kazakh language, spoken from the Caspian Sea region into central Siberia and northwestern China, is one of the major languages of the Kipchak language group. Originally written in an Arabic script during the Soviet period, it was mostly written in the Russian Cyrillic alphabet though now there is a movement to adopt the Latin alphabet. The Kazakh population in China and Mongolia uses a modified Arabic script similar to the script used by the neighboring Uyghur. The Kazakh language is the language of daily life, but Russian remains the language of business and is used as a lingua

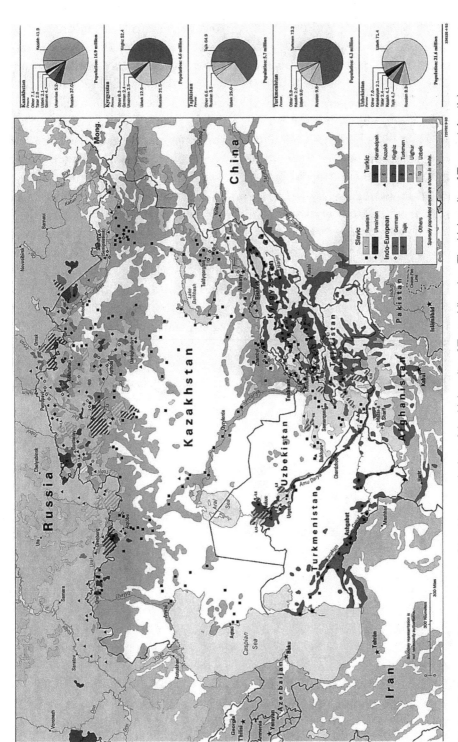

Major ethnic groups in Central Asia. (Used by permission of the University of Texas Libraries, The University of Texas at Austin)

Kazakh nomads on the road, northern Xinjiang Province, China. (Lihui/Dreamstime.com)

franca for communications between the Kazakh and other ethnic groups. Most Kazakh are practicing Muslims, the majority adhering to the Sunni branch of Islam. Because the spread and adoption of Islam was a long slow process in the vast steppe lands, Islam has long existed alongside the early belief system. Traditional beliefs head that there existed a parallel spirit world, with separate spirits inhabiting and animating the sky, water, fire, and animals. To the present, particularly honored guests may be treated to a feast of freshly butchered lamb and are sometimes asked to bless the spirit of the lamb and ask for its permission to partake of its flesh. Although lamb is very important, other traditional foods also retain symbolic value in the Kazakh culture. Livestock remain a central part of Kazakh culture, even among the urban population,

with traditional games played on horseback popular parts of any large event.

Increasing Russian interference in their culture and daily lives provoked resentment and growing tensions in the first decades of the 19th century. Serious Kazakh revolts erupted in different districts between the 1820s and the 1840s. The Kazakh Khanate, founded in the 15th century, was finally dismantled in 1847. By the mid-19th century, nearly the Russian authorities directly administered the entire huge Kazakh Steppe region. A string of Cossack forts and a large military presence acted as a parallel government to the Russian civil authorities. Taxes, much resented by the nomadic clans, were paid in the form of animals, hides, furs, or other valued goods. In 1868, the huge territory was organized into three provinces roughly based on the three historical hordes. The three provinces, known as the Steppe Province, Tugai Province, and Ural Province, were opened to colonization by Europeans moving east from European Russia. Conflicts over land, water, and authority were frequent and often violent. Possibly as a reaction to Russian attempts to convert the Kazakh to Orthodox Christianity, the majority of the Kazakh adopted the Muslim religion, making them the only Central Asian people to embrace Islam after the Russian conquest. From the 1890s, large numbers of Slav settlers began colonizing the Kazakh Steppe. The completion of the Orenburg–Tashkent Railroad in 1906 linked Central Asia to European Russia. The rail link brought an influx of new settlers with migration to the region encouraged and overseen by a specially created Migration Department in St. Petersburg. The railroad also allowed the Russian government to quickly move soldiers into areas of unrest. The competition for land and resources accelerated as the Kazakh and the colonists repeatedly clashed. During the 19th century, more than 400,000 Slavs migrated to the region, and an estimated 1 million Slavs, Germans, Jews, and others, mostly from European Russia, settled in the Kazakh lands in the early 20th century. Revolutionary ideas began to penetrate the region in the wake of the aborted 1905 Russian Revolution. The Kazakh were not directly involved in the events of World War I until the massive losses of manpower and the faltering Russian war effort became so acute that minorities were conscripted for the first time. The need for manpower persuaded the imperial government to extend conscription to the Muslims of Central Asia. In 1916, local government authorities attempted to forcibly conscript 250,000 Central Asian into labor battalions. The conscription was widely resisted, setting off a local rebellion that spread from the Kazakh to the Uzbek regions than across Central Asia. The Kazakh defeated the small garrisons remaining in the region and attacked Slavic settlements and outposts. Thousands of European colonists were slaughtered with the survivors fleeing to military outposts or attempting to return to European Russia. Tsarist troops, though badly needed at the front, were hastily dispatched to Central Asia and sent against the rebel groups. The Russian troops, unable to find the elusive mounted Kazakh warriors, often fell on peaceful villages or unarmed civilian populations. The revolt resulted in a series of clashes and in brutal massacres perpetuated by both sides. The Russian Revolution of 1917 and the rapid collapse of Russian authority in Central Asia overtook the widespread rebellion. The scattered Kazakh clans organized as Russian civil government collapsed. Kazakh leaders demanded an end to European colonization and the return of all stolen lands. The Bolshevik coup in late 1917 was rapidly embraced by many Russians in the Kazakh Steppe region. Outraged by the Bolshevik's antireligious rhetoric and threatened by the arrival of Bolshevik troops from Europe, the Kazakh leaders declared their enormous homeland independent of Russia. Allied to the anti-Bolshevik White forces in the region, the ill-equipped Kazakh troops were quickly defeated by the advancing Red forces. The Red Army overran most of the region in 1919 and by 1920 had taken firm control of all of Central Asia.

Though a minority of Kazakh supported the revolution, which as often seen as ending the hated colonialism, a ruling adopted in July 1919 excluded Muslims from local government posts and the new authorities adopted a harsh antireligious stance. Kazakhstan became an autonomous republic of the new Soviet Union. Repression of the traditional Kazakh elite, along with forced collectivization of the huge Kazakh herds, resulted in widespread famine and further conflicts that were brutally put down. Between 1926 and 1939, the Kazakh ethnic population declined by 22 percent due to starvation and the flight of many refugees into Chinese territory. During the 1930s, periodic purges eliminated most Kazakh writers, poets, thinkers, politicians, and historians. In 1936, Kazakhstan became a full member republic of the Soviet Union, while mass deportations continued to decimate the Kazakh population while millions exiled from other parts of the country were forcibly resettled in Kazakhstan. The demands of World War II greatly increased industrialization as large populations were shifted from war-torn Europe to the Kazakh region. The testing of a nuclear bomb in Kazakhstan in 1949 was a catastrophe for the region, with ecological and biological effects still being felt. Kazakh anger with the Soviet system continued to grow and quickly gained support during the relaxation of harsh Soviet rule in the late 1980s. Caught up in the groundswell of nationalist sentiment as the Soviet Union collapsed, the Kazakh leadership declared the sovereignty of the republic. Following the aborted coup in Moscow and the subsequent dissolution of the Soviet Union, the Kazakh communist leaders, quickly embracing nationalist ideals, declared Kazakhstan independent on December 16, 1991. Hesitation and confusion made Kazakhstan the last of the former Soviet republics to declare full independence. During the 1990s and to the present, the Kazakh republic remains under the authoritarian control of the communists-turned nationalists who took control of Kazakhstan in 1991.

Further Reading

Hall, Awelkhan, Zengxiang Li, and Karl W. Luckert. *Kazakh Traditions of China.* Lanham, MD: University Press of America, 1998.

"Kazakhstan." *New York Times.* Accessed July 31, 2013. http://topics.nytimes.com/top/news/international/countriesandterritories/kazakhstan/index.html

Laumulin, Chokan, and Murat Laumulin. *The Kazakhs.* Leiden, Netherlands: Brill/Global Oriental, 2009.

Shayakhmetov, Mukhamet. *The Silent Steppe: The Story of a Kazakh Nomad under Stalin.* London: Stacy International, 2006.

Ket

The Ket, sometimes known as Jugun, Ostyak, or Yenisei Ostyak, are a Siberian people living in the middle and lower basin of the Yenisei River in the Krasnoyarsk Krai region of Russian Siberia. The estimated 1,500–3,000 Ket mostly use Russian as their first language though there are several hundred who speak the Ket language, the sole surviving language of the Ket Assan or Yeniseian language family. Most of the Ket are officially Orthodox Christian though they tend to practice a combination of Christian traditions and customs alongside their traditional shamanism.

The ancestors of the Ket are believed to have originated with the ancient peoples of the Sayan Mountains and the Yenisei River basin. According to Ket tradition, they were driven out of their homeland in the south by "mountain people" and crossed several mountain ranges before they reached their present homeland along the middle Yenisei River. Scholars believe that the Ket are the only surviving descendants of an ancient nomadic people who roamed throughout central and southern Siberia. The modern Ket are probably a mixture of the tribal peoples of the Yenisei taiga and the migrants from southern Siberia. The early Ket engaged in hunting, fishing, and in some areas reindeer herding. Russian explorers and traders began to visit the Ket homeland in the late 16th century. In 1607, Cossacks established an outpost at Imbat in the Ket territory as a center for the collection of the *yurga*, the fur tax imposed on the indigenous peoples. The yearly tribute was set at between 5 and 12 pelts per person, forcing many Ket to abandon fishing or their reindeer herds in order to fulfill the demand for furs. The Ket resisted Russian incursions, but their bows were of little use against the firearms of the invaders. European diseases and violent confrontations decimated the Ket tribe. In order to break Ket resistance, the Russian authorities deported the bands from their traditional territories. The strictly organized Ket culture disintegrated and tribal functions ceased. Part of the Ket people were resettled in the territory of the Selkup people. The Russian authorities cared little for the well-being of the indigenous populations as their primary concern was the collection of valuable furs. Gold miners and traders moved into the region, often abusing or defrauding the Ket tribesmen.

The Ket culture is a Siberian culture that evolved through the nomadic lifestyle of the original inhabitants of the vast Siberian region. The Ket are the sole surviving group of the Yeniseian or western Paleo-Asiatic peoples. The other peoples of the group have been absorbed into the Russian culture or by other Siberian indigenous peoples. Traditionally, the culture is divided between a northern group known as Imbak, Inbak, or Imbat and a southern group, the Yugh, organized into two fraternal kinship groups, the *kentandeng* and the *bogdedeng*. Anthropologically and linguistically, the Ket are unique as the descendants of the ancient inhabitants of south-central Siberia. The neighboring Siberian peoples are relative newcomers in comparison. The Ket language is also entirely different from any other language spoken in modern Siberia. Traditionally, the Ket were hunters and fishermen. Reindeer herding, adopted from their Samoyedic neighbors, always remained a secondary occupation to hunting, foraging, and fishing. The Ket allowed their reindeer herds to roam freely during the summer but kept them close to the winter camps. The Ket, particularly the southern clans, lived on large, flat-bottomed houseboats called *ilimka*, a convention borrowed from the Russians in the 18th century. In the warmer months, the Ket also constructed tepees called *qus* as temporary homes as they moved from region to region. In the winter, the Ket occupied dugout cabins made of logs and earth known as *banggus*, where the families lived while the men were out hunting. Traditionally, the Ket are a patriarchal society, with women in a secondary role. Like their Siberian neighbors, the Ket traditional religious beliefs are based on shamanism, with the shaman serving as the local priest and healer. The shamans interceded between the human and the spirit worlds in an effort to avoid the sicknesses and misfortunes caused by the evil spirits. Officially converted to Russian Orthodoxy in the 19th century, most Ken now practice a form of Orthodox Christianity that incorporates many of their pre-Christian shamanistic beliefs. The Ket language is spoken in two dialects, Sym and Imbat, whose differences are mainly phonological. The Ket language is distinguished from other Siberian languages by its category of gender and the distinction between animate and inanimate objects. The Ket culture possesses a rich vocabulary in regard to traditional life, with many words to describe the local flora, fauna, hunting, fishing, and the weather. Russian loanwords began flooding the language when a written script was devised, and the radical social reforms were imposed in the 1930s. The majority of the Ket now use Russian as their first language, and the Ket language is considered in danger of extinction.

By the early 19th century, the devastated Ket culture could no longer survive without food aid from the Russian state. The disappearance of their traditional hunting and fishing grounds and the Russian habit of hunting their domesticated reindeer resulted in many deaths from hunger and abuse. Russian Orthodox missionaries established missions and some schools in the Ket region. Local officials organized a mass baptism of the Ket though most retained their traditional beliefs alongside their new Christian teachings. The outbreak of World War I eased pressure on the Ket as soldiers and administrators returned to European Russia. The Russian Revolution and the subsequent civil war between 1917 and 1920 further devastated the region. The Soviet victory was quickly followed by the arrival of communist cadres in the territories of the Siberian peoples. The traditional way of life of the Ket was denounced, and all self-initiative was suppressed as antirevolutionary. The seminomadic Ket were forced to settle in permanent villages where they worked as employees of the state. Their herds of reindeer were confiscated, and the former owners were made to care for them on Soviet collective farms. Those who resisted and the most prosperous herders and hunters were persecuted as enemies of the state and were deported. Resistance to the collectivization of their territories and herds was brutally suppressed. By 1938, there were 72 cooperatives and 6 collective farms in the Ket region. To fulfill the objectives set by the Soviet administration, Ket women were forced to work outside the home. Furs, known as the Soviet hard currency, remained the most important economic activity. To the Ket, the Soviet system was little different from the old *yurga* fur tax of the 19th century. In the 1950s, collectivization of the Ket territory was officially completed. Most of the Ket lived in Russian-style cabins with schools, clubs, and public baths built to Soviet standards. Russian culture and tradition was forced on the Ket as progressive. The disintegration of the Ket society that began in the 1930s was also completed in the 1950s with education and administration only in the Russian language. The Russian language replaced the Ket language as the first language and was used in most Ket homes. By the 1980s, Russian-Ket bilingualism had mostly disappeared as Russian became the major language of the ethnic group. In 1986, a revived written form of the Ket language was introduced, but its effect on the Ket cultural revival was mostly lost during the upheaval of the collapse of the Soviet system in 1991. A modest cultural revival took hold in the 1990s with many Ket taking a new interest in their unique culture and language. In subsequent census figures, the number of people registering as ethnic Ket has grown though the actual number is probably much larger as many Ket register according to their primary language, Russian.

Further Reading

Haywood, A.J. *Siberia: A Cultural History.* New York: Oxford University Press, 2010.

Slezkine, Yuri. *Arctic Mirrors: Russia and the Small Peoples of the North.* Ithaca, NY: Cornell University Press, 1996.

Vajda, Edward J. "The Ket and Other Yeniseian Peoples." *East Asian Studies 210 Notes.* http://pandora.cii.wwu.edu/vajda/ea 210/ket.htm

Vitebsky, Piers. *The Reindeer People: Living with Animals and Spirits in Siberia.* Boston: Mariner Books, 2006.

Khakass

The Khakass, some times known as the Khakas, Khakassians, Khaas, Khorray, Tadar, Abakan Tatars, Minusinsk Tatars, Abakan Turks, or Yenisei Turks, are a Turkic people concentrated in the Khakassia Republic of southern Siberia in the Russian Federation. The estimated 90,000 Khakass are of mixed Turkic and Mongol background, physically resembling the Mongols but culturally and linguistically more closely related to the Turkic peoples of Central Asia. Outside Khakassia, there are Khakass communities in the neighboring Krasnoyarsk Krai with smaller groups in Kemerovo Oblast and the Tuva Republic. The Khakass language, a Yenisei Turkic language belonging to the Southern Siberian Turkic group, is spoken in several closely related dialects that take their names from the five major Khakass tribes. The Khakass are officially Orthodox Christian though they continue to practice their pre-Christian beliefs, a mixture of shamanism and Buddhism.

First mentioned in Chinese records in the early fifth century CE, the inhabitants of the area were listed as mostly nomadic groups. The indigenous peoples, more closely related to the early North Americans, were killed or absorbed by migrating Turkic nomads, and a Turkic khanate, the core of the historic Kyrgyz people, dominated the region from the sixth to eighth centuries. Defeated by the invading Mongol hordes in the 13th century, the majority of the Turkic people migrated southwest to the territory of the present-day Kyrgyzstan. The Khakass regard themselves as the descendants of the Kyrgyz who remained in Siberia. The Siberian Kyrgyz remained under Mongol rule for more than two centuries, gradually mixing with the conquerors to form the modern Khakass. Even after the dissolution of the Mongol Empire, the Golden Horde, the Yenisei tribes were the targets of periodic Mongol incursions. A powerful tribal federation, dominated by the Oirat tribe, began to expand in the 16th century and eventually extended its authority to the Yenisei Basin. Slavic Cossacks, the spearhead of the expanding Russian presence in Siberia, began to penetrate the federation and regularly collected a *yasak* or fur tax from the northern Khakass tribes. Drawn by the rich copper deposits in the Yenisei region, the Russians annexed Khakassia in 1707. A Russian protectorate over the region was proclaimed in 1727. The Russians collected taxes in the form of furs and occasionally put down tribal uprisings, but mostly left the Khakass tribes to govern themselves. The tribal Khakass, called Tatar by the Russians, were slowly pushed aside as Russian colonization to the Yenisei River basin in the late 18th century.

The mixed ancestry of the Khakass, comprising Turkic, Mongol, Kettic, and Samoyed strains, is still evident though the Turkic influence is the strongest in the culture and language with many still with Mongol physical features. The Khakass are divided into five principal tribal groups that are further divided into subgroups and clans, and loyalty to the tribe and clan remains strong. The designation "Khakass" was not used until 1923, when the Soviet authorities settled on the name for all the related tribal groups of the region. Since 1930, the various tribal groups have begun to use the Khakass name and to identify with the larger tribal grouping. Khakass identity, though still focused on family, clan, and tribe, has strengthened since the collapse of Soviet power in 1991. The Khakass language, a Uyghur-Oguz language belonging to the eastern branch of the Turkic languages, is spoken in five primary dialects and a number of subdialects. The Khakass language is believed to have evolved from the ancient Uyghur language, which remained a group of tribal dialects until its standardization under Soviet rule in the early 20th century. Though nominally Russian Orthodox Christians, the bulk of the Khakass population retain their traditional beliefs in the spirit world, most still worship milk and fire, and there is widespread respect for the wisdom of the shamans. Their shamanistic beliefs not only survived and outlasted the Soviet's oppression, but also have renewed itself as part of the post-Soviet Khakass cultural revival.

During the 19th century, the Russian government deported convicted criminals and political dissidents to camps and forts in the region. Many prisoners stayed in the area after their release, adding to the growing Slavic population in Khakassia. The colonial process, including a constant debt owed the Russian authorities in the form of valuable furs, the ever-increasing number of European colonists, and the despotism of the Russian bureaucrats and missionaries, quickly decreased the self-confidence and independence of the Khakass tribes. In 1876, Orthodox missionaries, ignorant of the local language or customs, simultaneously baptized 3,000 Khakass, naming all the men Vladimir and all the women Maria. Though the missionaries made superficial conversions to Orthodox Christianity, what emerged was a unique fusion of traditional shamanistic and Buddhist beliefs and Christian doctrine. The completion of the Trans-Siberian Railroad, extended through the region in the 1890s, facilitated the migration of colonists from

A Khakass man next to a harnessed buffalo poses for a portrait. (George Kennan/National Geographic Society/Corbis)

European Russia leaving the Khakass marginalized, their best lands stolen, while tsarist functionaries demanded more and more furs as taxes and tribute, up to six sable furs per person each year in the tribal areas. Untouched by World War I until the news of the Russian Revolution reached the region in 1917, the Khakass quickly organized to prevent local Bolsheviks from taking power. In spite of their efforts, the Red forces, victorious in the Russian Civil War, took control of Khakassia in 1920. The nomadic clans were forced to settle, their herds collectivized, and much of their remaining land turned over to the flood of European migrants entering the region.

The Soviets created a Khakass national territory, the Khakass National Okrug, which supposedly gave the Khakass some autonomy, but the reality was an urbanizing Russian culture with the Khakass relegated to rural poverty. Daily life came to be dominated by Soviet values and Russian culture, and the importance of the Khakass language and culture was denigrated as local Soviet officials constantly highlighted the prestige of the Russian culture and language. The marginalized Khakass began to decline, alcohol abuse became widespread, and pressure increased to embrace the universal Soviet culture. A modest cultural revival took hold in the 1950s and 1960s as the Khakass population again began to increase. The disintegration of the Soviet Union, in the early 1990s, allowed local officials to gain membership in the new Russian Federation for the Khakassia Republic, but life for the Khakass remained a calamity of social apathy, alcoholism, drug abuse, and afflictions such as tuberculosis and venereal diseases.

Further Reading

Gorenburg, Dmitry P. *Minority Ethnic Mobilization in the Russian Federation.* Cambridge: Cambridge University Press, 2003.

Kazachinova, Galina, and Kira Van Deusen. *Mountain Spirits.* Vancouver, BC: Udagan Books, 2003.

Olson, James Stuart. *An Ethnohistorical Dictionary of the Russian and Soviet Empires.* Westport, CT: Greenwood, 1994.

Vahtre, Lauri, and Jüri Viikberg. The Red Book of the Peoples of the Russian Empire. "The Khakass." Accessed July 31, 2013. http://www.eki.ee/books/redbook/khakass.shtml

Khanty

The Khanty, sometimes known as Khant, Khanti, Khande, Kantek, Hanty, Ostyak, Obdor, Yugra, or Jugra, are a northern Siberian people living in the Khanty-Mansi Autonomous Okrug in western Siberia and in neighboring regions of the Russian Federation. Their homeland, often called Yugra, lies along the lower reaches of the Ob River, a region of Arctic tundra and taiga with deep forests and swamps that remain frozen for much of the year. The estimated 30,000 Khanty speak an Ob-Ugrian dialect of the Ugrian branch of the Finno-Ugrian language group. The Khanty language is related to Magyar, the language of the Hungarians far to the west in Europe. The Khanty are nominally Orthodox Christians though they mix their belief system with traditional beliefs and its pantheon of gods, both great and small.

Scholars' beliefs differ as to the origins of the Khanty. Archaeologists have found evidence that the ancestors of the Khanty, the neighboring Mansi, and the Hungarians inhabited the western Siberian forests 3,000–4,000 years ago. One theory suggests that they evolved in the valley of the Pechora River in Northern European Russia and crossed the Ural Mountains to the Ob River basin in the first century BCE. Other scholars believe that they developed east of the Urals from a mixing of Uralian and other groups before being forced to leave their homeland and migrate northeast to settle the Ob lowlands while their kinsmen continued west, eventually settling in the present-day Hungary. In the 11th century, traders and explorers moving east from the Novgorod Republic encountered the Khanty tribes. They became tributary to the Novgorodians in the 13th century. From the 1440s to the 1570s, the Khanty territories were under the loose authority of the Siberia Khanate, a Tatar state in west-central Siberia. Slavic expeditions explored the Khanty homeland in 1483 and 1499. In the late 16th and early 17th centuries, the Khanty came under the rule of the expanding Russian Empire. They are mentioned in Muscovite chronicles of 1572 as a tributary tribe. Following the Russian defeat of the powerful Tatar khanates, the Russians established colonial center at the mouth of the Ob River in 1595. Russian fur traders and government functionaries took effective control of the region, taxing the Khanty for the furs so valued in European Russia. The Khanty were officially converted to Orthodox Christianity by the middle of the 18th century, though traditional Khanty beliefs and social structures survived the colonial experience.

The Khanty culture is unique, having developed in response to a harsh environment. It retains a set of distinct social and economic practices and traditions. Historically, the Khanty tribes were grouped into tribes, each divided into a system of strong patrilineal clans. The clans formed part of local tribes, each being a member of a regional ethnographic group—eastern, northern, southern—with differing cultural features and dialects. The system severely restricted the rights of women, as their presence was believed to defile religious idols and to tempt clan or family members; therefore women were forced to wear a veil. Modern Khanty culture is a unique blend of their traditional way of life and European customs. The Khanty language, despite the small number of speakers, is spoken in 10 distinct dialects loosely grouped into three dialectal groupings. The number of dialects reflects the vast distances and small population of their traditional homeland. Russian missionaries developed an alphabet, turning Khanty into a literary language in the mid-19th century. The first publication, part of the Bible, appeared in 1868. Elementary school primers, also written by Orthodox clerics, came into use in 1897. The modern literary language is based on the Kazym

dialect, though most education in the region is in the Russian language. Khanty religious beliefs, blending ancient customs and later Christian doctrines, include a belief in reincarnation. Each newborn baby is viewed as the reincarnation of a deceased member of the clan. Traditionally, each dwelling had wooden idols representing clan ancestors and animal spirits. Government pressure in recent decades has curtailed the ritual slaughter of animals at funerals and other gatherings.

In the early 1800s, even the rural Khanty clans were subjugated with the help of a combination of debt, to be paid in furs, and alcohol provided by Russian merchants and officials. Though some officials attempted to shield the Khanty from exploitation, the remoteness of the region and the small government presence prevented effective enforcement. Russian entrepreneurs stole large sections of land and fishing ground from the unsuspecting Khanty elders. Russian influence increased greatly following the Russian Revolution and the establishment of the Soviet system. A special governmental board, known as the Committee of the North, was created in 1924 to deal with the small peoples like the Khanty. The committee introduced modern medicine and primary schools and campaigned against the Khanty subjugation of women. The creation of a nominally autonomous district in 1930 was accompanied by the execution of shamans and tribal chiefs during the process of collectivization. The kidnapping of many Khanty children, who were sent to Russian-speaking boarding schools, provoked a widespread Khanty uprising in 1933. Efforts to modernize and "Sovietize" Khanty life included the oppression of their traditional religious beliefs and the promotion of a unitary Soviet culture. Efforts to modernize Khanty life continued after the death of the Soviet dictator, Joseph Stalin, in 1953. In the 1960s, the local government sponsored "open-faced" ceremonies to encourage Khanty women to give up their veils. By the 1980s, misguided Soviet policies had devastated western Siberia. A massive oilfield, prone to oil and chemical spills, badly polluted the rivers and swamps and devastated the traditional fishing villages. A variety of large-scale engineering projects ruined the grazing lands of the reindeer herders in the northern districts. Modern Khanty life, other than some seminomadic reindeer herders in the north, is based on small agricultural and fishing villages. These villages, largely Russian speaking, retain much of the Khanty culture and its yearly cycle of ceremonies and events. But the environmental catastrophe has incited activists and environmental groups to demand a more cautious development policy that would permit the survival of the land and the indigenous peoples and their ancient cultures.

Further Reading

Balzer, Majorie Mandelstam. *The Tenacity of Ethnicity: A Siberian Saga in Global Perspective.* Princeton, NJ: Princeton University Press, 1999.

Jordan, Peter. *Material Culture and Sacred Landscape: The Anthropology of the Siberian Khanty.* Lanham, MD: Altamira Press, 2003.

Uralic Peoples of Siberia and Russian Northern Europe. "Khants or Ostyaks." Accessed July 30, 2013. http://www.suri.ee/eup/khants.html

Widget, Andrew, and Olga Balalaeva. *Khanty: People of the Taiga Surviving the Twentieth Century.* Fairbanks: University of Alaska Press, 2011.

Korean

The Koreans, sometimes known as Hanguk-in, Han-in, Hanja, Hanguk-saram, Choson-in, Choson-saram, or Koryo-saram, are concentrated in the Republic of Korea (South Korea), the Democratic People's Republic of Korea, and adjacent areas of China. Outside the region, there are sizable Korean communities in the United States, Japan, Canada, Russia, Australia, Uzbekistan, the Philippines, Kazakhstan, Vietnam, Brazil, the United Kingdom, Thailand, Ukraine, Indonesia, Germany, New Zealand, Argentina, and elsewhere. The estimated 85 million Koreans speak a language of the Koreanic branch of the Altaic languages, though the relation between Korean and the Altaic languages is debated. Though many Koreans are not religious, Buddhism, Confucianism, Ch'ondogyo, and Christianity are all practiced, mostly in South Korea and the Korean Diaspora.

Archaeological evidence suggests that the ancestors of the Koreans originated in south-central Siberia. From there, they migrated south to populate the Korean Peninsula in successive waves from the Neolithic era to the Bronze Age. Koreans trace their history back to the founding of the Gojoseon kingdom by the legendary Dan-gun Wanggeom in 2333 BCE. Around 1500 BCE, the Korean Peninsula and the adjacent areas of the Manchuria region of northeastern China semisedentary agricultural settlements occupied the region. Around 400 BCE, the capital of the kingdom was moved to Pyongyang. In the southern part of the peninsula, the rival Jin kingdom was founded in the third century BCE. The Gojoseon kingdom was overrun by invading Han Chinese in 108 BCE, which resulted in the splintering of the state into many small states. Eventually three states emerged, Baekje and Silla in the south and Goguryeo in the north. The so-called Three Kingdoms dominated the Korean Peninsula and parts of Manchuria for much of the period from 57 CE to 668 CE when Silla conquered Goguryeo during the unification wars. The Korean homeland was then divided into Silla in the south and Balhae in the north during the period known as the North and South States era from 698 to 926. During the supremacy of Silla, Korean arts and literature flourished and Buddhism became an important part of the Silla culture. Buddhist monasteries became the centers of advanced architecture and learning. Unified Silla lasted for 267 years until it fell to the Korean kingdom of Goryeo in 935. Goryeo, also known as Koryo or Korea, was established in 918 and united the Korean homeland until 1392. Two of the most notable achievements of this period were the creation of the distinctive celadon pottery and the *Tripitaka Koreana*, Buddhist scriptures carved into roughly 80,000 woodblocks that are one of the modern Korean treasures. The first metal-based movable type was invented in 1234, with the oldest surviving example of a movable metal-type book, the *jikji*, dates from 1377. By the 14th century, the Goryeo state has lost much of its power under pressure from the Mongol Yuan dynasty of China. The Joseon dynasty, also known as Choson or Chosun, was established with the overthrow of Goryeo in 1392, beginning a succession of kings who ruled Korea until the late 19th century. Japanese invasions of Korea began with attacks by Japanese pirates on coastal communities and full-scale Japanese invasions between 1592 and 1598. During the war with the Japanese, the Koreans developed powerful firearms and used Turtle ships, warships completely enclosed, to defeat the Japanese naval force. A Chinese force sent by the Ming emperor of China aided the Koreans in expelling the Japanese invaders. The country, devastated by the Japanese incursion, became embroiled in the growing conflict between the neighboring Manchu and the Ming dynasty. Pressured by both the Manchu and the Chinese, the Koreans attempted to maintain neutrality. In 1627, a Jurchen (Manchu) army of 30,000 overran the country's defenses. Korea became a tributary state to the powerful Manchu kingdom. Following the imposition of loose authority by the Manchu Qing dynasty following the Manchu conquest of China, Korea's rulers became increasingly isolationist, seeking to avoid the alliances and conflicts that had repeatedly ravaged the country since the Japanese invasion of the late 16th century. A Korean Confucian social reform movement gained support in the kingdom. Known as Silhak, it developed as a response to the increasingly metaphysical nature of Korean religious thought that seemed disconnected from the rapid industrial, agricultural, and political changes taking place in the kingdom between the 17th and 19th centuries.

The traditional culture of Korea is shared between the two modern Korean states and the large Korean populations in adjacent areas of China, Japan, the United States, and other countries. Modern Korean culture has developed distinct contemporary forms since the political division of the Korean Peninsula in 1945. Historically, the culture has been heavily influenced by that of the neighboring Han Chinese and the Manchu, though the Koreans developed a unique cultural identity that remains distinct from the neighboring cultures. The industrialization and urbanization of the South Koreans has introduced many outside influences, particularly since the country joined the world's most advanced industrial states in the 1960s. In the north, a Stalinist-style communist regime has isolated the North Koreans from the influences of the outside world for nearly seven decades. Poverty and political excesses have destroyed many historical sites, shrines, and monasteries in the North, while the South Korean government subsidizes traditional cultural arts and traditions. Korean architecture is historically characterized by its harmony with nature. Many architectural treasures have survived, often standing alongside modern Korean architecture stimulated by the economic expansion of the 1970s and 1980s. While North Korea has stagnated, often with widespread hunger and suffering, it has built the world's fourth largest military forces, overseen by a communist dynasty. Tensions between the two Koreas often include cultural elements that seep into the North despite the regime's efforts to limit contacts between the two states. While the North remained mired in poverty and early

20th-century–style dictatorship, the South is among the most advanced states in the world. South Korean arts are flourishing, with music, television, and film popular outside the country in other parts of Asia. Korean technology is among the world's most innovative, and South Korean brand names are known throughout the world. South Korean mobile telephone technology, automobiles, and manufactures are exported throughout the world. Many of the Koreans living in North Korea and neighboring areas of China now consider themselves nonreligious though traditional shamanistic beliefs still survive to the present. Throughout Korean history, the traditional beliefs of Korean shamanism, Mahayana Buddhism, and Confucianism have remained an underlying influence as well as a vital element of Korean culture. These influences remain even among the large Christian community in South Korea and the largely atheist North Korea. The Korean language, the official language of both Korean states, is also one of two official languages in China's Yanbian Korean Autonomous Prefecture in adjacent parts of China. The language is also spoken by the large Korean Diaspora population around the world. The language forms the Koreanic branch of the Altaic language, though according to some linguists, it is not closely related to any other living language. Modern Korean is traditionally divided into a number of geographic dialects, with the dialect spoken in Jeju, an island off the southern coast, often considered a second Koreanic language. The language is usually written in the Korean Hangul script though it has been adapted to the Latin script and Cyrillic in Russia and Central Asia. Since the political division of Korea in 1945, dialectical differences have developed in standard Korean, including variance in vocabulary, pronunciation, and verb inflection. In the South, many English words have been incorporated into the language, particularly in the fields of technology, manufacturing, and entertainment, while in the North, specific words are invented to cover the linguistic needs.

The Joseon dynasty declined rapidly in the 19th century due to internal power struggles, foreign incursions, and rebellions. Western influence grew as trade and contacts increased. The Sino-Japanese War (1894–1895), fought between the Manchu Qing dynasty of China and the Japanese, was primarily over their rivalry for influence in Korea. China considered Korea a vassal state, but with defeat, power in the region shifted to Japan. The war, partially fought on Korean territory, devastated many areas in the west of the Korean Peninsula. The Japanese Empire, already expanding its industries and military power, viewed the Korean modernization as a threat to Japanese influence. The Treaty of Shimonoseki, at the end of the Sino-Japanese War, stipulated the end of the traditional ties between Korea's Joseon dynasty and the Qing dynasty of China. In 1897, the Korean kingdom was officially replaced by a new political entity known as the Korean Empire. The government was partially successful in its modernization of the military, the economy, various industries, the land system, and education. Russian influence increased in Korea until the Russo-Japanese War (1904–1905), after which Korea was made a protectorate of Japan. In 1910, Japan annexed Korea, beginning 35 years of often brutal military rule. After the annexation, the Japanese attempted to suppress Korean traditions and culture and rearranged the Korean economy primarily for the benefit of Japan. Anti-Japanese and pro-liberation demonstrations erupted across Korea on March 1, 1919. Japanese troops fired on the demonstrators, killing an estimated 7,000 people.

Continued anti-Japanese uprisings, particularly widespread in 1929, resulted in a more severe military rule. Following the outbreak of war following the Japanese invasion of China in 1937 and later World War II, the Japanese authorities redoubled their efforts to extinguish traditional Korean culture. The Korean language was banned, and Koreans were forced to adopt Japanese family names. Numerous Korean cultural artifacts and sites were destroyed or were taken to Japan. Resistance groups operated across the country but were particularly effective against the Japanese forces along the border with China. During World War II, the Koreans were forced to work for the Japanese war effort. Tens of thousands of Korean men were conscripted into the Japanese military, and around 20,000 Korean girls and women were abducted to serve as "comfort women," virtually sex slaves, for the Japanese military forces. Japanese rule ended with their defeat and the end of World War II in 1945. Soviet troops, even though the Soviet Union had not declared war on Japan until the end of the war, occupied the northern provinces of Korea, while American forces occupied the southern provinces in 1945. United Nations–supervised elections were to be held, but as the Cold War mentality took hold, elections were postponed. By 1948, the division of the Korean Peninsula into two states, a communist government in the North, and a Western-style anticommunist state in the South, was put in place. Soviet and American forces withdrew from the peninsula, but the weakened South encouraged communist leader Kim Il-sung to consider a plan for the invasion of the South. At first rejected by Joseph Stalin in the Soviet Union, the victory of the communists in the Chinese Civil War in 1949 encouraged the Chinese to send troops and other support for North Korea. The invasion of the South led to the start of the Korean War in 1950. With the endorsement of the United Nations, the United States and other allied countries intervened to aid the reeling South Koreans. After initial rapid military advances by the North Koreans and their Chinese allies, the war became a standoff between the two sides. Fighting ended in July 1953, with an armistice that restored the border between the two Koreas. More than a million Korean civilians and soldiers died in the conflict, along with tens of thousands of Allied and Chinese military personnel. The war was the first armed conflict of the escalating Cold War between the democracies and communist dictatorships that divided the world in the 1950s. Relations between the two Korean states have remained tense since 1953 with the Korean populations of the two living in radically different cultures. In the South, the postwar reconstruction, a long-standing alliance with the United States and its allies, and the large number of Koreans who escaped from the North during the war and its aftermath, resulted in an economic miracle that dramatically transformed South Korea from one of the world's poorest regions in 1950 to one of the world's richest countries by 1990. In North Korea, a cult-figure dictatorship, an enormous and costly military, and poor management of the economy resulted in widespread famine in the 1980s, 1990s, and into the 21st century. Military spending in the North, including a program to construct nuclear weapons, at the expense of the civilian population has resulted in increasing instability, aggression against South Korea and Japan, and strained relations with the United States and other states with interests in the region.

Further Reading

BBC News. "North Korea Profile." Last updated July 23, 2013. http://www.bbc.co.uk/news/world-asia-pacific-15256929

BBC News. "South Korea Profile." Last updated June 7, 2013. http://www.bbc.co.uk/news/world-asia-pacific-15289563

Demick, Barbara. *Nothing to Envy: Ordinary Lives in North Korea.* New York: Spiegel & Grau, 2010.

Oliver, Robert T. *A History of the Korean People in Modern Times: 1800 to the Present.* Newark: University of Delaware Press, 1993.

Tudor, Daniel. *Korea: The Impossible Country.* Clarendon, VT: Tuttle Publishing, 2012.

Koryak

The Koryak, sometimes known as Koriak, Chavchu, Chauvu, Nemelan, or Nymylan, are a Paleo-Asiatic or Hyperborean people divided into 12 clan or tribal groups. The Koryak homeland, the Koryak Autonomous Okrug, called Chav' Chiiv by the

Koryak, lies in northeastern Russia. Ethnically and linguistically, the Koryak are related to the Native American peoples across the narrow Bering Strait in North America. The estimated 12,000 Koryak, including the closely related Alyutor, speak the Koryak-Alyutor dialect of the Chukotko-Khamchatian languages of the Luorawetlan language group. The majority of the Koryak are Orthodox Christians with a minority, mostly in the more remote districts, having retained their traditional shamanistic beliefs.

Though little is actually known about the prehistory of the Koryak, many scholars believe that ancient peoples from the Ural Mountains on the eastern borders of continental Europe may have spread eastward from 40,000 to 20,000 BCE. Other peoples from the Aral Sea region of Central Asia may have gone north and east from about 20,000 BCE. There were also migrations of people from the Lake Baikal region of southern Siberia. The Paleo-Asiatic Koryak are probably descended from a mixture of two or three of the peoples of these migrations. In prehistoric times, small nomadic groups migrated across the vast territories later known as Siberia. In pursuit of game or better fishing, many of the small migrant bands crossed the narrow land bridge that connected Asia and North America some 30,000 years ago. The small nomadic groups that remained on the Asian side were gradually pushed north by stronger peoples. They spread out across the harsh landscape, some to take up herding in the more temperate grazing lands and others to settle as fishermen along the coasts. Around 2,000 years ago, the Koryak lived along the coast of the Sea of Okhotsk as fishermen and hunters of sea mammals. They slowly spread down the coasts of the Kamchatka Peninsula. Between the 11th and 16th centuries, the bands in the interior adopted reindeer herding. Taking their names from geographic areas, religious totems, or ancestors, the bands had no name for their ethnic group as a whole and often warred among themselves. Russian expeditions, led by explorers and Cossack warriors, moved across northern Siberia to reach the Kamchatka Peninsula and the Pacific Ocean in 1640. The Russians constructed forts that were used by Slavic traders, fur trappers, and hunters. By 1649, the estimated 25,000 Koryak had come under loose Russian authority. A wave of European diseases, to which the Koryak had no immunity, devastated the tribes. The Russians imposed a fur tax, the *yasak*, on every able-bodied male, forcing many Koryak to abandon their villages to go to the forests to hunt the valuable fur-bearing animals. As the number of fur animals decreased, the Russians lost interest in the area, leaving the surviving Koryak to their traditional way of life. By the mid-1700s, the Koryak were dependent on Russian traders for alcohol, iron tools, firearms, and tobacco, for which they traded reindeer hides, furs, and walrus tusks. Resistance to the encroaching Russians weakened the Koryak tribes. They became easy prey to the warlike Chukchi to the north, whose raids, and a serious smallpox epidemic in the late 18th century, reduced the number of surviving Koryak by about half. A Russian trade monopoly forbade foreigners trading in the coastal settlements. The

Russian traders enforced their demands for furs by taking hostages and selling them as concubines or slaves when their demands were not met. Only a few thousand Koryak survived the first century of Russian rule.

Koryak culture is divided into two distinct subcultures, that of the seminomadic reindeer herders and that of the settled coastal groups who fish or hunt sea mammals. The traditional occupations are used to classify the various clans in the vast region. Koryak tradition obliges a man to marry outside his clan, often leading to a mixing of the two occupational cultures. Dancing is an important element in the social and religious lives of the Koryak bands. Anthropologists have found remarkable parallels between the myths, dwelling types, and religious rituals of the Koryak and those of the indigenous peoples of the United States and Canada, particularly the Haida and Tlingit peoples living on the Pacific coast in Washington state and British Columbia. Linguistically, the Koryak-Alyutor language is very closely related to the language of the Chukchi to the north and more distantly related to languages in North America. Assimilation into Russian culture has resulted in a loss of language as Koryak speakers adopted Russian, but in recent years, a concerted effort has reversed the long linguistic decline. Though the majority of the Koryak are officially Orthodox Christian, they retain much of their pre-Christian beliefs, including reverence for the mythological first man and protector of the Koryak, the supernatural shaman Quikil or Big Raven. Big Raven myths are also found among the Tlingit, Tsimshian, and Haida in North America. Each Koryak family has a member who is skilled at drumming and is thought to have special influence with the spirit world. Soviet atmospheric nuclear testing in the region in the 1950s left behind a legacy of disease, particularly cancer, which exceeds the Russian national average by three times. Infant morality is also very high, and the life expectancy of the Koryak is now less than 50 years.

The Koryak tribes began to slowly recover during the early 19th century, and the long decline in population began to reverse. A series of penal camps was established, and Russian and Polish intellectuals deported to the region began the first studies of the Koryak culture and language. The deportees, who also set up schools, devised a written form of the Koryak language. Russian Orthodox missionaries also established schools and converted many of the tribesmen to Christianity. Revolutionary ideas were also brought to the region with the deportees. The small educated minority led Koryak demands for land rights, particularly the right to fish in the streams and rivers of their historic homeland, rights denied under the Russian trade monopoly. In 1920, the Soviets, having taken control of the Russian state, sent cadres into the northeast. The Soviet commissars outlawed the traditional nomadic lifestyle of the interior tribes and confiscated their herds. The coastal fishing villages were collectivized, the ancient religious beliefs were suppressed, and the shamans were eliminated or disappeared into the many labor camps in the region. Alcohol abuse became widespread, and alcohol became a sort of currency, used for barter. Official efforts to curb the sale of alcohol to the native peoples in the northeast met fierce resistance. Soviet policy that stressed production, not the well-being of the indigenous peoples, further decimated the Koryak, destroying ancient social structures, while misguided Soviet development schemes devastated the fragile Koryak homeland. Many of the herdsmen and fishermen, without experience or any training, were summarily assigned to the new coalmines in the north of the Kamchatka Peninsula. Many Koryak children were taken from their families to be raised in Soviet boarding schools where they learned the Russian language, state socialism, antireligious rhetoric, and scorn for ancient traditions and shamanistic practices. Over many decades, the number of Slavic settlers in the region increased, particularly when oil and natural gas were developed in the 1950s and 1960s. The settlers took the most productive lands, further restricting the Koryak settlements and collectives. The Soviet liberalization that began in the late 1980s gradually seeped into the remote Koryak region. The Koryak joined other small northern ethnic groups to demand redress of numerous Soviet abuses and their rights to recuperate their culture, language, and way of life. The Koryak and other groups established ties to the Native Americans across the Bering Strait and began to integrate into the Pacific Rim peoples. Many of the Slavs settled in the region during the Soviet era left to return to western Siberia or European Russia giving the Koryak greater control over their historic homeland. In the 21st century, many younger Koryak, with a new appreciation of their historic culture and language, have led a cultural and linguistic revival.

Further Reading

King, Alexander. Koryak Language and Culture. Last updated April 22, 2013. http://www.koryaks.net/

King, Alexander D. *Living with Koryak Traditions: Playing with Culture in Siberia*. Lincoln: University of Nebraska, 2011.

Slezkine, Yuri. *Arctic Mirror: Russia and the Small Peoples of the North*. Ithaca, NY: Cornell University Press, 1996.

Vitebsky, Piers. *The Reindeer People: Living with Animals and Spirits in Siberia*. Boston: Mariner Books, 2006.

Kyrgyz

The Kyrgyz, sometimes known as Kirgiz, Kirghiz, Khirghiz, Oyrqyz, or Qyrghiz, are a Turkic people of Central Asia. Concentrated in the Kyrgyz Republic, there are also large Kyrgyz populations in neighboring Uzbekistan, numbering 250,000; China, 145,000; Russia, 105,000; and smaller groups in Tajikistan, Kazakhstan, and Ukraine. The Kyrgyz homeland, most of which now forms the independent Kyrgyz Republic, lies at the western end of the Tian Shan Mountains. The estimated 4.5 million Kyrgyz speak a South Kipchak Turkic language of the Kazakh-Nogai branch of the Turkic languages. The Kyrgyz are predominately Sunni Muslim though many, particularly in the northern districts, espouse the Soviet ideal of atheism or define themselves as cultural Muslims. In the 18th and early 19th centuries, many Russian and European writers used the name *Kirghiz*, an Anglicized form of a contemporary Russian name, to refer not only to the Kyrgyz but also to their more numerous northern neighbors, the Kazakh. Only under Soviet rule was definite distinction established between the two peoples.

The Kyrgyz, often known as the Yenisei Kyrgyz, first appeared in written Chinese record around 100 BCE. The Kyrgyz emerged as a historically important people in 840 CE, when they revolted against rule by the Uyghur khanate in northwestern Mongolia and took control of the territory between the Yenisei and Orkhon Rivers in southern Siberia. Between 840 and 925, the state known as Great Kyrgyz was the most powerful in Central Asia. The declining Kyrgyz Empire was forced to surrender to the invading Mongols in 1218, when a majority of the Kyrgyz population fled southwest to the western end of the Tian Shan Mountains and into Xinjiang. Subjugated by various Turkic invaders and finally under Mongol rule, the Kyrgyz maintained the unity of their various Turkic tribes. The devastation of the Mongol invasions was responsible for a severe regression of Kyrgyz culture, including the loss of their writing system. With the breakup of the Mongol Empire around the late 14th century, the tribes in the Tian Shan region came under the control of a Mongol successor state. For several centuries, the Kyrgyz remained an obscure tribal people often conquered by more power invaders but lacking the tribal unity to defend their homeland. Despite the devastation of the Mongol invasions, the region was known as part of the Silk Road that linked the Orient with the Middle East and Europe. Islam, first introduced by Arab traders moving along the Silk

Road, the trade routes that crossed Central Asia, was first adopted by the inhabitants of the caravan centers and trading towns in the seventh and eighth centuries. During the period of the Mongol invasions, the Kyrgyz began to convert to the Sunni branch of Islam. As reflected in their famed epic poetry, many Kyrgyz viewed the struggle against the Mongol as a holy war. Overrun by the Oirat tribal federation in the 16th century, the Kyrgyz remained under the rule of the Alliance of the Four Oirat and the Dzungar, which succeeded the alliance. In 1510, the Kyrgyz finally gained their freedom, and in 1514, a new khan of the Kyrgyz was invested. Kyrgyz independence lasted only until the Kalmyk conquered the region in 1683–1685. Nearly all the Kyrgyz were driven from their highland region into other parts of Central Asia and Xinjiang. The Kyrgyz remained in a historical eclipse in the history records of the region until the 17th century, known to history only in the chronicles of the region's various conquerors. The Manchu rulers of China sent an army into the Central Asia in 1758, leading to the defeat of the Kalmyk/Oirat Federation. Gradually, many Kyrgyz tribes moved back to their grazing lands in the Tian Shan highlands as nominal Chinese subjects. Their nomadic way of living made Chinese control very difficult with most of the Kyrgyz tribes virtually independent. The destruction of the Kalmyk/Oirat Empire in 1758 allowed the expanding Russian Empire to begin interfering in Kyrgyz territory. In 1775, one of the Kyrgyz tribal chiefs established the first diplomatic ties to the Russian Empire.

The Kyrgyz culture is made up of a number of tribal groups and cultures. Officially, there are 40 Kyrgyz clans, symbolized by the 40-ray golden sun in the center of the Kyrgyz national flag. Kyrgyz society is based on kinship relationships, though governed by strict traditions of endogamy. Though a modern economy and capitalism accelerated the end of the authoritarian clan system, endogamy or marriage within the home village, especially between cousins, remains a strong part of the modern culture. Kyrgyz families are usually large, with four to six children the average family size. In the cities, the number of children per family has decreased but is still large by Western standards. The Kyrgyz were nomads throughout most of their history, which is still reflected by Kyrgyz culture despite rapid urbanization. A long tradition of epic oral tales dates back at least 1,000 years. One of the most famous of the poems tells the story of Manas, the father of the Kyrgyz people, now considered the national hero. The epic, about twice as long as the *Iliad* and the *Odyssey* combined, can take up to three weeks to recite and was not available in written form until the 1920s. The Kyrgyz language, promoted by the government of Kyrgyzstan, is now more widely spoken, but Russian remains the language of business and commerce. Increasingly, English is taught as a third language of communication. Historically, the Kyrgyz religious beliefs focused on horses, as it was believed that a horse carried the spirit of a dead person to a better world. The Muslim religion, dominant in the Fergana Valley in the southwest for many centuries, did not gain a strong presence in many Kyrgyz districts until the 19th century. The Kyrgyz tend to be more secular and nonreligious in their daily life

than some of the neighboring Muslim peoples though Islam is now spreading into the northern districts where Soviet influence was the strongest, and many Kyrgyz had embraced Soviet atheism. Pre-Islamic beliefs, including shamans, most of whom are women, still play a prominent role in Kyrgyz funerals, memorials, ceremonies, and rituals. The nature of their nomadic lifestyle and the need for women's labor made the Islamic tradition of female seclusion an impractical extravagance. Kyrgyz women enjoy considerable rights and status; they are not veiled, and they are not forbidden from contact with non-kinsmen. Alcoholism, a serious problem during the decades of Soviet rule, has again resurfaced, and public drunkenness is now a visible problem in the cities, partly due to rising unemployment.

In the 1830s, one of the Kyrgyz tribes, backed by the Uzbek Khanate of Khokand, defeated the other Kyrgyz tribes, bringing them under the rule of the Uzbek khan as vassals. Under Khokand Uzbek rule, the Kyrgyz were heavily taxed, and other ethnic groups were resettled in their traditional territory. It was during this long period of upheaval that Islam became more firmly established among the Kyrgyz tribes. Continued conflicts between Kyrgyz tribes led to a request by one of the tribes for Russian protection in 1854. The Russians established a fort in the Kyrgyz town of Pishpek. In 1867, most of the northern Kyrgyz tribes accepted Russian protection against incursions by other tribes and against the Khokand tax collectors. Some Kyrgyz tribes, fearing Russian domination, migrated into the Pamir Mountains or into Afghanistan. The southern tribes launched

A Kyrgyz family in a traditional yurt. (Vassiliy Mikhailin/Dreamstime.com)

a widespread revolt against the Khokand Khanate in 1870. Russian advances into Uzbekistan ended Khokand's domination, but the Kyrgyz soon found themselves fighting the Russians. The southern tribes launched a *jihad* or holy war against the Christian Russians, but all the Kyrgyz tribes were forced to accept Russian rule in 1876. The Russian conquest of Central Asia began the destruction of the political and cultural unity of the Kyrgyz tribes. The situation was made more chaotic by the Russian policy of encouraging Slavic, Cossack, and German immigration to the region. The colonists took the best and most productive lands, greatly restricting the grazing lands available for the Kyrgyz herds of horses and cattle. Famine in the western parts of the Russian Empire

in 1891 and 1898, plus the completion of rail links to European Russia, brought a new wave of colonists to the region, further marginalizing the Kyrgyz clans to the less productive mountain and steppe regions. The loss of grazing lands began a long cycle of declining living standards in the region. Northern Kyrgyzstan was particularly hard hit, with economic hardships making it one of the most neglected and least developed areas in Russian Central Asia. Though the Kyrgyz were mostly untouched or unaware of the bloody war in Europe from 1914 to 1916, the acute need for manpower brought the war to the region. Some 250,000 Kyrgyz and other Central Asians were rounded up for military conscription into work battalions setting off a widespread revolt. The rebels attacked the Russian forts and garrisons and turned on the Christian colonists. Russian troops, hastily withdrawn from the front, were sent against the rebels, often attacking peaceful villages or clan groups that had not joined the rebellion. More than 150,000 Kyrgyz and others abandoned their homelands to flee across the border into Chinese territory. The rebellion was soon overtaken by the Russian Revolution of 1917, bringing new fighting to the region as the Bolsheviks, known as the Reds or Soviets, fought the supporters of the Russian Empire, known as the Whites. A Red victory in the region established Bolshevik rule in 1919. The complete defeat of the Whites in 1920 allowed the Reds to take complete control of Central Asia. The new Soviet authorities divided the Kyrgyz lands among several provinces of the newly created Turkestan Autonomous Soviet Socialist Republic. During the 1920s, the Soviets continued the policy of encouraging European colonization of the Kyrgyz territories. All groups advocating autonomy or ethnic rights were ruthlessly suppressed, and ethnic Russians filled the government posts in the region. The Soviet government divided Turkestan along ethnic lines in 1924, giving the Kyrgyz territory the status of an autonomous province, which was upgraded to the status of an autonomous republic in 1926. Ten years later, the area became a full member republic of the Union of Soviet Republics. In theory, the new republic was to be self-governing, but the reality was strict Soviet control, and a local government heavily dominated by communist cadres drawn from the European minority. The rise of Joseph Stalin, in the 1920s, began a process that profoundly affected the Kyrgyz people. The collectivization of all private property, including the vast Kyrgyz herds, and the political purges that eliminated most of the Kyrgyz political and cultural leadership, devastated the Kyrgyz. Brutal Stalinist polices were met by Kyrgyz resistance with many slaughtering their herds before fleeing south to Chinese territory, which brought even more repression and hardship to the region. Despite widespread resistance, by 1933, an estimated 67 percent of all Kyrgyz households had been collectivized. The traditional nomadic life ended with forced settlement on collectives and state farms. Irrigation projects increased cultivation and drew many former nomads to agriculture. Migration to the Russian-dominated towns and cities where Kyrgyz menial workers were needed also helped to end the power of the clan and tribal system in the 1960s and 1970s. The relaxation of strict Soviet rule that was inaugurated in the late 1980s had little effect on the Kyrgyz until ethnic rioting broke out in the Fergana Valley on the border between Kyrgyzstan and Uzbekistan left more than 200 dead and many injured or driven from their homes. Soviet attempts to quell the rising chaos and violence ended with the attempted coup in Moscow in 1991 leading to the collapse of the Soviet Union. Suddenly, the Kyrgyz were free of harsh Soviet control though the local Kyrgyz communist leadership quickly consolidated their hold on the republic. The Kyrgyz leadership declared the former Soviet republic independent of the collapsing Soviet Union on August 31, 1991. The former communist hierarchy quickly took on nationalist rhetoric as the new republic was consolidated. In the early

21st century, attempts to promote Kyrgyz culture and language have not been heavily pursued as it is opposed by the large non-Kyrgyz population in the republic, though cultural and religious activists are gaining support.

Further Reading

Antipina, Claudia, Temirbek Musakeev, and Rolando Paiva. *Kyrgyzstan*. Milan, Italy: Skira, 2007.

Embassy of the Kyrgyz Republic to the USA and Canada. "About Kyrgyzstan." Accessed July 31, 2013. http://www.kgembassy.org/index.php?option=com_content&view=article&id=99&Itemid=219&lang=en

Igmen, Ali. *Speaking Soviet with an Accent: Culture and Power in Kyrgyzstan*. Pittsburgh: University of Pittsburgh Press, 2012.

Tranum, Sam. *Life at the Edge of the Empire: Oral Histories of Soviet Kyrgyzstan*. Seattle: CreateSpace, 2012.

L

Lahu

The Lahu, sometimes known as Lahuna, Launa, Mussuh, Muhso, Musso, Massur, Masur, Co Sung, Co Xung, Guozhou, Kha Quy, Khu Xung, Kucong, or Kwi, are an ethnic group inhabiting the mountainous regions of Yunnan Province in southern China and neighboring regions of Myanmar, Vietnam, Thailand, and Laos. The Lahu population of China is estimated at 455,000 out of a total population of 750,000. The Lahu comprise the 56 officially recognized nationalities in the People's Republic of China. Their language forms part of the Loloish branch of the Tibeto-Burman language family. It is an official language in the Lancang Lahu Autonomous County in Yunnan. The Lahu traditionally practice an animist religion with pantheon of gods and spirits. Many of the Lahu in China have adopted the Buddhist religion of the neighboring peoples.

The ancestors of the Lahu are thought to have originated in the region of the upper Salween River basin in Yunnan. According to Lahu legend, their forebearers, who were hunters, began migrating southward to the lush grasslands of the Shan Plateau region that they discovered while pursuing a red deer. The early Lahu lived in tribal groups that often warred among themselves. Gradually, stronger peoples pushed them out of the fertile grasslands and into the less accessible mountains. Invading

Tai peoples took control of the plateau region in the seventh century CE. The Lahu retreated to mountain strongholds whenever their territories were threatened. In the eighth century CE, the rise of the Nanzhao state in Yunnan pushed the Lahu tribes even further south. In the ninth century, ethnic Burmans invaded the region from the south while the Han Chinese took greater control of the Lahu tribes in Yunnan. The Lahu tribes often paid tribute to the Chinese officials in exchange for being left to their traditional lifestyle. In the 14th century, Mahayana Buddhist monks entered the Lahu highlands converting many to the religion of the lowlands. Several peasant uprisings were supported by the Lahu between the 15th and 17th centuries, but military suppression by troops of the Qing dynasty ended the unrest, which was often led by Buddhist monks. By the early 18th century, the Lahu tribes in China had settled in their present homeland. Influenced by the feudal system of the neighboring Han Chinese and the Dai people, the Lahu adopted many of their customs and traditions. Under the influence of the neighboring peoples, most of the Lahu settled as farmers formed part of the feudal hierarchy dominated by Chinese officials, landlords, and rich peasants. Most of the Lahu lived as poor peasants or sharecroppers on marginal lands in the higher elevations.

The Lahu culture, divided by international borders, is basically the same across the region sometimes known as Lahuland. There are four major divisions based on geography and the color of their traditional clothing. The four—the Lahu Na or Black Lahu, Lahu Nyi or Red Lahu, Lahu Shi or Yellow Lahu, and She-Leh Lahu—mostly live in small villages at high altitudes along the Lancang River in Yunnan. Traditionally, Lahu culture is patrilineal, with inheritance passed down through the male line. Extended families often live together in large houses constructed on stilts, though in recent years, many of the traditional ways of life are changing. Most Lahu are free to choose marriage partners, though in areas heavily influenced by the Han Chinese, arranged marriages are common. The language of the Lahu belongs to the Loloish or Yi branch of the Lolo-Burman languages of the Tibeto-Burman language family. The Lahu language, like the Chinese dialects, is tonal with seven distinct tones. Because of the heavy cultural influence of the Han Chinese and Dai cultures, many Lahu also speak Mandarin or Dai as a second language. The majority of the Lahu retain their traditional spiritual beliefs that revolve around a supreme being, Geusha or Exia, who controls all other deities and the spirits that inhabit all living things. The large Buddhist minority often retain many of the customs and beliefs of their pre-Buddhist ancestors.

By the 19th century, the majority of the Lahu had settled in permanent villages, often under the control of Han Chinese or Dai landlords. Christian missionaries entered the region from Burma bringing Western-style education and new ideas to the region. The oppression of the landlords often led to conflict and local uprisings, resulting in punishments or the intervention of Chinese troops. Gradually, their tribal identities began to give way to the idea of larger ethnic group encompassing the many culturally and linguistically related tribes in the Yunnan highlands. During World War II, the fierce Lahu warriors harassed Japanese troops as guerrilla troops behind the front lines. At the end of the war, violence between the Chinese government and communist rebel groups escalated into the Chinese Civil War, often drawing in the non-Chinese ethnic groups in Yunnan. Lahu tribesmen in Yunnan often shunted aid to Lahu rebels fighting the domination of the Burmans in neighboring Burma in the 1950s. The victory of the communists in the civil war brought cadres to the region to reorganize the Lahu villages into communes with the farmers, hunters, and even women worked for the Chinese state. In the 1980s, new economic laws allowed many Lahu to work for themselves or to leave the farming communes to work their own land. A modest prosperity spread through the region in the 1990s. Renewed contact with the Lahu in neighboring countries resulted in a cultural revival that continues into the 21st century.

Further Reading

Gall, Timothy L. *Worldmark Encyclopedia of Cultures and Daily Life*. Farmington Hills, MI: Gale, 2009.

Lewis, Paul, and Elaine Lewis. *Peoples of the Golden Triangle*. London: Thames and Hudson, 1984.

The People's Daily Online. "The Lahu Ethnic Minority." Accessed July 30, 2013. http://english.people.com.cn/data/minorities/Lahu.html

Walker, Anthony R. *Merit and Millennium: Routine and Crisis in the Ritual Lives of the Lahu People.* New Delhi: Hindustani Publications, 2003.

Lhoba

The Lhoba, sometimes known as Luoba or Lhopa, are one of the 56 ethnic groups recognized as official nationalities by the government of the People's Republic of China, which is in reality a small group of diverse tribes living in Southeastern Tibet. The term *Lhoba* was created and is used by the government, while those designated as Lhoba refer to themselves by local or tribal names, names recognized by the communities themselves. The estimated 6,000 Lhoba in China are part of a much larger group that lives across the border in the Arunachal Pradesh region of India. The Lhoba speak various dialects of Tibetan and often speak Mandarin Chinese as a second language. The major religion is Tibetan or Mahayana Buddhism, the major religion in the Tibetan Autonomous Region of China.

The area that is home to the modern Lhoba is historically known as Lhoyü, the larger part of which is now in India. In the seventh century CE, Lhoyü came under the rule of the Tibetan state. Over centuries, the small tribes were oppressed, bullied, and faced discrimination by the Tibetan government, the powerful Tibetan landlords, and the even more powerful monasteries. A feudal system that relegated the Lhoba to the lower rungs of society as serfs, sharecroppers, or poor peasants persisted in the region until the modern era.

Considered by the sophisticated Tibetans as wild or savage, the Lhoba were forbidden to leave their home areas without permission and were not allowed to trade or interact with other ethnic groups. Intermarriage with ethnic Tibetans was banned. Their primitive farming methods resulted in low yields, so they supplemented their diets with gathering, hunting, and fishing. Though largely poor farmers, the Lhoba were skilled at making bamboo object and other crafts. They bartered their crafts, animal hides, musk, bear paws, dye, and live game for farm tools, wool, salt, clothing, grains, and tea from itinerant Tibetan traders. Their mandatory pilgrimages to the monasteries proved good opportunities to engage in barter and trade.

The Lhoba people designated as a distinct ethnic group by the Chinese government do not traditionally self-identify as a single people. The two major tribal groups that are included in the Lhoba designation are the Yidu or Idu Mishmi and the Bo'gaer or Bokar Adi, both of which are found in greater numbers in Arunachal Pradesh in India. The Chinese government also includes the Na or Bangni people as part of the Lhoba ethnic group. Each of the tribal groups maintains their own distinct culture and dialect often using Tibetan or Mandarin Chinese as a lingua franca. As a result of long contact with the Tibetans, their clothing, food, and other cultural elements are increasingly influenced by the Tibetans. The Lhoba tribes speak at least three mutually unintelligible languages, Idu Mishmi, Bokar (Adi), and Na, languages more widely spoken in Arunachal Pradesh. Hunting remains an essential part of the local culture with young boys taught to hunt at a young age. The game they catch is partially distributed to villagers, while the hunter keeps just enough for himself and his family. Traditionally, there were two classes among the tribal groups, the *maide* and the *nieba*. The *maide* considered themselves nobles while regarding the *nieba* as inferior. The *nieba* could never become nobles no matter the accumulation of wealth or learning. Intermarriage between the classes was forbidden. Many of the *nieba* were held as slaves until the mid-1950s. Women's status within the family, as well as in the culture, is particularly low. The Tibetan Buddhist religion is an integral part of the tribal cultures.

Members of Lhoba ethnic group wearing traditional costumes in Nyingchi, in the Tibet Autonomous Region in 2012. The Lhoba costume has been listed as part of China's intangible cultural heritage. (Liu Kun/Xinhua Press/Corbis)

Many of the Lhoba suffered endemic diseases caused by a lack of salt in the 19th century. The population of the poor, undernourished Lhoba tribes continued to decline well into the 20th century. Abuses by the noble class, the Tibetan authorities, and even rich peasants added to the suffering of the majority of the Lhoba. The Chinese invasion of Tibet in 1951 brought communist cadres to the region. The noble class was decimated, and the commoners were allowed to buy land, which was later collectivized by the state. In recent years, the Lhoba have adopted more advanced farming methods and have opened up new farmlands in the hills while developing sidelines such as hunting, bamboo weaving, and other handicrafts to sustain them during the winter. Advances in education, including adult evening classes, brought new spirit to the Lhoba cultures. Modern medicine has allowed the Lhoba to eliminate the many endemic diseases and the high infant morality rate. Transportation and communications with newly built bridges have opened up more of the region to trade and commerce.

Further Reading

Bell, Charles. *The People of Tibet.* New Delhi: Motilal Banarsidass, 2011.

Guo, R., and Luc Guo. *China's Provinces in Transition: Tibet.* New York: CreateSpace, 2012.

Ministry of Foreign Affairs of the People's Republic of China. "The Lhoba Ethnic Minority." Modified November 15, 2000. http://www.fmprc.gov.cn/eng/ljzg/3584/t17897.htm

Nyori, Tal. *History and Culture of the Adis.* London: SOS Free Stock, 1995.

Li

The Li, sometimes known as Hlai, Say, or Sai, are a large ethnic group living on Hainan Island off the southern coast of mainland China. The estimated 1.3 million form one of the 56 officially recognized nationalities of the People's Republic of China. The Li speak their own language, called Hlai, which forms one of the primary branches of the Tai-Kadai language family. Many of the Li still revere their traditional animist religious beliefs with a large and important Theravada Buddhist minority.

Mentioned in historical records of the Chinese Tang dynasty between 619 and 907 CE, the Li are believed to be the descendants of the ancient Yue people who established a kingdom known as Nanyue that flourished on the southern coast of the present-day mainland China from 204 BCE to 111 CE. A conflict with the Chinese of the Han dynasty resulted in a war that left Nanyue destroyed. The Li are believed, by many scholars, to have been refugees from the fallen kingdom who sought sanctuary on Hainan Island where they mixed with indigenous peoples who had inhabited the island as early as 3,000 years ago. Han Chinese began to settle on the island before the Qin dynasty (221–206 BCE) as farmers, fishermen, and traders. Under the Han dynasty, from 206 BCE to 220 CE, imperial troops were sent to pacify the island and to create prefectures and strengthen Chinese control. In the seventh century, under Han Chinese influence, the Li changed their historical communal form of living for a feudal society overseen by a noble class and powerful landlords. Many of the Li were

forced to work as serfs or sharecroppers on large Han or Li estates. Between the 7th and 10th centuries, Chinese rule of the island was reinforced, and the central government control of the Li territories was extended by setting up five Li prefectures made up of 22 counties overseen by Han Chinese administrators. Between the 10th and 13th centuries, rice cultivation was introduced from the mainland and irrigation of paddy fields developed. Due to the tropical weather, Li farmers were able to produce four crops annually. By the 14th century, most of the land on the island was in the hands of a small number of landlords who exploited the Li peasants by usury and exorbitant rents and tributes. The oppression of the Li kindled resentment and resulted in 18 large-scale Li uprisings between the 14th and mid-17th centuries, and 14 serious rebellions from the 17th to the early 19th centuries.

The Li culture forms one of the Tai cultures of southern China and is related to the cultures of the peoples of Thailand, Laos, and parts of Vietnam. Traditionally, the Li are divided into five regional and linguistic branches, known as Qi, Ha, Run, Sai, and Meifu, each with distinctive cultural traits and dialects. Traditionally, the Li were divided into clans or extended families that often lived in a single village and shared the labor and benefits of communal farming. Traditionally, the Li are monogamous, and close relatives are not allowed to marry. The communal farms, known as *hemu,* were divided into two types, a smaller farm based on maternal or paternal blood relations and larger farms that accepted outsiders or families with no blood ties to the member families. The village headman not only was in charge of production and distribution, but also officiated at religious ceremonies assisted by his wife. While cattle were owned communally, farm implements, hunting and fishing gear, and work tools were privately owned. The Li language, Hlai, forms a distinct branch of the Tai-Kadai language family. It is spoken in several dialects, some of which are divergent enough to be considered separate languages. In 2010, an estimated 25 percent of the Li were monolingual, while many spoke Mandarin Chinese, Cantonese, or the local Chinese dialect known as Hainanese along with Hlai. The majority of the Li continue to practice their traditional animist religion that includes belief in spirits, witchcraft, and ancestor veneration.

The feudal political and social system continued in the 19th century with increasing poverty and suffering of the Li farmers, often no better than serfs or slaves. With the extension of feudal privileges, many of the landlords and headmen were officially chosen to represent the central government in the island's administration. Abuses of power and the poor condition of most of the Li people resulted in a series of conflicts and minor uprisings well into the 20th century. The victory of the communists in the Chinese Civil War resulted in an invasion of the island in May 1950. Officially, the new Red Army remained on Hainan to fight bandits and despotic landlords, but a vicious campaign against the Li ended resistance to the new regime. Communist cadres dismantled the traditional villages and destroyed the upper classes. The Li were forced to move to communal farms and collectives under tight communist control. The Hainan Li-Miao Autonomous Prefecture was created in July 1952. Their language, written in Chinese characters prior to the mid-1950s, was given a Latin script by linguists in 1957. Though rapid advancement in education and modern farming methods aided the recovery of the Li culture, the Chinese Cultural Revolution, from 1967 to 1977, was a disaster. Red Guard units descended on the island to destroy ancient temples, shrines, and other Li cultural symbols. Assimilation into the Han Chinese culture, already well advanced in some areas, became the official policy. The rapid changes that swept through China in the 1980s also reached Hainan. The island, with a dependable climate, tropical fruits, and beautiful beaches and scenery, became a favorite holiday destination for the newly prosperous peoples of the Chinese mainland. By 2010, the Li, once the poorest of the island's inhabitants, had gained a modest prosperity.

Further Reading

Diller, Anthony, Jerry Edmondson, and Yongxian Luo. *The Tai-Kadai Languages.* London: Routledge, 2008.

Rossabi, Morris. *Governing China's Multiethnic Frontiers.* Seattle: University of Washington Press, 2005.

Schafer, Edward H. *Shore of Pearls: Hainan Island in Early Times.* Warren, CT: Floating World Editions, 2009.

Lisu

The Lisu, sometimes known as Anung, Lasaw, Lashi, Lasi, Lesou, Lisaw, Lishu, Liso, Loisu, Lusu, Shisham, Yaoyen, Yawyen, or Yawyin, are a mountain ethnic group concentrated in China's Yunnan Province with a large population in neighboring areas of Myanmar and smaller groups in Thailand and India. The Lisu are one of the 56 officially recognized nationalities in the People's Republic of China. The estimated 730,000 Lisu of Yunnan form part of the extended ethnic group numbering around 1.2 million. The Lisu language forms part of the Lisu-Lalo branch of the Loloish or Yi languages of the Tibeto-Burman language family. It is an official language in the Weixi Lisu Autonomous County and the Nujiang Lisu Autonomous Prefecture in Yunnan. Most of the Lisu practice a religion that is partly animistic, partly ancestor veneration, and partly place-based religion. There is also a Christian minority, the result of the 19th-century missionary activity.

The Lisu are believed by scholars to have originated in the eastern part of the Tibetan plateau. According to Chinese historical records and Lisu folk legends, their ancestors once lived along the banks of the Jinsha River and were ruled by two powerful tribes, the Wudeng and the Lianglin. In the 12th century, the Lisu of Wunnan came under the prefectural administration of the Mongol Yuan dynasty of China. Under the authority of the Ming dynasty, in the 17th century, the Lisu, who had no clans and therefore no family names, were arbitrarily given the last name Mu. Patriarchal slavery was established in the Nujiang River region in the 16th century and continued well into the 20th century. Gradually, the rural Lisu population split into classes with a class of landowners, including individual peasants, clan communal ownership, and public ownership by a clan or village. A landlord class developed, often owning the most fertile lands worked by slaves or Lisu serfs tied to the land by debt usury or local laws. As a result of the spread of the landlord economic system and the instability of the small peasant economy, more land came under the control of powerful clans, village chieftains, or rich landlord households. By the 18th century, an increasing number of Lisu had become landless, forced to work as sharecroppers or as hired farmhands on lands owned by Han Chinese, Naxi, and Bai landlords and hereditary chieftains.

In Lisu culture, the clan and village plan important part of the society. The *ka* or village is defined as a place where close family relatives lived together though some villages were inhabited by families of different clans. Every village has an acknowledged headman, generally an influential village elder. Apart from communal land and work, the clan members shared everything from wine or pork to the catch of fishermen or hunters. When a Lisu girl married, the clan shared in the betrothal gifts to her parents, and when a young Lisu man took a wife, the gifts to the bride's family were provided by the clan. Debts are also considered a clan matter, to be paid by all. These collective obligations and rights make daily life in the Lisu regions possible with clan relationships continuing from generation to generation. Traditionally, the Lisu worshiped a pantheon of gods, both of nature and of inanimate things. Shamans were consulted to make sacrifices to ghosts and were considered accurate fortune-tellers. The basic unit of Lisu society is the monogamous family with the youngest or the only son obliged to remain with the parents to care for them and to inherit their property. Female children have no right of inheritance. The Lisu of Yunnan speak two similar but mutually unintelligible dialects known as Lisu and Lipo or Eastern Lisu. The two are further divided into several regional dialects that have various amounts of loanwords from neighboring peoples. A Latin Lisu alphabet was introduced by the Chinese government in 1957, but the majority of the Lisu continue to use their former alphabet developed by two Protestant missionaries in the early 20th century.

In the 1820s, the Qing government of China sent officials to the Lijiang, Yongsheng, and Huaping regions, where the Lisu clans live in compact communities. The officials replaced the hereditary chieftains, mostly ethnic Naxi or Bai, with Han Chinese landlords. The changes soon ended the feudal system and replaced it with a landlord system, but for the poor Lisu peasants' life barely changed. The changes allowed closer control of the Lisu and other ethnic minorities in the region. Around the turn of the 20th century, large numbers of Han Chinese, Bai, and Naxi farmers moved into the traditional Lisu lands. Until the mid-1950s, the Lisu, under exploitation and oppression by landlords, petty officials, and local traders, were considered an inferior people to be used or abused. The arrival of communist officials, following the victory of the communists in the Chinese Civil War, greatly changed the life of the Lisu people. The landlord class was destroyed, either

Lisu in traditional clothing in Yunnan Province, China. (National Geographic Society/Corbis)

resettled or eliminated, while the official policy of glorifying the peasant helped the majority of the Lisu to gain access to fertile land. In 1954, the Nujiang Lisu Autonomous District was established, giving the Lisu some powers of self-government. Land redistribution allowed many Lisu to own farms of their own, though they were later taken over and added to communes or collectives worked by employees of the Chinese state. The excesses of the Chinese Cultural Revolution, in the 1960s and 1970s, gave way to the economic and political reforms of the 1980s. New capitalist incentives changed the way the Lisu farmed, with many turning to cash crops or tourism as these industries were allowed to profit from their work. In the early 21st century, many Lisu, having gained from the educational programs in Mandarin Chinese and their own language, prospered as merchants, teachers, and artists.

Further Reading

Durrenberger, E. Paul. *Lisu Religion.* Southeast Asia Publications Occasional Papers, No 13. DeKalb: Northern Illinois University, 1989.

Hattaway, Paul. *Operation China: Introducing All the People of China.* Pasadena, CA: William Carey Library Publications, 2003.

OMF International: *The Minority Peoples of China.* Singapore: Overseas Missionary Fellowship, 2006.

M

Macanese

The Macanese, sometimes known as Macaense, Makista, or Patuá, are a people of mixed Portuguese and Asian, mostly Chinese, ancestry with roots in the Macao Special Administrative Region, formerly the Portuguese colony of Macau in southeastern China. The estimated 50,000–75,000 Macanese live in Macao, with sizable communities in Portugal, Brazil, Hong Kong, the United States, Canada, and Peru. The Macanese usually speak the Cantonese dialect of Chinese, with many also speaking Portuguese and Patuá, a Creole language of mixed Portuguese, Cantonese, and other influences. The majority of the Macanese are Roman Catholic, with smaller numbers of Buddhists, Evangelical Christians, and Protestants.

The history of Macao, called Macau in Portuguese, can be traced back to archives of the Qin dynasty, 221–206 BCE, when the region formed part of the Nanhai prefecture. The first inhabitants of the coastal area were refugees fleeing the invading Mongol hordes in the 13th century. In 1535, Portuguese fishermen and their families gradually migrated to the coastal villages from Guangdong and Fujian Provinces, but Macao became an important settlement only after the settlement of Portuguese traders in the 1550s. The Chinese Empire, seeing advantages for trade, leased the settlement to Portugal as a trading post in 1557. Most of the colonists and traders sailed to Asia alone, leaving wives and families behind in Portugal. In Macao, the Portuguese men married or lived with Malay, Sinhalese, and Japanese women from the other Portuguese settlements in Asia, and later the local Cantonese people. By 1564, Portugal dominated European trade with Asia. Pope Gregory XIII created the Roman Catholic Diocese of Macau to administer to the needs of the growing Catholic population. Though demands by the increasing Portuguese population for self-administration were rejected, in 1583, the Chinese government allowed the formation of a local legislature to handle questions concerning the colony's social and economic affairs, but under strict supervision of the Chinese authorities. In 1631, the Chinese government restricted Portuguese commercial activity to the port of Macao. In the mid-17th century, the port town had a population of around 30,000 people, including 20,000 Chinese, 5,000 slaves, 2,000 Europeans, and some 3,000 people of mixed race that later came to be called Macanese. Macau prospered, and the population increased, including a large population of mixed European and Asian background. The colony's golden age, in the late 16th and 17th centuries, coincided with the political union of Spain and Portugal, opening Macau and the other Portuguese colonies to attacks by the Dutch, then at war with the Spanish. Despite Dutch attempts to conquer the colony, Macau slowly became one of the most important trade centers on the Chinese coast with both European and Chinese merchants settling in the port. As well as its importance as a trading post, Macao was the center of activity for Roman Catholic missionaries. Religious schools offered education in Portuguese to the growing number of mixed race children, making them among the first to experience European-style education in the colony. In 1685, the Portuguese lost their privileged position in the trade with China when the emperor decided to allow trade with all foreign countries. Over the next century, other European nations and the United States established offices and factories, often locating them in Macao.

The Macanese culture is a mixed culture of both European and Chinese influences. Portuguese traditions are dominant, but Chinese cultural patterns are also significant. For centuries, the Macanese acted as the contact point between the Portuguese colonial government and the Chinese. As the Portuguese officials sent to Macao knew little about the Chinese, who made up more than 90 percent of the colony's population and knew little about the Portuguese, the Macanese became the interpreters and the transmitters of information, laws, and business. Initially, the local Cantonese population refused to marry Europeans, but many Chinese became Macanese simply by converting to Roman Catholicism. Rejected by the non-Catholic Cantonese population, the Christian Cantonese began to marry into the European and Macanese elite. There is some dispute about the exact makeup of the Macanese ethnic group, which includes descendants of Chinese Christian converts along with the largely European descendants of the old Portuguese trading families. Traditionally, the basis of ethnic affiliation has been the Catholic religion and integration into Portuguese cultural patterns. The language of the Macanese, known as *Patuá*, meaning "patois," is a Creole language derived mainly from Portuguese, Cantonese, Malay, and Sinhalese and is now spoken by a few families in Macao and in the Macanese Diaspora. The language is listed by UNESCO as critically endangered as the number of speakers continues to decline. Most Macanese now speak Cantonese, Portuguese, or the language of the country where they live. The Roman Catholic faith of the Macanese is one of the elements of the culture that remains despite a decline in the language and traditions. Catholic traditions that evolved over many centuries in Macao often mark the difference between the Macanese and the other Eurasian groups.

The colony continued as an important trading center, but competition from other European trading posts on the Chinese coast took much of its Chinese trade in the early 19th century. Following the Opium War of 1839–1841, the British took control of nearby Hong Kong with its deepwater harbor that soon became the destination of most shipping in the region. The Portuguese authorities occupied nearby Taipa in 1851 and expanded to take control of Coloane in 1864. The addition of the two islands greatly expanded the territory of the colony. In 1887, the Chinese and Portuguese governments signed a new treaty recognizing the right of "perpetual occupation and government of Macao by

Portugal." Macao officially became a territory under direct Portuguese administration. Following the Chinese Revolution in 1911 and the later creation of a republican government, the status of Macao remained unchanged, and the port continued as one of the major smuggling centers on the Chinese coast. During World War II, the Japanese respected Portugal's neutrality, and Macao enjoyed a brief economic boom as the only neutral port in southern China. This period was seen as the height of the Macanese culture in Macao when the culture, music, dance, and cuisine were acknowledged by visitors to the neutral enclave. After Japan's surrender in 1945, the Chinese Civil War resumed until the victory of the Chinese communists in 1949. Although the new People's Republic of China denounced the Portuguese control of Macao as the product of "unequal treaties," they left the question of sovereignty until a more appropriate time. The overthrow of the Portuguese dictatorship in 1974 began the period of Portuguese decolonization. The African and other Portuguese possessions were granted independence, but Macao was redefined as a Chinese territory under Portuguese administration. Granted a large measure of administrative, financial, and economic autonomy, Macao experienced a resurgence of trade and a new flowering of the Macanese culture. The question of Macao's future, including negotiations between the Portuguese and Chinese governments in the late 1980s, began the exodus of the Macanese who feared for their future. Many left for Portugal, Brazil, and North America, while others adapted to the local Cantonese culture. The numbers in the Macanese exile grew

rapidly as agreements were made to turn Macao over to China in 1999. The transfer of power spurred yet another exodus of the Portuguese and Macanese from the territory, mostly to nearby Hong Kong, which was already under loose Chinese authority. The transfer agreement allowed Macao to continue as an autonomous region of the Chinese republic. By the early 21st century, the territory was one of the most important tourist destinations on the Chinese coast. The tourists, drawn to the territory by the large number of casinos, also enjoy the cuisine and unique culture of the remaining Macanese in Macao.

Further Reading

De Pina-Cabral, João. *Between China and Europe: Person, Culture and Emotion in Macao.* London: London School of Economics monographs on social anthropology, 2002.

Miu Bing Cheng, Christina. *Macau: A Cultural Janus.* Hong Kong: Hong Kong University Press, 1999.

Porter, Jonathan. *Macau the Imaginary City: Culture and Society, 1577 to Present.* Boulder, CO: Westview Press, 1999.

Zhidong, Hao. *Macau: History and Society.* Hong Kong: Hong Kong University Press, 2011.

Manchu

The Manchu, sometimes known as Man, Manchurians, Mandzhu, Mandju, Mandzhuri, or Niuchi, are a Tungus people, the indigenous people of the region known as Manchuria. The Manchu population of China is estimated to number between 10.5 and 11.5 million. The largest of the Tungus peoples, the Manchu are the fourth largest ethnic group in the People's Republic of China. Linguistically, the Manchu now speak dialects of northeastern Chinese or the standard Mandarin Chinese with only a few speaking only the Manchu language. The Manchu language belongs to the geographically widespread Manchu-Tungus group of Altaic languages. Most of the Manchu are officially Buddhist though there are sizable groups that adhere to their traditional belief system, have adopted Chinese Confucianism, or describe themselves as atheists or agnostics. The government of the People's Republic of China asserts that the Manchu people do not now, and never did, exist as a separate ethnic group but were merely one of the many regional and cultural groups that made up China's dominant Han Chinese ethnic group.

The ancestors of the Manchu, known since the seventh century CE as Jurchen or Sushen, appear in historic Chinese documents as Tungusic people inhabiting the northern Manchurian plains. The early Tungusic tribes were sometimes considered vassals of various Chinese dynasties, paying tribute but not under direct Chinese rule. In the 10th century, the Jurchen were chronicled by Chinese scholars as the inhabitants of the state of Balhae, traditionally founded in 698. At its height, the kingdom covered nearly all of Manchuria, eastern Mongolia, and northern Korea. Invading Khitan Mongol destroyed the kingdom in 926 with the Jurchen later becoming vassals of the Chinese Liao dynasty. In 1114, a Jurchen leader, Wanyan Aguda united the Jurchen tribes under a single ruler. His brother and successor, Wanyan Wuqimai, destroyed the Chinese kingdoms of the Liao and Northern Song and established the Jin dynasty.

During the rule of the Jin dynasty, the first Jurchen scripts, written in a script mainly derived from that of the Khitan Mongol, were produced in the 1120s. In 1206, the Mongol groups under Jin rule rose in eastern Mongolia. Their leader, Genghis Khan, led the Mongol warriors against the Jurchen, who were finally defeated in 1234. Under Mongol rule, the Jurchen were divided; those in the southern districts were treated as ethnic Chinese, while those in the Manchurian heartland were treated as ethnic Mongol, often adopting Mongol customs, names, and the Mongol language. The Chinese threw off Mongol rule in 1368, again relegating the Jurchen to the status of a vassal people. A second Mongol invasion of China, in 1449, began a period of chaos and widespread violence with some tribal leaders joining the Mongol attack while others remained loyal to the Chinese Ming dynasty. During this time, the Jurchen script was mostly abandoned as most adopted the Mongol script for use in written Jurchen. Ming reprisals against the Jurchen left many districts in ruins with many chieftains killed and populations displaced. A century after the time of chaos in the Jurchen homeland, a chieftain named Nurhaci, seeking revenge for the Ming slaughter of his family, including his father and grandfather in 1586, set about unifying the Jurchen tribes. He established a military system known as the Eight Banners and ordered scholars to create a new Jurchen script. In 1603, the tribal leaders and his Mongol allies recognized Nurhaci as the ruler of the Jurchen. In 1616, Nurhaci took the throne as the khan or emperor of the Jurchen. He then launched a widespread attack on the hated Ming dynasty of China, moving his capital to Mukden following the conquest of parts of northeastern China. His son and successor, Hong Taiji, changed the name of the ethnic group from Jurchen to Manchu and called their northern homeland Manchuria. In 1644, the Manchu defeated the Chinese and moved the capital to Beijing, thus establishing the Manchu Qing dynasty in China. Some four million Manchu formed an elite nobility, ruling a vast empire of more than 400 million Chinese subjects. Many Manchu followed the court to Beijing or scattered throughout China as military garrisons, government officials, or colonists. Following a series of border conflicts with the Russians, the Qing emperors realized the strategic importance of their Manchurian homeland and gradually sent many ethnic Manchu back to the region. The government protected the region as a place where traditional Manchu virtues could be encouraged and preserved, and as a reservoir of loyal military manpower. The emperors attempted to protect the traditional Manchu culture in a variety of ways, but most importantly by restricting the migration of Han Chinese to the region.

The Manchu, calling themselves Niuchi, which is thought to mean simply "people," are a robust people, on average some five inches taller than the majority of the Han Chinese. Even though most Manchu now speak Chinese dialects, they have maintained their distinct culture and traditions, particularly those living in the Manchu towns and villages in the northeast. The traditional beliefs of the Manchu are rooted in the early shamanism of their ancestors. Magical healers—the shamans—help women to bear children, cure illness, and shield people from danger or harm with their spells. Shamanism still exists in Manchu villages, but it disappeared long ago among the urban Manchu population. Traditional festivals such as the New Year festivities, when Manchu decorate their doors with red, yellow, white, and blue banners, are still celebrated by the majority of the Manchu. Some customs are related to sacrificial ceremonies, such as the sacrificial pig or other animal each family dedicates to its ancestors in the autumn. In spite of decades of communist rule, the Manchu tend to be better educated and more prosperous than the neighboring Chinese. Traditionally, the Manchu are farmers, though by 1990, more than half lived in urban areas. The extended family remains

The Last Emperor

Puyi, an ethnic Manchu, was the last emperor of China and the 12th and final ruler of the Manchu Qing Dynasty. While still a child, he became the Emperor of China, ruling from 1908 until his abdication, following the Chinese Revolution, in 1912. Briefly restored to the throne by a local warlord in 1917, Puyi remained a private citizen until 1934, when he was declared the Kangde Emperor of the Japanese-controlled Empire of Manchukuo in Manchuria, the land of his ancestors in northeastern China. He remained the figurehead ruler of Japanese Manchuria until the end of World War II. Puyi's life is the subject of Bernardo Bertolucci's 1987 film *The Last Emperor*.

the basis of the Manchu culture with three or four generations often living under one roof. Until the 1980s, the Chinese government published that the Manchu had been completely assimilated into Chinese culture, but since then, a cultural revival has arisen to reclaim their ancient culture and heritage. Successive Chinese governments since 1911 officially discouraged the Manchu language, a Southwest Tungusic language of the East Altaic group of languages, so it is now mostly spoken by older people and their grandchildren, who have taken a new interest in the Manchu language and culture.

The Manchu elite managed to maintain a brilliant and powerful Chinese government until about 1800, when they seemed to rapidly lose ability and energy. Manchu territory was threatened by the expansion of the Russians into the territories just to the north, while British, French, and other Europeans encroached on other parts of the empire. In 1860, the territory known as Outer Manchuria, now the southern part of the Russian Far East, was ceded under pressure to the Russian Empire. Increasingly, the imperial and provincial governments fell into deep financial problems and were unable to maintain order. The rapidly growing population also presented a serious problem. The Manchu government, having preserved Manchuria for the Manchu for decades, was finally forced by severe population pressure to allow non-Manchu settlement from 1878. Even restricted immigration quickly reduced the Manchu to the position of a minority in their own homeland. By 1900, the immigrant Han Chinese population made up around 80 percent of Manchuria's population. The Russians established a virtual protectorate over Manchuria as Manchu power waned. The Japanese, after defeating Manchu China in a brief war in 1895, sought to extend their influence in the mineral-rich region. Continuing Russian encroachments prompted the government to allow unlimited immigration in 1896. The rivalry between Russia and Japan for control of Manchuria led to war in 1904–1905 allowing the victorious Japanese to consolidate their economic and political influence in Manchuria. Under Japanese influence, the region was industrialized and large urban centers evolved, bringing new waves of Han Chinese immigration. The long decline of the once powerful Manchu finally ended with the Chinese Revolution of 1911. The last of the Manchu dynasty, the child Pu-Yi, was deposed, and China was proclaimed a republic. The Manchu Qing dynasty ruled China from 1644 to 1912, one of the longest dynasties to ever rule China. The Manchu language was eliminated as a national language, and Manchu culture was scorned as a foreign culture. Chinese nationalists portrayed the Manchu as foreign colonizers even though many reform-minded Manchu supported the revolution. Many Manchu took on Chinese names to avoid persecution. The official Manchu population in China fell by half by 1920. The Japanese took advantage of the chaos in China to take control of most of Manchuria in 1931. Encouraged by the Japanese authorities, a small group of Manchu nationalists declared the independence of Manchukuo, the Manchu State, in 1932. The deposed emperor of China, Pu-Yi, was crowned as the emperor of Manchukuo though the Japanese actually governed the state. Japan's defeat in World War II ended the separate existence of Manchuria, which was reincorporated into China, and the Manchu were recognized as one of China's ethnic minorities. The communist government of the Soviet Union supported the Chinese communists during the post–World War II civil war against the pro-Western government from 1945 to 1949. With the Chinese communist victory, the Soviet Union retained considerable influence in Manchuria. The Manchurian leader Kao Kang, for his support of the communists, was made head of an autonomous Manchurian state in 1949. Accused of attempting to resurrect Manchu independence in 1954, he was dismissed and disappeared. Manchuria was divided into three Chinese provinces. The communist authorities decreed that no separate Manchu people had ever existed and banned the use of the names Manchu or Manchuria and all references to over 200 years of Manchu rule in China. Following the communist revolution, the Manchu received better treatment. In the 1953 official census, some 2.5 million people self-identified as ethnic Manchu. Persecuted during the Cultural Revolution from 1967 to 1977, tens of thousands of Manchu registered as ethnic Han Chinese. The relatively relaxed period of the 1980s allowed the Manchu to begin the recuperation of their history and culture. In 1990, for the first time in decades, the Manchu were counted as a minority people in the official Chinese census. Between 1982 and 1990, the official count of ethnic Manchu more than doubled, making them China's fastest-growing ethnic group. The rapid increase was not due to natural increase but instead was due to people formerly registered as Han Chinese applying for official recognition as ethnic Manchu. In the 1990s and into the early 21st century, there has been a renaissance of the distinctive Manchu culture and language, even among large numbers of Han Chinese fascinated with the history of the Manchu period of China's past. The Northeast Region, formerly Manchuria, has seen its heavy industries fading and a serious economic decline among the prosperous Manchu population as the provinces farther south became the engines of Chinese economic growth. The modern Manchu are more similar to an ethnic community that encompasses not only the descendants of the ancient Jurchen but also a large number of Manchu-assimilated Han Chinese and Mongol groups. However, groups considered Manchu under the Qing dynasty until the early 20th century, such as the Solon, Xibe, and Nanai peoples, have been separated from the Manchu as distinct ethnic groups by the government of the People's Republic of China. The Manchu cultural revival has been accompanied by a new interest in traditional activities, including riding, archery, and Manchu wrestling. Ice-skating, long a Manchu pastime, has become a popular activity across the northeastern provinces.

Further Reading

Crossley, Pamela Kyle. *The Manchus.* Hoboken, NJ: Wiley-Blackwell, 2002.

Elliott, Mark C. *The Manchu Way: The Eight Banners and Ethnic Identity in Late Imperial China.* Palo Alto, CA: Stanford University Press, 2001.

Giles, Herbert. *China and the Manchus.* Seattle: CreateSpace, 2012.

Manchu Studies Group. Accessed July 30, 2013. http://www.manchustudiesgroup.org/

Society for Anglo-Chinese Understanding. "Barbarian Empire." Accessed July 31, 2013. http://www.sacu.org/manchu.html

Mansi

The Mansi, sometimes known as Maansi, Vogul, Yugra, or Jugra, are an Ob-Ugrian people living in the basin of the Ob River in western Siberia. The Mansi homeland, originally known as Yugra, now forms part of the Autonomous District of Khanty–Mansi, part of Tyumen Oblast in the Russian Federation. The Mansi, who call themselves *Maan's'I*, originally meaning simply "human being" or "man," were formerly known as Vogul, their name in the Komi and Khant languages. Komis often guided Russian expeditions into the Ob River so their name for the ethnic Mansi was adopted. The estimated 15,000 Mansi speak a language of the Ob-Ugrian subgroup of the Ugric language group, which also includes Hungarian. The Mansi are nominally Orthodox Christians, but retain many of their pre-Christian traditions.

The origins of the Mansi are not clear, with several theories espoused by scholars and historians. Archaeological research indicates that the ancestors of the Mansi, the Khanty, and the Hungarians inhabited the western Siberian taiga and forested tundra 3,000–4,000 years ago. One theory suggests that the ancestors of the three ethnic groups originated in the basin of the Pechora River in Northern European Russia before migrating across the Ural Mountains to the Ob River region in the first century BCE. Others believe that the Ugrian peoples originated east of the Urals from a mixture of Uralian and other indigenous peoples. Many scholars believe that around 500 CE, the Ugrian peoples were forced to abandon their original homeland and move northeast across the Urals to settle in the Ob River valley, while their kinsmen moved farther west in a great migration to settle in the Hungarian Plain in Central Europe. The first European reference to the Mansi, then known as Yugra, appeared in the *Tale of the Bygone Years*, published in Novgorod in 1096. Archives of the 12th and 13th centuries record frequent expeditions from Novgorod to the region to collect tribute from the Ob-Ugrian tribes in the form of sable, ermine, Arctic fox, and other valuable furs much in demand in Europe. By the 14th century, the Mansi had been renamed Vogul. In the late 16th century, the Cossacks that led Russia's expansion across the Ural Mountains into Siberia took control of the Ob region. The Mansi, amazed by iron and steel implements, and later by firearms, were slowly brought under the authority of the colonial administration. Russian towns founded in the region became trading centers. In 1708, the Ob region was made part of the new province of Siberia, created to exploit the riches of the vast territory. Under tsarist rule, the region gained notoriety as a place of exile in Siberia for criminals and political prisoners. Missionaries from the Russian Orthodox Church began the conversion of the Mansi in the late 1700s. Though most of the Mansi tribes were officially converted to Christianity, they also retained powerful elements of their indigenous religious beliefs. As the numbers of fur-bearing animals rapidly decreased, the tsarist government lost interest in the region and in the well-being of its indigenous peoples.

Mansi culture reflects the harsh environment of their homeland with customs and traditions based on the forests and frozen swamps of the Ob River valley. Traditionally, the Mansi were grouped into a tribal system of patrilineal clans divided geographically into three distinct ethnographic groups—northern, southern, and eastern. Each of the three groups maintained distinct cultural and dialectical elements as part of the larger Mansi culture. The ancient traditions of the Mansi severely restricted the rights and movements of women. The presence of women was thought to defile religious articles, and women were considered a temptation to clan and family members; therefore, they were veiled to hide their faces. The Mansi language, spoken over a large area along the Ob River and its tributaries, is closely related to the neighboring Khanty language and more distantly related to modern Hungarian. The Mansi

now routinely use Russian, the language of education and administration, so that their own language is considered in danger of extinction. Two of the four major dialects are already considered extinct, and less than a third of the Mansi ethnic group is now able to speak their indigenous language. The written form of the language, invented by Orthodox missionaries in the 19th century, was first published in 1868, and in 1937, the Mansi alphabet was replaced with the Russian Cyrillic script. Officially, the Mansi are Orthodox Christians though their beliefs are an eclectic mix of institutional Christian religion and a large, rich folk belief system that revolves around the environment, fauna, and flora of western Siberia.

A member of the Mansi tribe, one of the indigenous tribes of the Khanty-Mansiy region of western Siberia, near his small wooden home in Yasund, near Saranpaul, Russia. (Jerome Levitch/Corbis)

European traders and colonists from Russia began encroaching on the historic grazing and hunting grounds of the Mansi in the early 19th century. Economically subjugated by a combination of accumulated debt and alcohol provided by Russian merchants and government officials, the Mansi were often held as virtual slaves. Well into the 20th century, the Mansi remained largely a nomadic people living by trapping, hunting, and fishing, while those in the northern districts engaged in reindeer herding. In the wake of the Bolshevik revolution in 1917, the European presence in their homeland intensified. A special government department, the Committee of the North, created in 1924, introduced the basic elements of communist administration, along with primary medical care and schools. The new Soviet authorities also launched a campaign to end the subjugation of women and to persuade Mansi women to unveil their faces. As part of the Soviet reorganization of western Siberia, an Ostyak-Vogul National Area was created in 1930–1931. Even though in theory the Ob-Ugrian Mansi and Khanty were to be allowed self-government, the reality was a program of assimilation of the tribal peoples into the larger Soviet culture. Compulsory attendance of Mansi children at Russian language schools introduced younger Mansi to the Russian-Soviet culture. Over decades of Soviet rule, the Mansi were inducted into a wider Soviet culture, losing much of their traditional culture and language. The homeland, rich in minerals and petroleum, began to be heavily exploited in the 1960s, drawing in tens of thousands of settlers and inundating the region in an ongoing environmental crisis. The collapse of Soviet power in 1991 brought demands for Mansi and Khanty participation in the decisions affecting their ancient homeland, but the reality is a highly endangered culture and language and rapidly increasing medical problems due to oil spills and chemical pollution.

Further Reading

Forsyth, James. *A History of the Peoples of Siberia: Russia's North Asian Colony 1581–1990.* Cambridge: Cambridge University Press, 1994.

Olson, James S. *An Ethnohistorical Dictionary of the Russian and Soviet Empires.* Westport, CT: Greenwood, 1994.

Quartly, Alan. "Siberia's Dying Mansi People." *BBC News, World Edition.* September 5, 2002. http://news.bbc.co.uk/2/hi/europe/2238333.stm

Slezkine, Yuri. *Arctic Mirrors: Russia and the Small Peoples of the North.* Ithaca, NY: Cornell University Press, 1996.

Maonan

The Maonan, sometimes known as Anan, are one of the officially recognized nationalities of the People's Republic of China. The estimated 118,000 Maonan are concentrated in the rugged northern part of the Guangxi Zhuang Autonomous Region in southwestern China and the southern part of Guizhou Province. The Maonan speak a language of the Tai-Kadai language group spoken across southern China. The majority of the Maonan follow Daoism with a sizable minority that continues to revere their traditional animist beliefs.

The Maonan believe that their ancestors migrated from the north to settle in the subtropical highlands north of the related

Zhuang people. A system of classes with the majority under the authority of a ruling class developed under the influence of the Zhuang and the growing number of Han Chinese in the region. Historically, the Maonan are believed to be the descendants of the Liao and Linren peoples, derived from the larger Tai-Kadai ancestral people, the Baiyue. Chinese historical archives note the presence of the Maonan in the area near the border of Guangxi and Guizhou Provinces some 1,800 years ago. They were known as Junnan or Ainan, which means people of Maonan or Three Souths. In the first and second centuries CE, the Maonan homeland was mentioned as a subtropical region characterized by a mild climate and beautiful rugged scenery and patches of flatlands available for farming. The many small streams were used to irrigate rice paddies though in the mid-17th century, the Maonan still used wooden hoes and ploughs. Over the next century, iron tools were introduced when the fertile lands were gradually concentrated in the hands of the ruling class, and the division of the classes became distinct. The growth of a ruling landlord class was paralleled by the appearance of farm laborers who did not own land, poor peasants holding just small amounts of land, self-sufficient peasants with sufficient land, and the landlords and rich peasants who owned the majority of the fertile lands in the region. The peasants were often exploited by high rents and usury. The region was famous for the slave girls either bought from the poor peasants or forced into slavery by unpaid debts.

The Maonan culture is a Tai culture heavily influenced by Han Chinese and Zhuang Tai influences. Maonan with the same surname and from the same clan usually live together in small villages of not more than 100 households. More than 80 percent of the Maonan share the same family name of Tan. The people named Tan believe that their ancestors moved south from Hunan to settle in the region and to marry local Tai women. Other frequent surnames are Lu, Meng, Wei, and Yan, who claim that their ancestors came to the region from Shandong and Fujian Provinces. The Maonan, besides being farmers, are expert herdsmen of beef cattle, which are marketed as far away as Shanghai, Guangzhou, and Hong Kong. Marriage patterns are mostly monogamous, while historically marriages were arranged by the parents. Old customs regarding marriage are still honored such as "never settle in the home of the husband" or "a widow should be married to the deceased younger brother." The Maonan population grew from about 38,000 in 1982 to 72,000 in 1990. Most of the population growth was not biological, but resulted from the official inclusion of the Yanghuang people as part of the official Maonan ethnic group in 1990. The Maonan language forms part of the Dong-Sui branch the Zhuang-Dong group of the Tai-Kadai languages. Only about half the Maonan now use their mother language as their first language, and its use is decreasing. Many now speak Mandarin Chinese or Zhuang, the language of their populous neighbor to the south. The Maonan Daoist beliefs, influenced by Buddhism and animism, include an annual temple festival. It is held to commemorate the patron of the Maonan people, San Jie. He is honored as the man who taught the Maonan to breed oxen for plowing, therefore enabling them to grow sufficient food to escape famine.

By the early 19th century, the landlords and rich peasants, making up less than 4 percent of the population, controlled more than 35 percent of the fertile lands. The sharecroppers and peasant farmworkers, who made up 54 percent of the population, owned only some 18 percent of the fertile land. Rents for farmlands were very high, and most of the Maonan peasants were constantly in debt to the landlords. Many daughters of Maonan households were seized and became slaves of the landlords if the family was unable to pay the high rents and the accumulated debt. In the early 20th century, many of the discontented Maonan joined organizations seeking to better the lives of the ordinary people. Some joined the new communist group organized in the 1920s. Conflicts between the communists and the government continued through World War II, then erupted into a widespread war known as the Chinese Civil War. The victorious communists arrived in the Maonan region in the early 1950s. They confiscated the lands of the landlord class and the rich peasants, who were eliminated or sent to reeducation camps, and began the redistribution of the farmlands. The individual farms were later taken back to form part of communes and cooperatives worked by the Maonan peasants. The relative relaxation of stringent communist rule in the 1980s allowed the Maonan to again hold personal property and to augment their incomes selling handicrafts, beef cattle, and the clothing for which they are famed throughout the area.

Further Reading

Ethnic Groups. "The Maonan Ethnic Minority." Accessed July 31, 2013. http://www.china.org.cn/e-groups/shaoshu/shao-2-maonan.htm

Harrell, Stevan. *Cultural Encounters on China's Ethnic Frontiers.* Seattle: University of Washington Press, 2000.

MacKerras, Colin. *China's Minorities: Integration and Modernization in the Twentieth Century.* Oxford: Oxford University Press, 1994.

McCarthy, Susan K. *Communist Multiculturalism: Ethnic Revival in Southwest China.* Seattle: University of Washington Press, 2009.

Miao

The Miao, sometimes known as Meo, Miautso, or Hmong, form one of the largest of the 56 officially recognized nationalities in the People's Republic of China. Miao is the official government name for four distinct groups who are only distantly related through culture or language, including the Hmu people of southeast Guizhou, the Qo Xiong in western Hunan, the A-Hmao people of Yunnan, and the Hmong people of Guizhou, Guangxi, Yunnan, and Sichuan. There are an estimated 9.8 million people designated as Miao in China, of whom the Hmong make up about a third. Outside China, there are large Miao/Hmong populations in Vietnam, Laos, the United States, Thailand, Myanmar, France, Australia, and French Guiana.

Scholars believe that the Miao peoples were among the first to settle in the territory of present-day China. Scientists have connected the Miao to the Daxi culture that flourished in central China from about 5,300 to 6,000 years ago. The Daxi culture, which occupied the middle Yangtze River region, has been credited with being the first to cultivate rice in East Asia. The Daxi, also known as Jiuli, fought a long series of wars with the ancestors of the Han Chinese to the north. As the Han Chinese expanded in the Daxi lands, a major war was fought near the site of present-day Beijing. Miao legends tell about victories in the first 9 battles but a devastating defeat in the 10th, prompting the Daxi to migrate south into the lower reaches of the Yellow River, where they established a new kingdom some 4,000 years ago. History repeated itself, and the ancestors of the Han Chinese again threatened the Miao kingdom known as San-Miao. In the ensuing war in about 2200 BCE, the Miao were again defeated and were largely exterminated by the Han Chinese leader known as Yu the Great. The remnants of the Miao people, also known as the Chiyou tribe after a legendary leader, under attack by tribes moving in the region from the north and west, moved south, southwest, and southeast while splitting into two smaller tribes, the Miao and the Li. The Miao continued moving to the southwest, while the Li moved to the southeast as the ancestors of the Han Chinese continued to expand southward. The name *Miao* was first used by the Han Chinese before the advent of the Qin dynasty in 221 BCE. The name was used to designate non-Han groups in the south. Successive Chinese dynasties mostly left the Miao peoples to govern themselves, demanding only an annual tribute. In the 1300s and 1400s, a series of uprising by the various Miao peoples and other indigenous groups in southern China came to be known as the Miao rebellions. During one of the first uprisings, in the 1370s, several thousand Muslim Uyghur warriors were sent by the Ming emperor to crush the rebels. The Muslims ended the rebellion and were settled in the region, often on lands confiscated from the defeated rebels. Another serious rebellion broke out in 1449 led by the Miao peoples. The uprising spread throughout the provinces of Guizhou and Huguang. Guizhou was overrun and sacked by imperial troops in 1459–1460. The Ming commander ordered many of the surviving Miao boys to be castrated so they would be unable to reproduce. Many towns were looted and destroyed and their surviving inhabitants sold into slavery. Several serious rebellions broke out in the 1460s, which were often brutally crushed during campaigns of extermination that left thousands dead. Many of the Han Chinese soldiers sent to crush the Miao uprisings were then settled in the depopulated districts as colonists, often given land and captured Miao women. In 1502, the Ming government began to abolish the rule of Miao feudal lords, appointing court officials that were subject to the Qing and could be recalled. The Qing dynasty, established following the Manchu conquest of China in 1644, sought to control the aboriginal peoples through direct control resulting in three separate wars between the Miao peoples and the Chinese Empire. In 1735, in the southeastern province of Guizhou, the Miao rose up against attempts at forced assimilation into Han Chinese culture. By the time the revolt was ended in 1738, an estimated half of the Miao population had been affected by the war. The second war, fought between 1795 and 1806, spread through the provinces of Guizhou and Hunan. The revolt again ended in failure, but it required the Qing dynasty 11 years to quell the uprising.

The Chinese name for the aboriginal peoples, Miao or Meo, means "savage" or "uncivilized," which is one of the reasons many Miao now use the name *Hmong*, meaning "free." The Miao/Hmong populations of China and Southeast Asia, now numbering as many as 12 million, represent between 70 and 80 separate groups, each with its own dialect, customs, and style of dress. Due to centuries of warfare, forced assimilation, and migrations, the Miao peoples have been divided into five major branches: Hong (red), Hei (black), Bai (white), Hua (flowery), and Qing (green), designations often based on the color of the clothing. The legends, folktales, religious beliefs, and music of all Miao groups are similar, and all still venerate the legendary leader Chiyou. Though their culture and traditions are very similar, a few important practices and traditions are peculiar to the Miao/Hmong of China and those in Southeast Asia. The Miao usually prefer to live in exclusively Miao villages or districts of larger towns but not in mixed ethnic neighborhoods. The Miao languages belong to the Hmongic branch of the Hmong-Mien group of the Austo-Thai branch of the Sino-Tibetan languages. The language is broadly divided into three major dialectical branches further divided into 30 to 40 mutually unintelligible subdialects. The Miao dialects, like the Chinese dialects, are tonal with the number of tones varying from dialect to dialect. The Hmu dialect spoken in Guizhou Province is designated by the Chinese government as the standard. The majority of the Miao practice their own animist religions, which usually involves the worship or veneration of demons, nature spirits, and the spirits of the ancestors. The spirits are traditionally appeased through animal sacrifices and the burning of "paper money." Over time, some groups have adopted Buddhism with a small number belonging to various Christian sects, the result of missionary activity in the early 20th century.

An elderly Miao (Black Hmong) woman selling goods in the Bac Ha market in northern Vietnam in 2013. (Pal Szilagyi-Palko/Demotix/Corbis)

Politically and militarily, the Miao peoples continued to be a problem for the Chinese Empire. In the mid-19th century, the largest of the three modern Miao wars broke out in 1854 in Guizhou Province. The revolt affected more than a million people and spread to all the neighboring provinces. By the time the widespread revolt had been defeated in 1873, only an estimated 30 percent of the Miao population were left. The war and defeat resulted in a large migration of Miao/Hmong out of Chinese territory into the northern parts of Southeast Asia in Vietnam, Laos, Thailand, and Myanmar. The imperial government established many military garrisons in Miao regions with many of their descendants still present in these regions to the present. Political and monetary means were used to speed the assimilation of the Miao, including the creation of many prestige posts for Miao willing to work for the Qing dynasty. Opium became the largest cash crop in the region, mostly sold to government agents or foreign firms. The landlord system continued to expand with more and more fertile land coming under the control of landlords and rich peasants, while the number of landless Miao peasants continued to rise. Many Miao joined subversive and antigovernment organizations, including the nascent communist party, in the early years of the 20th century. The growing conflict between the communists and the government drew in many Miao communities in the years before World War II. A truce between the two sides in order to fight the common Japanese enemy ended in 1945, and the Chinese Civil War resumed. The victorious communists moved into the Miao regions in 1950–1951, overthrowing the landlords and rich peasants while glorifying the simple peasants. Land redistribution continued until the government decision to collectivize all land in communes worked by the peasants as employees of the state. The Miao made great strides in education, health, and production until the Chinese Cultural Revolution (1967–1977) that resulted in many Red Guard units destroying Miao temples, shrines, and historic sites. Assimilation was once again official government policy and remained so until the relaxation of stringent communist rule in the 1980s. The new economic incentives and China's opening to the world market allowed many Miao to reestablish ties with their kin in other countries and to begin developing industries and trade goods instead of staying on unproductive small farms.

Further Reading

China: Facts and Details. "Miao Minority: History, Religion, Men, Women." Last updated April 2010. http://factsanddetails.com/china.php?itemid=174&catid=5

Jenks, Robert Darrah. *Insurgency and Social Disorder in Guizhou: The Miao Rebellion, 1854–1873.* Honolulu: University of Hawaii Press, 1994.

Schein, Louisa. *Minority Rules: The Miao and the Feminine in China's Cultural Politics.* Durham, NC: Duke University Press, 2000.

Tapp, Nicholas, Jean Michaud, Christian Culas, and Gary Yia Lee, eds. *Hmong/Miao in Asia.* Chiangmai, Thailand: Silkworm Books, 2004.

Mongol

The Mongol, sometimes known as Mongolians, are more properly described as Mongolic peoples. They are a Central–North Asian ethnolinguistic group encompassing up to 30 million people in China, Mongolia, and Russia with smaller groups in South Korea, the United States, Europe, Japan, and Central Asia. The largest Mongol population centers are in Mongolia, in the Inner Mongolia and Xinjiang regions of northwestern China, and the Buryat and Kalmyk republics in the Russian Federation. The groups forming the core of the Mongol peoples in Mongolia and Chinese Inner Mongolia include the Khalkha, numbering around 2.2 million, the largest ethnic group in Mongolia, and the 4.75 million Mongol, also known as Southern Mongol, divided into the Chakhar, Khorchin, Kharchin, Bairin, and Ordos (Tumet), in Inner Mongolia. An estimated six million Mongol, including such groups as the Oirat and Buryat, are counted as Mongol in China. These groups speak various dialects of what is known as Mongolian proper, the dialects spoken in the Mongol heartland of Mongolia and Inner Mongolia. The Tibetan form of Buddhism, Lamaism, is the most widely practiced religion in the region, with smaller numbers of Muslims, Christians, and other religions. In some areas, the ancient shamanistic beliefs are still revered.

The name *Mongol* originated from a tribal group called Mengwushiwei in the 10th century CE Chinese chronicle known as *Jiu Tang Shu, The Ancient History of the Tang Dynasty*. During the rule of the Yuan dynasty, from 1271 to 1368, the name was changed to Mongol and was gradually used as a common name for many nomadic tribes on China's borders. The Mongol tribes originally inhabited the east bank of the Erguna River in the central part of present-day Inner Mongolia. Around the seventh century, the Mongol nomads began to migrate into the grasslands to the west. By the 12th century, they had spread to the upper reaches of the Onon, Rerulen, and Tola Rivers east of the Kente Mountains. A local tribal chief, Temujin, began to unify the various tribal confederations in the vast plains that now make up Mongolia and Inner Mongolia. Later known as Genghis Khan, the great leader, he launched the Mongol invasions of the neighboring khanates, and farther into the Caucasus, the Middle East, and south into China. The neighboring Turkic peoples were annexed to the emerging empire, becoming part of the Mongol hordes. The Mongol invasions were often accompanied by wholesale massacres of the conquered civilian populations, the destruction of cities and irrigation systems, and the death of most humans and animals in the regions overrun by the Mongol hordes. By the end of his life in 1227, his Mongol empire occupied a large portion of Central Asia, China, and parts of Siberia. He divided the empire among his sons and grandsons, each to receive a separate khanate. Genghis Khan was buried somewhere in present-day Mongolia at an unknown location. His heirs continued the expansion of the Mongol Empire across most of the Eurasian landmass, creating vassal states in China, Korea, the Caucasus, Central Asia, and large parts of Eastern Europe, Russia, and the Middle East. The expanding Mongol Empire carried out military campaigns across a territory that stretched from the Adriatic Sea in Europe to Java in Southeast Asia and from Japan to the Middle East. By 1240, the Mongol, known as the Golden Horde, established their rule over Russia, and by 1279, the Mongol hordes had brought all of China under their rule. Many of these conquests were accompanied by the large-scale slaughter of local populations, giving Mongol a fearsome place in local histories. Genghis Khan also advanced the Mongol peoples in culture and politics. He decreed the adoption of the Uyghur writing system for the Mongol languages, promoted religious tolerance within the expanding empire, and created a firm bond between the nomadic tribes later collectively known as Mongol. The Khalkha consider Genghis Khan the founding father of the modern

Mongolian state. Under the rule of Kublai Khan, in the mid to late 13th century, the Mongol Empire began to splinter and, by the time of his death in 1294, had fractured into four separate empires or khanates, each under a descendant of Genghis Khan but each pursuing its own separate objectives and interests. The Khanate of the Golden Horde ruled Russia, Siberia, and the northwestern territories, the Chagatai Khanate in Central Asia and the Ilkanate in the southwest, from present-day central Turkey into Pakistan, and the Mongol Yuan dynasty controlled the Chinese Empire. In 1304, the three western khanates agreed to the nominal authority of the Yuan emperors, but after the overthrow of the Yuan by the Han Chinese Ming dynasty in 1368, the great Mongol Empire was finally ended though Mongol-descended states continued to control larges areas of Asia, the Middle East, and Europe. In the late 14th century, the supremacy of the Mongol in Mongolia and Central Asia was challenged by the Oirat, sometimes known as Western Mongol tribes. The Mongol groups of Mongolia and Inner Mongolia came under the rule of Dayan Khan, who reunited the central Mongol peoples in the mid-15th century. Under Dayan Khan, the Khalkha emerged as the dominant tribe in Mongolia and Inner Mongolia. The Manchu conquered the southern Mongol confederation of Inner Mongolia in 1635. The Manchu then moved south to conquer China in 1644. The Khalkha and other Mongol tribes of Outer Mongolia maintained their independence until they had to seek the aid of the Manchu Qing Dynasty against the Oirat Dzungar in 1688. By 1691, all of the central Mongol tribes had been brought under the loose authority of the Manchu rulers of China. In Inner Mongolia, the Mongol territories were added to Manchu China, while Outer Mongolia retained much autonomy under local khans and nominal Manchu rule. The Manchu extended their rule to the west in the 18th century, bringing other Mongol and Turkic peoples under their rule. The destruction of the Oirat Dzungar Empire in northern Xinjiang in 1755–1757 ended the largest threat to Manchu authority in the Mongol lands.

The Mongol culture is a collection of similar historical cultures that, over many centuries of interaction, has evolved into the modern Mongol societies mostly distinguished by dialectical rather than cultural differences. The largest of the Mongol groups of Mongolia is the Khalkha, who make up about 86 percent of the population of the Republic of Mongolia. Other large Mongol groups, living mostly in Chinese Inner Mongolia, Xinjiang, Qinghai, Gansu, and in the northeastern provinces of China are the Khorchin, with an estimated population of 2.5 million; the Kharchin, numbering around 1.8 million; the Chakhar, with an estimated 750,000 people; the Ordos or Tumet, with an estimated 300,000; and Bairin, with some 200,000, and a number of smaller groups. The Mongol language, known as Mongol khel, is spoken by five to six million across its various dialectal divisions. In Mongolia, the Khalkha dialect is the standard and is written in the Cyrillic alphabet and increasingly in a modified Latin script more adapted to social networking. The dialects of Inner Mongolia are written in the traditional Mongol script, also known as the Soyombo script. The Chinese authorities have synthesized a literary standard for the dialects spoken in China based on the Chakhar dialect that is commonly known as Southern Mongolian. Historically, the Mongol peoples evolved a belief system based on the belief in spirits and shamans, a combination of witch doctor, dream interpreter, and an intermediary between the living and the spirit worlds. In some areas, remnants of Mongol shamanism still exist, including sacrificial offerings to ancestors and a special reverence for the sun, moon, and nature. The Tibetan form of Buddhism, Lamaism, spread among the Mongol tribes in the 16th century and has had a strong impact on Mongol culture for centuries. Under communist rule in Mongolia and China, Lamaist practices and beliefs have been drastically curtailed, particularly in China since 1949. The Feast of Genghis Khan, held annually in Mongolia, is one of the largest celebrations in the country. Since the 1990s, the festival has also been observed in Inner Mongolia.

China's Manchu rulers, as they did in Manchuria, forbid Han Chinese immigration to the Mongol territories, which helped preserve the Mongol culture and dialects. The Qing dynasty maintained control of Mongolia through a series of intermarriages and alliances, as well as through military and economic means. Divided into ever more feudal and ecclesiastical holdings, Outer Mongolia's feudal nobility and clergy increasingly ignored the well-being of the people. By the late 19th century, poverty was widespread in the region. In 1878, to relieve severe population pressure and a lack of fertile land, the Chinese government opened the border districts to Han Chinese settlement.

Sporadic violence and widespread resistance accompanied the colonization of Inner Mongolia in the 1880s and 1890s. In 1904, the resistance in Inner Mongolia turned to riots, which quickly spread across the region. Mongol attacks on immigration offices and Han Chinese settlements left many dead and wounded. Serious anti-Chinese disturbances continued up to the revolution that ended the Manchu domination of China and the borderlands. With the fall of the Qing dynasty, a descendant of Genghis Khan, Bogd Khan, declared Outer Mongolia independent of China. Inner Mongolia, with its already large Han Chinese population, remained part of the new Chinese republic. In 1915, the Russian and Chinese governments, both opposed to Mongol sovereignty, signed the "Kiakhta Agreement" effectively dividing the historical Mongol territory between them. An uprising in Inner Mongolia was savagely put down leaving some districts virtually depopulated. In 1919, following the Russian Revolution, Chinese troops occupied Mongolia. During the Russian Civil War, White forces moved into Mongolia and defeated the Chinese military expedition. In order to eliminate the White threat, communist or Red Russian authorities decided to support the establishment of a communist Mongolian state. Supported by the new Soviet Union, communist Mongol forces liberated the former Outer Mongolia, which was again declared an independent Mongol State in 1921. Following the death of the religious leader and khan, Bogd Khan, a Mongolian People's Republic was proclaimed. In 1928, Khorloogiin Choibalsan became the head of the communist government. He quickly instituted Soviet-style collectivization of the Mongol herds and began the destruction of hundreds of Buddhist monasteries, and the mass killings of monks and others deemed a threat to the new communist state. In the early 1930s, Japanese intrusions and the invasion of neighboring Manchuria in 1931 alarmed the governments of both Mongolia and China. The Japanese encouraged Mongol nationalism in Inner Mongolia and supported anticommunist Mongol groups in Mongolia. Japan's war with China resulted in the Japanese occupation of Inner Mongolia in 1938. The puppet government installed by the Japanese collapsed with the Japanese defeat in World War II. In mid-1945, a Mongol army moved south from Mongolia to occupy the region. The Mongol of Inner Mongolia, welcoming the army as liberators, organized a provisional government and voted for unification with Mongolia. The Chinese communist forces, in the midst of a widespread civil war in China, appealed to Joseph Stalin in the Soviet Union. Stalin blocked the reunification of Mongolia and Inner Mongolia and asserted his influence to force the Mongol army to withdraw from Chinese territory. The victorious Chinese communists moved into Inner Mongolia in 1947. Under the communist nationalities policy a nominally autonomous Inner Mongolia region was created. Despite the official rhetoric of cultural autonomy, the Chinese government pressed assimilation and the sinicization of the Southern Mongol groups. Continued Han Chinese migration to the region resulted in minority status in their own homeland. By 1951, the Southern Mongol population was outnumbered 2 to 1; in 1957, they numbered only 1 in 8; and by 1980, the Southern Mongol constituted just 1 in every 17 people in the region. Mongolia's close alliance with the Soviet Union, mostly to offset Chinese threats and expansionism, resulted in a society closely copied from the Soviet model. Events in the Soviet Union, especially the relaxation of the late 1980s and the collapse of the Soviet government in 1991, strongly influenced politics in Mongolia leading to a peaceful democratic revolution and the introduction of a multiparty political system and a market economy. In Inner Mongolia, the Southern Mongol minority has benefited from the economic reforms and an end to the harsh communist doctrines. In the early 21st century, the region has seen rapid growth, largely owing to the exploitation of the Inner Mongolia's abundant natural resources.

Further Reading

Inner Mongolian People's Party. Accessed July 31, 2013. http://www.innermongolia .org/english/index.html

Morgan, David. *The Mongols.* Hoboken, NJ: Wiley-Blackwell, 2007.

Rossabi, Morris. *The Mongols: A Very Short Introduction.* Oxford: Oxford University Press, 2012.

Sneath, David. *Changing Inner Mongolia: Pastoral Mongolian Society and the Chinese State.* New York: Oxford University Press, 2000.

Monpa

The Monpa, sometimes known as Moinba, Menba, Monba, Mon pa, or Menbazu, are one of the 56 officially recognized nationalities in the People's Republic of China, where they are officially designated as the Moinba nationality. The estimated 25,000 Monpa, mostly living in the Cuona region of Tibet, form part of the larger Monpa population living in the Arunachal Pradesh state of India and a smaller community in Bhutan. The Monpa language is an East Bodish language belonging to the Tibeto-Kanauri branch of the Tibeto-Burman languages. The majority of the Monpa adhere to Mahayana (Tibetan) Buddhism, with a minority that retains the region's pre-Buddhist Bön religion.

The early records of the region discuss a Monpa kingdom known as Lhomon or Monyul that existed from about 500 BCE to 600 CE. Around the first century CE, part of the Monpa migrated from southern Tibet into eastern Bhutan and present-day Arunachal Pradesh. In the 11th century, the northern Monpa in the Tawang region came under the influence of the Tibetans and the Tibetan form of Buddhism. The Monpa adopted the Tibetan script and adapted it to their own language. Tibetan missionaries spread through the Monpa territories in the 13th century. At that time, the Monpa kingdom was divided into 32 districts, covering the area of eastern Bhutan, northern Arunachal Pradesh, and southern Tibet. The Monpa state remained an autonomous political entity, with the local monks holding great political and religious power. Direct rule by Tibet was established in the 17th century. In subsequent centuries, the Monpa came under increasing Tibetan cultural and political influence, with an ethnic Monpa named Tsangyang Gyatso becoming the sixth Dalai Lama from 1683 to 1706. In 1793, the Manchu rulers of China laid claim to the region along with Tibet proper.

The name *Monpa* means "people of the lower country" or "people of the south," from *Mon* or "lower country," and *Pa* meaning "from" or "belonging to." Monpa life revolves around their Buddhist religion and their *gompa* or temples. Historically, the Monpa, particularly the Northern (Tawang) Monpa, were divided into three classes based on their wealth and social status. Traditional Monpa society was administered by a council of six ministers known as *Trukdri*. The members of the council were subordinate to the *Kenpo*, the Lama or Abbott of the monastery of Tawang. The lamas were often considered both the political and religious leaders of the Monpa communities. Since the invasion of Tibet and the conquest of the region by the Red Army, many monasteries and lamaseries have been closed, and political power is now in the hands of local administrators assigned to their posts by the Chinese government. Traditionally the man is the head of the household and makes all important decisions. Socialist egalitarianism has changed the system in an effort to give women equal status in the region, but much remains to be accomplished. Most of the Monpa are farmers or herders. To prevent soil erosion in the higher elevations, many of the hillsides are terraced. Cash crops such as rice, maize, wheat, barley, chilies, beans, tobacco, and cotton are now raised for trade or income. The Monpa language is an East Bodish language of the Bodish group of Tibeto-Kanauri languages. Many Monpa also speak Tibetan or Mandarin Chinese as second languages or as a means of communicating with neighboring peoples. For many centuries, the majority of the Monpa have adhered to Lamaism, also known as Mahayana or Tibetan Buddhism, with a minority that has retained elements of their pre-Buddhist religion, Bön.

In the 19th century, the entire Tibetan area began to be of interest to the British in India to the south. A traveler from British India to Monyul, Nain Singh, who visited the Monpa homeland in 1875–1876, noted that the Monpa were a conservative, religious people who shunned contact with outsiders and seemed intent on monopolizing trade between India and Tibet. Due to the strategic location of Monyul, the British sought to extend their influence to the region. In 1914, the British colonial authorities in India drew the McMahon Line across the map to delineate the border between British India and Tibet. The line divided Monyul, leaving the southern districts within territory claimed by the British. The McMahon Line continued to be a bone of contention between Tibet and British India over Tibet's claims to the southern part of Monyul. The dispute continued following India's independence and the claims of the People's Republic of China to territory south of the McMahon Line following the communist invasion and conquest of Tibet in 1951. In 1962, tensions along the border erupted into a brief conflict known as the Sino-Indian War. During the war, the Chinese invaders took control of the entire Monpa territory south of the McMahon Line as well as surrounding districts. The cease-fire obligated the Chinese to surrender the occupied territory, but Chinese claims to the region remain to the present. The war, often fought in regions inhabited by the Monpa, left not only a legacy of fear in the region, but also demands for the unification of the Monpa people in one political entity.

Further Reading

Ethnic Groups. "The Moinba Ethnic Minority." Accessed July 30, 2013. http://www.china.org.cn/e-groups/shaoshu/shao-2-moinba.htm

Kapadia, Harish, and Geeta Kapadia. *Into the Untravelled Himalaya: Travels, Treks, and Climbs.* New Delhi: Indus Publishing, 2005.

McRae, Michael. *The Siege of Shangri-La: The Quest for Tibet's Sacred Hidden Paradise.* New York: Broadway Books, 2002.

Schaller, George B. *Tibet Wild: A Naturalist's Journeys on the Roof of the World.* Washington, DC: Island Press, 2012.

Mulao

The Mulao, who call themselves Mulam, Kyam, or Mu Lao, are one of the officially recognized nationalities of the People's Republic of China. The estimated 262,000 Mulao are concentrated in the Luocheng Mulao Autonomous County of Hechi, in the Guangxi Zhuang Autonomous Region in southern China. The Mulao language, known as Mulam, forms part of the Kam-Sui branch of the Tai-Kadai language family. Most Mulao are Buddhists or Daoists but with strong influences from their earlier animist religious beliefs.

The origins of the Mulao have been traced to the Ling and Liao tribes that inhabited the region in the third and fourth centuries CE. The historical records of the period known as the Southern and Northern dynasties from the late fourth century to the end of the sixth century refer to them as an aboriginal people to be assimilated into the dominant Han Chinese culture of the empire. During the rule of the Manchu-dominated Qing dynasty, in the 17th and 18th centuries, the traditional

Mulao lands were divided into territories known as *dong*, each of which was composed of units of 10 dwellings. Each of the *dong* had its own leader responsible for maintaining order, collecting taxes, and overseeing the twice annual tribute sent to the Chinese capital. Each of the *dong* was usually formed by families that shared the same surname. Later, when the territories increased in population, the *dong* were divided into small units known as *fang*. By the 18th century, the Mulao were relatively advanced in comparison with other Tai peoples of the region. Their agriculture was relatively advanced with farming techniques, crop varieties, and farming tools basically the same as the neighboring Han Chinese and Zhuang.

The Mulao culture is a Tai culture similar to those of the other Tai peoples of southern China and Southeast Asia. One of the unique features of the culture is the Mulao cooking pit or oven. Mulao houses usually consist of three rooms and are typically one-storied with mud walls and tile roofs. Inside, always on the lift of the entrance door, the ground is dug away to form a coal-burning pit or ground stove. The region is home to many of the most exotic food in China, including grilled or roasted dog, snake soup, roasted bamboo rat, short-tailed monkey brains, ants, roasted fruit fox, and armadillo. Mulao families bearing the surname of Luo or Wu are not allowed to eat dog meat or the internal organs of other animals. The Mulao are famous for their spinning, dyeing, and weaving, particularly their cloth of deep blue. Marriage traditions included arranged marriages, though a bride did not live with the husband until the birth of the first child. Legends, folktales, and *caidiao*, a form of local drama, remain very popular and are important elements in Mulao culture.

Officially, the majority of the Mulao are Buddhists or Daoists though their traditional beliefs in spirits and witchcraft remain strong. After decades of official communist atheism, many Mulao now consider themselves as nonreligious. The Mulao language is a Kam-Sui language spoken in Luocheng County, Hechi, in northern Guangxi. Since the Ming dynasty period, in the 15th and 16th centuries, Chinese characters have been used to write the Mulao language. A Latin-based script was developed by the Chinese government in the 1950s, but most Mulao continue to use the traditional Chinese script. Many Mulao speak Mandarin Chinese, Zhuang, or other of the languages of neighboring ethnic groups.

Mulao craftswoman shows embroidery skill during a Mulao embroidery exhibition in Luocheng Mulao Autonomous County, southwest China's Guangxi Zhuang Autonomous Region in 2012. Mulao embroidery was listed as one of the intangible cultural heritages of Guangxi in 2010. (Wei Rudai/Corbis)

In the 19th century, the Mulao farming economy was comparable with that of the neighboring Han Chinese with oxen or water buffalos as the main draft animals, though increasingly horses were used for plowing. Some 60 percent of the most fertile land was made up of rice paddies based on a well-developed irrigation system that was mostly under the control of local landlords who channeled most of the water off for themselves. Poorer Mulao often turned to sidelines such as collecting medicinal herbs, raising livestock, weaving, making pottery, or blacksmithing. Land, especially the most fertile tracts, was heavily concentrated in the hands of wealthy landlords. The landlords demanded that the Mulao workers pay rent with part of their harvest and with unpaid labor services. The communist takeover of mainland China in 1949 began a series of radical changes in the Mulao region. Communist officials came to the region in 1950–1951 to end the domination of the landlords, who were effectively eliminated or sent to reeducation camps, and to glorify the Mulao peasants. Land redistribution proceeded until the government decision to gather all private land in government-owned communes worked by Mulao peasants as employees of the state. Devastated by the Cultural Revolution of the 1960s and 1970s, the Mulao began to recover with the new economic policies and an end to forced assimilation in the 1980s. Since that time, the Mulao have made great strides in education, production, and prosperity.

Further Reading

Gall, Timothy L. *Worldmark Encyclopedia of Cultures and Daily Life.* Farmington Hills, MI: Gale, 2009.

MacKerras, Colin. *China's Minorities: Integration and Modernization in the Twentieth Century.* Oxford: Oxford University Press, 1994.

West, Barbara A. *Encyclopedia of the Peoples of Asia and Oceania.* New York: Facts on File, 2008.

N

Nanai

The Nanai, sometimes known as Nani, Golds, Goldi, Samagir, or Hezhen, are a Tungusic people inhabiting the border region between Russia's Far East and China's Heilongjiang Province. The estimated 20,000 Nanai live in widely scattered settlements along the Amur, Ussur, and Girin Rivers in Khabarovsk Province in Russia and along the Sungar River in northeastern China. The Nanai language belongs to the southern group of Manchu-Tungus languages, closely related to the languages of two other small groups, the Ulch and Orochi. The majority of the Nanai retain their traditional shamanistic religious beliefs with a minority that has embraced Lamaism, Tibetan Buddhism.

Ancient Chinese documents mention a people called the Sushi in the Amur, Sungar, and Ussur regions as early as the second and first centuries BCE. The Nanai, like the other Tungusic peoples, were sometimes considered vassals of the Chinese dynasties, sometimes paying tribute but not under the direct rule of the Chinese authorities. Around the end of the seventh century CE, the Nanai came under the rule of the early Manchu state of Balhae, which was destroyed by invading Khitan Mongols in 926. Most of the Nanai clans remained closely tied to the Manchu, then known as Jurchen, who destroyed the Chinese dynasties of the Liao and the Northern Song to establish their rule in northern China as the Jin dynasty. In 1206, the Mongol tribes under Jurchen rule rebelled under a new leader later known as Genghis Khan. The Mongol hordes defeated the Jurchen and took control of the region in 1234. Under Mongol rule, all the Tungusic peoples, including the Jurchen-Manchu and the Nanai, were divided. Those in the southern region were treated as ethnic Chinese and those in the northern region were treated as ethnic Mongol, bringing Mongol cultural and linguistic influences to the Nanai. Mongol and Chinese incursions continued for centuries, scattering the Nanai peoples over a wide area. The unification of the Jurchen in the late 16th century again brought the Nanai together under one government. In 1644, the Jurchen, called Manchu, defeated the Chinese and took control of the vast Chinese Empire. Many Nanai joined the related Manchu in the region often forgetting their Nanai heritage. Under Manchu rule, Han Chinese settlement in the huge Amur Basin and other areas known as Manchuria was closely restricted, allowing the Nanai and other peoples to maintain their distinct cultures and languages. Russian Cossacks began to explore the Amur region in the 1640s, but the terms of the Treaty of Nerchinsk between Russia and China in 1689 confirmed the region, known as Outer Manchuria, as part of the Chinese state. The

Chinese attempted to impose their authority and to levy taxes on the Nanai villages, but were successful only in those districts where Chinese farmers were settled alongside the Nanai.

The name *Nanai* or *Nani*, meaning "people of this place" or simply "people," has been in use since the 1920s to describe the indigenous people of the Amur Basin. The Russians originally called them Golds, a name also applied to the related Ulch, Orochi, and Negidal. The Chinese Nanai are known as Hezhen, taken from the local name for the Nanai groups of the lower Amur River valley. Historically, Nanai culture is based on river fishing with most Nanai villages built on the banks of the region's rivers. Traditional clothing was made out of sturgeon skins that were left out to dry. When dry, the skins were worked with a mallet until completely soft and then they were sewn together. This distinct practice earned them the name "Fish-Skin Tatars" by early Russian explorers of the region. The Nanai language, spoken in two distinct dialects, has been declining for most of the last century as the Nanai adopted either Russian or Chinese as the language of education and government. In recent years, in the Nanai Autonomous District in Russia, there has been a movement to publish in the language and to extend its use in schools. The Nanai are mainly shamanists, reserving great reverence for the bear, *Doonta*, and the tiger, *Amba*. They consider the shamans as intermediaries between them and the spirit world, the spirits of the sun, the moon, the water, trees, and the mountains. Traditional Nanai beliefs have their ancient homeland a great flat plain until serpents gouged out the river valleys. In the 20th century, some Nanai settlements began to adopt Tibetan Buddhism, but without losing their traditional beliefs.

Around 1800, when the Manchu rulers of China began to wane, Russian expeditions returned to the Amur region, trading with the Nanai settlements and the other groups in the region. Increasing debility in China finally resulted in the cession of Outer Manchuria, now the southern part of the Russian Far East, to the expanding Russian Empire. The Nanai in the region came under Russian rule, often forced to pay taxes in the form of fish products or furs. Russian colonization often meant that the Nanai were driven away from their traditional fishing grounds. The Nanai settlements in Chinese Manchuria, though traditionally isolated, came under rapid pressure when Han Chinese settlement was finally allowed after 1878. The Russo-Japanese War of 1904–1905 brought Japanese influence to Manchuria. In 1931–1932, the Japanese took control of Manchuria, which was rapidly industrialized and militarized. The Nanai felt Soviet rule in Russia after 1924, when a Native People's Department was created in the Soviet Far East. Between 1926 and 1928, the Nanai were forced to settle in larger villages, which served to create a sense of national identity that encompassed all Nanai for the first time. Harsh Japanese rule in Manchuria decimated the Nanai, with only some 300 surviving at the end of World War II in 1945. In recent years, as relations between Russia and China improved, the Nanai on both sides of the international border have reaffirmed family and cultural ties.

Official encouragement of the cultures of ethnic minorities has allowed the Nanai to retain much of their ancient traditions, but their language remains endangered despite efforts to extend its use.

Further Reading

Forsyth, James. *A History of the Peoples of Siberia: Russia's North Asian Colony 1581–1990.* Cambridge: Cambridge University Press, 1994.

Hutton, Ronald. *Shamans: Siberian Spirituality and the Western Imagination.* London: Continuum, 2007.

Olson, James S. *An Ethnohistorical Dictionary of the Russian and Soviet Empires.* Westport, CT: Greenwood, 1994.

Vahtre, Lauri, and Jüri Viikberg. The Red Book of the Peoples of the Russian Empire. "The Nanais." Accessed July 31, 2013. http://www.eki.ee/books/redbook/nanais .shtml

Naxi

The Naxi, sometimes known as Nakhi, Naqxi, Na-khi, Nahi, Moriayi, or Mosha, are one of the 56 officially recognized nationalities of the People's Republic of China. The estimated 310,000 Naxi inhabit the foothill regions of the Himalayas in the northwestern part of Yunnan and southwestern Sichuan Province in China. The Naxi language forms the Naxish branch of the Loloish languages of the Tibeto-Burman language family. The Naxi mostly adhere to an indigenous religion known as Dongba, with important groups that practice Lamaism or Tibetan Buddhism, Daoism, and a small group of Christians.

Historical Chinese chronicles place the forebears of the Naxi people with the tribe called Maoniu Yi during the Han dynasty between 206 BCE and 220 CE. Scholars believe that the Naxi are descendants of the early Qiang, a nomadic ethnic group that inhabited the Tibetan Plateau region since ancient times. Later known as Moshi Yi or Yoxie Yi, they are believed to have lived in the region for several thousand years. The ancestors of the Naxi are believed to have come originally from northwestern China. Migrating south into the Tibetan-populated regions, they usually took control of the most fertile river valleys, driving the other tribal groups into the less accessible and less fertile areas. The Naxi engaged in trade with Tibet and India on the so-called Tea and Horse Caravan routes. Originally livestock herders and breeders, the Naxi adopted settled agriculture between the 10th and 13th centuries. During that period, a group of prosperous slave-owing farmers gradually gained land and power as evolved into a feudal ruling class. In 1278, under the rule of the Mongol Yuan dynasty, the Naxi heartland was organized as Lijiang Prefecture with representation at the imperial court. In the 14th century, the leader of the Naxi people, a chieftain called Mude, was raised to the position of hereditary chief of Lijiang with authority over the Naxi and other ethnic groups in the region. Throughout the next centuries, the Naxi leaders of the Mu family kept tax monies and tribute flowing to the Ming court in the form of silver, grains, and slaves. The Ming authorities relied on the Mu family to maintain control of the various ethnic groups in northwestern Yunnan Province. In the 17th century, with the development of better production methods, the buying, selling, and renting of farmland began to spread through the Naxi region, marking the end of the feudal system and the beginning of a landlord economy. After 1723, under the rule of the Manchu Qing dynasty, the hereditary Naxi chieftains in Lijiang began to be replaced by court officials, and the Mu family were appointed as local administrators.

Naxi culture has been largely formed by the ancient Dongba religion and the proximity of the neighboring Tibetan peoples. Traditionally, the Naxi are an agriculture people raising rice, maize, potatoes, wheat, beans, cotton, and hemp. Their homeland is extensively forested and contains many valuable wood varieties along with many types of herbs, bulbs, and fungus used in local medical practices. Dongba is actually the ancient culture of the Naxi people; though now it is considered a religion, it remains an important part of the Naxi society. Naxi priests or practitioners of the Dongba religion, which evolved from the Tibetan Bön belief system, are called *dongba*, which means "wise man" in the Naxi language. The *dongba* play a major role in the culture, which stresses their beliefs of harmony between man and nature. Religious rituals are commonly conducted by the *dongba* to propitiate the spirits that are believed to inhabit every part of the natural world. The core of the Dongba religion is the belief that both man and nature are two half-brothers born of two mothers but the same father. This creates a situation of revenge from heaven on humans who use up too much of nature's resources. Over the centuries, many Naxi have embraced Tibetan Buddhism and many *gompa* dot the Naxi region. The Naxi language is spoken in two major dialectal groups, Western Naxi or Naxi proper, which is fairly homogeneous, and Eastern Naxi or Na, mostly spoken by the Mosuo people, who are officially considered part of the Naxi ethnic group.

In the 19th century, Naxi culture still showed remnants of a matriarchal family structure that had slowly given way to the Chinese patriarchal system. In most of the Naxi areas, a feudal landlord system was prevalent, with some elements of capitalism beginning to be adopted. The landlords and rich peasants, who made up about 10 percent of the Naxi population, owned between 60 and 70 percent of the land. Lands rented to peasant farmers were often charged between 50 and 80 percent of the farmer's crop. Forced labor, debt slavery, and exorbitant rents allowed the small landowning classes to flourish, while the majority of the Naxi lived in poverty. In the early 20th century, a small portion of the Naxi people began to urbanize, often as traders or storekeepers. During the war between China and Japan in the 1930s and 1940s, foreign trade was blockaded resulting in a great expansion of trade with India. Lijiang, the major Naxi city, became a center of the new trade routes to India, Tibet, and the interior Chinese provinces. The Chinese Civil War ended with a communist victory in 1949, with communist cadres moving into the Naxi homeland in 1950s. The landlords and rich peasants were overthrown and eliminated, often brutally. The peasants were first given land under a redistribution scheme, but these farms were later collectivized with the Naxi farmers working for the Chinese state as employees. The relaxation of stringent communism in the 1980s began a period of rising prosperity and a rapid expansion of traditional handicrafts, such as ironwork, copper, carpentry, tannins, weaving, papermaking, and sculpture, as export items in the newly capitalist China.

Further Reading

Chao, Emily. *Lijiang Stories: Shamans, Taxi Drivers, and Runaway Brides in Reform-Era China.* Seattle: University of Washington Press, 2012.

Ethnic Groups. "The Naxi Ethnic Minority." Accessed July 31, 2013. http://www.china.org.cn/e-groups/shaoshu/shao-2-naxi.htm

Legerton, Colin, and Jacob Rawson. *Invisible China: A Journey through Ethnic Borderlands.* Chicago: Chicago Review Press, 2009.

Mathieu, Christine, and Cindy Ho, eds. *Ancestral Realms of the Naxi.* Stuttgart, Germany: Arnoldsche Verlagsanstalt, 2011.

Wiens, Mi Chu. "Living Pictographs: Asian Scholar Unlocks Secrets of the Naxi Manuscripts." Library of Congress Information Bulletin, June 1999. http://www.loc.gov/loc/lcib/9906/naxi1.html

Nenets

The Nenets, sometimes known as Nentsy, N'enyts, Khasava, Hasavan, Hasaba, Yurak, Yurak Samoyeds, or Samoyeds, are the most numerous of the indigenous peoples of the Russian Arctic region. The Nenets homeland occupies a huge region of tundra, taiga, and permafrost just north of the tree line stretching from the Kola Peninsula in northwestern European Russia to the Taimyr Peninsula in north-central Siberia. The region forms three ethnic districts of the Russian Federation—Nenets, Yamalo-Nenets, and Taimyr. The estimated 43,000 Nenets now form minorities in all three of the autonomous districts. The Nenets language, actually two distinct dialects, is a Samoyedic language of the Uralic language family. The modern Nenets normally adhere to their traditional shamanistic beliefs with only about 4 percent belonging to Christian sects, primarily Russian Orthodox.

Many scholars believe that the Nenets are descended from early clans that split from the Finno-Ugrian migrations moving west around 3,000 years ago. The small clan groups probably mixed with Turkic-Altaic peoples around 200 BCE. For centuries, the Nenets and the related tribal peoples of the region herded reindeer across the vast reaches of the Arctic territories, moving their herds to the seasonal grazing lands in the tundra and taiga regions north of the tree line. Nenets society was carefully organized into well-defined clan units, each with its own grazing, fishing, and hunting territories. European chronicles first mention the Nenets reindeer people in the 11th century CE. Around 1200, some of the Nenets clans came under Slavic influence. The Russians called the Nenets clans *Samoyeds*, a word denoting "cannibal," for their practice of eating raw reindeer meat, particularly at ceremonies. The reindeer provided the nomadic clans with food, shelter, and clothing. The Nenets never slaughtered more of their reindeer than their immediate needs required as the reindeer herds were closely tied to their traditional way of life and even their religious beliefs. The western Nenets clans came under the authority of the mercantile republic of Novgorod in the 13th century. The Novgorodians demanded taxes and tribute, often in the form of valuable furs. In the 14th century, some of the clans were taxed by the powerful Tatar khanate to the south. In the 16th and 17th centuries, the Russians practiced a form of indirect rule. Cossack forts were established across the region to collect the *yasak*, the fur tax, but daily life continued under the traditional clan leadership. Citizenship was offered to any Nenets who converted to Orthodox Christianity, a process often leading to forced baptisms and serfdom in order to increase the number of Nenets involved in fur trapping. As the number of fur-bearing animals rapidly decreased, the Russians lost interest in the area and its inhabitants. Over centuries, Russian merchants took control of most commerce in the region, first enticing the Nenets with iron and steel tools, and later with firearms and alcohol. Diseases brought from European Russian decimated many of the Nenets clans. The Russian colonizers were dismayed at the number and ferocity of the frequent Nenets uprisings, which continued until the mid-18th century.

The Nenets are the largest of several closely related ethnic groups living in the Russian Arctic region. The Nenets encompass two distinct groups based on their economic activity: the Tundra Nenets, mostly reindeer herders, hunters, and trappers in the north, and the Forest Nenets, mostly herders and fishermen living below the tree line in the subarctic districts. A strong and determined people, the

Nenets have resisted oppression and assimilation for many centuries, both under tsarist rule and later communist dictatorships, but their resistance cost many lives. Decades of Soviet disregard for the environment has left a legacy of pollution by heavy metals and chemicals, which is a serious health risk for the Nenets, whose average life expectancy is only 45–50 years. The Nenets speak a language of the Samoyed group of Finno-Ugrian languages divided into two major dialects, Tundra and Forest. Due to their vast national territory, both of the dialects are spoken in dozen of subdialects. Most of the Nenets continue to adhere to their traditional beliefs, a type of Siberian shamanism that reveres the natural environment, animals, and plants, all of which are believed to have their own spirits. Reindeer are considered to represent purity and are accorded great respect. In some districts, elements of Orthodox Christianity have been mixed with the traditional Nenets gods and spirits. Forbidden to conduct religious ceremonies and rituals during the decades of Soviet rule, the Nenets religious has survived and is now enjoying a strong revival.

Russian intervention in the Nenets way of life increased in the early 1800s. In 1824, the government launched a campaign of large-scale conversion to Orthodox Christianity. In the 1870s, the tsarist authorities confiscated large portions of the Nenets territories in the west. Many clans were resettled to the northwestern border regions of European Russia. Though most Nenets remained nomadic and poor, a few Nenets families had amassed herds numbering in the thousands, though most reindeer herds were much smaller. The arrival of the

A Nenets father and son herding reindeer in Russia's Arctic region in northern Siberia. (Stphoto/Dreamstime.com)

victorious Soviets after the Russian Civil War of 1918–1920 began the implementation of a socialist society in the region. At first, the Soviets favored large reservations to allow the Nenets to continue their traditional way of life. Instead, it was decided to forcibly integrate the Nenets into the universal Soviet system. The plan included the confiscation of all surplus wealth from the Nenets. The reindeer herds were confiscated, and each Nenets herder was allowed just four animals. All of the clan's hunters were relieved of any furs they had stored. As an average Nenets band needed at least 250 reindeer just to survive, thousands of Nenets perished from hunger and disease. In the late 1920s and 1930s, nominally autonomous regions were organized across the north. Over decades of Soviet rule, all signs of dissent were severely punished, the traditional religion was suppressed, and the nomads were forced to settle in permanent villages. The collapse of the Soviet system, in 1991, allowed the Nenets to resume much of their pre-Soviet way of life, including the revival of their culture, language, and religion.

Further Reading

Golovnev, Andrei V., and Gail Osherenko. *Siberian Survival: The Nenets and Their Story.* Ithaca, NY: Cornell University Press, 1999.

"The Nenets." BBC Home. Last updated March 2008. http://www.bbc.co.uk/tribe/tribes/nenets/

Slezkine, Yuri. *Arctic Mirrors: Russia and the Small Peoples of the North.* Ithaca, NY: Cornell University Press, 1996.

Vitebsky, Piers. *The Reindeer People: Living with Animals and Spirits in Siberia.* Boston: Mariner Books, 2006.

Nivkh

The Nivkh, sometimes known as Nivikh, Nivkhi, or Gilyak, are an indigenous people inhabiting the northern half of Sakhalin Island and the Amur River estuary in Siberia's Pacific coast in eastern Russia. The Nivkh historically occupied a much larger territory, including all of Sakhalin and parts of Japan's northern island of Hokkaido. The estimated 6,000 Nivkh mostly use Russian as their first language though about 10 percent still speak the Nivkh language, which is considered a language isolate. The majority of the Nivkh continue to follow their traditional shamanistic belief system, with a minority of Russian Orthodox.

The ancestors of the Nivkh are believed to have originated in the Transbaikal region of southern Siberia in the late Pleistocene Era. The migrant tribes crossed the land bridge that today forms the Tartar Strait during the last Ice Age to settle on the island of Sakhalin and possibly moved south into Hokkaido. When the Ice Age finally receded, the oceans rose leaving the Nivkh split into two groups, one in the North Asian mainland and the other in the islands of Sakhalin and Hokkaido. As the ice receded and the northern lands warmed, other more powerful peoples moved into the region where they mostly assimilated the indigenous peoples. The Nivkh, like the Ainu in Japan, are considered the descendants of the original peoples who were not assimilated into the larger ethnic groups. Though linguistically and ethnically isolated, the Nivkh maintained trade and marriage relations with the Nanai, the Jurchen (Manchu),

and other Tungusic peoples in the region. Around the early 12th century CE, the Nivkh in northern Manchuria and southeastern Siberia often paid tribute to the increasingly powerful Jurchen people, the ancestors of the Manchu. Around the same time, they came into contact with the Han Chinese, trading furs for Chinese textiles, alcohol, tobacco, beads, and metal disks that were fashioned into jewelry. Though nominally independent under their tribal chiefs, the Nivkh were often included in the sphere of influence of the Manchu or later the Chinese Empire. The Nivkh in Hokkaido and Sakhalin, though often hostile to the Ainu populations of the islands, maintained their independence as individual tribal groups. In 1644, the Manchu expanded rapidly to conquer China and extended their influence north to the lands of the Nivkh. Regarded as subjects of the Manchu Qing dynasty in China, the chiefs were often appointed by Qing officials who collected taxes in the form of furs. The expansion of the Russians into the Far East region, in the 16th and 17th centuries, resulted in conflicts in the region for control of the tribal areas. The Russians first encountered the Nivkh salmon fishing settlements along the Amur River in the early 17th century. Nivkh resistance to Russian attempts to impose a fur tax often ended in violence. Following the Treaty of Nerchinsk between the Russian and Chinese empires, the Nivkh functioned as intermediaries between the Russians, the Manchu, and through their vassal, the Ainu and maintained contacts with the Japanese. In Hokkaido, the Japanese took control of the southwestern part of the large island. Conflicts between the Japanese and the

Nivkh tribes in the late 1600s decimated the tribes, and within a century, the Nivkh had disappeared from their ancient homeland in Hokkaido.

Nivkh culture is traditionally based on tribe, and clan was mostly destroyed during the early years of Soviet rule in the 1920s when the scattered Nivkh settlements were uprooted and the populations shipped to a handful of large villages. Forestry, mining, oil-drilling, and industry took a heavy toll on the Nivkh and their lands, leaving a legacy of pollution, endemic illness, and the depletion of the region's natural resources. In recent years, many Sakhalin Nivkh have returned to their ancient manner of living in small villages shared by several families. Clan membership is again permitted and has again become an important part of the small Nivkh society. Hunting and fishing, the major occupations, are most often organized at a clan level. The Nivkh language is often classified together with Chukchi, Koryak, and other Siberian languages of the Paleo-Asiatic language family, but the Nivkh language shares very few features in common with them. Most linguists consider Nivkh a language isolate—a language that cannot be proven to be related to any other known language. The language is divided into two mutually unintelligible dialects known as Amur and Sakhalin, which are further divided into subdialects. The language was an oral language until 1931 when Soviet linguists created a Nivkh script based on the Amur dialect and written in the Latin alphabet. The Cyrillic (Russian) alphabet was substituted for Latin in 1936. The written language based on the Amur dialect remained the only written

form until 1979, when a written form was devised for the Sakhalin dialect. Despite efforts by the Russian colonial administration to convert the Nivkh to Orthodox Christianity, the majority retain their traditional beliefs in a pantheon of vaguely defined gods that control mountains, rivers, the seas, and the sky. Nivkh shamans traditionally preside over the annual Bear Festival, a tradition possibly borrowed from the Ainu, when a young sacred bear raised by the Nivkh women is sacrificed and eaten in an elaborate religious ceremony. The Bear Festival was prohibited during the Soviet regime but has had a modest revival in recent years.

The Nivkh suffered massacre and displacement during the Cossack conquest of the region in the early 1800s. The Russians called the Nivkh *kinrsh* or devils for their fierce resistance to outside authority. The Russian Empire gained complete control over the Nivkh lands in the Amur region and Sakhalin following the Treaty of Aigun in 1858 and the Treaty of Peking in 1860, which ceded the Amur region to the Russian Empire. The Nivkh population declined rapidly due to violence, displacement, and epidemics of smallpox, plague, and influenza, European diseases to which they had no immunity. Japan and Russia jointly ruled the island of Sakhalin as part of the terms of the 1855 Treaty of Shimoda, but Russia took control of the island in 1875. Following the Russo-Japanese War in 1904–1905, the island was partitioned between Russia and Japan along the 50th parallel north. Overexploitation of fish stocks in the waters off Japanese southern Sakhalin drove many Nivkh to starvation or migration to the northern part of the island. The remaining Nivkh population under Japanese control succumbed to forced assimilation and disappeared from the southern half of Sakhalin. The Russian Revolution and the subsequent Russian Civil War between 1917 and 1920 ended with the victory of the communists. The Soviet regime established by the communists brought substantial changes to the Nivkh culture. In the 1920s, the Nivkh were forced to abandon their villages and to settle in communes. The first collective was established in Nivkh territory in 1930, forcing the Nivkh to abandon their traditional system of summer and winter settlements developed over millennia to maximize the benefits of local resources. During the 1950s and 1960s, the smaller collectives and settlements were closed, and the Nivkh were again moved into larger multiethnic settlements under closer government control. By the 1980s, the majority of the Nivkh lived in Russian-style houses, wore ready-made clothing, bought their food at shops, and mostly communicated in the Russian language. The decline of the language and assimilation continued until the collapse of the Soviet Union in 1991. The enduring traditions of hunting and fishing, revived in the 1990s and in the early 21st century, became the basis of a modest cultural revival that aims to preserve the language and culture of the small Nivkh ethnic group.

Further Reading

Colombi, Benedict J., and James F. Brooks, eds. *Keystone Nations: Peoples and Salmon across the North Pacific.* Santa Fe, NM: School for Advanced Research Press, 2012.

Ensemble XXI. "Journey to the Indigenous Nivkh People of Sakhalin." YouTube, January 16, 2008. http://www.youtube.com/watch?v=rGhJJQpOplU

Forsyth, James. *A History of the Peoples of Siberia: Russia's North Asian Colony 1581–1990.* Cambridge: Cambridge University Press, 1994.

Hutton, Ronald. *Shamans: Siberian Spirituality and the Western Imagination.* London: Continuum, 2007.

Vahtre, Lauri, and Jüri Viikberg. The Red Book of the Peoples of the Russian Empire. "The Nivkhs." Accessed July 31, 2013. http://www.eki.ee/books/redbook/nivkhs.shtml

Nu

The Nu, sometimes known as Anoong, A-Nung, Anong, Anu, Lutze, Luzi, Nung, Noutzu, Nu-tsu, or Nusu, are one of the officially recognized ethnic groups in the People's Republic of China. The estimated 35,000 Nu are concentrated in Yunnan Province with smaller groups in Sichuan, in the Tibetan Autonomous Region, and in neighboring Myanmar, where they are called Kwinpang. The Nu speak various dialects belonging to the Tibeto-Burman language family. The majority of the Nu adhere to the Tibetan form of Buddhism, with a large minority that continue to practice their traditional animist religion along with a few Christians.

The Nu region along the Nujiang or Nu (Salween) and Lancangjiang Rivers is thought to have been the original home of the peoples known as Nousu and Anu, both closely related to the neighboring Yi people. Historically, the tribes in the region lived by hunting, using crossbows and poisoned arrows. Poison arrows played a significant role in the history of the Nu people, being the only means they had to defend themselves. Slowly, larger and more aggressive ethnic groups drove them from the river valleys into the higher elevations where cultivation was difficult. In the eighth century, the Nu came under the authority of the Bai rulers of Nanzhao and later the Dali principality. These states, which ruled most of Yunnan, were often threatened by the advancing Han Chinese. In the early 13th century, the invading Mongols took over the region, bringing the Nu into the Chinese empire ruled by the Mongol Yuan dynasty. During this period and under the Manchu rules of the later Qing dynasty, the Nu villages were mostly ruled by a Naxi chieftain in Lijiang. From the 17th century, the Nu people were dominated by various Tibetan and Bai headmen and later by Tibetan lamaseries. These rulers took the best of the Nu lands and carried off many Nu as slaves.

Though the Chinese government has attempted to end the historic clan system, clan ties remain strong and an extended clan network continues to unite the peoples of the small ethnic group. The clan is the center of Nu life with often three generations living in the same household. Most of the surrounding households are related family and clan members. The Nu are among the least educated and poorest of the ethnic groups in Yunnan. Few of the adult Nu have a good command of Mandarin Chinese though educational opportunities are beginning to improve. Most Nu children now attend Chinese language schools, while older Nu learn Mandarin from their

newly acquired televisions and radios. The Nu have been slow to adapt to new ways of living and farming despite the determined efforts of the Chinese government. Social development among the various Nu groups remains very uneven. In some areas, the Nu farming methods and standard of living are similar to those of the neighboring Han Chinese, the Bai, and the Naxi. In other areas, there are vestiges of the communalism historically practiced by the Nu tribes. The Nu ethnic group gets it name from the nearby Nu or Nujiang River, with those living in the upper reaches of the river calling themselves Nu or Anu. Those living in the lower reaches of the river normally call themselves Nusu. Together with several smaller tribes, they were consolidated by the Chinese government to form the official Nu nationality. The languages of the Nu peoples, though forming part of the Loloish group of Tibeto-Burman languages, are not mutually intelligible. The languages have no written form and use Chinese characters for writing. Some of the Nu groups are Buddhists, belonging to the Tibetan form, while others have retained their historical indigenous religious beliefs. Christianity is professed by some of the southern groups.

By the 19th century, landownership in the Nu regions took three regional forms, a primitive communal style, private ownership, or group ownership, though most of the land was controlled by non-Nu landlords. The clan system remained strong, and clan alliances helped to alleviate the grinding poverty of the Nu villages. The remoteness of their villages precluded the modernization that began to be seen in the lowlands in the early 20th century.

By the mid-20th century, only a handful of Nu had received primary education. The Nu remained isolated until the communist victory in the Chinese Civil War in 1949. Government agents entered the Nu villages in 1950, often offering seeds, farm implements, and articles of daily use. By the mid-1950s, the Nu villages had been collectivized with the Nu working on communes or cooperatives run directly by government agents. The Nu made rapid gains in education, health care, and infant morality. The excesses of the Chinese Cultural Revolution brought renewed misery to the Nu, but the economic and political reforms of the 1980s began a new era with many Nu turning to handicrafts such as carving and jewelry instead of cash crops. A majority of Nu children now attend schools, and a string of health clinics and health-care centers have done much to alleviate the diseases that formerly ravaged the small tribal groups.

Further Reading

Ethnic Groups. "The Nu Ethnic Minority." Accessed July 31, 2013. http://www.china.org .cn/e-groups/shaoshu/shao-2-nu.htm

Foley, Peter J., "A Snapshot of the Nu," *Cultural Survival Quarterly*, 30.1 (Spring 2006). http://www.culturalsurvival.org/pub lications/cultural-survival-quarterly/china/ snapshot-nu

Harrell, Stevan. *Cultural Encounters on China's Ethnic Frontiers*. Seattle: University of Washington Press, 2000.

Mullaney, Thomas, and Benedict Anderson. *Coming to Terms with the Nation: Ethnic Classification in Modern China*. Berkeley: University of California Press, 2011.

Olson, James S. *An Ethnohistorical Dictionary of China*. Westport, CT: Greenwood, 1998.

Nuristani

The Nuristani, sometimes known as Kalasha, Nuri, Nurestani, or Nooristani, are an Indo-European people mostly living in the Nuristan region of eastern Afghanistan. Prior to their conversion to Islam in the late 19th century, the Nuristani were often called Kafir or infidel by the surrounding Muslim peoples. Nuristan occupies the valleys on the southern slopes of the Hindu Kush Mountains. Outside Nuristan, there are Nuristani communities in neighboring Afghan provinces and in adjacent areas of Pakistan's Chitral District. The Nuristani are closely related to the Kalash people of Chitral though distinguished by their adoption of Islam. The Nuristani have a distinctly European physical appearance, with fair skin, light eyes, and often blond or red hair. The estimated 150,000–300,000 Nuristani speak a number of dialects that make up one of three divisions of the Indo-Iranian language family, alongside the much more numerous Indo-Aryan and Iranian language groups. The Nuristani are overwhelmingly Sunni Muslims, with many pre-Islamic folk customs being integrated into their rituals and ceremonies.

The origins of the Nuristani are unknown, though they are thought to represent the remnants of a very early Indo-European migration. The ancestors of the Nuristani are thought to be the original inhabitants of the plains and lowlands of Afghanistan, possibly settling the region as early as 200 BCE. Over time, the small groups were forced into the higher valleys, leaving the plains to the waves of conquerors. The Nuristani are mentioned in the Indian

Rigveda, a collection of sacred Vedic Sanskrit hymns written between 1700 and 1100 BCE. In the fourth century BCE, the Greek invaders of Alexander the Great finally defeated the Nuristani after a stubborn and prolonged war. The Greeks noted in their chronicles that the peoples of the Nuristani valleys were fair and culturally and linguistically distinct. Living in the high mountain valleys, the Nuristani retained their ancient culture and their religion, a form of ancient Hinduism with many customs and rituals developed locally. Certain deities were revered only by one tribe or community, but one deity was universally worshipped by all Nuristani as the Creator, the Hindu god Yama Râja, called *imr'o* or *imra* by the Nuristani tribes. Around 700 CE, Arab invaders swept through the region now known as Afghanistan, destroying or forcibly converting the population to their new Islamic religion. Refugees from the invaders fled into the higher valleys to escape the onslaught. In their mountain strongholds, the Nuristani escaped conversion to Islam and retained their ancient religion and culture. The surrounding Muslim peoples used the name *Kafir*, meaning "unbeliever" or "infidel," to describe the independent Nuristani tribes and called their highland homeland Kafiristan. In the 10th century, the Ghaznavid ruler claimed that the Nuristan region launched a crusade against the idolatry and paganism practiced by the Nuristani tribes. The invaders captured the major Nuristani center at Nardain, which was destroyed and the temples looted. The Ghaznavid invaders, unable to sustain the occupation far from their lowland bases, finally withdrew leaving the Nuristani to continue with their

traditional religion. In the 14th century, the Mongols invaded the region, slaughtering much of the lowland population but were unable to penetrate the Nuristani mountain strongholds. The first European to visit the region is traditionally a Portuguese Jesuit missionary, Benedict de Goes, who mentioned the place and the people in his writings while on a journey from Lahore to China.

The Nuristani are sometimes called Kalasha though this name is more appropriate for the closely related Kalash in the neighboring Chitral region of Pakistan. The differences between the Nuristani and the Kalash are religious as the Kalash mostly retain their ancient religious beliefs. Both the Nuristani and the Kalash are known for their physical characteristics such as fair skin, light eye color, and blond, red, or light brown hair. Genetically, the Nuristani are related to the Kalash but have little genetic relation to the neighboring peoples. The historic isolation of the Nuristani valleys resulted in a genetically and culturally isolated population. Since the 19th century, many Western explorers have wondered if they might be descendants of the Greek soldiers of Alexander the Great's army. One of the huge mountains that tower over the Nuristani territory is known as Qala Iskanderiya, the Fort of Alexander. The Nuristani speak five different, though related, Indo-European languages that are believed to form a third branch of the Indo-Iranian language family. Many Nuristani now speak other languages, such as Pashto or Dari, the two official languages of Afghanistan. Never subjugated or under any real central authority until modern times, the Nuristani retain many ancient customs, rituals, and traditions that have disappeared from the lowland cultures of Afghanistan and Pakistan. The culture remained intact even though Nuristan was conquered, and the people forcibly converted to Sunni Islam in the 1890s. Their Islamic practices are often a blend of Islamic traditions and earlier folk customs associated with their pre-Islamic religion. The Nuristani were depicted, as their pre-Islamic past as Kafir, in Rudyard Kipling's book, *The Man Who Would Be King*, which was made into a movie in 1975.

In the early 19th century, incursions by Muslim groups from the plains often disrupted life in the Nuristani valleys. Kafiristan, as the region was called, was viewed as an abomination, an affront to all Muslims. British adventurer Colonel Alexander Gardner wrote that he visited Kafiristan twice, in 1826 and 1828. The first time when the Afghans killed members of his expedition and he and his men escaped through Kafiristan. Two years later, he visited the Kunar Valley while returning to Afghanistan. In 1893, the Durand Line was agreed to as the dividing line between Afghan territory and British India. Most of the Nuristani were included in the territory officially under Afghan rule, but the tribes remained independent in their mountain strongholds. In 1895, Emir Abdur Rahman Khan, the emir of Afghanistan invaded Kafiristan and forcibly converted the Nuristani tribes to Islam as a symbolic end to his campaigns to bring all of the country under centralized rule. The Kalash, on the British side of the line, retained their traditional religion. In 1896, the emir renamed the people as

Nuristani Mujahideen during the Soviet occupation of Afghanistan, 1985. (Reza/Webistan/Corbis)

Nuristani, meaning "enlightened ones," and *Kafiristan*, "the land of the infidels," became *Nuristan*, "land of the enlightened." Some of the tribespeople escaped across the Durand Line into the Princely State of Chitral in British India to join their kin there, though many converted to Islam in the 1930s, and many of their kin, the Kalash, were forcibly converted in the 1970s. The upheavals in Afghanistan during the 1970s were mostly confined to the lowlands until the overthrow of the Afghan government in 1978 and Soviet invasion of the country in 1979. The Nuristani were among the first to take up arms against the invaders. They played an important part in the conquest of neighboring provinces though Nuristan remained a battleground with some of the bloodiest guerrilla fighting in the war against the Soviet forces from 1979 to 1989. The withdrawal of the Soviet forces in 1989 undermined the communist government installed in Afghanistan, which collapsed in 1992. The Nuristani were hailed as an example to other Afghan peoples in leading the battle against the Soviet invasion. The Nuristani demanded their own province as the Soviets withdrew. A plan for a separate Nuristani province was put in place in 1989 but set aside as civil war swept the country. The victory of the Taliban in 1996 obliged many Nuristani to return to their highland valleys as harsh Taliban rule spread across the lowlands. The overthrow of the Taliban, implicated in the terrorist attacks in the United States in 2001, brought a democratic government to power in Kabul. In 2001, the Nuristani were rewarded for their bravery as their historic homeland was carved out of Laghman and Kunar Provinces to officially become the new province of Nuristan. In the 21st century, many Nuristani have migrated to Kabul and other areas where they are well regarded and often prospered as merchants, soldiers, or merchants.

Further Reading

Barrington, Nicholas, Joseph T. Kendrick, and Reinhard Schlagintweit. *A Passage to Nuristan: Exploring the Mysterious Afghan Hinterland.* London: I. B. Tauris, 2006.

Robertson, George Scott. *The Kafirs of the Hindu Kush.* Seattle: Amazon Digital Services, 2012.

Strand, Richard, Nick Dowling, and Tom Praster. *Nuristan Provincial Handbook: A Guide to the People and the Province.* Brighton: IDS International, 2009.

Oirat

The Oirat, sometimes known as Oirad, Oy-irad, Eleuth, Dzungar, or Zunghar, are the westernmost group of the Mongol peoples living primarily in Mongolia and China. Historically, the Oirat were composed of four major tribal groups: Dzungar, also known as Choros or Ööled, Torghut, Dör-bet, and Khoshut, each further divided into a number of minor tribes. An estimated 200,000 people in western Mongolia and another 150,000 in China, mostly in the northwestern region of Xinjiang, speak the Oirat language, spoken in a number of regional dialects. Most Oirat adhere to La-maism, the Tibetan form of Buddhism, which is also the primary religion of their Mongol neighbors. Minorities in some areas continue to practice their traditional religions or consider themselves to be athe-ists, the result of decades of antireligious teachings under communist rule. In north-western China, some Oirat groups are Sunni Muslim.

The Oirat or Western Mongol people share some culture and language along with parts of their history and geogra-phy with the Mongol because at various times, the two groups were united under the same leader. The name *Oirat* may de-rive from a corruption of the name *Dörben Öörd*, meaning "the Four Allies" or "the Allied Four," referring to the historic alli-ance of the Oirat tribes. One of the earliest mentions of the Oirat in a historical chron-icle is found in *The Secret History of the Mongol*, the 13th-century CE text that fol-lows Genghis Khan's rise to power. The Oirat are mentioned as a forest people orig-inally ruled by shaman-chiefs. The Oirat fought against the Mongol expansion but were defeated and absorbed into the grow-ing Mongol Empire in 1207. In 1256, an Oirat horde spearheaded the Mongol in-vasion of Persia. Others aided the Mongol conquest of China and helped to establish the Mongol Yuan dynasty in 1279. Follow-ing the overthrow of the Yuan rulers and the expulsion of the Mongols from China, the Oirat reorganized as a loose alliance of the four major West Mongol tribes. The alliance, known as the Four Oirats or the Alliance of the Four Oirats, began to ex-pand into the steppe lands of Central Asia, challenging the powerful states of the re-gion. In 1409, the Chinese emperor de-manded that the Oirat Alliance accept his supremacy, but a force sent to subdue them was defeated and the Oirat invaded the ter-ritories of the Mongol tribes. The Mongol chiefs refused to accept Oirat rule, and they were constantly at war with each other. In the mid-15th century, the Oirat hordes de-feated the Eastern Mongol and expanded their empire to the borders of China. The death of the Oirat leader in 1454 ended the unity of the Oirat tribes, who fought each other for leadership of the alliance. From 1480 on, the Eastern Mongol hordes pushed the Oirat westward, but by 1510, the Oirat formed part of a unified Mongol state. Relations between the Oirat and Mongol tribes remained tense with raids and fighting that continued until peace was made in 1640, and a new set of laws, the Mongol-Oirat Code, was accepted. In the early 17th century, the Oirat mostly converted to the Tibetan form of Buddhism, making themselves the chief defenders of the Dalai and Panchen lamas. The Mongol script, until 1648–1649, was replaced by a specifically Oirat alphabet. In 1678, Galdan, the chief of the Dzungar tribes, traditionally the left wing of the Oirat tribes, received from the Dalai Lama the title of khan, thus confirming the Dzungar as the new leading tribe of the Oirat. The Oirat homeland, often called Dzungaria, is in present-day northern Xinjiang from which the Oirat expanded. The new Oirat state, a confederation of nomadic tribes led by the Dzungar, was known as the Dzungar or Zunghar Khanate or sometimes the Dzungar Empire. The khanate continued to expand at the expense of neighboring states until the newly powerful Manchu, having conquered China, defeated the confederation and gained control of Outer Mongolia. In 1717, the Manchu sent an army to Tibet to expel the Oirat and to proclaim Tibet a Chinese protectorate. In 1750–1757, the Manchu Qing dynasty, taking advantage of a civil war in the khanate, invaded Dzungaria and laid waste to large parts of the Oirat territories. Some historians estimate that about 80 percent of the 600,000 Dzungar Oirat population of the conquered khanate were destroyed by a combination of warfare and disease during the final Chinese conquest of Dzungaria and

Central Asia in 1755–1758. The massacres and planned extermination of most of the Dzungar Oirat is considered the great genocide of the 18th century.

The modern Oirat are the survivors of the Qing Chinese destruction of their homeland, and most now live in western Mongolia and northern Xinjiang in western China. They are primarily the descendants of surviving Torghud and Khoshud Oirat. A smaller group is located in the Aixa region of Inner Mongolia, where they settled in the late 17th century. Many members of the group, known as the Aixa Mongol, are Muslim. Another group, called the Ejine Mongol, lives along the Ejine River in Inner Mongolia. Modern Oirat culture is now often considered a subculture of the Mongol peoples due to many similarities and common traits. The Oirat language belongs to the Mongolic language family, and scholars differ as to whether Oirat is a distinct language or a major dialect of the Mongolian language. In the Oirat regions of western Mongolia and northwestern China, the Oirat language is either endangered or even extinct in some districts as a direct result of government actions or due to social and economic policies. During the 20th century, the various *ulus* or peoples of the Mongolian plateau region were subjected to deliberate homogenization projects in the Soviet Union, China, and Mongolia. Over many decades, Buddhist practitioners and traditions were either eliminated or forced into hiding. After the 1990 revolution in Mongolia, the Oirat began to regain their hidden culture, language, and religion. For the first time since the early 20th century, the Oirat could select their *yastan* or clan for official purposes. Unlike other Mongol groups, the Oirat emerged from the socialist experiment with their ancient identity nearly intact. Relaxation of stringent communist rule in China allowed the two Oirat groups to reestablish cultural, clan, and family ties that reinforced the reculturation that continues to the present. Though the Oirat share many traditions and customs common to the peoples of the Mongolian Plateau, they have always had a strong sense of identity separate from the more numerous Khalkha or Eastern Mongol groups.

Further Reading

Golden, Peter B. *Central Asia in World History*. New York: Oxford University Press, 2011.

Kitinov, Baatr U., and Thupten Ngodub. *The Spread of Buddhism among Western Mongolian Tribes between the 13th and 18th centuries: Tibetan Buddhism in the Politics and Ideology of the Oirat People*. Lewiston, NY: Edwin Mellen Press, 2010.

Perdue, Peter C. *China Marches West: The Qing Conquest of Central Eurasia*. Cambridge, MA: Harvard University Press, 2005.

Oroqen

The Oroqen, sometimes known as Oroqin, Orochon, or Oronchon, are one of the smallest of the 56 officially recognized ethnic groups in the People's Republic of China. The estimated 8,000 Oroqen are divided with about half living in Inner Mongolia and half living along the Heilongjiang River in Heilongjiang Province in northwestern China. The Oroqen language is related to Ewenki and forms part of the northern group of Tungusic languages.

The indigenous religion remains the primary belief system with a smaller Buddhist minority.

The ancestors of the Oroqen mostly lived as hunters and gatherers following the food animals from area to area in the vast grasslands north of ancient China. Originally, part of the Bei Shiwei people, the Oroqen are believed to have broken away to form a distinct ethnic group sometime between 420 and 589 CE. One of the most ancient ethnic groups in Northern China, the *Oroqen* name means "people living on the mountain" or "people using reindeer." The original Oroqen homeland, a vast area south of the Outer Xing'an Mountains and north of the Heilongjiang River, was suited to their nomadic lifestyle. Gradually, the Oroqen bands acquired reindeer and horses and became herders as well as hunters and gatherers. Both men and women were accomplished hunters, both on foot and on horseback. To defend themselves, the mounted warriors would engage in guerilla war tactics until the invaders were driven from their territory. Under loose Chinese authority, the Oroqen bands were known as Soulun or other names often meaning hunters or reindeer herders. The name *Oroqen* was first used during the rule of the Kangxi emperor of the Manchu Qing dynasty in the late 17th century. Horses gradually became indispensable to the Oroqen culture both for hunting and for carrying the family belongings and provisions. The Oroqen horses evolved an extra-large hoof that prevented the animals from sinking into the marshy lands the Oroqen crossed. A Russian invasion in the mid-1600s drove many Oroqen deep into the less accessible mountains and forests of the northern Chinese border regions.

Oroqen hunters and their wives sit under a tarp and clean their rifles before their afternoon hunt in China. (Earl Kowall/Corbis)

The Oroqen culture is rich in folklore, legends, and oral traditions. Men, women, and children often gather to dance and sing when hunters return with a bountiful catch. The many tales, fables, riddles, and proverbs have been handed down from generation to generation. The culture has been greatly transformed in the last 50 years. As late as the 1950s, the Oroqen lived as hunter–gatherers in the relative isolation of the mountains just south of the Russian border in Northern China. The Oroqen language forms part of the Ewenki group of northern Tungusic languages, but its lack of a written form and inroads by Mandarin Chinese has endangered the survival of the language. Many Oroqen speak, along with Mandarin Chinese, the language of the neighboring Ewenki and Daur peoples. The majority of the Oroqen continue to revere nature as part of their traditional animist religion. Sacrifices to ancestral spirits are routinely made, and most believe that the elements of nature all have spirits that must be revered or appeased. Historically, the Oroqen had a special veneration for the bears and the tigers that shared their highland homeland.

In the early 20th century, the Oroqen fought alongside the other ethnic groups in the region to repulse Russian attempts to take control of the region. In the 1930s, the Japanese took control of Manchuria, including the Heilongjiang region. Many Oroqen took to the mountains to carry on a guerrilla war against the invaders. By the end of World War II in 1945, the Oroqen had been decimated and were facing extinction. The communist victory in the Chinese Civil War in 1949 at first brought shipments of shotguns, cartridges, and supplies of food, grains, and clothing, but by the 1950s, the Oroqen herds had been collectivized and the Oroqen forced to settle in permanent collectives and cooperatives as employees of the Chinese state. Farming was introduced in 1956, and within 20 years, the Oroqen region became self-supporting in grain. The reforms adopted in China in the 1980s gradually made inroads in the region with some Oroqen returning to herding to make a living, while others produce handicrafts for sale as souvenirs.

Further Reading

Akiko, Yosano. *Travels in Manchuria and Mongolia.* New York: Columbia University Press, 2001.

Ethnic Groups. "The Oroqen Ethnic Minority." Accessed July 31, 2013. http://www.china .org.cn/e-groups/shaoshu/shao-2-oroqen.htm

MacKerras, Colin. *China's Minorities: Integration and Modernization in the Twentieth Century.* Oxford: Oxford University Press, 1994.

West, Barbara A. *Encyclopedia of the Peoples of Asia and Oceania.* New York: Facts on File, 2008.

Whaley, Lindsay. "The Growing Shadow of the Oroqen Language and Culture," *Cultural Survival Quarterly*, 25.2 (Summer 2001). http://www.culturalsurvival.org/ourpublica tions/csq/article/the-growing-shadow-of-the-oroqen-language-and-culture

P

Pamiri

The Pamiri, formerly known by the older, generic name Pamir People, and sometimes known as Pamirian, comprise several small ethnic groups calling themselves Pomir or Pamiri, though they usually identify with their specific ethnic group or call themselves Badakhshani. The Pamiri have sometimes been collectively called Mountain Tajiks, Pamirian Tajiks, or Galchahs. The Pamiri are an Indo-European group estimated to number over 350,000 in the Pamir Mountains in the Gorno-Badakhshan Autonomous Province of Tajikistan and the neighboring Badakhshan Province of Afghanistan. Outside the region, there are Pamiri communities in the Xinjiang region of northwestern China and the Upper Hunza, Chitral, and Gojal regions of Pakistan. A precise population estimate is difficult as they have not been counted separately but have been included in successive census material in all regions as ethnic Tajik except in Afghanistan, where they are known as Pamiri and are mentioned in the list of Afghan ethnic groups. The Pamiri speak a group of related Eastern Iranian dialects only distantly related to the Tajik language spoken by the majority in the Badakhshan region of Tajikistan and Afghanistan. Most of the Pamiri follow the Aga Khan as adherents of the Nizari Ismaili form of Shi'a Islam. A smaller number, particularly among the Yazgulem, Wakhan, and Bartang, are Sunni Muslim of the Hanafi school.

Pamiri tradition holds that they are the descendants of the Greek leaders of Alexander the Great's army that invaded the Pamir Mountains around 327 BCE. The Pamiri first appear in historical chronicles in the second century CE when Chinese scholars mentioned the Rushans, Shugnans, and the Wakhan peoples. Though the Pamiri peoples enjoyed periods of independence over the centuries, most often they were under the political control of some foreign power. The region was an important trading center, trading precious gems and lapis lazuli from as early as the fourth century. One of the trading routes known as the Silk Road passed through the region, giving the Pamiri access to imported goods. For centuries, a long line of kings who traced their descent to Alexander the Great ruled the region, known as Badakhshan. The last of the Pamiri sultans, Sultan Muhammad, was killed in the 15th century and supplanted by Abu Sa'id Mirza, ruler of the Timurid Empire, one of the successor states of the Mongol Empire. The region, often overrun by invaders, provided the small Pamiri clans refuge in the high valleys and strongholds in the Pamir Mountains. During the 16th century, the area changed hands a number of times before the great empires of the region left the small mountain peoples to govern themselves in small, often warring states. In the 18th century, Badakhshan was conquered by Ahmad Shah Durrani and brought under Afghan rule. Afghan and Uzbek rulers of neighboring states fought for control of the Pamiri region throughout the 18th and into the 19th century.

The Pamiri peoples are considered the oldest small nation to have survived in the Central Asian region. After thousands of years, they have preserved their European appearance, with many very fair with blue or brown eyes. All of the Pamiri peoples, including the Shugnan, Rushan, Bartang, Yazgulem, Ishkashmi, Wakhan, Bajui, and Kuf, share close linguistic, cultural, and religious ties across the Badakhshan regions of Tajikistan and Afghanistan. The Pamiri speak a group of Eastern Iranian languages that form part of the Southeastern group of Indo-Iranian languages. The literary language is based on Tajik, which is spoken by most of the Pamiri as a first or second language. The Tajik government asserts that the Pamiri dialects are closely related to the Tajik language, but scholars and linguists classify the Pamiri languages as part of a branch of the Into-Iranian languages that includes only Pashto, the language of the Pashtun people, as closely related. The language group is considered endangered, with the total number of speakers declining. The religion of the vast majority of the Tajiks is Sunni Islam, so the Pamiri minority adhering to the Ismaili faith is further removed from the Tajik majority in the region by language, culture, and religion. The Pamir Mountains, known in the Persian language as the "roof of the world," has protected the Pamiri peoples for thousands of years, allowing them to preserve not only their Caucasian physical features but also many cultural traits

and traditions unique to the region. Many traditional Pamiri beliefs and rituals have to do with agriculture and animal herding. Tradition determines when planting and watering should be done. Pamiri women enjoy greater freedom than Tajik women, often participating in public gatherings just like men. Women are allowed to work outside the home and, unlike neighboring peoples, have never been veiled, nor are they restricted to particular parts of houses.

In the early 19th century, the Afghan kingdom and the Uzbek Emir of Bukhara contested the Pamir region. In the latter part of the century, Bukhara, which had become a Russian protectorate, continued to expand to the south, while Afghanistan, under loose British control, expanded toward the Hindu Kush and the Pamir Mountains. Between 1840 and 1859, the Afghans and Uzbeks of Bukhara often sent expeditions into the region that disrupted Pamiri life. The ruler of Badakhshan, Mir Shah, signed a treaty agreeing to accept nominal Afghan authority but little changed for the Pamiri peoples. In 1895, to prevent a serious conflict, the United Kingdom and Russia agreed to delimit the border between Bukhara and Afghanistan at the Pyanzh River, effectively partitioning Badakhshan and the homeland of the Pamiri peoples. The Emir of Bukhara controlled the territory north of the river, with the Afghans controlling the land to the south. Russia annexed the entire Badakhshan region from Bukhara in 1904, bringing the northern Pamiri under direct Russian rule. The Pamiri were mostly left to their traditional way of life until the end of the Russian Civil War and the arrival of Bolshevik cadres in Central Asia. The government of the new Soviet Union organized the Gorno-Badakhshan Autonomous Province within the newly created Tajik Soviet Socialist Republic in 1924. Contact between the Pamiri in the Soviet Union and those in Afghanistan and China were discouraged and restricted. Only with the collapse of Soviet power in 1991 were ties reestablished among the scattered Pamiri peoples.

Further Reading

"About Pamirians." YouTube, November 16, 2007. http://www.youtube.com/watch?v= mwvEMj0WSqM

Bergne, Paul. *The Birth of Tajikistan: National Identity and the Origins of the Republic.* London: I. B. Tauris, 2007.

Countries and Their Cultures. "Pamiri." Accessed July 31, 2013. http://www.everyculture.com/wc/Tajikistan-to-Zimbabwe/Pamiri.html

Forbes, Andrew. *Silk Road.* London: Insight, 2013.

Koen, Benjamin D. *Beyond the Roof of the World: Music, Prayer, and Healing in the Pamir Mountains.* New York: Oxford University Press, 2008.

Pashayi

The Pashayi, sometimes known as PaSai, Pashai, Pashi, Safi, or Kohistani, are a Dardic people living primarily in eastern Afghanistan and the neighboring Khyber Pakhtunkhwa Province and the Chitral district of Pakistan. The estimated 550,000 Pashayi are mostly highlanders. In Afghanistan, they are concentrated in the northern districts of Laghman and Nangarhar Provinces and the eastern districts of Kapisa Province with smaller communities in Nuristan and Kunar. The language of the Pashayi belongs to the Dardic branch of the Indo-Aryan group of Indo-European languages. Pashto, the language of the dominant Pashtun people of Afghanistan, is spoken as a second language. The majority of the Pashayi are Sunni Muslim, with an important minority adhering to Nizari Ismaili Islam.

Historically, north and east Afghanistan was considered part of the Indian cultural and religious sphere. Early accounts of the region mention the Pashayi as living in a region producing rice and sugarcane, with many wooded areas. Many of the people of the region were Buddhists, though small groups of Hindus and others with tribal religions were also noted. The Pashayi region formed part of the ancient kingdom of Gandara, which was centered on the great river valleys where an advanced civilization flourished from the early first millennium BCE to the 11th century CE. Alexander the Great and his Greek warriors conquered Gandara in 327 CE, but Greek influence remained slight. Traditionally, the Pashayi were converted to Islam by the Pashtun Ghaznavids led by Abu Mansur Sebük Tigin in 1021, when the name *Gandara* disappeared. According to accounts of the conquest, the Ghaznavids slaughtered all non-Muslim populations, razed their towns and cities, and converted the lowland survivors to the Islamic religion. Venetian explorer Marco Polo wrote of a Pashai region during his travels there in the 13th century. The Mongol invasions of the 14th century pushed many of the Pashayi into the more mountainous regions as the Mongols devastated the lowland regions. The Pashayi in the highlands mostly retained their traditional beliefs until many were forcibly converted to Islam in the late 16th century. In the 16th century, the region was under the rule of the Mughal successors to the Mongols in India. Mughal nobility spent time in the highlands, which were famed for the beauty of the forested hillsides and the fertility of the river valleys. In the early 18th century, the Afghan territories became part of the kingdom ruled by the Pashtun Hotaki dynasty. Pashtun influence on the Pashayi increased as the Pashtun culture and language spread across the non-Pashtun regions in the north.

Because of a lack of written records or a written tradition among the Pashayi, the origins and descent of the ethnic group are shrouded in obscurity. Traditionally, the Pashayi are believed to be the descendants of the ancient Gandarans. The Pashayi language belongs to the Dardic group of Indo-Aryan languages and is related to Kashmiri, the most widely spoken of the Dardic languages, and to the Shina language spoken in Gilgit-Baltistan and Khowar or Chitrali spoken in northern Pakistan. The Pashayi homeland is often referred to as *Kohistan*, meaning "land of mountains or peaks," referring to the high peaks of the Hindu Kush Mountains that rise in the region. The Pashayi remain a tribal people though most live in villages or towns. Personal disputes are traditionally resolved by the injured party, often leading to feuds. The Pashayi value honor above all else, and the Pashayi ideal is a proud warrior who is loyal to his tribe and family, dangerous to his enemies, and always prepared for the necessities of a feud. Every Pashayi adult male carries a

knife or a gun. The culture has a rich tradition of songs and folklore that is mostly oral traditions passed from generation to generation. The Pashayi language, though spoken for more than 2,000 years, used Pashto as the literary language. In 2003, a written form of the language was devised, with the written language now beginning to be introduced into elementary schools. The Muslim religion is an integral part of modern Pashayi culture with many parts of the Koran memorized, even among illiterate groups in the most remote areas. Traditionally, the Pashayi women are not secluded and may interact freely with men not belonging to their immediate family. Many clans permit women a degree of sexual freedom that is not often found in most areas of Muslim Afghanistan.

The Pashayi homeland, lying along the volatile region between Afghan and British authority, was often subject to tribal raids, feuds, and uprisings. The Pashayi men were known as formidable warriors, quick to take offence. In 1893, the British and the Afghan government established the Durand Line, which fixed the borders between their respective spheres of influence. The new border divided many Pashayi clans and families and was mostly ignored though smuggling became a widespread occupation. In the late 1920s, King Amanullah Khan moved to end Afghanistan's long isolation and to modernize the kingdom. Reforms such as education for women, the abolition of the tradition of veiled women, or the supremacy of secular laws over Islamic traditions raised tensions in the more conservative Pashayi regions. Many Pashayi warriors joined a widespread uprising that forced the king to abdicate in 1929. The warriors returned to their homes when a new king was enthroned, remaining distant from the political upheavals of Kabul and the Afghan lowlands until the early 1970s. The end of the monarchy and the imposition of a republic in 1973 began a long decline that resulted in a communist coup and a massive Soviet invasion of Afghanistan in 1979. The Pashayi joined the anti-Soviet guerrilla forces, and heavy fighting devastated many of their valleys over the next 10 years. The Soviets finally ended the occupation in 1989, leaving between 850,000 and 1.5 million Afghan dead, including many Pashayi leaders and warriors. Weak governments, corruption, and ethnic disputes brought on a vicious civil war from 1992 to 1993, pitting the Pashtun, aided by the Pashayi, against the Tajik, Uzbek, and other peoples of northern Afghanistan. The violence of the war resulted in a takeover of the country by the Taliban, radical Pashtun students who imposed a strict Islamic government, banned entertainment, music, and forced women to wear the burka, a tentlike covering from head to foot. Taliban complicity in the 2001 terrorist attacks in the United States brought a U.S.-led invasion and the overthrow of the Taliban government in 2003. A more moderate government, still dominated by the Pashtun peoples, won the support of the Pashayi though their homeland remains poverty stricken and underdeveloped.

Further Reading

Adamec, Ludwig W. *Historical Dictionary of Afghanistan.* Lanham, MD: Scarecrow Press, 2011.

Ewans, Martin. *Afghanistan: A Short History of Its People and Politics.* New York: Harper Perennial, 2002.

Keiser, R. Lincoln. *Muslim Peoples: A World Ethnographic Survey.* Westport, CT: Greenwood, 1984.

Yun, Ju-Hong. "Pashai Language Development Project: Promoting Pashai Language, Literacy, and Community Development." SERVE International Afghanistan, 2003. http://www-01.sil.org/asia/ldc/parallel_papers/ju-hong_yun.pdf

Pashtun

The Pashtun, sometimes known as Pushtun, Pahktun, Patan, Pakhtoon, Pashto, Pukhto, or Pashtu, are an Indo-Iranian people living mostly in northwestern Pakistan and southern and eastern Afghanistan, a large area sometimes known as Pashtunistan or Pakhtunkhwa. The estimated 50 million Pashtun made up one of the largest ethnic groups in the region. The Pashtun form the largest ethnic group of Afghanistan and have dominated the country for over 300 years, with nearly all Afghan rulers being ethnic Pashtun. In Pakistan, the Pashtun population forms the largest ethnic group in the province of Khyber Pakhtunkhwa, the Federally Administered Tribal Areas, and northern Baluchistan in Pakistan. Outside the traditional Pashtun territories, there are large Pashtun communities in other parts of Pakistan and Afghanistan, the United Arab Emirates, the United States, Iran, Kashmir, the United Kingdom, Germany, Canada, India, and smaller groups in Russia, Australia, Malaysia, Chile, and Tajikistan. The Pashtun language, called Pashto, belongs to the southeastern group of the Indo-Iranian language family. Many Pashtun speak Urdu, Dari, or English as second languages. The majority of the Pashtun are Muslims, divided into the often conflicting Sunni and Shi'a branches of Islam, with smaller numbers of Ahmadi, Ismaili, and Christians.

Scholars continue to debate the origins of the Pashtun people. According to Pashtun traditions, they are descended from Afghana, the legendary grandson of the Hebrew King Saul. The most widely held belief is their origins lie with ancient Aryan tribes that intermingled with various subsequent invaders. From about the third century CE onward, the Pashtun were most often known as Afghan, a name now used to describe every citizen of Afghanistan. Their mountainous homeland, containing the passes leading into the great Indian Plain, has been a corridor for invaders for thousands of years. A center of the ancient Buddhist realm known as Gandhara when it was reached by the soldiers of Alexander the Great, the Pashtun homeland has archeological evidence of a Greek-inspired Buddhist society. In the first century CE, the invading Kushans overran the region. Fair Aryan groups, driven from the Iranian Plateau region, occupied the mountains in the seventh century and created small tribal states in the highland valleys, gradually

A Muslim Pashtun man and boy walking a road in the Urak Valley just outside Quetta city, Balochistan Province, Pakistan, 2008. (Joe Lapp/Dreamstime.com)

absorbing the earlier inhabitants. Persian traders introduced Islam to the western Pashtun tribes between 632 and 661. The new religion gradually spread to the east, and by the 10th century, most of the Pashtun had become Muslim. The Muslim centers in the Pashtun territories formed one of the main centers of the Muslim world during the so-called Islamic Golden Age that ended with the Mongol conquests of the 13th century. The destruction caused by the invading Mongol hordes in Pashtunistan depopulated major cities and forced many of the survivors to revert to an agrarian tribal existence. Waves of invaders converted the Pashtun tribes into a warrior people, often considered the best guerrilla fighters in the world. The various tribal groups united only with threatened, more often warring among themselves. Historically, the Pashtun territories formed part of the lands ruled by successive kingdoms centered on Kabul. Expanding to the north and east, the Pashtun tribes settled in many lowland areas, reaching the Peshawar Valley probably in the 15th century. Because of their division into powerful tribal groups, the Pashtun only began to feel a sense of shared identity in the 16th century. The Afridi Pashtun rallied the tribesmen to defeat an invading Mughal army of 40,000 in the 17th century. Only able to partially subdue the warlike tribes, India's Mughal rulers initiated the practice of paying local rulers and chiefs to keep the peace on the volatile frontiers of the Mughal Empire. From the 16th century to the early 18th century, Pashtunistan was divided between the Shi'a Persians in the west and a larger territory nominally ruled by the Mughal Empire. Mughal power declined rapidly in 1707, allowing the Pashtun to unite under the rule of the Durrani Sultanate of Afghanistan in 1747. As the Pashtun gained domination over the many ethnic groups in Afghanistan, many settled in other areas, particularly around the capital at Kabul.

The Pashtun people, until the 20th century, more commonly known as Patan or Pathan, comprise four major geographic divisions. The major group in Afghanistan is known as the Durrani. The other three divisions are in Pakistan, including the Ghilzai

Sword Dance

The Sword Dance, also called the Khattak or the Khattak Dance, is a swiftly moving martial sword dance performed by the agile warriors of the Khattak tribe of Pashtun in Afghanistan and Pakistan. The dance, performed by Khattak warriors before a battle, originated in the 17th century as a war preparation exercise. Developed over centuries, the warriors perform the dances with their weapons in their hands. The warriors display their physical fitness through complex body movements while holding up to three swords at a time. The dance, with many regional versions, is now performed by many of the Pashtun tribes in Afghanistan and Pakistan.

or Gilzai, the second largest Pashtun tribal confederation, the highland groups called Tribals, which includes a number of distinct tribal groups, living along Pakistan's border with Afghanistan, and the Lowland Pashtun, the most integrated into modern Pakistani society. The major divisions are further fragmented into some 60 tribal groups. The tribal and subtribal or clan groups remain the focus of Pashtun loyalty even though the Pashtun culture now encompasses a highly diverse population, from highly educated urban dwellers to tent-dwelling nomads. The Pashtun have evolved a strong sociocultural ethnic identity that transcends the numerous tribal divisions and the international border that divides Pashtunistan between Afghanistan and Pakistan. All Pashtun groups honor the *pashtunwali*, the "way of the Pashtun," a strict unwritten historical code of honor that includes 10 main principles and obligations—*melmastia*, extending hospitality to all strangers; *nanawatai*, giving asylum to any refugee, even mortal enemies; *badal*, to seek justice or take revenges for wrongs; *tureh*, defense of Pashtun land, property, family, and women; *sabat*, loyalty to family, friends, and tribe; *imandari*, righteousness in thought, word, and deed; *inteqamat*, trust in God; *ghayrat*, always show courage; *namus*, protection of women; and *nang*, preserve honor and defend the weak. It is considered the personal responsibility of every Pashtun male to discover and rediscover essence and meaning of *pashtunwali*. The Pashtun language is divided into two major dialectal groups, the northern dialect known as Pakhto, and the softer southern dialect, Pashto. The language is further divided into four major dialects that roughly correspond to the ethnic divisions—Pakhto or Eastern Pashto, the major dialect spoken in northwestern Pakistan; Southern Pashto in central Pakistan and eastern Afghanistan; Durrani or Western Pashto, in western Afghanistan and Iran; and Mahsudi or Central Pashto, spoken in Pakistan's tribal districts. Each of the regional dialects is divided into several subdialects and numerous regional variants. Written in a modified Perso-Arabic script, the Yusafzai dialect of Eastern Pashto is the basis of the literary language in Pakistan while the Kandahari dialect is the standard in Afghanistan. Pashto is one of two official languages in Afghanistan, but in Pakistan, only Urdu and English are official, with Pashto allowed in elementary education since 1984 though higher education is in the Urdu language. The religious beliefs of the Pashto are overwhelmingly Muslim, mostly Sunni of the Hanafi school, though adherents of the two major sects, the Sunni and the Shi'a, are often in conflict. Smaller groups such as the Ismaili or Ahmadi are often considered heretics while the small Christian population is often seen as apostates. Violence among the religious groups is common, particularly in Pakistan.

The Sikhs of the Punjab, expanding their empire to the north, drove the Durrani government from the territory east of the Khyber Pass in 1823. The Afghan king initially sought the aid of the British in India to recover the territory taken by the Sikhs, but the eastern Pashtun territories remained under Sikh rule until the British defeat of the Sikhs in 1849. Despite demands by the Afghan government for the return of the eastern districts, the largely Pashtun districts remained under British rule. The frontier between British territory and Afghanistan was fixed at by arbitration between 1872 and 1875 with an 1893 agreement establishing the Durand Line that divided historical Pashtunistan as the international border. The British garrisoned the main towns of British Pashtunistan but were unable to pacify the lawless tribal areas so they adopted their predecessor's practice of paying local rulers and chiefs to maintain the peace. The British stipends became the region's major source of legal income, though smuggling and other prohibited activities continued across the mountain passes. Various military expeditions attempted to bring the tribal areas under direct British control in the 1880s and 1890s, but with little success. In 1901, having failed to conquer the Pashtun tribes, the British created a semi-autonomous region called the North-West Frontier District with British garrisons in the major towns controlling only about a third of the Pashtun territory. Indirect rule through the Pashtun *jirgas*, local tribal leaders or councils, remained the policy in British Pashtunistan. The Pashtun majority in Afghanistan, though under British influence, remained the dominant ethnic group led by the Afghan king and the nobility. Tribal groups in Waziristan, in the mountainous districts along the Afghan border, rebelled against British rule in 1919–1920. The rebellion rapidly spread, forcing the authorities to mobilize 30,000 British and Indian troops before the rebels were finally subdued. In the 1930s, the Afridi Pashtun, led by a local religious leader, declared a holy war against the British. More than 10,000 Pashtun died before the rebellion

was ended, leaving a lasting hatred of the British and other Westerners. Afghanistan was recognized as an independent multiethnic kingdom in 1921, under a royal government dominated by the Durrani Pashtun. The Afghan government laid claim, on historical and ethnic grounds, to the Pashtun territories under British rule. The Pashtun in the North-West Frontier District acknowledged neither the Durrani Pashtun ruler of Afghanistan nor the British authorities. The Afghan government, like the British, was forced to pay local rulers to keep the mountain passes open and to control local smuggling and tribal uprisings. Following World War II, as the British began preparing British India for independence, including its partition into secular India and Muslim Pakistan, the Afghan government proposed that the North-West Frontier District be allowed a wider choice of joining Pakistan, India, Afghanistan, or separate independence. Allowed to choose only India or Pakistan, the Pashtun territories voted for Muslim Pakistan. The Afghan government, opposed to eastern Pashtunistan's inclusion in the new Pakistani state, voted against Pakistan's membership in the new United Nations organization. The Soviet invasion of Afghanistan in 1979 sent a wave of six million refugees fleeing across the border, mostly into the Pashtun Province in the northwest. About 85 percent of the refugees were ethnic Pashtun, often with tribal or family ties to Pashtun in Pakistan. The Afghan civil war that followed the Soviet withdrawal in 1986 pitted the Pashtun tribes in the south against the non-Pashtun groups in the north of the country. A group of radical students, mostly from religious schools in

Pakistan's North-West Frontier Province, known as the Taliban, gradually gained power in the Pashtun regions of Afghanistan. Initially seen as peacemakers after years of civil strife, they imposed a harsh form of Islamic law. Women were particularly targeted, being forbidden work outside the home, receiving education after the age of eight years, or being allowed medical care. Afghan men were required to stop shaving and to grow untrimmed beards, while all music, sports, and other forms of entertainment were banned in the Taliban-controlled provinces. Taliban ties to a radical Islamic group known as Al Qaeda gave the radicals material support and training facilities in Afghanistan. Following the Al Qaeda attacks in the United States on September 11, 2001, the Taliban and Al Qaeda were targeted as terrorists. In October 2001, American and British forces launched a new phase in the long Afghan civil war designed to remove the Taliban from power and to dispel Al Qaeda from their Afghan hideouts. The Taliban government was quickly toppled, and a moderate government took power with Western backing. The Taliban, with widespread support in Pakistan, were able to regroup and to launch attacks inside Afghanistan that continue to the present. Among the Pashtun people, women continue to have their rights curtailed in favor of their husbands or male relatives. Despite the obstacles, Pashtun women have begun a process of change in both Pakistan and Afghanistan. The ongoing ethnic and religious conflicts in Afghanistan and Pakistan have reinforced the ethnic identity of the Pashtun, often leading to demands for the reordering of international borders to reflect the historic and ethnic geography of historic Pashtunistan.

Further Reading

Akbar, M. J. *Tinderbox: The Past and Future of Pakistan.* New York: Harper Perennial, 2012.

Knudsen, Are. *Violence and Belonging: Land, Love, and Lethal Conflict in the North-West Frontier Province in Pakistan.* Copenhagen, Denmark: Nordic Institute of Asian Studies, 2009.

Lindhom, Charles. "Respect Essential for Survival in Pashtun Culture." Accessed July 31, 2013. http://home.honolulu.hawaii.edu/~pine/Phil100/pashtun.htm

Nichols, Robert. *Settling the Frontier: Land, Law and Society in the Peshawar Valley, 1500–1900.* New York: Oxford University Press, 2001.

Pumi

The Pumi, sometimes known as P'umi, Primi, Pimi, or Prummi, are one of the officially recognized nationalities of the People's Republic of China. The estimated 38,000 Pumi are concentrated in the southwestern Chinese province of Yunnan with a smaller community in neighboring Sichuan. The Pumi language, commonly known as Prinmi, belongs to the northern group of Qiangic languages of the Tibeto-Burman language family. The majority of the Pumi adhere to a form of the pre-Buddhist Bön religion locally known as Zanbala. A smaller group has adopted the Tibetan Buddhism of the nearby Tibetan populations.

The Pumi are believed to have originated as nomads in the Qinghai-Tibetan plateau region. Around the fourth century BCE, they migrated south, probably following game animals, into the warmer valleys in the Hengduan Mountains in the eastern part of the plateau just west of the Sichuan Basin. By the seventh century, the Pumi had migrated into Sichuan, where they formed one of the major ethnic groups in the Xichang region. Under the influence of the neighboring Tibetans, the Pumi adopted much of the Tibetan's pre-Buddhist religion known as Bön, which they adapted to their own traditional belief system. Later, Tibetan Buddhism was introduced through the Pumi's close contact with the neighboring Tibetan peoples. A further migration, possibly as part of the displacements of the Mongol invasion of the region, in the 13th and 14th centuries, brought the Pumi south into the mountainous Ninglang, Lijiang, Weixi, and Lanping areas of present-day Yunnan. The migrants settled as herders, gatherers, hunters, and farmers. By the 17th century, most of the Pumi had adopted agriculture, which became the mainstay of their local economy. Local landlords, mostly Han Chinese or Bai, dominated the Pumi communities. Except for a number of communal regions shared by Pumi villages, most of the land was held by landlords who collected rents from the peasant farmers. A lucrative sideline for the Pumi chieftains and the other landlords in the region was the trade in domestic slaves, many of them ethnic Pumi. Despite some 2,000 years of history, the population of the Pumi tribes remained relatively small due to disease, famine, war, and assimilation into other cultures.

The official Pumi nationality was organized in 1960 from a number of small tribal groups, each with a different name. The name *Pumi* means "white people." The Pumi culture, through centuries of close contact with the Tibetans and their close proximity to Tibet, closely resembles that of their Tibetan neighbors, though in recent years, they have borrowed many traditions from the neighboring Han Chinese in Yunnan. Unlike the Tibetans, rice is the staple food. Even the Pumi villages in areas too cold for rice often trade their potatoes for rice. Generally, the Pumi are patrilineal and monogamous, though polygamy is accepted in some of the northern communities. A traditional beer-like drink called *priis* is an essential element of the culture and is normally served at ceremonies, rituals, and marriage celebrations. The word for "marry" is literally "to drink *pri*" in the Pumi language. The language is spoken in at least five regional dialects. Some scholars believe that Pumi was originally a Qingic language though the modern language has a large number of Tibetan and Mandarin Chinese loanwords. Most of the Pumi adhere to a mixed belief system known as Zanbala, which is based on the ancient Bön religion of the Tibetans with later admixtures from Buddhism and the beliefs of nearby ethnic groups. The Pumi believe in a spirit world that if offended can release a deluge of fierce, predatory beasts to devour their livestock and destroy their crops. Despite a growing number claiming Lamaism or Daoism as their religion, the majority continue to believe in a pantheon of gods and the influence of their revered ancestors in their lives.

By the early 19th century, the Pumi culture was still at a prefeudal level of organization. Generally, clan members grouped together with different clans bearing different names. Families belonging to the same clan, which acted as an extended family, regularly ate together to commemorate their common ancestry. Marriage was primarily between members of different clans. Village patriarchs or respected elders wielded great influence and were often consulted to settle disputes. Clan members shared a responsibility to help each other in difficult times. In some areas, landlords owned most of the land, relegating the majority of the Pumi to the position of sharecroppers or debt slaves on large estates. By the early 20th century, more than 90 percent of the Pumi were farmers working land scattered on the slopes of hills. Many also raised livestock, primarily sheep and cattle. Most of their tools were made of wood as blacksmithing was unknown though some iron goods were traded from the Han Chinese. Except for a limited number of "public hills," the landlords owned the land, taking at least 50 percent of the harvest as rent. Pumi and Naxi landlords owned domestic slaves, which they could sell or give away as gifts. The Pumi remained relatively isolated until the end of the Chinese Civil War in 1949. Communist agents of the new Chinese government moved into the region. They quickly eliminated the landlords and their families and began the redistribution of land to the Pumi peasants. However, these lands were later collectivized, and the Pumi farmers became employees of the state. In 1960, the Chinese government grouped together a number of small related tribes into the official Pumi ethnic group. The relative relaxation of stringent controls in the 1980s allowed many Pumi to buy land of their own, begin businesses selling wood products and handicrafts, and extend the rice-growing paddy fields on the terraced hillsides.

Further Reading

Ethnic Groups. "The Pumi Ethnic Minority." Accessed July 31, 2013. http://www.china.org.cn/e-groups/shaoshu/shao-2-pumi.htm

McCarthy, Susan K. *Communist Multiculturalism: Ethnic Revival in Southwest China.* Seattle: University of Washington Press, 2009.

Mitchell, Sam. *Ethnic Minority Issues in Yunnan.* Kunming, China: Yunnan Fine Arts Publishing, 2004.

Mullaney, Thomas, and Benedict Anderson. *Coming to Terms with the Nation: Ethnic Classification in Modern China.* Berkeley: University of California Press, 2011.

Q

Qiang

The Qiang are sometimes known as Qiang zu, Qiang Min, Ch'iang, Chiang-min, Erma, R'ma, Rimai, Rima, Ma, or Zangzu. The estimated 327,000 Qiang live in the Maowen Qiang Autonomous Prefecture in China's Sichuan Province with smaller communities in Yunnan, Gansu, and Guizhou. The Qiang form one of the 56 official nationalities of the People's Republic of China. Though officially all Qiang speak the Qiang language, the linguistic diversity among the group is bewildering. The majority of the Qiang adhere to a polytheist religion known as Ruism, with smaller communities who practice Tibetan Buddhism or the Daoism borrowed from the Han Chinese.

The name *Qiang*, probably meaning "herdsmen," was originally given by the ancient Han Chinese to the nomadic peoples to the west some 4,000 years ago. The Qiang, as they are known in historic Chinese archives, were not a single ethnic group but many non-Han ethnic groups and tribes. The history of the Qiang goes back as far as the Western Zhou dynasty between 1100 and 771 BCE. During the rule of the Qin and Han dynasties, between 221 BCE and 220 CE, the Qiang peoples mostly migrated south from Inner Mongolia to settle the highlands of western Sichuan. Because of the repeated threats, they built imposing stone fortresses. During

that time, considerable Han Chinese migrations moved into the region to sometimes form mixed communities of Han and Qiang peoples. For many centuries, the Qiang peoples were squeezed between the great Chinese and Tibetan states that controlled most of the territory. Numerous armies overran the region along with raiders and bandits that ravaged the Qiang regions. Between 600 and 900 CE, many Qiang assimilated into the Tibetan or Han Chinese cultures, greatly reducing the number of people known as Qiang in the region. For many centuries, the successive Chinese dynasties maintained political and military units in the Qiang-occupied regions. Many of the Qiang headmen and leaders were officially named by the Chinese court as the official authorities in the various regions. During the rule of the Manchu in China, known as the Qing dynasty beginning in the mid-17th century, the system of appointing local hereditary headmen to rule over the Qiang gave way to rule by officials dispatched to the region directly from the Qing court.

The culture of the Qiang varies from region to region though oftentimes the matrilineal society allows women to wield considerable power in the Qiang communities. Primarily monogamous, the Qiang also accept polyandry and cross-cousin marriages. Due to its tribal diversity, Qiang culture has been influenced and has influenced many other cultures. Generally, those Qiang living near the Tibetan populations have adopted many Tibetan cultural traits, while the majority have been heavily influenced by Chinese culture. Historically, the Qiang lived in areas often attacked by raiding armies, bandits, and ethnic warriors so that a tradition of living in stout stone houses, often part of larger fortress villages, continues to the present. The Qiang religion, known as Ruism, involves belief in the white stones that are revered as representing the sun god, who can bring good luck to their daily lives. According to Qiang legends, the white stone began as markers left along the route of their early migrations to show those who wished how to return to their original homes and to honor those they left behind. Later, white stones were placed on the corners of Qiang roofs and towers and at the pinnacle of their square stone pagodas. The Qiang dialects are broadly divided into Northern Qiang and Southern Qiang, the latter of which is tonal. Each of the divisions is composed of several different dialects. Both groups form part of the Qiangic branch of the Tibeto-Burman language family. Many of the dialects diverge greatly and are not mutually intelligible.

In the early 1800s, the majority of the Qiang were mountain dwellers, living in fortress villages composed of between 30 and 100 households mostly belonging to a single clan structure. Close trade and cultural relations with the Han Chinese and the Tibetans allowed the Qiang to trade their horses, medicinal herbs, and other produce for farm implements and other necessities. A feudal landlord economy dominated farm production. Landlords and rich peasants,

A Qiang tower, traditional architecture of the Qiang ethnic group in Taoping, Sichuan Province, China. (Jinfeng Zhang/Dreamstime.com)

who accounted for about 8 percent of the Qiang population, controlled some 43 percent of the cultivated land. Poor peasants, sharecroppers, and hired farmhands made up the bulk of the Qiang population. The administration of the region during the last decades of the Qing dynasty, in the late 19th and early 20th centuries, mostly relied on corrupt officials and avaricious landlords to gather taxes and send tribute to the Chinese court. By the advent of communist rule in China in 1949, most of the Qiang were illiterate peasants with little or no education. Communist cadres arrived in the region in early 1950. They quickly eliminated the landlord class and redistributed land to the Qiang peasants. These lands were later collectivized, and the peasants became employees of the Chinese state. Through the early years of Chinese communism, many of the Qiang were sent to reeducation camps or were eliminated as enemies of the state. The gradual ending of stringent communism, in the 1980s, allowed many Qiang to reclaim their ethnic heritage. An ethnic revival spread through the Qiang regions in the 1990s with a renewed interest in their traditional music, dance, and oral history. In the early 21st century, many Qiang have turned to occupations other than farming, mostly trade in handicrafts or other products. In 2008, a serious earthquake rocked the Qiang region in western Sichuan. The epicenter, in Wenchuan County, was the worst hit, but many Qiang communities suffered great damage. A second large quake, in 2013, further damaged already devastated Qiang villages and towns.

Further Reading

Chen, Yong, and David C. Booth. *The Wenchuan Earthquake of 2008: Anatomy of a Disaster*. Berlin: Springer, 2011.

Legerton, Colin, and Jacob Rawson. *Invisible China: A Journey through Ethnic Borderlands*. Chicago: Chicago Review Press, 2009.

Magnier, Mark, and Demick, Barbara. "Quake Threatens a Culture's Future." *Los Angeles Times*. May 21, 2008. http://articles.latimes.com/2008/may/21/world/fg-qiang21

Ming-Ke, Wang. "From the Qiang Barbarians to the Qiang Nationality: The Making of a New Chinese Boundary." In Shu-min Huang and Cheng-Kuang Hsu, eds. *Imaging China: Regional Division and National Unity*, 43–80. Taipei, Taiwan: Institute of Technology, 1998. http://ultra.ihp.sinica.edu.tw/~origins/pages/barbarbook4.htm

Simpson, Andrew. *Language and National Identity in Asia*. New York: Oxford University Press, 2007.

R

Ryukyuan

The Ryukyuan, sometimes known as Okinawan, Lewchewan, Riukiuan, Riukiu Islanders, Ryukyu Islanders, or Luchu, are the indigenous people of the Ryukyu and Amami Islands that stretch south from the Japanese island of Kyushu to Taiwan off the east coast of China. The estimated 1.5 million Ryukyuan make up the majority of the inhabitants of the Ryukyu Islands and the Amami Islands, which form part of Kagoshima Prefecture of the southern Japanese island of Kyushu. The Ryukyuan speak dialects of the Ryukyuan branch of the Japonic languages. Most Ryukyuan adhere to Buddhism or Shintoism, with a small Christian minority.

The early inhabitants of the islands are believed to have been a people distantly related to the Caucasians or to the Altaic or Uralic peoples of eastern Siberia. Over thousands of years, this population absorbed migrants from the Asian mainland to form the modern Ryukyuan people. The islanders retained their ancient dialects and culture while borrowing from the Chinese and later the Japanese cultures. The islands were early divided into three distinct kingdoms corresponding to the three island groups. Japanese contacts were frequent between the sixth and ninth centuries CE; then Chinese influence became stronger. The three small domains often warred among themselves

while sometimes uniting to face an outside threat. In the mid-14th century, a powerful Sho king began to unite the islands in one kingdom. Under the Sho dynasty, the kingdom, known as Ruujchuukuku in the Ryukyu dialects, by 1429 had united the three small states and extended its rule to the Amami Islands just south of Kyushu and to the large island of Taiwan in the south. Despite its small size, the Ryukyu kingdom played a central part in the maritime trade between mainland Asia and Southeast Asia. The Ryukyuan, from the 14th century, were forced to swear allegiance to the Chinese emperor and to pay annual tribute though the kingdom remained independent under its Sho kings. The kingdom experienced a golden age of prosperity, art, music, and literature in the late 15th and early 16th centuries. In 1609, the imperial government of Japan gave the Satsuma Samurai clan its permission to invade the Ryukyu kingdom. The Japanese occupation forces disarmed the Ryukyuan of all bladed weapons to forestall rebellions. A system of self-defense using only farm tools as weapons developed as the forerunner of modern karate. The Japanese maintained the kingdom in order to benefit from the Ryukyuan trade ties to mainland China. Forced to pay tribute to both China and Japan, the Ryukyu kingdom began to decline, quickly losing Taiwan to Chinese colonization. For the next two centuries, the Ryukyu kingdom retained a precarious independence amid increasing poverty as the Chinese and Japanese empires sought to assert their control.

The Ryukyuan culture is a fusion of the ancient society of the islands with later Chinese, Japanese, and American influences. Ethnically, the Ryukyuan are thought to be more closely related to the Ainu of northern Japan than to the ethnic Japanese. Generally taller than the Japanese, the Ryukyuan include the early possibly Caucasian inhabitants of the islands in their ancestry, with later admixtures of Chinese and Japanese influences. Geographically, the Ryukyuan are divided into seven major dialectical and cultural groups that correspond to the regional grouping of islands. Through centuries of close contact with China and Southeast Asia, the Ryukyuan developed a unique culture with a distinct language, social customs, and traditions. The family is the center of Ryukyuan life, with extended families often living together. Tightly knit families and close personal relationships are part of the island culture. Unlike the reserved Japanese of the main islands, the Ryukyuan are known for their courtesy, warmth, humor, generosity, and directness. Though most Ryukyuan adhere to the beliefs of Buddhism or Shintoism, they retain much of their traditional religious beliefs. Ryukyuan women have historically played a strong role in the culture and religion of the islands, holding positions of shamans and guardians of the home. Traditional reverence for nature, including the belief in spirits in the elements of nature and an ongoing fear of unseen demons, gods, and ancestral spirits, remains part of the culture. The spirits of the ancestors are believed to dwell in the ornate tombs that dot the islands. These spirits must be invited back into the lives of their descendants so that the ancestors may continue to exist. The Ryukyuan language, known as Nantö, is spoken in six major dialects and is thought to be related to Ainu spoken by the indigenous people of Hokkaido in northern Japan. Assimilation into Japanese culture, especially among young Ryukyuan, has decreased the use of the dialects as Japanese is the language of administration and education.

The Japanese allowed the Ryukyuan people to continue to rule themselves and to maintain the important trade links from China through the islands to Japan. In the Amami Islands, just south of Kyushu, the assimilation of the Ryukyuan population was official policy. The Ryukyuan relationship with Japan changed with the arrival of European and American ships in the region. Commodore Matthew Perry of the U.S. Navy landed at Naha, the Ryukyuan capital, in 1853. The Americans established friendly relations with the Ryukyuan population and used the islands as a base for the eventual penetration of the "hermit kingdom," Japan. During one of his visits to the islands, Commodore Perry acquired an ancient temple bell, the Gokokuji Bell, that was taken back to the United States where it was used to ring out the score at Army–Navy football games until its return to the Ryukyu Islands in 1988. Increased tensions and rivalry with China prompted the Japanese imperial government to dispatch an occupation force to the kingdom in 1872. Two years later, the Japanese annexed the kingdom over fierce Ryukyuan resistance. The last Sho king was deposed in 1879 amid an official policy of full assimilation of the population into Japanese culture. Discrimination against the Ryukyuan increased as the military hierarchy took control of Japan in the 1920s and 1930s. Japan's military government, always suspicious of the loyalty of the Ryukyuan people, heavily fortified the islands as World War II began in the Pacific. In early 1945, American troops landed in the islands, beginning a three-month battle to dislodge the Japanese troops in the islands. The Ryukyuan population, forced by the Japanese military to continue resistance long after the battle was lost, suffered civilian losses of about a third of the prewar population. The scale of the slaughter during the fighting was one of the major factors in the decision to drop atomic bombs on Nagasaki and Hiroshima rather that risk repeating the bloodletting of the Battle of Okinawa. In 1945, the Ryukyu and Amami Islands were placed under American military occupation. With American aid, the islands quickly recovered. The Amami Islands, over Ryukyuan opposition to the division of their islands, were returned to Japanese sovereignty in 1953. The United States and Japan, with much popular support in the islands, reached an agreement to return the Ryukyu Islands to Japan in 1972. The Ryukyuan, with incomes higher than the Japanese central islands in 1972, began to lose their economic base. Japanese companies, without the restrictions in the main islands, opened heavily polluting factories in the region. By the 1990s, the living standard of the Ryukyuan people had fallen to just 70 percent of the Japanese average. Japan's postwar ideology of a single Japanese culture, while denying the existence of the Ryukyuan as a distinct ethnic group, resulted in discrimination and a widespread annoyance with the Ryukyuan for their resistance to assimilation. Tensions and discrimination continue to color relationships between the Ryukyuan people and the Japanese of the main islands. The ongoing resistance to a continuing American military presence in the islands as part of the alliance with Japan is another point of tension. Many Ryukyuan would like to close the military bases or at least to share in the financial benefits that go directly to the central government. In the 1990s, the Japanese government officially apologized for the ongoing discrimination, past neglect, and renewed a pledge to raise the island incomes to the level of those in the main islands. However, in the 21st century, the dismal view of the national minorities by the majority of the Japanese remains a major problem for the Ryukyuan people.

Further Reading

"Daily Publishes Challenge to Japanese Sovereignty over Okinawa." *South China Morning Post*, May 9, 2013.

Figal, Gerald. *Beachheads: War, Peace, and Tourism in Postwar Okinawa.* Lanham, MD: Rowman & Littlefield, 2012.

Kerr, George. *Okinawa: The History of an Island People.* Clarendon, VT: Tuttle Publishing, 2000.

McCormack, Gavan. *Resistant Islands: Okinawa Confronts Japan and the United States.* Lanham, MD: Rowman & Littlefield, 2012.

Minority Rights Group International (2008). *World Directory of Minorities and Indigenous Peoples—Japan: Ryukyuans (Okinawans).* Accessed July 31, 2013. http://www.refworld.org/docid/49749cfdc.html

S

Sakha

The Sakha, sometimes known as Saha, Yakut, or Jeko, are a Turkic ethnic group, considered the largest group belonging to the Altaic branch of the Turkic peoples and the largest indigenous ethnic group in the Russian Far East. The Sakha homeland forms the Sakha Republic, a member state of the Russian Federation. Though considered a Turkic people, the Sakha are of mixed Turkic, Mongol, and Paleo-Siberian background. The estimated 485,000 Sakha speak a Northern Turkic language belonging to the Siberian Turkic branch of the Turkic languages. A majority of the Sakha are Orthodox Christian, with a minority retaining their pre-Christian shamanistic beliefs.

Sakha traditions trace their origins to the region around Lake Baikal in southern Siberia. A revered Sakha legend tells of the first Sakha, the result of the union of a Tatar hero and a Buryat maiden living on the shores of Lake Baikal. The early Sakha fled the region around the lake to escape the 13th-century Mongol invasion. Moving north into central Siberia, they adopted a nomadic existence as herders of cattle and horses. The Sakha migrated again to the region of northeastern Siberia during the Middle Ages, probably forced to move north by Buryat invaders during the turbulence following the collapse of the Mongol Empire in the 14th cen-

tury. By the 15th century, the Sakha had spread across the basin of the Lena River. They first settled along the lowlands of the middle Lena, along the lower Vilui and Aldan Rivers, where they found grass for grazing and some protection from the extremes of the northern winter. Maintaining their traditional way of life as herdsmen, the Sakha adapted to the rigors of their new homeland with remarkable flexibility. From their new heartland along the middle Lena River, they gradually expanded northeast and west beyond the Lena Basin toward the Arctic Ocean. The Sakha migration brought them into contact with the earlier inhabitants of the region, Evenk and Yukagir, who were absorbed or pushed farther north. The Sakha learned from these people to adapt their culture to Arctic conditions, adopting the hunting, fishing, and reindeer herding that meant survival in the Arctic and subarctic territories. Unlike their Turkic kin in southern Siberia and Central Asia, the Sakha were never affected by the introduction of the Islamic religion but retained their ancient shamanistic belief system. Traditional Sakha society was divided into a number of tribal groups dominated by *tonjon*, tribal chiefs. Gradually, the Khangala tribe came to dominate the other tribes of the region. Russian traders and explorers visited the Sakha region in the 16th century, trading tobacco for valuable furs to sell in European Russia. The chief of the

Khangala, in return for military aid against other peoples in northeastern Asia, granted the Russians the right to construct a trading post and stockade known as Fort Lensky in 1632. The fort became an important military center during the Russian wars to subdue the tribes they called Yakut between 1634 and 1642. The defeat of the Sakha began a period of Slavic settlement. By 1710, colonists from European Russia had occupied the more productive lands in the southern river valleys forcing the Sakha into the harsh taiga and tundra. Several serious Sakha rebellions erupted over the dispossession of various tribes from their traditional territories and the imposition of the *yasak*, the fur tax that required a quota of valuable furs from each able-bodied Sakha. The fierce Sakha horsemen bravely resisted Russian domination but were finally subdued after a brutal campaign by mounted Cossack troops. In the late 1600s, Russian Orthodox missionaries settled in the region and began to convert the Sakha to Christianity. Many of the Sakha accepted the new Christian religion,

but not out of conviction but because Christians were exempt from the hated fur tax. Over time, the Sakha blended the Christian traditions and rituals with their shamanistic beliefs in a uniquely Sakha belief system. The Sakha homeland was made part of the Siberian Governorate created as part of Tsarist Russia in 1708. In an administrative reform in 1782, the region became part of the new region of Irkutsk and was divided into Sakha administrative units based on traditional clan territories, often governed through tribal chiefs. Fort Lensky, renamed Yakutsk, became the center of Slav colonization of the huge Sakha homeland. The Slavic influx, mostly limited to the more fertile southern districts, had little effect on the majority of the Sakha tribes until the arrival of political and criminal deportees at slave labor camps established after 1773.

The Sakha culture is a unique Turkic culture combining traditions and influences from many sources. The Sakha emerged as a distinct culture in the 14th century encompassing many disparate groups. Gradually,

The Sakha Holocaust

Russians began to encroach on Sakha territory in the 1620s, imposing a hated fur tax and suppressing rebellions in 1634 and 1642. The rebellion of 1642 spread from the Sakha to the other peoples of the region. The Russians forces, under the command of Peter Golovin, responded with a reign of terror. Sakha villages were burned, with the few surviving captives raped, tortured, and then killed. Thousands of Sakha fled, but the massacres continued. Between 1642 and 1682, the Sakha population declined rapidly, with most estimates of between 70 and 75 percent of the population eliminated in just 40 years.

the groups merged into the two modern divisions based on economics and geography. The northern Sakha group is mostly seminomadic hunters, fishermen, and reindeer herders. The southern group, living in the more temperate zones, is mostly horse and cattle herders or farmers. During the 20th century, an urbanized Sakha population developed mostly not only in Yakutsk, called *Joküskai* in the Sakha language, but also in the towns that grew up around the economically important diamond mines. Physically, the Sakha display two distinct types, Turkic and Mongol, which reflects their mixed ethnic ancestry. Like the Turkic cultures to the south, the Sakha are known for their oral epics, the *toyons* that tell of their ancient leaders and heroes. The Sakha homeland is about twice the size of Alaska, partly mountainous and partly lowland with some 40 percent of the region lying within the Arctic Circle. Known to the Sakha as Sakha Omuk, officially the region forms the Sakha Republic, one of the member republics of the Russian Federation. Traditionally, the Sakha were divided into a number of tribes known as *aymakh* or *d'on*, which were often engaged in tribal warfare with each other. The Sakha language, Sakha Tyla, is a Northern Turkic language spoken over an enormous geographic area but without dialects and little regional variations. The largest part of the Sakha population is Orthodox Christian, though in the more remote districts, shamanistic beliefs remain the local religion. Since the 1990s, the traditional shamanistic beliefs have been revived, even among the urbanized Sakha, and now form an active part of their Christian rituals.

Slavic settlement continued in the 19th century, often encouraged by the Russian authorities. The number of labor camps grew rapidly as political dissidence increased in European Russia. Many of the political prisoners, Poles and Russians particularly, were highly educated scholars and scientists who devoted themselves to the study of the Sakha language and culture. The Sakha language became a literary language when political exiles created a modified Cyrillic alphabet. The exiled scholars opened a Yakut museum in 1891, others devised an alphabet to fit the Sakha language, and a political exile compiled the first dictionary of the Sakha language. Primary schools developed by political prisoners and Russian Orthodox missionaries aided the development of a Sakha literary language. Revolutionary ideals espoused by the deportees found fertile ground in the Sakha region, where poverty and malnutrition were endemic. The upheavals of World War I, followed by the Russian Revolution in 1917, brought chaos to the region. The Bolshevik coup and the resulting Russian Civil War pushed most Sakha into an alliance with the anti-Bolshevik White forces. Sakha leaders joined with the Whites to form the Autonomous Government of the Yakut Region, turning their vast homeland into an anticommunist bastion. Far from the battlefields of the Russian Civil War, Sakha Omuk escaped the devastation and chaos, but in 1920, the victorious Red Army occupied the major towns in the region. Soviet attempts to force the Sakha to settle in permanent villages and collectives provoked a widespread Sakha uprising in 1921. The last of the Sakha rebels and anti-Bolshevik forces in the region were defeated and liquidated in 1923. In spite of continuing suspicion of Soviet authority and a renewed rebellion in 1928, the Sakha benefited from Soviet policies that helped to spread education and supported the Sakha culture. The period of Soviet collectivization, widely resisted in the 1930s, began a long decline in the Sakha population. Thousands of shamans, targets of Soviet repression, were eliminated or disappeared into the slave labor camps established across the region after 1931. Soviet policies under the dictator Joseph Stalin aimed at ending ethnic cultures in favor of a universal Soviet culture. Sakha cultural organizations, schools, and publications were banned. In the years after World War II, the development of the region's enormous diamond, gold, and coal deposits drew in a large Slavic settler population in the 1950s and 1960s. The Sakha percentage of the population of their historic homeland dropped from 80 percent in 1946 to less than 50 percent by 1965 and just 33 percent in 1989. As the only form of protest possible under strict Soviet rule, the Sakha fiercely resisted giving up their language and culture. In the late 1980s, as reforms loosened harsh Soviet rule, the Sakha demanded that they be allowed to de-Russify family names. The demand opened the way for a torrent of grievances and discussion of past abuses and oppression. The Sakha leaders put forward a plan for local control of the region's mines, long controlled by ministries in Moscow. In the wake of the collapse of the Soviet Union, in 1991, the Sakha region, renamed the Sakha Republic, became a member republic of the newly reorganized Russian Federation. Thousands of Slavs, settled in the region during the Soviet era, began to return to European Russia. The Russian population dropped from more than half the total in 1991 to about 40 percent in 2000, while the Ukrainian percentage dropped from 7 to 5 percent. The Slavic decline allowed the Sakha majority to occupy many government posts and to win local control of the important mining sector. By 2010, the Sakha formed about 50 percent of the multiethnic population of the republic, with their language recognized as an official language, along with Russian. Sakha nationalism is a strong force in the republic, but moves toward greater autonomy or even independence have been tempered by the prospect that the important mining region, with a Slavic majority, would stay with Russia should the Sakha attempt to secede from the Russian Federation. Although the enormous ecological damage to the region by the uncoordinated extraction of Sakha's raw materials is one of the major themes of the Sakha national movement, the loss of part of their historic homeland would be an even greater disaster.

Further Reading

Argounova-low, Tatiana. *The Politics of Nationalism in the Republic of Sakha 1900–2000: Ethnic Conflicts under the Soviet Regime.* Lewiston, NY: Edwin Mellen Press, 2012.

Bychkova Jordan, Bella. *Siberian Village: Land and Life in the Sakha Republic.* Minneapolis: University of Minnesota Press, 2001.

Scott Polar Research Institute. "Republic of Sakha." Last modified January 8, 2000. http://www.spri.cam.ac.uk/resources/rfn/sakha.html

Tichotsky, John. *Russia's Diamond Colony: The Republic of Sakha.* London: Routledge, 2000.

Salar

The Salar people, sometimes known as Salar'er, Salor, or Salur, are one of the 56 officially recognized ethnic groups in the People's Republic of China. The estimated 110,000 Salar are concentrated in the Qinghai-Gansu border region on both sides of the Yellow River in western China. Outside that region, there are Salar communities in Xinjiang, farther to the west. The Salar speak a language belonging to the Oghuz branch of the Turkic languages. Most also speak Mandarin Chinese, and both languages are official in the autonomous counties with large Salar populations. The Salar are overwhelmingly Sunni Muslim.

Salar traditions place their origins around the city of Samarkand in present-day Uzbekistan. Then part of the Western Turkic Khaganate, a confederation of many Turkic tribes that was established in the beginning of the seventh century CE, the Salar or Salur formed one of the member nations. Their name is believed to have meant "those who wave swords and spears." Salar legends tell of two brothers, Haraman and Ahman, highly regarded Muslim leaders living near Samarkand in the 11th century. Jealousy and persecution by King Galamang resulted in their flight to the east. With 18 followers, they tied a Koran to the head of a white camel. When the camel found a waterfall and bent to drink, it turned to stone, indicating the place where the Salar should settle in present-day Qinghai Province. Later, others left the region around Samarkand to join the Salar colony in Chinese territory. Around 1370, the Salar clan leaders accepted the authority of the Chinese Ming dynasty officials. The Salar leaders were appointed as the Ming representatives in the region with control over the taxes and tribute to be sent to the court each year. Under the Ming government, the Salar were allowed to govern themselves and to retain their Muslim religion. Following the Manchu conquest of China, the autonomy of the Salar was curtailed. Many of the officials of the Manchu Qing dynasty viewed the Muslim Salar as a fierce and troublesome minority. Between the 1670s and 1780s, various Muslim teachers brought competing schools of Muslim thought to the region, often leading to violence between adherents of different teachings. In 1781, concerned by the spread of subversive teachings, Qing officials arrested Ma Mingxin, a Salar leader, and took him in chains to Lanzhou in Gansu. The Salar responded by killing all local government officials and defeating a military expedition sent against them. They moved into Gansu hoping to free Ma Mingxin. Arriving at the walls of Lanzhou, they demanded the release of their leader, who was summarily beheaded. Outraged, the Salar besieged Lanzhou but were unable to penetrate the thick walls. The Qing officials organized Mongol and Tibetan warriors to attack the Salar camp, where the Salar were defeated and most were killed. Historians estimate that the uprising of 1781 decimated some 40 percent of the total Salar population. Over the centuries, the Salar intermarried with the neighboring Tibetans, Hui, Han

Chinese, and Mongols to form the modern Salar people. During the rule of both the Ming and Qing dynasties, Muslim men were constantly subjected to military conscription, which placed a heavy burden on their families and the Salar villages.

The Salar, as a Muslim culture, are a patrilineal people divided among clans in a unique kinship clan system. Clan members are encouraged to marry into other clans as marriage within the clan is forbidden. As Muslims, Salar villages are dominated by the central mosque and the Muslim clergy. Though they are considered a distinctive Chinese nationality and are recognized as such by the government of the People's Republic of China, they are very similar to the Uyghur of Xinjiang, with little difference in language and culture. Despite modernization, the Salar maintain many of their traditional taboos and conventions. It is impolite to pass in front of Salar people during ceremonies. Coughing during conversations is considered rude. Brides leaving for the wedding must cry while singing to demonstrate her reluctance to leave her family. Friends and relatives of the bride then escort her to the bridegroom's home, where they force open his door so the bride can enter. The Salar diet is based on wheat flour, supplemented by potatoes and other root vegetables. They eat beef, lamb, and chicken, but are prohibited from eating pork, donkey, or horse. Their Muslim religion belongs to the Sunni branch of Islam, with the Salar maintaining their own particular form known as *gazui*. This organizational form of Islam originated with an elected leader, but now the *gazui* is the hereditary leader of the Salar Muslims. The Salar language, part of the Oghuz or Western Turkic languages, is spoken in two distinct dialects. The two dialects diverged as one was influenced by Tibetan and Chinese dialects, the other by the Uyghur and Kazakh languages. Most writing in the Salar language is adapted to the Chinese script.

Violence between the various Muslim groups in the Salar region continued into the 19th century. In the 1880s and 1890s, sectarian strife spread through all the Salar communities. The conflict arose between traditionalists and a reform teaching with the Qing officials finally supporting the reformists. Qing troops were dispatched to restore order but were repulsed. The Salar led a revolt that spread to the neighboring Hui and Dongxiang Muslims. The uprising turned into the Dungan Revolt of 1895–1896, which swept across western China. It was finally brutally put down by imperial troops and a loyalist Hui army. A widespread slaughter of the rebels and their clans left many districts virtually depopulated. In the early 20th century, the landlord economy was predominant in the Salar regions. Relying on feudal and religious traditions, Salar landlords maintained ownership of most of the land and the farm animals, as well as water sources and oil mills. Religious leaders often owned large tracts of land and demanded heavy unpaid labor by the Salar peasants. Following the Chinese Revolution in 1911, many Salar left their landlords to join the army, then known as being given eating rations. Many Salar soldiers fought the Japanese during World War II. After 1945, the Chinese Civil War engulfed the country with heavy fighting between communist rebels and government troops. Many of the Salar troops, promised greater political and religious freedom, defected to the communists and fought alongside the rebels until their victory in 1949. The initial stance of the new government was conciliatory, but soon antigovernment legislation and restrictions on the Salar culture were implemented. Land was collectivized, making Salar farmers employees of the new government. With a long history of entrepreneurial enterprises, the Salar quickly took advantage of the capitalist reforms that have swept China since the 1980s. Many have opened new businesses to export the region's products to the booming Chinese cities in the east, while others have set up construction and manufacturing. The opening of the Chinese economy has allowed the formerly very poor Salar to enjoy a modest prosperity in the early decades of the 21st century.

Further Reading

Akasoy, Anna, Charles Burnett, and Ronit Yoeli-Tlalim. *Islam and Tibet: Interactions along the Musk Routes.* Farnham: Ashgate, 2010.

Lipman, Jonathan Neaman. *Familiar Strangers: A History of Muslims in Northwest China.* Seattle: University of Washington Press, 1998.

Ma, Wei, Ma Jianzhong, and Kevin Stuart. *The Folklore of China's Islamic Salar Nationality.* Lewiston, NY: Edwin Mellen, 2001.

Selkup

The Selkup, sometimes known as Solkup, Sholkup, or Ostyak-Samoyed, are a Siberian ethnic group concentrated in the Taz River region and on the middle reaches of the Ob and Yenisei Rivers. The Selkup are the only surviving representative of the Southern Samoyed peoples. The estimated 3,000–5,000 Selkup speak a Samoyedic language of the Uralic language group though now more than 50 percent of the population uses Russian as their first language. The majority of the Selkup retain their traditional belief system, which includes shamanism and belief in spirits, though a minority have adopted Orthodox Christianity.

Linguistic evidence points to a common Samoyedic ancestry, probably in the areas west of the Ural Mountains. In the first millennium BCE, the Samoyed tribes began to migrate to the east, northeast, and southeast. They inhabited a vast area stretching from the Urals, on the boundary between European Russia and Siberia, to the basin of the Yenisei River in south-central Siberia. The Selkup are believed to be descended from a mixing of the aboriginal population of the Ob River basin and the early Samoyed migrants to the region. The Selkup tribes lived in relative isolation along the central reaches of the Ob River. Contact with neighboring tribes was difficult due to the long distances and rough terrain. In the 13th century, the Selkup and the other Southern Samoyed peoples came under the rule of the Tatar khanates of Kazan and Sibir. Though mostly left to govern themselves, they were forced to pay tribute and taxes, usually in the form of valuable furs. In the late 16th century, the Russians began to conquer parts of western Siberia. The building of a strong Russian fortress at Krasnoyarsk in 1628 brought an end to Tatar authority in the region and began the subjugation of the Selkup and the neighboring Siberian peoples to Russian rule. Harsh treatment and heavy Russian taxes pushed the Selkup to abandon their traditional homeland along the Ob and retreat into the basins of the Taz, Turukhan, and Yeloghuy Rivers in the 17th century. Despite their dispersal, they were unable to free themselves from the hated Russian tax collectors. The Selkup joined the other Samoyedic and Ugric peoples in uprisings against the Russians but were defeated by modern Russian firearms. They adopted a policy of strategic withdrawal, moving quickly away from areas of Russian penetration, but the Russians quickly followed. Suicide was often preferred to a life of slavery. A favored method was to dig a cave that, once crowded with people, the props would be cut and the people buried alive. The surviving Selkup were subjected to a policy of Christianization and Russification in the 18th century. The Selkup were given Russian names, and mass baptism was pronounced; however, the Selkup, as soon as the Russians left their villages, returned to their ancient religious beliefs and customs.

The Selkup people are the only surviving ethnic group of the Southern Samoyed group. The related Kamasins disappeared in the early 20th century, mostly absorbed into the local Russian-speaking peasantry. The culture of the Selkup is endangered, both by increasing urbanization and by the distance between Selkup groups. They inhabit large areas of Siberia, including communities in the northern parts of Tomsk Oblast and Krasnoyarsk Krai, and farther north in the Yamalo-Nenets and Nenets Autonomous Okrugs. The Selkup tend to be fairer and less Mongoloid in

appearance than the Northern Samoyed peoples, and they are unique among the Samoyeds as they are bearded. The Selkup are divided geographically and dialectically into the Taz, living along the Taz, Turukhan, Yeloghuy, and Yenisei Rivers, the Tym, along the Tym, Narym, Vakh, and Vasyugan Rivers, and the Southern or Ket, in the basins of the Ket and Ob Rivers. The geographic groups also respond to the major dialects spoken by the Selkup speakers. The Selkup language, which forms part of the Kamas-Selkup group of Samoyedic languages, is the only surviving representative of this language group and is severely endangered. By 2013, only around 45 percent of the Selkup are able to speak or understand the Selkup language. Since the 1930s, the influence of the Russian language has been increasing with many Russian words added to the Selkup language, and Russian equivalents are rapidly replacing Selkup words. Most of the Selkup continue to revere their traditional shamanistic beliefs. A belief in the spirits that inhabit all of nature is still vibrant with prayers and sacrifices offered to avert the problems caused by evil spirits. A minority of the Selkup, perhaps as high as 6 percent of the population, has adopted the Russian Orthodox faith.

In the early 19th century, the Selkup were still mostly hunters, reindeer herders, and fishermen, living in conical tents in summer and moving to log cabins in the winter. Fur-bearing animals such as sables, wolverines, and squirrels were favored game and their pelts were required to satisfy the Russian fur tax imposed on the Siberian peoples. Russian settlers appeared in the Selkup regions as permanent settlers along the rivers in the mid-19th century. European diseases, to which they had no immunity, decimated the Selkup and other aboriginal peoples of the region. The Russians often discriminated against and mistreated the Selkup, who retreated to areas farther from the Russian settlements. The Russians also took to hunting the reindeer that the Selkup used as draft animals, making reindeer breeding very difficult in many areas. The Russians introduced many European tools and improvements but also used alcohol, fraud, and force to secure the best lands and furs. The Soviet takeover of Russia in 1920 brought Soviet planned economy and collectivization. Forced to give up their nomadic way of life, the Selkup were forced to live in permanent settlements and work as employees of the Soviet state. Shamanism was outlawed and militant atheism introduced, further eroding the Selkup culture. Selkup children were rounded up and sent to Soviet boarding schools, accelerating their alienation from the traditional Selkup environment and occupations. The life and culture of the Selkup were governed by strangers from far away with little room for the advancement of the Selkup as a distinct ethnic group. In the 1950s, the survival of the Selkup as an ethnic group again came under threat. Many Selkup living in the permanent Soviet villages adopted a Russian way of life, including dependence on consumer goods such as clothing, furniture, tools, and household appliances. Both the Russian language and Russian mass culture were being rapidly assimilated. The assimilation would have been more rapid, but for the discrimination, they often had to endure from the ethnic Russians. In the wake of the collapse of the Soviet Union in 1991, activists began to work for the recovery of the Selkup culture and language. Discrimination, high unemployment, and alcoholism remain as severe problems for the small ethnic group in the 21st century.

Further Reading

Arctic Photo. "The Selkups." Accessed July 31, 2013. http://www.arcticphoto.com/selkups .asp

Atherstone, Pamela. *Like Footprints in the Wind: A Generation Lost.* Denver: Outskirts Press, 2012.

Forsyth, James. *A History of the Peoples of Siberia: Russia's North Asian Colony 1581–1990.* Cambridge: Cambridge University Press, 1994.

Olson, James S. *An Ethnohistorical Dictionary of the Russian and Soviet Empires.* Westport, CT: Greenwood, 1994.

Vahtre, Lauri, and Jüri Viikberg. The Red Book of the Peoples of the Russian Empire. "The Selkups." Accessed July 31, 2013. http://www.eki.ee/books/redbook/selkups .shtml

She

The She, sometimes known as Ho Ne, Ho Nte, or Shanha, are one of the 56 official nationalities recognized by the People's Republic of China. The estimated 900,000 She are concentrated in the coastal province of Fujian, where they form the largest minority, with smaller groups in Zhejiang, Anhui, Jiangxi, and Guangdong. There are also She living among the Hakka people in Taiwan. The She language is a She-Jiongnai language of the Hmong-Mien language group, though most She now speak

Hakka. Most She adhere to their traditional religion known as Panhu, based on ancestor worship, along with elements of Buddhism and Daoism.

Many scholars believe that the She originated in the Phoenix Mountains in present-day Guangdong Province. According to She traditions, they left their original homeland to escape the oppression of their feudal rulers, the Hakka people. Their flight from tyranny is commemorated in their oral history and in their name for themselves "guests from the mountains." The She came under the rule of the Han Chinese in the seventh century CE, when the Tang dynasty organized prefectures in the Fujian region. A feudal society was well established among the She by the time that the Song dynasty took power in 960. Many of the landlords were either She, Han Chinese, or Hakka, controlling the majority of the lands worked by She farmers growing rice, sugarcane, tea, and ramie. By the 14th century, many She had migrated into the highland areas in eastern Fujian, southern Zhejiang, and northern Jiangxi. The majority of the She lived in abject poverty under the arbitrary rule of local landlords and headmen. Many fled to other areas seeking a better life or a means to make a living. The situation for the She improved somewhat under the policies of the Ming dynasty from the 14th to the mid-17th centuries. Some local She headmen or prosperous landlords were picked to represent the Ming court in the She regions.

She culture retains many of its historic traditions even though the She have incorporated many Han Chinese customs. She society is organized by ancestral temples, a type of clan grouping with people of the same surname or clan. Each such temple has a headman or chieftain responsible for settling internal disputes, administering public affairs, and presiding over the sacrificial ceremonies of the Panhu belief system. Within each temple are units known as *fang*, of extended family groups. The basic social unit is the family within each *fang*, under a patriarchal system usually headed by the eldest male. She women enjoy more privileges and have higher status than that among the Han Chinese. She men often live with their wife's family and adopt the wife's family surname. Traditionally, each She clan is symbolized by a dragon-headed stick, a sign of the She's religious beliefs. She clans trace their ancestry to a legendary hero named Panhu, who helped the Chinese emperor to put down a rebellion and therefore won the hand of a Chinese princess. She beliefs trace the beginnings of the She ethnic group to Panhu and the princess, who had three sons and a daughter, the ancestors of the She people. The traditional She religion glorifies their legendary ancestors, and paintings of them are hung in every home for holidays and religious services. Sacrifices are made to Panhu every three years. Though Buddhism and Daoism have been adopted, many of their historic beliefs, particularly in spirits and ghosts, remain to the present. Many of the She traditions and customs have given way as the She adopt much of the neighboring Han Chinese culture.

By the 19th century, many of the She lived among the larger Han Chinese and Hakka populations both in the coastal provinces of China and on Taiwan. Near feudal conditions prevailed, with the majority living as peasant farmers paying rent for lands controlled by rich landlords. Parent-arranged marriages were normal, as were the outright sale of daughters. Bride dowries usually included bamboo hats, iron farm tools, and woven rain capes. As the feudal system evolved, She parents and matchmakers, intent on making correct alliances, drove up bride prices across the region. Dowries became exorbitant, and many of the poorest She peasants were unable to afford to marry. Due to the large number of arranged, loveless marriages, gatherings for folk singing became very popular as a means of spending time with lovers in defiance of the feudal marriage system. Well into the 20th century, tensions remained in the She regions as they struggled against the corruption and oppression of the landlord system. In the 1920s, She peasants in eastern Guangdong organized to fight the forces of the landlords with similar uprisings in Fujian and Zhejiang. The uprising lasted from 1924 to 1927. It was finally put down, but the tensions remained. A second She uprising, known as the Agrarian Revolution, broke out in Fujian in 1927. The revolt spread until most of the She districts were under a worker–peasant administration. The movement was finally defeated in 1937, when the war with Japan spilled into the region. The She fought with the neighboring peoples against the Japanese invaders until 1945. Many of the She regions supported the communists in the Chinese Civil War from 1945 to 1949, though others supported the government. The communist victory in 1949 drove the Chinese government to exile on Taiwan with many She joining the exodus to settle the plains of western Taiwan. The Chinese Cultural Revolution, from 1967 to 1977, was particularly hard on the She, who were forbidden to worship their ancestors or to celebrate other aspects of the Panhu religion. Many shrines and temples were destroyed by Red Guards, and She who were deemed antirevolutionary were arrested and sent to labor and reeducation camps. The economic and political reforms that were introduced after 1979 allowed the She to own land, open businesses, and worship their ancestors once again; however, by the early 21st century, the She had assimilated into Han Chinese culture to a great extent, including losing their language in most of the She regions where Hakka and Mandarin Chinese are now widely spoken.

Further Reading

Ethnic Groups. "The She Ethnic Minority." Accessed July 31, 2013. http://www.china .org.cn/e-groups/shaoshu/shao-2-she.htm

Legerton, Colin, and Jacob Rawson. *Invisible China: A Journey through Ethnic Borderlands.* Chicago: Chicago Review Press, 2009.

MacKerras, Colin. *China's Minorities: Integration and Modernization in the Twentieth Century.* Oxford: Oxford University Press, 1994.

Mullaney, Thomas, and Benedict Anderson. *Coming to Terms with the Nation: Ethnic Classification in Modern China.* Berkeley: University of California Press, 2011.

Shor

The Shor, sometimes known as Tadar, Mountain Shor, Mrassa Tatar, Kondoma Tatar, Chysh, or Kuznets Tatars, are a small

Turkic people living in the southern part of the Kuznetsk Basin region in southern Siberia. Though Turkic in language and culture, the Shor evolved from a mixture of Turkic, Ugric, Samoyedic, and Ket peoples. Culturally and linguistically, the estimated 20,000 Shor are closely related to the Khakass and Altay peoples. The Shor language belongs to the Khakass subgroup of the Turko-Tatar languages. Most of the Shor are bilingual, using Russian as the language of education and administration. Though the Shor are officially considered Orthodox Christians, they retain their pre-Christian shamanistic beliefs.

Indigenous Samoyedic and Kettic tribes were known to inhabit the Kuznetsk Basin, probably as early as the Paleolithic period. Pastoral nomads in the region were mentioned in Chinese records of the fifth century CE. Overrun by migrating Turkic tribes, the region came under the rule of a Turkic khanate from the sixth to eighth centuries. The intermingling between the indigenous peoples and the Turkic tribes began the evolution of the distinctive Shor people as the Samoyeds and Ket adopted the language and culture of the Turkic rulers.

In the eighth and ninth centuries, the Shor tribes emerged as a separate ethnic group. The expanding Mongol Empire absorbed the tribes of the region in the early 13th century. Under Mongol rule for more than two centuries, the Shor took on many Mongol traditions and customs. A powerful Oirat federation took control of the region in the 16th century. The Shor, living in the basin of the Tom River and along the Kondoma and Mras-Su Rivers, were mainly engaged in hunting, fishing, and some farming, and a specific craft, blacksmithing. Known as the "Blacksmith Tatar," the Shor supplied finished iron weapons and tools to the Oirat, Kyrgyz, and other neighboring peoples. Slavic Cossacks, the vanguard of the expanding Russian Empire, began to penetrate the Kuznetsk Basin in the late 16th century. The Cossacks called the Shor the "Blacksmith Tatar," with the name *Kuznetz*, blacksmith in Russian, being extended to the entire region. Over the next century, Russian authority was extended over the region known as Shoria or Mountain Shoria. The growing number of Russian colonists into the valleys of the upper Tom River in the late 18th and early

Protector of the Forests

The most internationally known member of the Shor people is Alexander Arbachakov, the current director of the Agency for the Research and Protection of the Taiga in the Siberian province of Kemerovo. He has worked for over 15 years to protect the cedar forests that are considered the green heart of the Shor people. Arbachakov is documenting the traditional knowledge of the Shor to show other Siberian peoples how they can use the forests without harming the fragile biodiversity. In 2006, Arbachakov was presented with the prestigious Whitley Award, the United Kingdom's top environmental award, by the Royal Geographic Society.

19th centuries greatly changed traditional Shor life. Russian merchants brought sophisticated metal tools that ended the Shor blacksmithing. Russians officials forced the Shor to pay the *yasak*, the fur tax, so large numbers of Shor left their villages for the forests seeking sable and other fur-bearing animals. Orthodox missionaries converted many to Christianity, though without the loss of their pre-Christian belief system.

The Shor are of mixed Turkic and Mongol background with earlier influences from the Samoyed and Ket peoples. Physically, the Shor resemble the Turkic peoples, with certain Mongol features. With relatively fair skin, light eyes, and straight, soft hair, most of the Shor physically resembles the Turkic peoples of Europe and Central Asia. Traditionally, the Shor are organized in clans, with each clan headed by a chief of *pashtyk*. The chiefs were elected at large clan gatherings, where all major decisions were made, conflicts settled, and offenders judged. Hunting areas were divided between the clans. Their ancient craft of blacksmithing was highly prized, giving the Shor protection by the powerful groups who bought their weapons and tools. Under Russian rule, they were forbidden to practice metalworking for fear that the larger tribes would use the weapons against the Russians. The Shor language is a Northern Turkic language of the Altaic language family. Use of the language is declining as many Shor adopt Russian, the language of education and administration, as their first language. In recent census, the number of Shor claiming Shor ethnic identity has fallen as many, though still part of the Shor culture, identify with the Russian language and are classified as ethnic Russian. Attempts to revive the language began in the late 1990s when a language society was formed and a chair of the Shor language was created at the Pedagogical University in Novokuznetsk. The majority of the Shor are officially Orthodox Christian, though they continue to observe many of their traditional rituals, and shamans are accorded great respect for their wisdom and knowledge of Shor history and customs.

The process of the unity of the Shor identity began in the early 19th century as the colonization of their traditional territory by European settlers ended intertribal conflicts and differences. A code of laws governing the laws applied to the non-Russian peoples of Siberia was published in 1822. The code dictated the administrative divisions, taxes, and tributes, as well as the legal status of the tribes. The constant debt owed the Russian officials in the form of the unpopular fur tax, the growing number of Slavic colonists, the despotism of the Slavic bureaucrats, forced Christianization, and Russification greatly affected the self-confidence and independence of the Shor. The Russian Revolution and subsequent civil war had little impact on the Shor until Bolsheviks took control of the region in 1920. In 1926, the Soviets created a Shor autonomous district. During this period, Shor traditional culture was encouraged, a Shor intelligentsia developed, and many books and texts were published in the Shor language. In the 1930s, huge deposits of coal, iron, and gold were discovered in the Kuznetzk Basin. By the late 1930s, tens of thousands of Slavs were settled in the region to work in the coal and iron mines and in the newly established steel production plants. The Shor, overwhelmed during the development of the region, often took jobs in the new industries in order to survive. In 1939, the Shor autonomous district was dismantled, leaving the Shor as a tiny minority in an overwhelmingly Slavic population. From that point on, the Shor traditional culture went into a rapid decline. Assimilation, the loss of their language and traditions, became a threat to their survival as a people. During the decades of the Stalin dictatorship, their former homeland was dotted with the slave-labor camps of the Gulag, which also had a devastating effect on the morals and spiritual ethics of the Shor. The Shor languished until the relaxation of Soviet rule in the late 1980s when a revival of the Shore culture and identity began. The Association of Shor People, created in the 1990s, set up branches throughout Mountain Shoria. Their ancient shamanistic beliefs, closely tied to their traditional culture, also revived as a cultural and religious asset alongside the cultural revival.

Further Reading

Forsyth, James. *A History of the Peoples of Siberia: Russia's North Asian Colony 1581–1990.* Cambridge: Cambridge University Press, 1994.

Mayer, Fred. *The Forgotten Peoples of Siberia.* New York: Scalo, 1993.

Olson, James S. *An Ethnohistorical Dictionary of the Russian and Soviet Empires.* Westport, CT: Greenwood, 1994.

Vahtre, Lauri, and Jüri Viikberg. The Red Book of the Peoples of the Russian Empire. "The Shors." Accessed July 31, 2013. http://www.eki.ee/books/redbook/shors.shtml

Shui

The Shui, sometimes known as Sui, Shuijia, Sui Li, or Suipo, are a Tai people, one of the officially recognized ethnic groups in the People's Republic of China. The estimated 430,000 Shui are concentrated along the upper reaches of the Duliu and Longjiang Rivers to the south of the Mioling Mountains in the Yungui (Yunnan-Guizhou) Plateau. There is a small community of ethnic Shui, known as Thuy, in Vietnam. The Shui language belongs to the Kam-Sui branch of the Tai-Kadai language group. Most Shui are polytheists, venerating a pantheon of gods, along with great reverence for their ancestors.

Shui history reaches back as early as 200 BCE in ancient Chinese archives. The Shui are probably the descendants of the ancient Luoyue tribes that inhabited China's southeastern coastal regions before the early Han dynasty that ruled China from 206 BCE to 24 CE. According to Chinese records, the first emperor of the Qin dynasty sent a large army to the region, forcing the Shui to retreat up the rivers to settle in the region between Guizhou and Guangxi. Separated from the Luoyue, the refugees evolved as a distinct ethnic group.

During the period of rule by the Song dynasty, 960–1279, the Shui settled in villages and gradually adopted the cultivation of rice. By the 13th century, the Shui had evolved the early stages of feudalism. A noble clan bearing the surname Meng controlled the upper reaches of the Longjiang River, where they established a feudal system under their authority though vestiges of the earlier communal village remained. The Mongol rulers of China, the

Yuan dynasty that governed from 1271 to 1368, established local prefectures with officials appointed by the court in an effort to appease the restive minority peoples of the region. From the late 14th century, the Shui communities experienced a marked economic growth due to the introduction of improved farming tools that allowed farmers to create new rice paddies on flatland and in terraced fields on mountain slopes. The advent of more advanced farming methods and the use of draft animals resulted in a greatly increased rice crop. The Ming dynasty, established in 1368, continued the prefectural system with appointments of hereditary Shui officials. Under the administration system, the Shui had to pay taxes and work as unpaid labor for both the court-appointed Shui leadership and the imperial court. The name *Shui* means "water," referring to the people living along the water, was adopted in the early 17th century. From 1640 to the end of the 18th century, the Shui economy continued to develop. Farm production increased with high yields of rice and other products. Shui prosperity allowed many to quit farming to become artisans or handicraftsmen.

Shui culture is organized around family clans living in villages of a few hundred families, usually with the same surname. The Shui homeland is a region known as a land of plenty, with abundant fishing and rice paddies. Wheat, rape, and ramie are also grown along with a great variety of citrus and other fruits. The forests of the region are rich in timber and medicinal herbs. The Shui have a large store of oral literature and art. Historically they not only excelled in poetry, but also have many legends, fairy tales, and fables. Usually, monogamy

is the rule in Shui communities though the strict rules of courtship and marriage have been discarded. Though marriages can be expensive and elaborate, the Shui funerals are even more so. Livestock is sacrificed as offering to the dead, followed by singing, dancing, and performances by local operas that continue until an auspicious day is found to bury the dead. The majority of the Shui continue to adhere to their traditional religious system of polytheism. In some areas, shamans are still employed to say prayers and to slaughter animals as offerings. The shamans are also summoned when a person is ill or has died. The Shui, with an ancient culture, have their own calendar and writing system though many now use Mandarin Chinese as their first language. The Shui language forms part of the Kam-Sui branch of the Tai-Kadai languages that are spoken across southern China. The language is divided into three dialects though there are only minor differences. The Shui script is now used only for ritual purposes, and modern written material uses the Chinese script. The script, known as Shuishu, is in danger of extinction though in recent years efforts have been made to preserve it as part of the Shui cultural heritage. The name *Shui*, meaning "water," was formally adopted for the entire group in 1956 and refers to their preference for dwelling along rivers and streams, their customs, worship, and folklore, which all revolve around water. Fish is the staple food and symbolizes the ancestors of the Shui and the prosperity of the group.

The Shui economic base continued to grow in the early years of the 19th century, with rice production reaching record levels.

The landlord system and the village commune remained the basis of Shui society. Clan relations remained important as a focus of economic activity and the cultural and social life of the Shui communities. Following the overthrow of the Qing dynasty during the Chinese Revolution of 1911, capitalist economic policies were introduced. Iron mines and mineral processing plants were established in the region, giving work to many young Shui. Rice production continued to expand allowing many Shui to join the ranks of the landlords and rich peasants. The outbreak of World War II not only brought a renewed boom to the region's industries but also resulted in conscription of many young Shui into the Chinese army. The end of the war saw the resumption of the long rivalry between the government and the growing number of communists. The Chinese Civil War, from 1945 to 1949, brought violence and fighting to the Shui region. The communist victory resulted in the confiscation and collectivization of their lands, factories, and paddies with the Shui forced to work as employees of the state. The upheaval of the Chinese Cultural Revolution (1967–1977) saw rampaging Red Guard units destroying Shui historical sites, cemeteries, and shrines. The chaos gave way to the reforms instituted in the 1980s, allowing the Shui to recuperate private property and to trade their products for the industrial goods and services that accompanied the modernization of the region in the late 20th and early 21st centuries.

Further Reading

Ethnic Groups. "The Shui Minority." Accessed July 31, 2013. http://www.china.org.cn/e-groups/shaoshu/shao-2-shui.htm

Harrell, Stevan. *Cultural Encounters on China's Ethnic Frontiers.* Seattle: University of Washington Press, 2000.

Mullaney, Thomas, and Benedict Anderson. *Coming to Terms with the Nation: Ethnic Classification in Modern China.* Berkeley: University of California Press, 2011.

Olson, James S. *An Ethnohistorical Dictionary of China.* Westport, CT: Greenwood, 1998.

T

Tajik

The Tajik, sometimes known as Sart or Sarjkoli, are an Indo-European people closely related to the Iranians and other Persian-speaking peoples. The Tajik homeland, mostly in Afghanistan and Tajikistan, is a landlocked region of mountains and highlands in the southeastern part of Central Asia. The estimated 20–23 million Tajik include an estimated 8.2 million in Afghanistan, 6.2 million in Tajikistan, 1.5 million in Uzbekistan, 400,000 in Iran, 200,000 in Russia, 50,000 in the United States, and smaller communities in Kyrgyzstan, China, Kazakhstan, Pakistan, Canada, and Ukraine. The Tajik language is a Persian language, a Central Asian variety of Persian closely related to the Persian language of Iran. The great majority of the Tajik follow the Hanafi school of Sunni Islam, with smaller groups of Shi'a Tajik, particularly among the Tajik populations in the Gorno-Badakhshan Autonomous Province in Tajikistan, and the Badakhshan Province of Afghanistan, and the Tashkurgan Tajik Autonomous County in the Xinjiang region of northwestern China.

The Tajik are considered the descendants of the early Indo-European civilizations that flourished in Central Asia as early as 2000 BCE. The Tajik mountains, a natural corridor leading to the plains and grasslands of Central Asia, were subject to numerous waves of conquerors during the long Tajik history. Known as Bactria, the Persian-speaking region formed part of the Persian Empire of Cyrus I in the sixth century BCE. In the fourth century BCE, the Greeks of Alexander the Great conquered the area, then known as Sogdiana. The great Persian-speaking states of Bactria and Sogdiana were often linked to the Persian kingdoms and empires to the west. Around the first century CE, the region was conquered by a people known as the Tocharians and formed the center of the powerful Tocharian Kushan Empire. By the fifth century, the last of the Tocharians was driven from the region by nomadic Huns, possibly the earliest of many subsequent waves of Turkic invaders in Central Asia. The Turkic migrations into Central Asia continued until the 10th century, broken only during the Arab conquest of the region in the mid-eighth century. In the 11th and 12th centuries, the Seljuk Turks overran the region, and the Mongol-Turkic hordes of Genghis Khan brought the region into the vast Mongol Empire in the 13th century. In the 15th century, Timur, also known as Tamerlane, one of the heirs of Genghis Khan, launched yet another Turkic and Mongol invasion of the Central Asian territories. By the 15th century, the majority of the peoples of Central Asia were Turkic-speaking and of Turkic culture, including a large part of modern Tajikistan and northern Afghanistan. Only the ancestors of the Pamiri, speaking East Iranian languages, and the

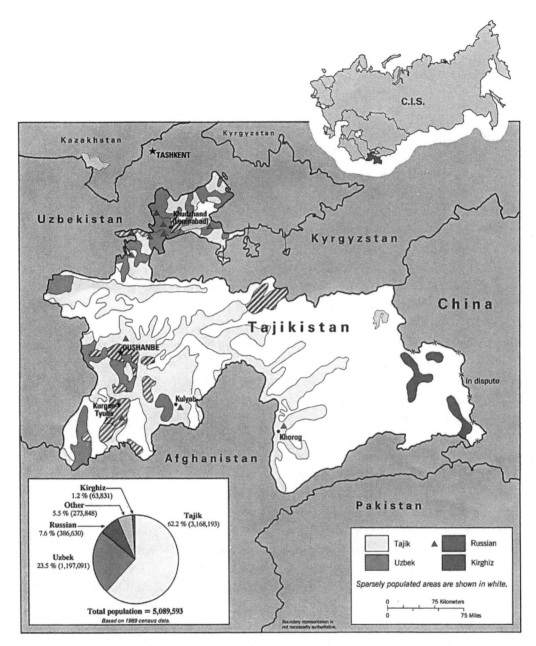

Major ethnic groups in Tajikistan. (Used by permission of the University of Texas Libraries, The University of Texas at Austin)

ancestors of the Tajiks, speaking a West Iranian language, remained as two enclaves of Indo-Europeans in the largely Turkic Central Asia. From this small surviving core, the Tajik evolved, possibly as early as the eighth century. Historically,

they included three distinct cultural groups: the lowland Tajik of the oases and valleys, related culturally but not linguistically to the neighboring Turkic Uzbek groups; the mountain Tajik, who share many cultural traits and a common religion with the sedentary lowlanders; and the Pamiri Tajik, often Shi'a Muslim and with a highland culture in eastern Tajikistan and northern Afghanistan. The three historic divisions remain to the present. Islam, brought to the Tajik territories in the wake of the Arab conquest in the eighth century, supplanted a variety of older religions and played an important part in the evolution and distinctiveness of Tajik society. Under Islamic influence, the Tajik established peace among the various clans and tribes and united to form the short-lived Perso-Arabic Samanid Empire, which flourished from 903 to 999 in eastern Iran and Central Asia following the overthrow of the Persian Empire by the invading Arabs. The Samanid Empire was the only specific Tajik state until the emergence of modern Tajikistan. The waves of Turkic conquerors from the 11th through 15th centuries converted the Tajiks into a Persian-speaking island in a Turkic sea connected to Persia and the outside world by the trade routes known as the Silk Road. Though the Tajik cities in the valleys and lowlands were destroyed and the population carried off or massacred, the Tajik culture continued in the highland valleys and strongholds. In the early 1500s, a minor branch of Genghis Khan's Mongol and Turkic hordes conquered the region south of the Aral Sea. The invaders, known as Uzbek, turned east to conquer the Tajik regions, setting up a series of semi-independent Tajik border states along the frontier with China. The Uzbek retain much of the Tajik territories when a resurgent Persia conquered the northwestern portion of Tajikistan in the 1760s. The Persians reinforced the Persian culture and language of the Tajik though they soon came under the rule of the Uzbek

Khokand Khanate. At the end of the 18th century, the Tajik population of Central Asia was divided between Afghanistan to the south, and the Uzbek-dominated states of Khokand, Bukhara, and Khiva in Central Asia.

Tajik people, with their long and often violent history, are now quite genetically diverse, though classified as belonging to the Mediterranean subgroup of the Caucasian peoples, physical types ranging from the European to the Mongol with many divisions in between. Culturally, the Tajik society also shows a diversity of influences from the Persian and Turkic to Mongol and later the Russian conquerors. Such cultural elements as the national sport, *gushtigiri*, Tajik wrestling, have a long and colorful history and have become very popular in recent years in both Tajikistan and Afghanistan. Another sport, *buzkashi*, which means "dragging the goat," has also been revived. The sport involves the carcass of a goat being dragged by horsemen who grab it from each other in attempts to deposit the carcass in a designated circle. The Tajik culture now forms part of a crescent running from Tajikistan through most of Afghanistan and into Iran with many similarities in culture and language throughout this area. The major contribution to this shared heritage is the famed *Shah-nameh*, "The Book of Kings," written by the Persian poet Firdawsi in the 11th century. The book is a chronicle of the early history of the region, telling the story of the cosmic battle between Good and Evil, the development of the divine right of kings, and is a detailed history of the region's early monarchs. Historically, the Tajik territory formed part of the ancient Persian Empire with its official religion Zoroastrianism, often associated with the worship of fire. Following the Arab conquest of Central Asia in the eighth century, Islam became the dominant religion. Tajiks are very family oriented, and extended families are quite large though the family is usually widely spread, giving it more opportunities for amassing resources. These extended families are then grouped into clans. There are at least four or five major clan groups in Tajikistan and even more in Afghanistan. The Tajik language is an eastern Persian dialect, often called Dari, as in Afghanistan, while in Tajikistan, where a Cyrillic alphabet is used, the language is known as Tajik. In Afghanistan, the Tajik language is still written in the Perso-Arabic script. The language, since

the 19th century, has absorbed many Russian and Uzbek works, further separating it from the Dari dialect spoken across the border in Afghanistan. The abrupt end of Soviet rule in 1991 began a strong cultural revival strengthened by the Tajik nationalism that led to the independence of Tajikistan.

In the early 1800s, internal disputes between the settled Sart (Tajik) population and the seminomadic Uzbek rulers of the Central Asian khanates, coupled with continuing warfare between Bukhara and the northern tribes, severely weakened the Uzbek states just as Russian expansion into the region began. By the mid-19th century, the Russians accelerated their encroachment on Central Asia as

Horsemen compete during a Buzkashi game near the Tajik capital of Dushanbe, 2012. The traditional central Asian sport of Buzkashi is played between two teams of horsemen competing to throw a beheaded goat into a scoring circle. (Nozim Kalandarov/Reuters/Corbis)

they moved south toward Afghanistan. The Russians annexed the Tajik areas of Khodzhent and Ura-Tyube and in 1867 created a government of Russian Turkestan. The next year, the Russians subjugated and established a protectorate over Bukhara, bringing more Tajik populations under Russian influence. The second of the three Uzbek khanates, Khiva, came under Russian rule in 1873. Heavy Russian taxes triggered a widespread Tajik revolt, the Vaase Uprising, in the 1870s, which was put down mercilessly. The Khokand Khanate, where the Russians put down a serious uprising in 1873–1876, was abolished, and its territory, including the Tajik portion of the large and fertile Fergana Valley, was joined to Russian Turkestan. By the end of the 19th century, all of the Central Asian Tajik were under Russian rule, while across the border British influence had been firmly established in Afghanistan. The Afghan Tajik, because they made up the bulk of Afghanistan's educated elite and possessed considerable wealth, had significant political influence in the largely Pashtun government in Kabul. Rivalry between Russia and the British along the Central Asian-Afghanistan frontier was known as the Great Game with the Tajik groups often used as pawns. In the wake of the overthrow of the Russian monarchy in 1917 and the subsequent Russian Civil War, guerrilla groups throughout Central Asia, known as *basmachi*, waged a widespread war against the openly antireligious Bolshevik armies in a futile attempt to maintain their independence. The Bolsheviks, calling themselves Soviet, finally wiped out most of the *basmachi* in a four-year

conflict that left many towns, villages, and mosques destroyed. The Soviet policy in the region suppressed the Islamic religion, with persecution of practicing Muslims and the closure of most of the region's many mosques. In 1924, the Soviet government divided Central Asia along ethnic and linguistic lines, establishing the Tajik Autonomous Soviet Socialist Republic as part of Soviet Uzbekistan, but in 1929, the Tajik state became one of the full member states of the Soviet Union. The predominately ethnic Tajik cities of Samarkand and Bukhara became part of Uzbekistan. Ethnic Slavs migrated to Tajikistan, often filling the middle and upper management and government positions. In terms of living conditions, education, and production, Tajikistan quickly fell behind the other Central Asian republics with the lowest household incomes and the lowest rate of university graduates. By the late 1980s, as the Soviet Union's government relaxed its stringent hold on the region, Tajik nationalist organized to demand increased ethnic and linguistic rights. In 1991, the Soviet Union collapsed, and Tajikistan was declared an independent republic under a government hastily organized along national line by the ruling communist hierarchy of the Soviet government. The first nation to establish an embassy in independent Tajikistan was Iran. The independence of the new Tajik republic was quickly threatened by a civil war among Tajik clans that nearly destroyed the country. The Tajik of Afghanistan are the second largest ethnic groups after the Pashtun, who dominate the south and east of the country. The Tajik population of Afghanistan is made

The Conflict over Fabled Samarkand

Samarkand, the city noted for its central position on the legendary Silk Road between China and the West, is known throughout the world for its exotic image in fiction, poetry, drama, and film. Though the city is the second largest in Uzbekistan and an important center of industry, tourism, and culture, the majority of the population are ethnic Tajik. Arbitrary Soviet boundaries placed Samarkand in Soviet Uzbekistan in 1924, but since the independence of Uzbekistan and Tajikistan in 1991, many of the ethnic Tajik population in Samarkand have supported efforts to separate the Tajik-majority provinces from Uzbekistan and to reunite the region with Tajikistan.

up of three important concentrations, the Plains Tajiks living in the Heart region on the Iranian border, in the Parwan region north of Kabul, and in the Kabul capital region. The Tajik of Afghanistan are largely urban traders, skilled artisans, and farmers, many prosperous enough to be termed middle class until the chaos that led to the Soviet invasion of Afghanistan in 1979. The Afghan Tajik joined the guerrilla groups fighting the Soviet occupation forces, often facing ethnic Tajik in the Soviet ranks. Some Tajik battalions mutinied and refused to fight their ethnic kin in Afghanistan. The Soviets withdrew from Afghanistan in 1989, leaving behind a vicious civil war that pitted the Tajik, Uzbek, and other northern groups against the predominately Pashtun southerners. The Taliban, organized by groups of students among the Pashtun populations of Afghanistan and Pakistan, took advantage of the chaotic situation to take control of the country. Their rule devastated the country while terrorist groups such as Al Qaeda set up training camps and received aid and weapons from the Taliban. The Al Qaeda attacks on the United States in September 2001 led to a military intervention in Afghanistan and the overthrow of the Taliban government. A democratic government was created in Kabul, but its authority is mostly confined to the region around the Afghan capital. In the northeastern Tajik regions, local leaders make most of the decisions. During the 1990s and in the 21st century, the Tajik populations of Tajikistan and Afghanistan have revived their historical, cultural, and family ties as one great ethnic group divided by the former colonial borders. The Tajik traditional reliance on familiar traditions and cultural patterns has aided the Tajik peoples in both Tajikistan and Afghanistan to weather the crises that have battered both regions since the 1970s.

Further Reading

Abazov, Rafis. *Tajikistan.* New York: Benchmark Books, 2006.

Bergne, Paul. *The Birth of Tajikistan: National Identity and the Origins of the Republic.* London: I. B. Tauris, 2007.

Countries and Their Cultures. "Tajikistan." Accessed July 30, 2013. http://www.everyculture.com/Sa-Th/Tajikistan.html

Howard, Ross. *Tajikistan: Loosening the Knot.* Seattle: CreateSpace, 2011.

Talysh

The Talysh, sometimes known as Talishi, Taleshi, Talyshi, Talish, Tolish, or Talush, are an ethnic group of mixed Caucasian and Iranian ancestry. Their homeland, often called Talyshtan, straddles the border between Azerbaijan and Iran. The Talysh population living in Azerbaijan numbers between 120,000 and 500,000; the different estimates are based on language as many ethnic Talysh now speak Azeri. The majority of the Talysh, like the majority of the Azeri and the Iranian peoples, belong to the Shi'a branch of Islam.

The Talysh trace their origins to the Talysh Mountains that lie in southeastern Azerbaijan and northwestern Iran. Early Caucasian tribes settled the mountains as early as 1500 BCE. Both Persian-speaking and Caucasian peoples settled the region, and the Talysh evolved from a mixture of the two groups. Traditionally, the Talysh culture revolved around cattle, with large herds that were moved seasonally between the mountains and the lowlands. Cultural activities and customs developed around the seasonal activities associated with the Talysh cattle herds. By the sixth century BCE, most of the Talysh lands were included in a province, a satrapy, of the ancient Persian Empire. Conquered by the Greeks of Alexander the Great in 334–331 BCE, many of the Talysh retreated to their traditional mountain strongholds.

Officially, their homeland formed part of the Greek province of Media Atrophene. In the second century BCE, the Persians reconquered the Caspian region. Persian influence in the Talysh culture and language became paramount. Muslim Arabs overran the region in 641 CE, bringing with them their new Islamic religion. The Arabs settled in the coastal regions with Islam gradually adopted by the highland Talysh people. Over many decades, the pagan Talysh gradually adopted the new religion with its strong cultural elements and strict rules. Beginning in the 10th century, the Talysh homeland formed part of the newly established linguistic and cultural frontier between the Turkic peoples, who had conquered and settled the territory to the north and the Persian peoples to the south. Devastated by the invading Mongol hordes in the 13th century and the conquest by Tamerlane a century later, the Talysh lands had declined to a poor backward region by the time the Persians regained control of the Caspian region in 1592. English traders, moving south from Russia, reached the Talysh Mountains in the late 16th century. The traders brought news and trade goods never seen before in the region, beginning a tradition of trade on the caravan routes to the west. Russian explorers and traders, led by Cossack horsemen, spearheaded the Russian colonial expansion into the Turkish and Persian provinces around the Caspian Sea and moved into the region in the early 17th century. A large Cossack raiding party overran the Talysh lowlands in 1636, causing considerable damage before withdrawing. In 1722, the Russians returned to conquer the region from Persia. The Russians held the area for 10 years, finally returning the province to Persian rule in exchange for territorial concessions elsewhere in the Caucasus. In the 1720s, during a turbulent period in Persia, minor members of Persia's ruling Safavid dynasty settled in the Talysh region. Seyyid Abbas, though acknowledging Safavid authority, established the Talysh Khanate, a semi-independent state under loose Persian rule. His son, Gara Khan, inherited the khanate in 1747 and expanded Talysh rule to the Caspian lowlands. Gara Khan followed a pro-Russian policy to offset the Persian and Turkish influence in the region, often bringing Talyshstan into conflict with the neighboring khanates. By 1785, the khanate had become a dependent of the neighboring Quba Khanate, but in 1789, the Talysh regained their independence under Mir Mustafa, the son of Gara Khan. In 1794–1795, the Persians called on the various khanates of the southern Caucasus to form a military alliance against the encroaching Russians.

The Talysh culture exhibits many unique traditions and customs along with borrowings from neighboring Caucasian and Persian peoples. Though traditionally the Talysh were cattle herders, many now farm, particularly the cultivation of rice in the lowlands and wheat and barley in the highlands. Known in Azerbaijan for their intellectual abilities and literacy, the Talysh tend to be more highly educated than the neighboring peoples. Their culture, though materially close to that of the Turkic Azeri, has retained many customs and rituals not found among other peoples of the Caspian region. Some Talysh groups claim an ethnic Talysh population in Azerbaijan accounting for 11 percent of the country's population, while government estimates place the Talysh population at just 2 percent of the population. The difference is in the use of the language, as many ethnic Talysh were forced to adopt Azeri as their first language during the decades of Soviet rule as Azeri and Russian were the official languages of Soviet Azerbaijan. Counting only the first language, Talysh speakers as representing the Talysh ethnic group have caused much confusion and conflict over the total number of Talysh in Azerbaijan. Since the 1990s, the Azeri-speaking Talysh have embraced their traditional culture and often learned Talysh. The Talysh language forms part of the northwestern Iranian language group, though it has considerable borrowings from Azeri and the Caucasian languages. The Talysh language is spoken in four major dialects in Azerbaijan that correspond to the four regions with Talysh majorities, Astarin, Lenkoran, Lerik, and Massalin. Under Soviet language policies, the Talysh literary language in Azerbaijan mostly disappeared, and the Azeri alphabet is used as the literary language. The majority of the Talysh are bilingual, speaking both Talysh and Azeri, with some also able to speak Russian or Farsi, the Iranian language. The Talysh are overwhelmingly Muslim, most adhering to the Shi'a branch of the religion. Traditionally, Talysh women wore traditional Muslim clothing, including veils and long robes that completely covered their bodies, but after decades of Soviet atheism and antireligious teachings, most Talysh women now wear Western-style clothing. Although Islamic traditions allow men to marry as many as four wives, most Talysh men marry only once. Custom dictates that the Talysh marry at a young age, with men between 15 and 20 years and girls between 12 and 16. The groom's family usually pays a bride price, the *kebin*, which includes money, household goods, and utensils. Though the Talysh have been Muslim for many centuries, some remnants of their pre-Islamic religious beliefs remain. They have a special reverence for trees and groves, with trees included in most of their most sacred sites. Many also believe in the presence of both good and evil spirits, particularly a dangerous spirit known as Alazhan or the Red Woman, an invisible spirit that is believed to assault women during childbirth as well as threaten newly born babies.

On the resentment of Persian encroachments on their land and culture, Mir Mustafa also followed a pro-Russian foreign policy. Mir Mustafa refused to join the Persian-led anti-Russian alliance that included most of the neighboring khanates and sought Russian aid against the Persians. The Russians were slow to respond, but finally sent a military expedition to the khanate, which was occupied and declared a protectorate of the Russian Empire in 1802. The Persians continued to contest control of Talyshtan, taking control of the southern districts in the early 1800s. In 1813, the Russians forced Persia, after a long undeclared war, to cede control of the formerly independent khanates. In 1814, Mir Mustafa died and was succeeded by his son, Mir Hasan, but only in name as the Russians retained control of the northern part of the khanate. The Russian defeat of Persia in the Russo-Persian War, 1826–1828, effectively divided the Talysh homeland between Russian and Persian parts. In 1828, the Persians signed the Treaty of Turkmenchay, which recognized Russian authority over the khanates

north of the Arras River. The Talysh khanate was abolished, and the various regions were incorporated into the Russian Empire. Under the rule of Tsarist Russia, the Talysh lands were cultivated, and many Talysh were forced to settle as farmers, particularly in the rice fields along the Caspian Sea. In the wake of World War I, the Russian Civil War spilled into the region, with many Talysh imitating their ancestors by moving into the mountains to escape the fighting. The Soviet victory in 1920 ended a brief period of Azerbaijan independence and established firm Soviet control of the northern Talysh region. The tight border controls between the new Soviet Union and Persia began a period of divergence between the Talysh in the two countries. The Soviet authorities encouraged assimilation of the Talysh into the larger Azeri culture. In 1939, the Talysh Latin alphabet was abolished and replaced with the Russian Cyrillic script, forcing the literate Talysh to use Azeri as their written language. Education, local administration, and entertainment were promoted in the Azeri language. By 1959, relatively few people self-identified as ethnic Talysh and Soviet ethnographers assumed that the Talysh, as planned, were disappearing as a separate people and were being absorbed by the Azeri, with whom they shared their Shi'a Muslim beliefs and many cultural traits. The Soviet authorities, convinced that the Talysh had disappeared as a distinct ethnic group, did not count them separately in the censuses of 1970 and 1979. But by the early 1980s, agitation and demands for cultural recognition forced the Soviet government of Azerbaijan to reconsider. By the late 1980s, it was evident that a core of Talysh continued to cling to their ancient culture and language, refusing to assimilate into either the larger Azeri culture or the Russian-dominated Soviet culture. The reforms introduced to Soviet society beginning in 1987 allowed the Talysh to mobilize and loosed a torrent of pent-up grievances. The Soviet authorities were forced to count the Talysh as a separate ethnic group in the 1989 census and were surprised to find that 21,914 people registered as ethnic Talysh. The collapse of the Soviet Union and the independence of Azerbaijan in 1991 allowed the Talysh to regain much of their culture and language despite official Azeri efforts to continue with the policy of assimilation. Controversy over the number of Talysh in Azerbaijan is only one of a number of grievances that has spurred the formation of a widely supported autonomy movement that demands recognition of their ancient culture and language in the districts with Talysh majorities.

Further Reading

Clancy, Tomas. *Countries of the World: Republic of Azerbaijan.* Seattle: CreateSpace, 2012.

Shoup, John A. *Ethnic Groups of Africa and the Middle East: An Encyclopedia.* Santa Barbara, CA: ABC-CLIO, 2011.

Zonn, Igor S., Aleksey N. Kosarev, Michael Glantz, and Andrey G. Kostianoy. *The Caspian Sea Encyclopedia.* New York: Springer, 2010.

Tat

The Tat, sometimes known as Tati, Tatian, Parsi, Daghli, Lohijon, or Caucasian Persians, are an Iranian people living primarily in the Caspian Sea region of northeastern Azerbaijan. There are also Tat communities in the neighboring regions of Dagestan in the Russian Federation, in Europe, and in the United States. The estimated 22,000–26,000 Tats living in Azerbaijan speak a southwestern Iranian language that is considered an endangered language due to the gradual adoption of the Azeri language by the Tat people. The majority of the Tat adhere to the Shi'a branch of Islam with a smaller number of Sunni Muslims and a community of Christians. Traditionally, the Tat people formed three distinct groups, the Muslim Tat, the Christian Tat, now mostly assimilated by the local Armenian population, and the Jewish Tat or Mountain Jews, who are now considered a separate ethnic group.

The origins of the Tat people are not known, and references are scarce. They are believed to be the descendants of the early inhabitants of the Caucasus region. Gradually, the early Caucasians adopted Persian speech and culture sometime in the third or fourth centuries CE when the Sassanid dynasty of Persia conquered the Caucasus. To secure their conquests, the Persians settled them with Iranian-speaking peoples among the indigenous Caucasians. The Iranian peoples eventually absorbed some of the local Caucasian groups to form the ancestors of the Tat people. The ancient Persian religion, Zoroastrianism, spread to the Caucasus and formed an important element in the local culture. Christianity was adopted by many of the Caucasian peoples later in the fourth century and remained the primary religion until the conquest of the Caucasian region by invading Arabs in 642. The Arab invaders, fired by religious fervor, forcibly converted the majority of the population to their new Muslim religion. Small communities of Christians survived in the high mountains where they remain to the present. In the 11th century, waves of Oghuz Turks, moving west from Central Asia, invaded the Caucasus. By 1030, the region of modern Azerbaijan was under Turkish rule. The Oghuz Turks were followed by the Seljuk Turks who conquered the region, adding it to their newly formed empire in 1055. The Seljuks adopted the Muslim religion and spread their Turkic language and culture to the Caspian lowlands. The highland communities that remained Iranian in culture and language were called Tat by the Turkish speakers. Tat signified plowman or settled farmer as opposed to the nomadic traditions of the Turkic peoples. The Mongol invasion of the Caucasus devastated the region. The Mongols destroyed most of the important cities and trading centers while many Tat fled to strongholds in the mountains. The Mongol domination of the Caucasus lasted until 1360–1370, though many Persian-speaking officials were incorporated into the local administration. At the end of the 14th century, the southern Caucasus was invaded by the forces of Tamerlane, again forcing many Tat to flee back to their mountains. By the end of the 15th century, a Turkic khanate ruled the region, with the Turkic Azeri culture predominating in the southeastern Caucasus. About a century later, the South Caucasus was joined to the Persian Empire of the Safavid dynasty. Persian rule allowed the Tat to retain their language and culture and to reverse a long period of assimilation into the local Azeri Turkic culture. By the end of the 18th century, the Tat culture was very similar to that of the neighboring Azeri people, with their language as the only distinctive Tat cultural element.

The Tat culture, after centuries of interaction with the Azeri and other cultures, is a mixed culture with both Iranian and Turkic elements and traditions. Traditional Turkic arts such as carpet weaving, embossing, and incrustation are highly developed and are considered important Tat arts. The Tat culture retains a rich tradition of oral folktales and poetry. As a result of their long association with the Turkic Azeri, there are many cultural features shared by both cultures, such as farming techniques, cuisine, and music. The Tat are traditionally a farming people, particularly cultivating fruits and cereals. Cattle herding is also an important economic pursuit in some districts. Historically, the Tat built their towns and villages in the high mountains of the Caucasus. The availability of water designated the location of the villages, often built on ledges or high mountain valleys. As early as the 19th century, Tat communities were settled in the region of the Apsheron Peninsula, the site of the important oil industry that employed many Tat. The proximity of the lowland Tat communities to the large Azeri cities, particularly Baku, has resulted in a particularly liberal and reform-minded Tat culture that is often in conflict with the conservative Tat living in the less accessible mountain areas. The assimilation of the Tat by the Azeri culture has been an ongoing process over many centuries, a process greatly assisted by their common Shi'a religion. The process was accelerated by the policies of the new Azerbaijan state that sponsored assimilation in the 1990s. The

Tat have somewhat resisted assimilation by a tradition of marriage only within the Tat ethnic group. The Tat language, which forms part of the Southwestern Iranian languages, is considered to form a bridge language between modern Farsi (Iranian) and the Caspian Iranian dialects. Assimilation has also threatened the survival of the language, which is considered an endangered language. The Tat have no written form of their language, most often using Azeri as their literary language. Azeri is also the language of administration and education. The majority, estimated at up to 99 percent, are adherents of Islam, mostly belonging to the Shi'a branch that is predominate in Azerbaijan and Iran. There is a small Christian community, probably only a few hundred in number, which is Tat by language but does not participate in the Muslim Tat culture.

Russian expansion south into the Caucasus region brought more devastation to the Tat people, who often resorted to their traditional retreat to mountain strongholds to escape marauding armies. The Russo-Persian wars fought between 1803 and 1828 ended with the southern Caucasus and the Tat lands becoming part of the Russian Empire. When the town of Baku was occupied by Russian forces in the early 1800s, nearly the entire population of some 8,000 people was ethnic Tat. The development of the Baku region on the Apsheron Peninsula, particularly the oil industry, brought a large influx of ethnic Azeri, Russians, and others to the region. According to Russian sources, the use of the Tat language was widespread in many of the lowland regions along the Caspian Sea. The *Calendar of the Caucasus*, published in 1894, counted 124,693 Tats in the southern Caucasus region. The gradual spread of the Turkic Azeri language replaced the Tat language in many of the lowland areas. The imposition of Soviet rule in 1920 greatly changed the ethnic balance in the region. The Azeri were considered the titular nationality of the Azerbaijan republic within the Soviet Union, and assimilation into the Azeri culture became official policy. In the Soviet census of 1926, only some 28,000 Tat were registered. Repression of their language, harsh assimilation policies, and the antireligious stance of the Soviet authorities affected the Tat ethnic group. By the late 1980s, only around 10,000 self-identified as ethnic Tat. The collapse of the Soviet Union and the emergence of independent Azerbaijan in 1991 were initially welcomed by the Tat leaders. Many Tat embraced their long-ignored culture as Soviet policies collapsed. The new leadership of Azerbaijan also enforced assimilation policies, but the revival of the Tat culture continued even as the use of the language has declined. By the early decades of the 21st century, a thriving cultural movement has promoted the use of the Tat language and the recovery of the traditional Tat culture.

Further Reading

Clancy, Tomas. *Countries of the World: Republic of Azerbaijan.* Seattle: CreateSpace, 2012.

Swietochowski, Tadeusz. *Russian Azerbaijan, 1905–1920: The Shaping of a National Identity in a Muslim Community.* Cambridge: Cambridge University Press, 2004.

Vahtre, Lauri, and Viikberg, Jüri. The Red Book of the Peoples of the Russian Empire.

"The Tats." Accessed July 31, 2013. http://www.eki.ee/books/redbook/tats.shtml

Zonn, Igor S., Aleksey N. Kosarev, Michael Glantz, and Andrey G. Kostianoy. *The Caspian Sea Encyclopedia.* New York: Springer, 2010.

Tibetan

The Tibetan people, sometimes known as Tibate, Tebilian, Bhotia, Phoke, or Zang, are an ethnic group native to the region of Tibet in Asia just north of the Indian subcontinent. The homeland of the Tibetans, often referred to as the "roof of the world," occupies the wide Tibetan Plateau region in the southwestern part of the People's Republic of China. The Tibetan ethnic group is concentrated in the Tibetan Autonomous Region, formerly known as Outer Tibet. Large Tibetan populations are also found in the Chinese province of Qinghai and in the western districts of the provinces of Sichuan, Gansu, and northern Yunnan, collectively known as Inner Tibet. Outside the Tibetan Plateau region, there are Tibetan communities in India, including the Tibetan government-in-exile, as well as in Nepal, Bhutan, the United States, Canada, Switzerland, Taiwan, Australia, and the United Kingdom. The estimated 6.5 million Tibetans speak dialects of the Tibetan language known as Tibetic or Bodic, which forms part of the Sino-Tibetan language group. Most Tibetans practice Lamaism, the Tibetan form of Buddhism, though a minority adheres to the pre-Buddhist Bön religion.

A Tibetan family taking a meal while working in the fields. (Gan Hui/Dreamstime.com)

Tibetan myths and folklore explain the origins of the Tibetan people as descendants of the monkey Pha Trelgen Changchup Sempa, considered the embodiment of the bodhisattva of compassion, and the rock ogress Ma Drag Sinmo. Chinese chronicles of the 10th century CE record the Tibetans' origin among the nomadic pastoral Ch'iang tribes of the great steppe region northwest of China as early as 200 BCE. Tibetan civilization probably began near the Yarlung Zanbo River in Tibet, where a Tibetan kingdom was created in the sixth century. A sophisticated theocratic state flourished in the region following the introduction of Buddhism in 630 CE. The Tibetan ruler Songtsän Gampo, founder of the state in 618, made Lhasa the center of the kingdom, where Tibetan laws, alphabet, calendar, and an advanced system of weights and measures were created. The kingdom established diplomatic relations with the Chinese Tang dynasty, and Songtsän Gampo married a Chinese princess, Wencheng, who came to Tibet in 641. She had great influence on the evolution of the Tibetan culture. Around 700, the Tibetan kingdom controlled an empire that controlled the Silk Road trade routes between East and West and exacted tribute from the Tang dynasty in China. Under Gampo's successors, Tibetan Buddhism became established as the state religion and Tibetan political power extended into Central Asia and China. Tibetan politics for many centuries focused on resistance to Chinese incursions and conquest. In the mid-800s, a civil war over the succession brought on the collapse of the Tibetan Empire and the beginning of the period known as the Era of Fragmentation, when Tibet split into numerous fiefs ruled by warlords and tribal chieftains.

Invading Mongol hordes conquered the region known as Outer Tibet in the 13th century, eventually extending their conquests to mountainous Inner Tibet. The abbot of the Sakya lamasery reportedly converted the Mongol emperor of China, Kublai Khan, to Tibetan Buddhism, then on a visit to the Chinese capital. The abbot later returned to Lhasa to become Tibet's first priest-king. During the rule of the Ming dynasty in China, Tibet was ruled as an independent theocracy under the priest-kings of the Pagmodru, Rinpung, and Tsangpa dynasties. In the 15th century, Tibet's religious leaders accepted the reform sect of Mahayana Buddhism known as Gelugpa, the Victorious Order of the Yellow Hat. In 1578, the khan of the Tumet Mongols, Altan Khan, gave the priest-king Sonam Gyatso, the high lama of the Gelugpa school, the name *Dalai Lama*, Dalai being the Mongol word for the Tibetan Gyatso or ocean. Neighboring China fell to Manchu rule in the latter half of the 1600s, ending Chinese threats to the Tibetan kingdom. To avoid maintaining a defensive military force, the fifth Dalai Lama negotiated a protective alliance with the Manchu emperor of China in the 1650s. However, the Manchu incorporated Inner Tibet into their growing empire and established nominal Manchu rule over Outer Tibet in 1720 though there was no attempt to incorporate Tibet into the territories of the Manchu Qing dynasty.

Modern Tibetan culture developed under influences absorbed from neighboring cultures in Nepal, India, and China, while Tibet's remoteness and inaccessibility have preserved distinct cultural elements. Tibetan society and culture is based on a historical mixture of the early Tibetan culture and their unique form of the Buddhist teachings. Tibetan Buddhism is a fusion of the lowland Buddhism of Asia with the pre-Buddhist Bön religion that produced a unique system of beliefs and rituals. The indigenous Bön religion of the Himalaya region contributed a pantheon of local deities and greatly influenced Tibetan art and material culture, particularly the unique Tibetan architecture. The Tibetan people comprise two distinct strains, the brachycephalic or roundheaded and the dolichocephalic or longheaded groups. The former, predominant in the cultivated lowland valleys, is more closely related to the early Chinese and Burman peoples. The latter, found primarily among the nomadic groups of the northern Tibetan populations and in the noble families in central Tibet, much more closely resembles the Turkic peoples. Besides the physical division, the Tibetans are divided into three major regional and linguistic groups—the Tibetans of Outer Tibet, known as Ü-Tsang, making up the majority the population of the Tibetan Autonomous Region; the Amdo Tibetans, mostly in Qinghai region in the northeast; and the Kham Tibetans in the eastern districts of the Tibetan Autonomous Region, and western Sichuan and northern Yunnan in China proper—further divided into 15 subgroups. The three major divisions correspond to the three dialects of the Tibetan language, all sharing the same literary language. Tibetan culture remains closely tied to the Tibetan Buddhist religion. Prior to the imposition of communist rule, daily life in Tibet revolved around the yearly religious calendar. Many Tibetans, particularly in Qinghai, are seminomadic, moving with their herds of yaks, cattle, goats, and sheep from the lowland to highland pastures. Polyandry, a Tibetan tradition that permits a woman to have several husbands, remains widespread and is socially acceptable, except among the Amdo Tibetans, who are usually monogamous. The culture exhibits elements related to the Tibetan ability to withstand the severe weather condition of the high Tibetan Plateau, giving them a reputation as rugged and hardy. Tibetan cultural and linguistic influences remain strong in areas that once formed part of the Tibetan Empire such as Bhutan, northern Nepal, and the Indian state of Sikkim and the Ladakh region of Kashmir.

Tibet's Fraternal Marriage System

Polyandry is a form of polygamy with women taking several husbands. In Tibet, this form of marriage has a long history. The multiple husbands are often brothers, therefore keeping lands from being divided among siblings and allowing farms to remain sufficiently large to continue to support a large family. There is also the sociobiological justification for brothers to raise all children together as brothers are closely related genetically. Another reason for polyandry in Tibet is the mountainous terrain, which makes farming difficult and requires more physical strength, so several husbands are available to help work the land.

As the Qing dynasty weakened in China, its authority over Tibet also weakened. The British, expanding from their Indian territories, took control of the vassal kingdoms south of the Himalayas. By the mid-19th century, Chinese influence was minimal with both the British and Russians suspicious of each other's influence in Tibet. The Tibetans repeatedly rejected British overtures. The British viewed Tibet as a trade link to China but feared that Tibet could become a route for Russian advances that might endanger their empire in India. When the Tibetans rejected a demand for trade concessions, the British authorities in India dispatched an expedition to occupy the country in 1903–1904. The British occupation forces took control of Lhasa and coerced the Dalai Lama to sign a new treaty that opened several Tibetan cities to outside trade in 1904. Two years later, the British signed a treaty with China, without Tibetan participation, recognizing Chinese suzerainty over Tibet. The Qing dynasty of the Manchu rulers, to reinforce their claim to Tibet, sent a large Chinese force to the region in 1910. The Chinese invasion sent the Dalai Lama and many followers fleeing across the Himalayas into British territory. The Chinese Revolution overthrew the Manchu Qing dynasty in 1911, greatly weakening Chinese control over the Tibetan kingdom. Tibetan soldiers succeeded in driving the last of the Chinese soldiers and bureaucrats from the region. The Dalai Lama returned from India to proclaim Tibet independent of China on February 18, 1912. The Tibetans, consolidating their authority in Outer Tibet, put forward a claim to the Tibetan-populated region of Inner Tibet in China, though the claim was put aside in 1918 when the Tibetans were forced to fight off an attempted Chinese invasion. The Tibetan state was organized as a theocracy ruled by the Dalai Lama with most of the land held by just 3 percent of the population made up of noble families, feudal lords, and some 6,000 lamaseries. Of the Tibetan majority, some 5 percent were slaves, 20 percent Buddhist monks, and most of the remainder lived as serfs attached to the feudal estates and the lamaseries. The Dalai Lama, the god-king of Tibet, was both the secular and religious ruler of the Tibetan state. In 1914, the Dalai Lama signed a new agreement with the British establishing the McMahon Line as the southern border of Tibet and ceding the Tibetan territory south of the line to British control. The Chinese government denounced the agreement as illegal. Tensions between Tibet and China continued, primarily over the poor Chinese treatment of ethnic Tibetans in Inner Tibet. A brief border war in 1931–1933 ended with the loss of additional Tibetan territory to China north of the Yangtze River in Qinghai. The closed Tibetan ruling class declined British and other offers of outside help, fearing that foreign influences would undermine their position in the country. Opening Tibet to the outside world could have posed a credible deterrence to the territorial claims of China, allowing Outer Tibet, like Outer Mongolia, to maintain a precarious sovereignty to the present day. Civil war in China and later war between the Chinese and Japanese eased Chinese pressure on the kingdom in the 1930s and 1940s. The civil war in China, suspended during the years of World War II, resumed in 1945 and lasted until the communist victory in 1949. Determined to extend their authority, the communist Chinese invaded eastern Tibet in October 1950, quickly overcoming the resistance of the poorly equipped Tibetan troops. The Dalai Lama's appeals for help to the new United Nations were ignored, as were pleas to the British and Indian authorities. In 1951, the Chinese invaders forced the Dalai Lama to sign a new treaty and to accept Chinese garrisons on the volatile southern border with India. The communist leader, Mao Tse-tung, announced his government's intention to end the Tibetan problem by changing the population of Tibet to a Chinese majority of five to one. Then the Chinese government launched a program of mass immigration to the Tibetan-populated Inner Tibet in 1954. The Tibetan population in the colonization districts in Inner Tibet revolted, attempting to reunite their region with Outer Tibet under the rule of the Dalai Lama. Fighting and refugees spread into Outer Tibet with the Tibetans there joining the uprising in March 1959. The communist authorities launched an invasion of Tibet, forcing the 14th Dalai Lama, Tenzin Gyatso, and at least 87,000 refugees into exile in northern India. India's decision to take in Tibetan refugees worsened already tense relations between the two countries, and in 1962, the Chinese Red Army invaded northern India, touching off heavy fighting in several areas of their long mutual border. The Chinese government, determined to finally crush the troublesome Tibetan people, ordered the destruction of 6,125 ancient lamaseries with their priceless treasures and libraries. More than 100,000 Tibetans were killed in mass executions,

while the Chinese government proceeded with the resettlement of millions of ethnic Chinese in the traditionally Tibetan territories. During the chaos and upheaval of the Cultural Revolution in China from 1967 to 1977, zealous Red Guards reduced most of the remaining lamaseries and shrines to rubble. Entire collections of ancient manuscripts were looted and often were publicly burned. Only 13 lamaseries remained of the 6,254 in existence in 1959. In the late 1980s, a slight relaxation of the heavy military presence in Tibet resulted in the revival of Tibetan demands for self-determination. A pro-independence demonstration in Lhasa in 1988 ignited similar demonstrations across Tibet and into the Tibetan regions of the neighboring Chinese provinces in 1989, the same year that the Dalai Lama was awarded the Nobel Peace Prize in acknowledgment of his and the Tibetan people's peaceful campaign to regain their lost freedom. From the 1990s to the present, the Chinese authorities have continued to crack down on any signs of dissidence in the Tibetan regions though news constantly leaks out of defiance by many Tibetans, particularly Buddhist monks and nuns.

Further Reading

Beech, Hannah. "Tibet's Next Incarnation." *Time Magazine.* October 1, 2011. http://www.time.com/time/magazine/article/0,9171,2095608,00.html

Kapstein, Matthew T. *The Tibetans.* Hoboken, NJ: Wiley-Blackwell, 2006.

Smith, Warren W. Jr. *China's Tibet: Autonomy or Assimilation.* Lanham, MD: Rowman & Littlefield, 2009.

Van Shaik, Sam. *Tibet: A History.* New Haven, CT: Yale University Press, 2011.

Tu

The Tu, sometimes known as Tuzu, Tu Zu, Donghu, Tangut, Xianbei, Monguor, Mongguer, Chaghan Mongguer, or White Mongols, are Mongol people, one of the 56 officially recognized ethnic groups in the People's Republic of China. The estimated 290,000 Tu mostly live in the western Chinese provinces of Qinghai and Gansu. The most widely spoken language is Monguor, which is a Shirongolic language of the Mongolic language family. A smaller group living in eastern Qinghai speak a mixed language known as Wutun. The religious beliefs of the Tu combine Yellow Hat (Tibetan) Buddhism with the elements of Daoism introduced by the Han Chinese in the region.

The Tu are mentioned in early Chinese chronicles as a warlike, robust people living west of present-day Liaoning. In the fourth century CE, the ancestors of the Tu migrated east to Gansu and Qinghai. In their new homeland, they created a kingdom, a federation of tribal groups, known as Tuguhun. The kingdom was defeated in a war with Tufan in the seventh century, forcing many refugees to flee south to the region of the Yellow, Huangshui, and Datonghe Rivers. These refugee bands became the ancestors of the modern Tu people. The Tu were first recorded as a separate people during the great expansion of the Mongol peoples. A Mongol army was dispatched to control the Tu area in 1227. The Mongol soldiers remained in the region, taking wives from the local tribal groups. Another group of Mongols, following a defeat by a rival group in the 16th century, settled to the east of Qinghai, where they were gradually integrated into the Tu culture. Most of the Tu were herders of sheep and goats, moving their herds from the lowlands to the mountains each year. Around the middle of the 17th century, farming was introduced in some regions. The Tu tribes came under the rule of 16 hereditary chieftains or headmen, whose titles and lands were granted by the Ming emperor. Over time, these headmen controlled most of the land, which was rented for herding or farming. Many of the feudal lords were Buddhist lamas representing powerful lamaseries, which also served as large landlords renting land to the Tu peasants.

Tu culture is a mixed culture with influences from the Mongols, the Han Chinese, and the other ethnic groups living in the region. Many Tu view the name given to them by the Chinese government, which means simply "indigenous people," as derogatory, while they continue to call themselves Chaghan Monguor, meaning White Mongols. In recent years, urbanization and the adoption of many Han Chinese traditions and customs have endangered their own traditional culture. Many historical songs, riddles, folktales, and proverbs are slowly disappearing. In most Tu villages, a Buddhist temple and a Daoist shrine are the two most important buildings. Buddhist monks are common in most Tu regions, though Daoist priests and shamans are less numerous. Though many Mongol traits form important elements in the Tu culture, they have been adapted and changed over time until now they form part of the unique features of Tu society. The language of the Tu belongs to the Shirongolic branch of the Mongol languages, sometimes known as the Gansu-Qinghai group of Mongol languages. The language is spoken in several dialects that show strong Tibetan and Chinese influences. Many of the Tu words associated with religion have Tibetan origins. The basic vocabulary is similar to that of the Mongolian language, but in form and influences, the Tu language is closer to the languages spoken by the Dongxiang and Bonan ethnic groups in China. The Tu language was adapted to a Latin script by the Chinese government, but most Tu continue to use the Chinese script for writing their language.

The role of the hereditary headmen gradually changed until in the 19th century, abuses were rampant and the Tu peasants were forced to labor many days each year for the landlords or lamaseries apart from paying taxes of various types. The headmen or lamas made inspection tours every three years to assess the state of their lands. The Tu were gradually being reduced to a class of serfs in the feudal society controlled by the headmen and the lamaseries. In the late 19th century, Christian missionaries entered the area. They introduced education to some of the Tu communities, and between 1915 and 1949, they constructed churches and primary schools in the region. A family of headmen of the Ma family gained control of the region during the upheavals of the early 20th century. Controlling the region as warlords, the Ma implemented 40 different kinds of taxes and forced labor. Utilizing debt slavery, exploitation, and high rents, the Ma controlled the Tu people for some 38 years until the outbreak of World War II. Many Tu resisted the oppression of the Ma warlords, including a number of serious uprisings in the region before 1949. The victorious communists in 1949 sent cadres to the region to overthrow the Ma warlords and to eliminate the influences of the landlords and the lamaseries. The Tu made rapid strides in education and productivity, even during the collectivization of their herds and lands in the 1950s. The first autonomous Tu district, the Huzhu Tu Autonomous County, was established in 1954. The Chinese Cultural Revolution, from 1967 to 1977, devastated the region. The lamaseries, shrines, churches, and church schools were destroyed by Red Guards. Many Tu were arrested and sent to labor or reeducation camps. The political and economic reforms of the 1980s permitted the Tu to reconstruct many of their ancient lamaseries and shrines, but the churches and church schools remained banned. The recovery of the means of production promoted greater prosperity in the region, but by the early 21st century, the culture was in danger of losing much of its historic elements as assimilation into Han Chinese culture advanced.

Further Reading

Bulaq, Uradyn E. *The Mongols at China's Edge: History and Politics of National Unity.* Lanham, MD: Rowman & Littlefield, 2002.

Ethnic Groups. "The Tu Ethnic Minority." Accessed July 31, 2013. http://www.china.org.cn/e-groups/shaoshu/shao-2-tu.htm

Morgan, David. *The Mongols.* Hoboken, NJ: Wiley-Blackwell, 2007.

West, Barbara A. *Encyclopedia of the Peoples of Asia and Oceania.* New York: Facts on File, 2008.

Tujia

The Tujia, sometimes known as Ba, Bizika, Bizeka, Mozhihei, Tudja, or Tuchia, are one of the largest of the 56 officially recognized nationalities in the People's Republic of China. The approximately 8.4 million Tujia inhabit the Wuling Mountains region, which straddles the borders of the Chinese provinces of Hunan, Hubei, and Guizhou, and the municipality of Chongqing. Most Tujia adhere to their traditional animist belief system, with smaller numbers of Buddhists, Daoists, and Christians.

The Tujia can trace their history back to the ancient Ba people, who are thought to have occupied the region around the modern city of Chongqing some 2,500 years ago. The Ba established a state structure encompassing a number of distinct tribes under an elected king. The kingdom, under pressure from successive Chinese dynasties, reached the zenith of its power and territorial expansion between 600 and 400 BCE. The kingdom was finally overrun and destroyed by the forces of the Qin dynasty in 316 BCE. The Ba state was dismantled and converted into a territory of the Chinese Empire. The Qin emperor allowed the Ba to retain indirect rule as his agents and did not force the Ba to accept large-scale Chinese immigration into the conquered territory. Called by different names in Chinese records, the Tujia were considered a distinct ethnic group by the early 10th century CE. Han Chinese migrations to the region beginning in the early 12th century greatly changed the ethnic makeup of the region. The Han migrants also brought modern tools and farming techniques. Tujia feudal lords sold some of their lands to the Han Chinese peasants and traders, some of whom became landlords. The Tujia, exploited by their own chieftains, the feudal lords, and the Han Chinese landlords, often turned to the army as a way of survival. Renowned as fierce fighters, the Tujia were often employed to put down uprisings among other ethnic groups. Later, they were sent east to fight incursions by Japanese pirates during the 16th century. The Manchu conquest of China in 1644 began the process of replacing local headmen with Manchu officials, particularly in the early 18th century. Resistance to the new administration was widespread though the majority of the Tujia returned to central control between 1728 and 1735. Though the Tujia peasants probably preferred rule by Manchu officials to that of the arbitrary tyranny of the Tujia chieftains they had replaced, the Tujia resented the attempts of the Manchu Qing dynasty to impose Han Chinese culture and customs on them. To distinguish themselves from the many immigrant Han Chinese, the Tujia began to use the Chinese word *tujia* meaning "local" to refer to themselves and *kejia* or guest to address the growing Han Chinese population. With the weakening of Qing authority in the 18th century, numerous large-scale uprising broke out.

Though Tujia culture is officially recognized as a minority culture, traditional Tujia customs are now mostly found in remote areas in the mountains. Assimilation into the dominant Han Chinese culture has resulted in the loss of the Tujia language in most areas and the adoption of Han Chinese traditions and customs. Elements of the culture that remain include

the renowned singing and song composi-
tions and the traditional dances such as the
Baishou Dance, which has been performed
for more than five centuries. The Tujia are
also famous for their brocades, known as
xilankapu, which once were prized as tribute to the Chinese government. Many of
the traditional taboos are still honored.
Pregnant women and young girls are not
permitted to sit on thresholds, while men
cannot enter a house wearing straw rain-
coats or carrying hoes or buckets. Young
women are not allowed to sit next to male
visitors, though young girls are permitted. At religious ceremonies, cats are kept
away as their meowing is considered in-
auspicious. Though their religious ceremonies and rites are dying out as they
become more assimilated, their traditional
religious beliefs still blend Daoism, ancestor worship, and a shamanistic belief
in gods, spirits, and demons. Most of the
Tujia revere a white tiger totem, though in
western Hunan, they revere a turtle totem.
The Tujia often refer to themselves as the
descendants of the white tiger. Only about
170,000–200,000 Tujia are still fluent in
the Tujia language, the rest speak Mandarin Chinese or the local dialect known as
Ghao-Xong. The Tujia language was traditionally spoken in two regional dialects,
with the speakers of northern Tujia calling themselves Bizika while the southern
Tujia calling themselves Mozhihei.

The Tujia living among the large Han
Chinese population adopted many Han
Chinese customs and traditions though
they retained much of their traditional culture. The distance to the central regions
of China left much of the Tujia under
the despotic rule of local warlords in the

A Tujia woman makes traditional brocade with
the help of a "Tiaozi," a knitting tool, in Longshan
County, central-south China's Hunan Province,
2011. Listed in 2006 as one of China's National
Intangible Heritages, the traditional Tujia
brocade is now protected as a national
treasure. (Bai Yu/Xinhua Press/Corbis)

19th century. The Taiping Rebellion, in
the mid-19th century, affected the Tujia
area very badly, and western traders
flooded the region with cheap foreign
goods, with local products purchased
at rock-bottom prices. The slowly collapsing Qing dynasty was finally overthrown by the Chinese Revolution in
1911. At Qing authority evaporated, the
Tujia found themselves caught between
various competing warlords. Many of the
wealthy landlords insisted in turning more
and more land over to the cultivation of

high-earning opium poppies. Banditry was rife with attacks on Tujia villages frequent and often violent. Many Tujia joined the rebels led by the communists that opposed the excesses of the republican government and promised to impose peace and order on the countryside. Many Tujia fought against the Japanese during World War II, then joined the communist forces in the Chinese Civil War that finally ended with a communist victory in 1949. The Tujia regions were brought under communist control. Banditry was quickly eradicated, the landlords and warlords eliminated, and the Tujia peasants glorified as the true people of the region. Land redistribution soon gave way to collectivization with the Tujia workers considered employees of the state. The Tujia were officially recognized as one of the country's ethnic minorities in 1957, with a number of autonomous prefectures and counties established to give the Tujia an illusion of self-government. The Chinese Cultural Revolution, active between 1967 and 1977, left most of the ancient Tujia shrines, totems, and historical buildings in ruins. Many Tujia, judged as antirevolutionary, were arrested. The reforms instituted in the early 1980s permitted the Tujia to recover much of their cultural sites, which were rebuilt, but assimilation, promoted during the 1960s and 1970s, continued to progress with a rapid loss of the Tujia language and many cultural traits. By the early 21st century, it is often difficult to distinguish the Tujia from their Han Chinese neighbors, with only the Tujia in the more remote and mountainous areas retaining the language and the traditional culture.

Further Reading

Chetham, Diedre. *Before the Deluge: The Vanishing World of the Yangtze's Three Gorges.* Basingstoke, UK: Palgrave Macmillan, 2004.

Guo, Rongxing. *China's Ethnic Minorities: Social and Economic Indicators.* London: Routledge, 2013.

People's Daily Online. "The Tujia Ethnic Minority." Accessed July 31, 2013. http://english.people.com.cn/data/minorities/Tujia.html

Xingliang, He. *Totemism in Chinese Minority Ethnic Groups.* Beijing: China Intercontinental Press, 2006.

Turkmen

The Turkmen, sometimes known as Turkomen, Türkmen, or Trukhmen, are a Turkic people of Central Asia. The largest Turkmen population is in Turkmenistan, with sizable populations in Iraq, Syria, northeastern Iran, and northwestern Afghanistan, and smaller communities in Turkey, Pakistan, and Russia. Descended from early Caucasian tribal groups and later Oghuz Turks, the estimated 8.3 million Turkmen speak an Oghuz Turkic language related to Turkish, Azeri, and Uzbek. The Turkmen are overwhelmingly Sunni Muslim, though because they still retain some pre-Islamic rituals and practices, they are sometimes described as half Muslim. In Iraq and Syria, there are small communities of Christian Turkmen.

The earliest inhabitants of the region known in Arab and Hindu legends as the birthplace of the Aryan race were Caucasian tribal groups living in the fertile oases scattered around the edges of the Karakum

The Turkmen Horse

The Akhal-Teke are a breed of horses important to Turkmen history. The horses, known as the golden horses in Turkmenistan, are well adapted to severe climatic conditions and are believed to be one of the oldest surviving horse breeds. The Akhal-Teke may date as far back as 3,000 years, when early tribes used the horses for travel and raiding. They selectively bred the Akhal-Teke, keeping accurate oral records of the complicated pedigrees. When Turkmenistan gained independence from the collapsing Soviet Union in 1991, the first president's Akhal-Teke horse was added to the official seal of the new state.

Desert, known in the Turkic languages as Black Sand. The Caucasians developed a settled agricultural civilization greatly influenced by ties to the other Persian-speaking peoples, particularly those of the powerful Persian Empire. In the sixth century BCE, the territory, then under the rule of the Persian Achaemenid dynasty, was the site of a string of powerful fortresses to protect the towns and cities from incursions by nomadic tribes. The conquest of the region by the Greeks of Alexander the Great in the third century BCE brought the region into contact with the Mediterranean cultures to the west. The Greeks founded new cities and Greek soldiers settled in the area, taking wives from the native Caucasian tribes. From about 225 BCE, most of the region formed part of the Greek-influenced Bactrian kingdom. The territory again came under Persian rule as part of the Parthian Empire. The Parthians, the only serious rival of the Roman Empire for domination of the Middle East, fought long wars with the expanding Romans. In 53 BCE, some 10,000 Roman prisoners of war were transported to the region and forcibly settled at the city of Mary, then known as Margian. Much of the vast region remained the domain of nomadic tribal groups, with a settled Persian-speaking population in the limited fertile lands and the oases. Tribal migrations overran the region in a long series of invasions until the Persians of the Sassanid Empire reestablished Persian rule over the oases towns. The Turkmen trace their origins to the early Caucasian groups and to the Oghuz, a loose confederation of Turkic tribes in the territory now forming part of Mongolia in the seventh and eighth centuries. Beginning in the seventh century, these nomadic Turkic tribes of the desert region periodically migrated west, some passing through Persian territory to settle in parts of present-day Iraq and Syria. Muslim Arabs invaded the territory between 651 and 716 CE. Joined to the Muslim Caliphate, the majority of the settled population embraced the new Islamic religion. The city of Mary, known as Merv, was established as a center of Arab administration for a large part of Persia and Central Asia, becoming one of the major centers of Arab-Persian Muslim learning and culture. Turkic-speaking nomads of the Oghuz Confederation overran the entire territory in 821. Taking control of the oases trading centers and the important trade routes that crossed the region, they established themselves as the rulers of the vast Karakum region. In the 11th and 12th centuries, the oases trading cities were important caravan stops on the Silk Road trading routes that connected the Orient with the Mediterranean. The Turkic rulers made Merv the center of the Seljuk Empire from 1118 to 1157, when the majority of the Turkic tribes left the region to migrate farther west. The remaining Turkic groups continued to dominate the Karakum region, gradually imposing their Oghuz language and tribal system on the settled Caucasian oasis dwellers. The Mongol hordes invaded the Karakum territory in 1219–1222, destroying the trading centers and the extensive irrigation system that had supported the large settled populations. According to Turkmen legends, the invading Mongols slaughtered more than a million people in the region. Their settled agricultural civilization in ruins, the survivors gathered together in small tribal groups that gradually spread across the region as nomadic herdsmen. Later renowned as horsemen and warriors, the Turkmen tribes again settled in the oases following the end of Mongol domination. Expanding from the oases, the Turkmen warriors conquered a huge territory that formed a loose Turkmen empire stretching from Central Asia as far west as Azerbaijan and Armenia from 1378 to 1500. Many of the Turkmen populations of Turkey, Iraq, Syria, and other areas far from the Turkmen homeland date from this period of Turkmen expansion. Turkic Uzbek groups subjugated all of Central Asia in the 16th century though their empire soon split into several successor states, including the Khanate of Khiva and the Emirate of Bukhara. The Turkmen tribes in the regions claimed by the Uzbek states resisted for more than two centuries, with the last of the Turkmen groups brought under the rule of the khan of Khiva only in the early 19th century. Members of the first Russian expedition to the region, seeking a trade route to Southern Asia and the Middle East, were murdered by Turkmen tribesmen in 1716. Diplomatic ties between Russia and the Uzbek states that dominated Central Asia were finally established in the mid-18th century.

Descended from the mixture of the early Caucasian peoples and the later Turkic tribes, the Turkmen culture remains a fusion of these two and other later influences. The Turkmen follow three traditional codes of conduct: *adat*, customary law; *sherigat*, Islamic law; and *edep*, rules for proper etiquette and behavior. Though some aspects of these traditions were lost during the decades of Soviet rule, they still continue to shape social behavior on a daily basis. Many of the Turkmen have the fair skin and light eyes of their Caucasian ancestors though most are Turkic in appearance with dark hair and eyes. The most traditional of the Turkic peoples of Central Asia, the Turkmen remain divided along tribal lines, the largest and most important of the tribes being the Tekes of Mary, the Tekes of Attok, the Ersaris, the Yomuds, and the Goklans. All of the tribes are divided into regional, clan, and family groups. The Turkmen tribes all speak dialects of the same Oghuz Turkic language of the West Altaic language family. The language is spoken in at least 11 regional dialects spread from Turkmenistan through Iran into Iraq and Syria. The Turkmen language in Turkmenistan borrows many words from Russian. In Turkmenistan, the language is officially written in the Täze Elipbiý, the so-called new alphabet based on the Latin writing system, though the old Soviet-era Cyrillic alphabet is still widely used as many Turkmen speak Russian as the second language. The adoption of the new Latin alphabet has facilitated communication with the Turkmen minorities and other Turkic peoples using the Latin alphabet in Turkey and Iraq and in other countries. Turkmen is not a literary language in Iran and Afghanistan, where the Turkmen are normally bilingual, usually speaking both Turkmen and the local variations of Persian. The Turkmen have a rich tradition of epic stories, heroic tales, and lyric poems, many about their mythical ancestor, Oghuz Khan, the believed ancestor of the Turkmen tribes. The most famous figure in Turkmen cultural history is the 18th-century poet, Magtymguly Pyragy, a spiritual leader and philosophical poet who worked for the independence and autonomy of the Turkmen people. Virtually all Turkmen know his quotations and poetry by heart. The Turkmen are overwhelmingly Sunni Muslim, with each tribal or clan group maintaining the legend or account of how it adopted Islam. Pre-Islamic rituals and traditions, such as belief in charms, lucky and unlucky days, and the evil eye, are common. Each of the Turkmen tribes and clans maintains its own cemetery and saint's shrine that dot the Turkmen landscape.

Several Turkmen clans were officially proclaimed Russian subjects in 1802. The tribes accepted Russian aid during the frequent Turkmen uprisings against the authority of the Uzbek rulers of Khiva and Bukhara. In 1865, aided by their Turkmen allies, the Russians invaded the region. The Governorate-General of Turkestan was created in 1867. The Emirate of Bukhara was made a Russian protectorate in 1868, while the Khanate of Khiva, weakened by ethnic disputes and Russian incursions, lost control of some of its Turkmen territories. Led by the powerful Teke tribes, the Turkmen attempted to create an autonomous state in the Transcaspian region. In 1869, a Russian army moved into the Turkmen lands, meeting the fiercest resistance and suffering the greatest losses of the long campaign to win control of Central Asia. The western Turkmen clans, fearing a return of Uzbek rule, accepted Russian rule, but the eastern and southern tribes fiercely resisted Russian attempts to take control of their tribal territories. In 1880, the Khanate of Khiva came under Russian authority as a protected state, allowing the Russians to claim the remainder of the Turkmen lands. The Battle of Gok-Tepe, in January 1881, ended with the slaughter of thousands of Turkmen tribesmen. The Russians took control of the Turkmen territories in a new Russian Transcaspian province south and west of the vassal states of Bukhara and Khiva, still in nominal control of parts of Turkmenistan. In 1884, Russian forces

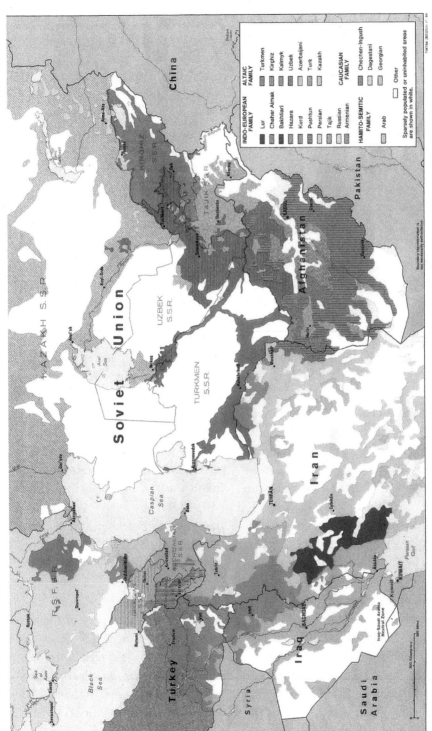

Ethnolinguistic groups in the southern republics of the former Soviet Union. (Used by permission of the University of Texas Libraries, The University of Texas at Austin)

overran the oasis city of Mary, officially completing the conquest of the Turkmen. However, many Turkmen warriors continued to fight the Russians until they were finally defeated in 1895. Under Russian rule, the Turkmen territories remained the least developed, poorest, and most backward of Russian Central Asia. Frequent Turkmen revolts and violent disputes over water and land were endemic. Russian authority extended only to the major towns, garrisoned oases, and the string of Russian forts. Though untouched by the bloodshed of World War I far to the west in European Russia, the attempted conscription of Muslims into work battalions in 1916 set off a widespread revolt throughout Central Asia. Led by Dzhunaid Khan, the Turkmen overran the Russian vassal state of Khiva, where they established an autonomous government. The Central Asian revolt was overtaken by the Russian Revolution and civil war in 1917–1920 that created chaos in the region. By July 1919, all of the Turkmen tribes had fallen under the authority of the new Soviet authorities. Many of the Turkmen warriors joined the *basmachi*, guerrilla bands fighting the imposition of Soviet rule between 1921 and 1924. The Soviet government divided Central Asia along ethnic lines in 1924, creating a nominally autonomous Turkmen state, which was admitted to the new Soviet Union as a constituent republic in 1925. During the collectivization of the region, in the 1930s, the Turkmen nomads, labeled parasites and antisocial elements, were forced into permanent settlements. Far from the centers of the Soviet Union, over the next decades, ethnic Russian or Turkmen bureaucrats whose only

qualification was unquestioning loyalty to the Soviet hierarchy controlled the Turkmen region. Wielding almost unlimited power, the communist bureaucrats systematically looted Turkmenistan, earning themselves the derisive name the "Turkmen Mafia." Despite the unsuitability of the crop, cotton production was extended across the fertile districts, ravaging the environment and endangering public health in the 1960s and 1970s. The Soviet leadership of the Turkmen Soviet Socialist Republic, grounded on obedience to the Soviet government, was increasingly based on clan, family, and influence ties. The Turkmen communists that controlled the republic were notorious for corruption, but loyalty to Moscow counted for much more than capability. Saparmurad Niyazov was named head of the Turkmen Communist Party in 1985. He led the republic during the Soviet reform era in the late 1980s. In early 1990, the announcement of the first open elections galvanized a Turkmen revival and such forbidden subjects as language use, environmental catastrophes, and social conditions. The decentralization of the Soviet Union allowed the local Turkmen Communist Party to increase its hold on the republic. The collapse of the Soviet government, in 1991, allowed the old Turkmen communist leadership to take full control of Turkmenistan, which was declared an independent republic in October 1991. Saparmurad Niyazov, the head of the Soviet government, quickly reinvented himself as a nationalist leader and became the first president of the new Turkmenistan republic. Since independence, Turkmenistan has remained a one-party state dominated by its president and his closest advisers with little progress in moving from the Soviet-era authoritarianism to a democratic system.

Further Reading

Edgar, Adrienne Lynn. *Tribal Nation: The Making of Soviet Turkmenistan.* Princeton, NJ: Princeton University Press, 2006.

Kropf, John. *Unknown Sands.* Houston: Dusty Spark Publishing, 2006.

Peyrouse, Sebastien. *Turkmenistan: Strategies of Power, Dilemmas of Development.* Armonk, NY: M.E. Sharpe, 2011.

Tuvan

The Tuvan, sometimes known as Tuvivinians, Tyvan, Tuwa, Tuba, Uriankhai, Uryankhay, Soyoty, or Soyony, are a Turkic people living in southern Siberia and adjacent areas of Mongolia and China. A people of mixed ancestry, the Tuvan resemble the Mongol peoples physically but culturally and linguistically are more closely related to the Turkic peoples. The estimated 280,000 Tuvans form the majority of the population of the Tuva Republic, one of the constituent states of the Russian Federation. The language of the Tuva, known as Tuvin, is a Northern Turkic language of the Southern Siberian branch of the Turkic languages. The largest numbers of religious Tuva adhere to the Tibetan form of Buddhism, Lamaism. A small number, estimated to number about 2 percent, converted to Orthodox Christianity under Russian influence.

Historically, the Tuvan have been herders for thousands of years, tending herds of cattle, goats, sheep, camels, and yaks. The nomads lived in yurts that they relocated seasonally as they moved with the herds to new pastures. Archaeological evidence confirms the presence in the region of the early Scythians, possibly in the seventh and sixth centuries BCE. They are thought to be the basis of the occasional blond, freckled, green- and blue-eyed Tuvans. Chinese chronicles record the existence of a tribal group called the *Dubo* in the region as early as 200 CE. Traditional history has the Tuvan people under the rule of a Turkish khanate in the sixth century. Chinese and Uyghur launched incursions against the nomadic Tuvan tribes. The Uyghur Khanate held the region for about a century until the Kyrgyz of the Yenisei region overran the Tuvan homeland in 840. They were mentioned by travelers in the 10th century as a nomadic herder people living in clans ruled by hereditary or elected chiefs. They were noted as inhabiting the grasslands north of the Silk Road trade routes, the ancient caravan trails that connected the Orient to the Mediterranean. In the 13th century, the invading Mongols conquered the region, which remained under Mongol rule for three centuries. The Mongol hordes ruled Tuva from 1207 to 1368, then the Oirat gained control of the region until the 16th century. Around 1650, the Dzungar Oirat added Tuva to their expanding empire. The various Tuvan tribes, often warring among themselves, merged as an identifiable ethnic group only in the early 18th century, about the time that Tibetan Buddhism was introduced through contact with the Mongol peoples to the south. The new Buddhist religion was adopted by all the Tuvan tribes, but most also retained many of the customs and rituals of their earlier shamanistic beliefs. The Manchu rulers of China launched an invasion of the region in 1757–1758, bringing the Tuvan clans under their rule as the Uriankhai or Urjanchai region of Manchu-ruled Mongolia.

The Tuvan culture reflects their mixed ancestry, which includes Turkic, Mongol, Samoyed, and Kettic strains. The Turkic and Mongol influences predominate in western Tuva, the Samoyed in western and eastern Tuva, and the Kets in eastern Tuva. Historically, the Tuvan are divided into two major subgroups—the Western Tuvan and the Eastern or Todzhin Tuvan concentrated in the Todzhinsky region of the republic. In spite of the destruction that over four decades of Soviet rule inflicted on the Tuvan people, education and professional training made great strides. The majority of the modern Tuvan are literate, and the number of trained professionals such as doctors, engineers, and teachers is much higher than that in neighboring Mongolia. The majority of the Tuvan remain herdsmen and hunters but some have settled as cereal farmers close to the growing urban Tuvan population. Since 1991, ethnic Tuvans returning to the region from China have introduced vegetable farming. Though the Tuvan revere their past as nomads living in yurts, the modern Tuvans are more likely to live in urban settlements in permanent brick houses or high-rise apartment buildings. The Tuvans are noted for their rich oral epic poetry and their music. Tuvan singing, called *khoomei* or throat singing, is famous for their ability to sing with two voices simultaneously, one voice usually a lower base drone and the second a higher-pitched flutelike sound. The two-note singing ability is unique to Tuvan, part

of Mongolia, and some Tibetan monks. The Tuvan language is closely related to the Turkic Uighur language spoken widely in Chinese Xinjiang to the south. Tuvan has literary status in Russia, but the Tuvan minority in Mongolia use Khalkha Mongol as their literary language, and in China they use the Chakhar Mongol language. The Tuva language is divided into five dialects—Central, Western, Northwestern or Todzhin, Southeastern, and Tuba-Kizhi. Sharp dialectical differences exist between the language spoken in Russia and the Kokchulutan and Khöwsögöl dialects spoken in Mongolia and China. Though Russian has made inroads over time, the Tuva language remains the mother tongue of 99 percent of the Tuva population in the Russian Federation with Russian often spoken as the second language. The Tuvan religion, a variant of Tibetan Lamaism, is an integral part of their culture. The Dalai Lama of Tibet, now living in exile in India, is revered as the spiritual leader of the Tuvan nation. The practice of their religion still often combines Buddhism with the elements of their traditional shamanistic belief in an unseen world of gods, demons, and ancestral spirits. Most Tuvan Buddhists continue to believe that all natural elements contain spirits that must be appeased with offerings. Shamans continue to have widespread respect for their ability to cure the sick and to communicate with the spirit world.

Russian expeditions first contacted the Tuvan tribes around 1860, when the terms of the Treaty of Peking between Russia and China opened the region for trade. Russian interest in the region grew as the power of the Manchu rulers of China waned in the

Tuvan family throat sings and plays the igil, or horse-head fiddle. (Lynn Johnson/National Geographic Society/Corbis)

1870s. Over the next two decades, several thousand Slavic colonists settled the region known as the Asian Switzerland. The Slavic settlers in the Tuvan region of Chinese Mongolia gradually took control of the region as Manchu Chinese authority withered away. Tuvan leaders, with Russian support, organized a national

Throat Singing

The famous Tuvan throat singing is a particular variant of overtone singing practiced for thousands of years. The art of throat singing is a style in which one or more distinct pitches sound simultaneously over a fundamental pitch, creating a unique singing form. The popularity of throat singing remains an important element in modern Tuvan culture. Formerly practiced only by males, women have mastered the technique in recent decades. Traditionally, it was believed that female throat singing could harm male relatives and cause difficulties in childbirth. Tyva Kyzy, meaning Daughters of Tuva, was founded in 1998 as an all-female ensemble performing all types of Tuvan throat singing.

government during the chaos of the 1911 Chinese Revolution, which overthrew centuries of Manchu rule. On December 18, 1911, the Tuvan leaders, supported by the powerful Slavic minority in the region, declared the Tuvan homeland independent of China. The weak Tuvan state, bowing to the demands of the influential Russian minority, was forced to accept Russian protection against Chinese or Mongol claims to their territory when World War I broke out in Europe in 1914. The tsarist government of Russia proclaimed Tuva a Russian protectorate and assumed responsibility for the country's defense and foreign affairs. A 1915 international agreement between the Tuvan leadership, the Chinese, and the Russians recognized Tuvan autonomy but under nominal Chinese authority. The majority of the Tuvan population remained indifferent to politics as they mostly lived in rural areas or small villages, often employed by members of the Tuvan aristocracy in a feudal system of local loyalties. The onset of the Russian Revolution allowed the Tuvans to reassert the independence of their homeland. Early in 1918, Tuvan revolutionaries, supported by local Russian Bolsheviks, rebelled against the country's traditional ruling class. The weak Tuvan militia was pushed aside as anti-Bolshevik White forces occupied the region and forces from China and Mongolia occupied the southwestern and southern districts. In mid-1919, the Bolshevik Red Army occupied Tuva. In August 1921, a Tuvan People's Republic, popularly known as Tannu-Tuva, was created. Tannu-Tuva maintained a precarious independence until 1944. During World War II, the Red Army returned to occupy Tannu-Tuva in 1944. In 1945, the Soviet

Union annexed Tannu-Tuva, supposedly at the request of its citizens. Granted the status of an autonomous republic in 1961, Tuva remained isolated, and the Tuvan people were forbidden contact with neighboring peoples. The Soviet antireligious stance resulted in the destruction of many Buddhist shrines and lamaseries until the late 1970s and early 1980s when the Soviet government relaxed the curbs on religion as part of its international peace campaigns targeted at the Buddhist countries of Asia. The liberalization of the Soviet Union, beginning in the late 1980s, allowed the Tuvans to reestablish long-forbidden cultural, family, and religious ties to the neighboring peoples of Siberia, Mongolia, and China. Closed to foreigners for more than two decades, the picturesque Tuvan homeland was finally opened to travelers in 1988. Freed of the hated Soviet restraints, Tuvan activists organized to demand increased Tuvan language education, help in rebuilding destroyed Buddhist monasteries and shrines, and an end to all interference in relations with the related peoples of the region. Tuvan nationalism grew rapidly until large demonstrations rocked the Tuvan region in June 1990. Activists demanded the dismissal of the passive local government and denounced the 1944 annexation of their country by the Soviet Union as illegal. The demonstrations continued through the summer of 1990, sending more than 3,000 ethnic Slavs fleeing back to Russia to escape the escalating anti-Russian violence. The complete collapse of the Soviet Union in 1991 raised nationalist expectations of a renewed Tuvan independence, but the new Tuvan leadership acknowledged that after nearly half a century of harsh Soviet rule, they suffered a lack of trained administrators and professionals making immediate independence impossible. Tuva, renamed the Tuva Republic, became a member state of the post-Soviet Russian Federation.

Further Reading

Giuliano, Elise. *Constructing Grievance: Ethnic Nationalism in Russia's Republics.* Ithaca, NY: Cornell University Press, 2011.

Gorenburg, Dmitry P. *Minority Ethnic Mobilization in the Russian Federation.* Cambridge: Cambridge University Press, 2003.

Hunmagyar.org. "Tuva." Accessed July 31, 2013. http://www.hunmagyar.org/turan/tuva/

Levin, Theodore. *Where Rivers and Mountains Sing: Sound, Music, and Nomadism in Tuva and Beyond.* Bloomington: Indiana University Press, 2006.

U

Ulch

The Ulch, sometimes known as Ulchi, Ulcha, Ulche, Olchi, Olcha, Mangun, or Gilyak, are a Siberian people living in the Khabarovsk region of the Russian Far East. The Ulch call themselves *nani*, though the name was applied to a neighboring people as Nanai in the 1930s. Some 90 percent of the Ulch live within the district of Ulchsky. The estimated 2,500–3,500 Ulch mostly speak Russian as their first language with fewer than 900 still able to speak or understand the Ulch language. The language forms part of the Nanai group of the Southern Tungusic languages spoken in Siberia. Most of the Ulch retain their traditional shamanistic belief system with a minority that have embraced Russian Orthodoxy.

The Ulch are an ancient people whose original home is believed to be in the basin of the Lower Amur River in eastern Siberia. They are considered a people of mixed ancestry, with cultural and physical traits from many of the local Siberian peoples and the ancient Manchu that inhabited the region just to the south. The Ulch bands were mostly hunters and river fishermen living in seasonal villages along the rivers and lakes of the region. Though the majority of the Ulch were fishermen on the Lower Amur River and the many lakes in the region, they also hunted the fur-bearing animals of their forests. Some Ulch also hunted marine animals in the Straits of Tatar after an annual journey via Lake Kiz and along various small rivers. They moved seasonally and traded with the neighboring Siberian peoples. Contact with the ancestors of the Manchu resulted in the adoption of some cultural traits and traditions. Intermarriage was common between the Ulch and other peoples of the region, leading to later complications in dividing the population into defined ethnic groups. Until the 17th century CE, the Ulch maintained their traditional way free of outside interference until officials of the Chinese Empire moved into the region and attempted to make the Ulch and other Siberian peoples pay tribute and taxes. The attempt to imposed taxes was unsuccessful, mostly because of the nomadic habits of the Siberians, but contact with China was maintained on a commercial basis. Chinese goods, tools, and textiles were imported in exchange for the valuable furs taken by the Ulch. In 1643, a Russian flotilla, led by Vassili Poyarkov, descended the Amur River to the Sea of Okhotsk. In 1649–1650, Russian Cossacks occupied the banks of the Amur River, but the Chinese resisted the encroachments and forced the abandonment of the Russian forts. The Treaty of Nerchinsk, signed in 1689, confirmed the basin of the Amur River as Chinese territory though China never laid claim to the lower course of the river.

The Ulch culture is based on their traditional culture that evolved through their close relationship with nature, as their survival depended on their knowledge and relations with all aspects of their homeland. The Ulch customs include a reverence for nature as they view trees, grasses, rivers, lakes, and mountains as living and feeling entities. Ancient rituals such as making offerings to the spirits of tobacco and food are still practiced. The offerings are made with requests for happiness, the well-being of the family, or success in work to the spirits, known as masters such as Master of the Water or Master of the Fire. Traditional dances are an important cultural element, historically imitating the movements of seals, reindeer, bears, or ravens, all accompanied by Ulch drummers. In ceremonies involving shamans or healers, the dances were often trance-inducing and involved whole villages. Rhythms played on the drums by shamans were believed to reveal what the spirits were commanding. The Bear Cult, common in Siberian cultures, is even found among the Ainu in northern Japan. Though suppressed by the Soviet authorities, it has been revived. The Ritual of the Bear, involving drums, dancing, and offerings, is the most important event that is believed to ensure the clan's harmony. The ritual also honors the ancestors of the Ulch and ensures their passage to a new existence in the Lower World away from what the Ulch call the Middle World. The Ulch also believe in helpful spirits known as *savin*. Effigies of these spirits are carved in wood that decorate Ulch dwellings and are used in healing. A long history of amateur theatrical performances has been revived in recent years. Though the Soviet era did great damage to the Ulch culture, it is still connected to its ancient traditions. The Ulch language belongs to the Amur or Southern group of Tungus languages. It is closely related to the languages of the neighboring Nanai and Orok peoples. The language is homogeneous, spoken without dialects or regional differences. Despite many local initiatives, the Ulch culture is giving way to a more Russian-style way of life. Though many traditions and customs have been saved or revived, the use of the language continues to decline with a majority of the Ulch speaking Russian as their mother tongue.

The Ulch maintained their trade links to the neighboring peoples and Chinese merchants often traded along the banks of the rivers though the Ulch and the other Siberian peoples remained free of outside authority. In 1852, a Russian expedition explored the Amur, and within a short period of time, Russian Cossacks and peasants were settled along the river. The Russian occupation of the Amur region was confirmed in a new treaty between Russia and China in 1858. The Treaty of Aigun recognized the Amur River as the boundary between Imperial Russia and Manchu China and granted the Russians free access to the Pacific Ocean. The Russians began fishing on a massive scale and set up fish-processing plants along the Amur River. The Ulch were forced to adopt commercial fishing, selling their catch to Russian traders and peasants. As Russian authority expanded, local officials sought to restrict the Ulch fishing grounds leading to conflicts and bloody confrontations. Because of the increased demands for fish, hunting became less important as the Russians hunted the declining number of fur-bearing animals in the region. The Ulch were forced to learn new occupations, including land cultivation and logging timber for riverboats. Over time, a small number of wealthy Ulch merchants emerged, who extended their trading networks with neighboring peoples and even into Manchuria. Russian Orthodox missionaries became active in the 1860s. Though they failed to eradicate shamanism, they created several clerical schools. New elementary schools were opened, partly by intellectuals exiled from European Russia, between 1913 and 1917. The Ulch way of life continued and adapted until the arrival of the Soviet authorities in the early 1920s. As the fishing industry was in crisis, many Ulch worked as loggers in the timber industry around Lake Kiz. Soviet authority was established in Ulch territory in 1922. The Ulch were collectivized, and the more prosperous merchants and landowners were ruthlessly eliminated. Nine ethnic Ulch village communes were established by 1927–1928, and in 1934, the district of Ulchsky was established. At first, Soviet cadres encouraged ethnic culture and studied the Ulch traditions and language. But collectivization began in 1930 with the Ulch population moved from their traditional villages to larger centers with mixed populations. The Ulch were treated as employees of the Soviet state, and private property was forbidden. Collectivization and forced relocations decimated the Ulch culture as the population began to assimilate into the Soviet-Russian culture. Regular shipping on the Amur River allowed the scattered Ulch to maintain ties to family and friends despite Soviet restrictions. By the 1980s,

the region was in crisis due to the unrestricted polluting of the Amur River and its tributaries that badly depleted fish stocks. The timber industry, particularly the large mill on Lake Kiz, effectively eliminated all fish in the lake. The Soviet authorities united the fishing collectives with the timber mills and state farms, but this did little to alleviate the suffering of the Ulch and other people of the region. The end of their traditional fishing further damaged the fragile Ulch culture in the early 21st century. Despite the revival of some folk music, dance, and theater, the Ulch culture, like their dying language, is in danger of disappearing completely.

Further Reading

Evans, John L. *Russian Expansion to the Amur 1848–1860: The Push to the Pacific.* Lewiston, NY: Edwin Mellen Press, 1999.

Forsyth, James. *A History of the Peoples of Siberia: Russia's North Asian Colony 1581–1990.* Cambridge: Cambridge University Press, 1994.

Olson, James S. *An Ethnohistorical Dictionary of the Russian and Soviet Empires.* Westport, CT: Greenwood, 1994.

Vahtre, Lauri, and Jüri Viikberg. The Red Book of the Peoples of the Russian Empire. "The Ulchis." Accessed July 31, 2013. http://www.eki.ee/books/redbook/ulchis.shtml

Utsul

The Utsul, sometimes known as Utset, Utsat, or Hainan Cham, are a small ethnic group living in the southern most tip of the Chinese island of Hainan. They have not been recognized as a distinct ethnic group by the Chinese government. The estimated

5,000–8,000 Utsul speak a language called Tsat, which forms part of the Chamic subgroup of the Malayo-Polynesian language group. The Utsul are a Muslim people; therefore, they were arbitrarily added to the officially recognized Hui ethnic group in China.

According to Utsul traditions, they are descended from Muslims who migrated southeast from their origins in Central Asia. However, most scholars believe that they are descendants of Cham refugees who fled their homeland in present-day Vietnam. Ancient Champa, the Cham homeland, emerged as a separate state in 192 CE, during the breakup of the Han dynasty in China. The Cham kingdom eventually expanded to control most of present central and southern Vietnam. The Cham, a Malay people, experienced a golden age of culture and prosperity between the sixth and eighth centuries. The expansion of the Cham kingdom resulted in conflicts with the Khmer peoples to the south and the newly independent Vietnamese to the north. By the 10th century, Champa was involved in a long series of indecisive wars with the Khmer and Viet states and with China. The Cham maintained a large and powerful fleet that carried on trade and piracy across the region. The constant warfare resulted in many Cham refugees, some fleeing north to Hainan as early as 986, as mentioned in Chinese chronicles. The Vietnamese kingdom of Dai Viet invaded Champa in the 10th century, taking first the principality of Amaravati in 1000 and the principality of Vijaya in 1069. The Vietnamese sacked the city of Vijaya sending tens of thousands of Cham refugees fleeing west into Khmer territory. A Cham prince and some 1,000 followers fled by ship north to the Chinese island of Hainan, where officials of the Chinese Ming dynasty allowed them to join the earlier Cham refugees and to create an exile kingdom. Culturally and religiously distinct from the other inhabitants of the large island, the Cham refugees clustered in one area where they maintained their culture and language. Over time, they were called Utsul or Utsat, and their language Tsat. The language, influenced by neighboring Chinese and Tai dialects, became the only known Malayo-Polynesian language spoken in the region that is a tonal language.

The Utsul culture is a Muslim culture more closely related to the Cham of Cambodia and Vietnam and the peoples of Indonesia and Malaysia than to the neighboring Li and Han Chinese populations of Hainan. The Utsul live primarily in the villages of Yanglan and Huixin on the outskirts of the large city of Sanya. Even though the Utsul are historically, linguistically, and ethnically unrelated to the Muslim Hui people of mainland China, because of their Muslim religion, they have been included as part of the official Hui ethnic group. The Utsul villages are visibly Muslim with mosques, religious schools, and women in headscarves. The Utsul form the only Muslim ethnic group on the island. Each Utsul family keeps a Koran and lives strictly by its terms. The Utsul belong to the al-Ikhwan subsect of Sunni Islam. The Utsul region is famous for the mosques known as Eastern, Western, Southern, and Northern, the most splendid buildings in the region. The Utsul wear white robes and turbans when they enter the mosques to pray. The main hall of each of the mosques is used for daily prayer and Muslim festivals. Dietary restricts are also followed, including the ban on pork, animal blood, and the meat of any animal that is not butchered according to ancient Muslim tradition. Utsul houses are unusual as they all have tablets over their gates with the word *peace* written in the Arab script though many now live in tall apartment buildings. Traditionally, the Utsul are fishermen rather than farmers. Legends tell of the early Cham/Utsul settlers who lived on sea algae during a prolonged period of poor catches. The unique Tsat language, still spoken by the Utsul along with Li and the Chinese Min dialect, belongs to the Chamic branch of the Malayo-Polynesian language family. The language is the only Chamic language spoken in China, though a large Cham population speaks the related Cham language in Cambodia and Vietnam. Over time, the original Cham of the early refugees, under the influence of the neighboring Li and Han Chinese peoples, became a tonal language, very unusual for a Malayo-Polynesian dialect.

Cut off from the other Muslim peoples for hundreds of years, the Utsul began to renew ties to the Muslim peoples to the south when several ports, including Sanya, were opened to foreign commerce in the 19th century. Contacts with the Muslim peoples of Malaya and Dutch Indonesia resulted in the modernizing of the Utsul culture and the decline of many archaic Muslim customs and traditions. Wealthy Muslim merchants supported the small Utsul community and partly financed the construction of the four famous mosques of the Sanya region. The southern part of Hainan was militarized in 1890 during the Chinese war with the French colonial military in nearby Vietnam. In the 1930s, the Utsul, promised religious freedom and an end to religious and ethnic persecution, supported the communist guerrilla bands that initially fought Chinese government troops but later attacked the Japanese invaders during World War II. In 1950, the island of Hainan was created a special administrative area of the new People's Republic of China. Official atheism and pressure to assimilate damaged the Utsul culture in the 1950s and during the Chinese Cultural Revolution in 1967–1977. The reforms adopted in China in the 1980s and 1990s opened the country to outside influences, including renewing religious and cultural ties. The Utsul have campaigned to change their status. Arbitrarily included in the large Hui ethnic group for official purposes because of their Muslim faith, the Utsul have no cultural or historical ties to the Hui. Petitions and pleas for separate ethnic group status have been ignored or rejected. Another controversy developed in the Utsul region in 2008, when the government began construction of a parachute training base that will effectively destroy a 700-year-old Utsul cemetery. When 10 ancient tombs were ravaged by the construction workers in December 2008, angry Utsul protesters took to the streets. Since that time, 20–30 Utsul guard the cemetery against further depredations. The Utsul point out that not even the Japanese, who occupied the island during World War II, dared to disturb the cemetery. Utsul leaders claim that the destruction of the ancient cemetery is yet another sign that their status as ethnic Hui does not give them the same protection as the status of a distinct ethnic group.

Further Reading

Brodsgaard, Kjeld Erik. *Hainan: State, Society, and Business in a Chinese Province.* London: Routledge, 2008.

Icon Group International. *Hainan: Webster's Timeline History, 40 BC–2007.* San Diego: Icon Group International, 2010.

Shafer, Edward H. *Shore of Pearls: Hainan Island in Early Times.* Warren, CT: Floating Worlds, 2009.

Uyghur

The Uyghur, sometimes known as Uighur, Uygur, Uighuir, Wei Wuer, East Turkestani, or Kashgar Turki, are a Turkic people living mostly in the Tarim Basin region of the southern Xinjiang Uyghur Autonomous Region in the People's Republic of China. Outside their homeland, which nationalists call East Turkestan, there are Uyghur communities in Hunan Province of China, in the Central Asian republics of Kazakhstan, Kyrgyzstan, and Uzbekistan, and in Afghanistan, Pakistan, Turkey, the United States, Canada, Australia, Russia, and in other parts of Europe. The majority of the Uyghur live in the large oases centers in the southern region of Xinjiang south of the Tian Shan Mountains. Southern Xinjiang is dominated by the huge Tarim Basin, part of which is fertile, and the Taklamakan Desert in the center of their territory. The estimated 10.5 million Uyghur speak Vigus, also known as New

Uyghur, a language belonging to the Uyghur-Chagatai branch of the Turkic languages. Population estimates are difficult as no reliable census figures are made available by the Chinese government. The Uyghur are overwhelmingly Sunni Muslim, and like the neighboring Muslim peoples of Central Asia, they often fuse Islamic traditions with earlier pre-Islamic rituals and customs.

The ancestors of the Uyghur originated as nomadic tribes called Tiele, who occupied the valleys south of Lake Baikal and the large basin of the Yenisei River. Besides herding, the Tiele practiced some agriculture and were highly efficient metalsmiths due to the abundance of easily found iron ore in the Yenisei River valley. Around 300 BCE, the Tiele tribes were subjugated by the Xiongnu, who appreciated their skills and metalsmiths and put them to work making weapons for the forces of the first large steppe empire. According to Chinese records, war broke out between the Han Dynasty and the Xiongnu in 129 BCE. Other Chinese archives place the early Uyghur tribes under Han Chinese rule from 206 BCE to 220 CE. The first official record of the Uyghur is in a Chinese chronicle of 357 CE. One of the Tiele tribes, made up of 12 clans, gained enough power to establish an independent tribal state from 481 to 520 in the region north of the Tarim Basin. The first state to encompass most of the Uygur tribes was established in 744 under Kutluk Bilge Kul. His son, Moyunchur, conquered neighboring Turkic peoples and extended Uyghur rule to Lake Baikal on the north, the Caspian Sea to the west, Manchuria to the east, and to the borders of India in the south. In 840, the

Kyrgyz overran the Uyghur confederation and took control of the capital. With the collapse of the Uyghur Khanate, smaller Uyghur states were created in present-day Gansu and Xinjiang. The expansion of the Mongols in the 13th century ended Uyghur autonomy as they were absorbed into the subject peoples of Genghis Khan. The Uyghur formed the left wing of the Turkic-Mongol hordes that eventually conquered most of the known world. The Muslim religion, first introduced by Arab invaders in 934, spread rapidly along the trade routes known as the Silk Road and became one of the major religions of the Mongol Empire. In the 14th century, as Mongol power waned, numerous small Uyghur states emerged along the trade routes, with many gaining fame as centers of Muslim learning and tolerance. The Uyghur cities, centers of the trade between the Orient and the Mediterranean, had large settled population of disparate ethnic and religious groups, and were adorned with extensive libraries, elaborate mosques, opulent palaces, and distinguished public buildings. The Manchu rulers of China dispatched a huge army to conquer the territories to the west. In a swift campaign in 1756–1759, the Chinese conquerors ended the celebrated ethnic and religious tolerance of the Uyghur territories. Under the Manchu Qing dynasty, the vast Xinjiang region became a cauldron of interethnic conflicts and sporadic uprisings.

The Uyghur, called *Wei Wuer* by the Chinese, form the largest Turkic minority in the People's Republic of China. The Uyghur are ethnically, culturally, and linguistically closely related to the Turkic peoples of Central Asia. Many Uyghur have settled in Central Asia to escape Chinese rule over the centuries. The descendants of the peoples of the legendary trading centers of the Silk Road, the Uyghur still dominate the bazaars of Xinjiang. The most numerous of the 40 distinct ethnic groups in China's Xinjiang region, the Uyghur culture has been adopted by many of the smaller Turkic peoples. The poorest of China's regions and provinces, about 90 percent of the Uyghur of Xinjiang live below China's established poverty line. Uyghur culture is a mixture of the early Turkic culture and the later Muslim culture brought to the region, mixed with influences brought from Europe and the Orient during the centuries of caravan travel on the Silk Road trade routes. The Uyghur, unlike other Muslim groups, generally do not oppose the education of male and female students together; however, women are generally excluded from public life. Prior to adopting Islam, the majority of the Uyghur practiced Buddhism or adhered to shamanistic beliefs. Numerous cave temples in the region contain depictions of the early Uyghur and the Buddha. Like the neighboring Central Asian peoples, the Uyghur practice a form of folk Islam, a distinctive blend of Muslim beliefs and rituals and ceremonies retained from their earlier Buddhist and shamanistic religions. The Uyghur continue to revere wolves, including the custom of giving birth while lying on a wolf skin. Uyghur men traditionally wear an embroidered cap known as a *doppa*, while Uyghur women of the more conservative families and regions cover their faces with veils. Unlike other Muslim peoples, the Uyghur are usually monogamous. The Uyghur language, known as Vigur or New Uyghur, is spoken in several regional dialects and numerous subdialects. The Arabic script, adapted to the Uyghur religion during the conversion to Islam, remains the basis of the Uyghur literary language. Officially, the Uyghur-Arab alphabet has been replaced by the Latin script that was adapted to suit Chinese phonology in the 1960s and 1970s. Uyghur music, an integral part of the culture, incorporated modern musical styles along with the classical style known as *muqam*. The *muqam* style developed over many centuries from the Arabic *maqamat* system. The 12 *muqam*, known as the "Twelve Great Songs," make up the national oral epic of the Uyghur, which is performed with classical and folk songs and music, and is often accompanied by dancers. The Uyghur *muqam* has been designated by UNESCO as part of the intangible heritage of humanity.

While the British hold all of colonial India with just 30,000 troops, Manchu China required a military force of 100,000 to control the Chinese Turkestan region in the early 19th century. Between 1759 and 1862, the Uyghur, often joined by the other Turkic peoples, rebelled 42 times. A widespread rebellion of the Turkic Muslim peoples in 1863–1866, encouraged by Russian and British agents, loosened the weakened Chinese imperial hold on the region. Tsarist Russian troops from Central Asia occupied Kuldja and the Ili Valley in 1871, and the British supported a Uyghur campaign to create a separate Uyghur state centered on Kashgar. The

Two Uyghur girls with veils at a market in Xinjiang, China. (Bbbar/Dreamstime.com)

independent Kashgar kingdom was formally recognized by the Turkish Ottoman Empire, tsarist Russia, and the United Kingdom. The Chinese reconquest of the Uyghur territories in 1876–1878 was notable for the savage reprisals against both rebels and civilian cities and towns. Thousands of Uyghur fled the Chinese onslaught to seek shelter in Russian Central Asia, where many remain to the present. The territory of Xinjiang, the name meaning "new dominion" or "new territories," was formally annexed to the Manchu Chinese Empire in 1884. The Chinese administration divided the huge region into four government regions, while the Uyghur population, considered rebellious, was subjected to an official policy aimed at destroying their pride, unity, and self-respect. A divide-and-conquer policy was initiated, and discord among the Turkic Muslim groups was encouraged. Many ethnic Uyghur were forced to marry Han Chinese, wear Chinese clothing, and show exaggerated respect for Chinese officials. Any complaints against Chinese brutality or Chinese officials brought savage reprisals against not only those who made the complaint but also their whole family and often their hometown or village. Government officials authorized the execution of thousands of Uyghur seen as a threat to Chinese rule. The number of people executed or massacred during the 19th century is estimated at up to a million by modern Uyghur activists. Another 500,000 Uyghur, to escape Chinese oppression, escaped to Russian territory or into the wilds of Afghanistan. Another 200,000 were driven from their homes in the Chinese settlement region of the Ili Valley.

The dispossessed Uyghur were forced to work as slave laborers to provide food for the Chinese occupation forces. News of the overthrow of the Manchu Qing dynasty during the Chinese Revolution in 1911 was greeted with celebrations in the region. A widespread uprising against the remaining Chinese troops began several decades of instability and turbulence in Chinese Turkestan. At first, the Chinese republican government took a conciliatory attitude to the Muslim populations in the northwest, but in 1924, power passed to Chiang Kai-shek, who proved far less tolerant of the minorities in Chinese territory. Thousands died in the upheavals surrounding the Chinese Kuomintang government's assimilation policies. The Uyghur rebelled against the Chinese excesses and abuses in 1931. The rebels drove the Chinese administrators and military from Uyghur territory. Aided and encouraged by agents of the Soviet Union, the rebel leaders declared Xinjiang independent of Kuomingtang China in 1934, naming the new republic the Islamic Republic of East Turkestan. Betrayed by Soviet duplicity, the independent Muslim state soon fell to returning Chinese troops. A renewed Muslim rebellion swept the region in 1936–1937 that culminated in the widespread collapse of the Chinese administration in the region just as World War II overwhelmed the Chinese heartland to the east. During the course of the war, the Muslim rebels continued to advance. In January 1945, they overran the last Chinese garrison at Kuldja. On January 13, 1945, the revel leaders declared the independence of Xinjiang as the Republic of East Turkestan under a government led by Ali Khan Türe. The government of the Soviet Union, fearing the spread of Turkic nationalism to Soviet Turkestan, pressured the rebel Muslim government to negotiate with the Kuomingtang government of Chiang Kai-shek. After eight long months of talks, the rebels finally agreed to accept autonomy under loose Chinese authority. They also agreed to disarm. Once their arms had been turned in, the Chinese authorities launched a brutal crackdown. The betrayal by the Kuomingtang Chinese government cost Chiang Kai-shek a major setback in the civil war that raged in China following World War II. The entire Xinjiang region, because of their hatred of the Kuomingtang, went over to the Red Chinese without a fight in late 1949. Under communist rule, the Xinjiang region became a region of vast Han Chinese agricultural colonies, strongly garrisoned military bases on the volatile frontiers, and the center of the notorious *laogai*, the slave labor camps. Communist rule proved as harsh as that of the Kuomingtang. The Red Chinese leader, Mao Tse-tung, ignored his promises of autonomy for Xinjiang and sponsored mass colonization of the region by loyal Han Chinese to dilute the Muslim majority. Only 3 percent of the regional population in 1950, the Han Chinese portion grew to nearly 50 percent by 1975. During the violent Cultural Revolution that swept the People's Republic of China from 1967 to 1977, Chinese cadres destroyed thousands of mosques and Muslim shrines. Public prayer was banned, Koranic schools closed, and pressed the Uyghur to assimilate into Chinese society. Isolated from the outside world during the

years of the Cold War, Xinjiang became a dumping ground for tens of thousands of criminals, mostly political prisoners. The dumping of nuclear and chemicals wastes heavily polluted many districts. The excesses of the Cultural Revolution gave way to a more relaxed post–Cold War era. The Uyghur language was returned to official status, some religious schools reopened, and a limited number of mosques were allowed to function. By the 1990s and 2000s, religious and ethnic grievances were again bringing unwanted attention to China's treatment of the Uyghur and other Muslim peoples in the region. Riots and demonstrations were met by force, leaving many Uyghur dead or injured and the Uyghur districts of several cities in ruins. By 2005, military experts estimated that China had a million soldiers stationed in the strategic region thought to be rich in natural resources. The Uyghur have resisted assimilation for decades, counting on their cultural, linguistic, and geographic differences to combat Chinese efforts to absorb them.

Further Reading

Bovingdon, Gardner. *The Uyghurs: Strangers in Their Own Land.* New York: Columbia University Press, 2010.

Dwyer, Arienne M. *The Xinjiang Conflict: Uyghur Identity, Language Policy, and Political Discourse.* Honolulu: East-West Center, 2005.

Starr, S. Frederick. *Xinjiang: China's Muslim Borderland.* Armonk, NY: M.E. Sharpe, 2004.

The Uyghur American Association. "About Uyghurs." Accessed July 31, 2013. http://uyghuramerican.org/about-uyghurs

Uzbek

The Uzbek, sometimes known as O'zbek, are a major Turkic ethnic group concentrated in the Republic of Uzbekistan in Central Asia. Outside the republic, there are large Uzbek populations in Afghanistan, Tajikistan, Kyrgyzstan, Kazakhstan, Turkmenistan, Russia, the Xinjiang region of China, Pakistan, Ukraine, Australia, the United States, and Turkey. Of mixed Turkic, Caucasian, and Mongol ancestry, the majority of the Uzbeks physically resemble the Turkic and Iranian peoples. The most numerous ethnic group in Central Asia, the estimated 28–30 million Uzbeks are divided into 92 distinct tribal groups. The Uzbeks speak a Turkic language of the Eastern Turkic or Karluk language group. Most Uzbeks are Sunni Muslim, mostly of the Hanafi school.

The Central Asian region was an early center of civilization and trade, particularly along the Silk Road, the legendary trade routes that connected China and the East to the Mediterranean and the West. The inhabitants of the region were mostly Persian-speaking nomads who settled the region in the first millennium BCE. Building their towns and villages along the rivers, they began to construct an extensive irrigation system. Cities such as Bukhara and Samarkand appeared as centers of government, trade, and culture. Known as Sogdiana and Bactria, the region flourished with a mixed population of Persian-speaking oases dwellers, early Turkic nomads, and travelers from Europe and the East. Zoroastrianism, Buddhism, and even Christianity were practiced alongside earlier shamanistic beliefs. Controlled by the various Persian empires, the Greeks of Alexander the Great, and other conquerors, each group added to the mixed ancestry of the population. The conquest of Central Asia by invading Muslim Arabs in the eighth century CE brought with it a new religion that continues to the region's dominant religion to the present. Called Mawarannahr by the Arabs, the Central Asian region continued to flourish with its cities becoming renowned centers of Muslim learning and culture. During the rule of the Abbasid Caliphate, the great Muslim Empire, in the eighth and ninth centuries, the region experienced a golden age. Bukhara became one of the leading cities of learning, culture, and art in the entire Muslim world. Turko-Mongol infiltrations by nomadic tribes started early in history, but in the 11th and 12th centuries, the Seljuk Turks conquered the region. Under Seljuk rule, the trading centers flourished, the tradition of open trade was maintained, and the vast areas of irrigated agriculture were protected. The Seljuk Turkic nomads mixed with the settled Persian-speaking population known as Sart to form the nucleus of the later Uzbek people. The Seljuk Turks founded the Khorezm state, later known as Khiva, one of the successor states that emerged with the end of the Seljuk Empire. In the 13th century, despite continued migrations by small Turkic tribal groups, the region's majority population was still the Persian peoples when the Mongol-Turkic hordes of Genghis descended on the region. Devastated by the invading hordes, the region later came under the rule of several successor states dominated by the Mongol descendants of Genghis Khan. The Mongol destruction of the extensive irrigation system had a profound influence on the culture and the decline that followed. The Mongol conquest quickened the Turkification in most of the region as the Turkic elements of his hordes drove many Persians south or absorbed the settled population. Central Asia again flourished under the rule of Timur or Tamerlane, who established his capital at Samarkand in the late 14th century. The Uzbek, a remnant of the Mongol hordes, conquered Central Asia between 1490 and 1505. They eventually expanded their conquests into present-day Afghanistan, Iran, and China. In 1555, the Uzbek leaders transferred the capital of Central Asia from Samarkand to Bukhara, the new center of the Uzbek Khanate of Bukhara. The ancient state of Khiva also became an Uzbek khanate with a mixed population. Tensions between the mainly Sunni Muslim Uzbek and the Shi'a Persians to the west and south gave a religious aspect to the rivalry between the two peoples. A new group of nomadic Turkic people, led by Shaybani Khan, moved into the region in the 16th century; settling mostly around Bukhara and Samarkand, they also began to mix with the settled population. At the end of the 16th century, the states of Bukhara and Khiva began to decline due to wars against each other and against constant Persian incursions. Trade also declined as the Europeans opened new sea routes for trade with China and India, bypassing the caravan routes of the Silk Road. Raids by Kazakh and Mongol groups disrupted the states. In the early 1700s, the Khanate of Bukhara lost the fertile Fergana Valley, where a new Uzbek khanate was formed with its capital at Khokand. All three of the Uzbek states had mixed populations dominated by the Uzbek elite, including Tajik, Turkmen, Kyrgyz, Arab, Persian, and Bukharan Jews. Various Uzbek dynasties ruled the states during the 18th century, with the khan of Bukhara upgrading his state to that of an emirate with himself as emir.

The Uzbek culture shows a wide mix of ethnic and religious influences with the Turkic and Muslim elements the most prominent. Ethnically, the Uzbek people occupy a kind of bridge culture between the Turkic and Persian worlds. Historically, various ethnic and tribal groups occupied different economic niches before they were united by their common history and their Islamic religion as the modern Uzbek people. Bilingualism has historically been seen as normal, not only among the governing elite but among the commercial and peasant classes as well. Traditional festivals, Uzbek cuisine, and many customs were incorporated from the Persians, Russians, and other peoples later exiled to Central Asia. Green tea, usually served at every Uzbek meal, is also a drink of hospitality, automatically offered to every guest. Uzbek teahouses, known as *chaikhanas*, are considered of cultural importance. The Uzbek language is a very important cultural element and is now the only official language of Uzbekistan. Since 1992, the language has officially been written in a modified Latin alphabet. Russian remains important for interethnic communication, especially in the cities, and is the language of business and technology. The Hanafi school of Sunni Islam remains the major focus of the religious Uzbek population, though many claim to be atheists, the result of decades of Soviet antireligious propaganda. The Uzbek Muslims tend to be more secular than the other Central Asian peoples, including allowing the production of alcoholic wines in Uzbekistan. When Uzbekistan gained independence in 1991, there was widespread concern that Islamic fundamentalism would spread across the region. However, despite the persecution of religion during the Soviet decades, moderate religious views have been retained though Islamic observance is increasing. The Uzbek literacy rate, at about 99 percent in Uzbekistan, is one of the highest in the region, though the Uzbek populations in other countries have lower literacy rates. Expenditure on education in Uzbekistan is very low, and in 2010, only about 75 percent of school-age children were enrolled in schools so the literacy rate will probably fall in the future.

The rivalry between the Uzbek states of Bukhara and Khiva weakened the response to growing Russian interest in the region. Cossack expeditions, the forerunner of the later Russian conquest, began to visit the region in the early 19th century. Russian troops invaded Central Asia in 1865, first taking control of the Uzbek stronghold of Tashkent. In 1867, the Russians, expanding across the steppe lands of Central Asia, established a colonial government, the Governorate-General of Turkestan, with its capital at Tashkent. The Uzbek states, under increasing Russian pressure and influence, were forced to accept the status of Russian protected states. The Emirate of Bukhara accepted protectorate status in 1868 and the Khanate of Khiva in 1873.

The Russians annexed the Khanate of Khokand outright in 1876, thus completing their conquest of Central Asia. Slavic colonists from European Russia were settled across the region, enjoying special privileges as the overseers of harsh colonial rule. American cotton was introduced in 1884 and rapidly changed the agricultural traditions of the Central Asian peoples. Serious Uzbek uprisings against the Russian authorities continued to undermine the colonial administration well into the 20th century. The completion of the Orenburg-Tashkent Railroad in 1906 opened a direct rail link between Central Asia and European Russia. The railroad brought an influx of new European settlers, manufactured goods, political prisoners, and revolutionary ideas to the region. It also made it possible to quickly send Russian soldiers to quell each of the series of threats to Russia's colonial hold on Central Asia. European revolutionary ideas greatly affected the Muslim intellectual elite, particularly in Bukhara and Khiva. Revolutionary groups such as the Young Bukharans, which included both Uzbek and other ethnic participants, were formed in the years before World War I. As Muslims, the Uzbek were exempted from Russian military service when World War I began in 1914. However, as the war continued and Russia's manpower losses reached into the millions, the authorities attempted to conscript 250,000 Central Asians into labor battalions in 1916. Resistance to the conscription ignited a widespread uprising among the Uzbek and other Central Asian Muslim peoples. The rebellion, often attacking reduced Russian garrisons and Slavic settlements, was overtaken by the onset of the Russian Revolution in 1917.

The revolutionary upheaval resulted in the establishment of two rival provisional governments in Turkestan, one a secular and Muslim supported government and the other the Tashkent Soviet, both based in Tashkent. A Muslim congress demanded the end of Russian colonization and a return of all confiscated lands. The October Revolution, the Bolshevik takeover of Russia, galvanized the local Bolshevik groups to take power in Tashkent. The Muslims, led by the Uzbek, meeting in Khokand, created a rival Muslim provisional government. Outraged by the Bolshevik antireligious rhetoric and threatened by the Soviets in Tashkent, the leaders declared Turkestan an autonomous state, with the Uzbek states of Bukhara and Khiva also declaring their sovereignty. Fighting broke out with the ill-equipped Muslims forces easily defeated. Soviet forces took control of the Muslim center at Khokand in February 1918. Given leave by the Soviet leaders, the Soviet troops looted the city, wantonly destroyed ancient shrines and monuments in an orgy of killing and rape. The Muslim population of the city, some 120,000 people, were either killed or dispossessed and dispersed. In Bukhara and Khiva, turmoil increased as competing ethnic groups fought over water and land while progressive groups clashed with the conservative leadership. The Russian Civil War lessened pressure on the two Uzbek states though only temporarily. The Soviet government in Tashkent voted to exclude Muslims from government posts in Turkestan, quickly alienating their Muslim revolutionary allies. Many Uzbek joined the *basmachi*, guerrilla groups operating across the region to oppose the Soviet conquest. In 1920, revolutionary groups in first Khiva, then in Bukhara, requested Soviet aid to overthrow the rulers of the two states, which were declared people's republics. In 1924, over strong Uzbek opposition, the states of Khiva and Bukhara were added to Turkestan, and the entire Central Asian region was reorganized along ethnic lines. The Soviet authorities abolished the name *Sart*, used for centuries as the name of the settled oases dwellers, as derogatory, and decreed that henceforth the settled Turkic population of Russian Turkestan would be known as Uzbek, even though many groups had no Uzbek heritage. An anti-Islamic campaign, begun in 1928, disbanded Islamic courts and religious schools. Mosques were turned into museums, factories, warehouses, or Soviet schools. The forced collectivization of the Uzbek territory was carried out with great brutality from 1928 to 1933, leaving many to starve as food, herds, and other provisions were confiscated. A local hierarchy of Uzbek cadres, organized as the Uzbekistan Communist Party, established a feudal hold on the Uzbek homeland, which became a member republic of the Soviet Union. Unquestioned loyalty to the Communist Party became the only requisite for holding office in the republic. Corruption and graft infiltrated all levels of the republican government. The liberalization of Soviet society, beginning in the late 1980s, allowed dissidents and activists to question the Uzbek leadership for the first time in decades. A growing nationalist opposition gained support though growing violence between the Uzbek and other ethnic groups, covertly provoked by the feudal communist leadership of Uzbekistan, quickly spread to all parts of the region.

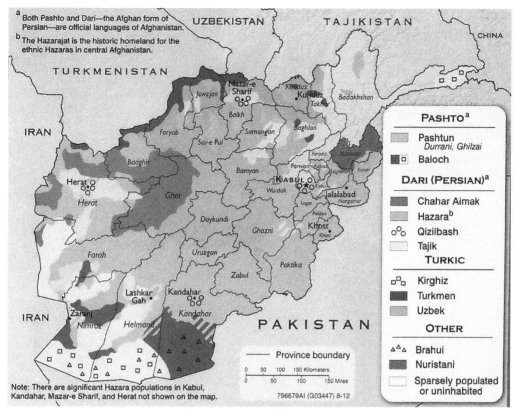

The ethnic groups of Afghanistan. (Used by permission of the University of Texas Libraries, The University of Texas at Austin)

The collapse of the Soviet Union in 1991 forced the Uzbek leaders, under nationalist pressure, to declare Uzbekistan an independent state in August 1991. In the Central Asian tradition, the old communist hierarchy quickly converted to nationalists to maintain their hold on the country. Many Slavs left Uzbekistan hampering efforts to modernize the country. The Uzbek language was declared the only official language, and a campaign to reassert the traditional Uzbek culture continues to the present.

Further Reading

Adams, Laura. *The Spectacular State: Culture and National Identity in Uzbekistan.* Durham, NC: Duke University Press, 2010.

Embassy of Uzbekistan to the United States. "About Uzbekistan." Accessed July 31, 2013. http://www.uzbekistan.org/uzbeki stan/history/

Kalter, Johannes, and Margareta Pavaloi, eds. *Uzbekistan: Heirs to the Silk Road.* London: Thames & Hudson, 2003.

Melvin, Neil J. *Uzbekistan: Transition to Authoritarianism.* London: Taylor & Francis, 2000.

V

Va

The Va, sometimes known as Wa, Ava, Parauk, or Ba rāog, are one of the 56 officially recognized ethnic groups in the People's Republic of China though about two-thirds of the Va/Wa people live in the northern part of neighboring Myanmar and in Thailand. In China, the Va live in compact communities in southwestern Yunnan Province. The estimated 400,000 Va in Yunnan speak the Va language, which belongs to the Palaungic branch of the Mon-Khmer language group, along with the local Chinese dialect known as Yunnanese Mandarin. Most Va adhere to their traditional animist religion with a sizable minority that has adopted Buddhism.

Believed to have originated in eastern Tibet, the ancestors of the Mon-Khmer peoples migrated south following the Mekong and Salween Rivers, known to the Chinese as the Lancang and Nujiang Rivers. The people later known as Va or Wa settled the upper reaches of the rivers, probably between the fifth and third centuries BCE. They may have occupied a larger area, including the lowlands, but were driven into the mountainous regions by stronger tribes. In 109 BCE, Emperor Wu Di of the Han dynasty established the Yizhou Prefecture that covered an area extending to the Gaoligong Mountains. As a result of the Chinese administration established in the prefecture, the forebears of the Va and other ethnic groups in the Yunnan region were brought under Han Chinese rule. While their kin to the south remained primitive tribal peoples, famous for head-hunting, the Va under Chinese rule mostly gave up *latou*, the taking of heads, and engaged in hunting, fruit collecting, and herding livestock, the primitive stages of an agricultural economy. In the 17th century, agriculture became the major occupation for the Va people, who mostly lived in communal villages. Interchanges with the neighboring Dai, Han Chinese, and Lahu peoples helped the Va in China to develop their culture and agricultural economy much faster than their kin in neighboring areas claimed by Burma. Their homeland, known as Ava, adopted private ownership in the 18th century, though remnants of their primitive communal system remained in the more remote areas. In some areas, under the influence of the neighboring Dai, many Va adopted Buddhism. In other areas, American and European missionaries introduced Christianity, often building churches and church schools.

The Va people, known as Wa in Myanmar and Lawa in Thailand, are believed to be one of the earliest inhabitants of the Yunnan plateau region. Ethnically and linguistically, the Va are related to the Mon people of Myanmar and the Khmer of Cambodia. Traditionally, the Va are divided into a large mass of commoners and a small elite known as the Kun. In China, the Va are an official ethnic group while the closely related Va group called the Blang were separated as a distinct nationality. The basis of the Va culture is the basic monogamous family unit. Family property is generally inherited by the youngest son, who remains in the family home to care for his aging parents. Daughters and older sons who leave the family home do not inherit. Traditionally, Va men were permitted to have more than one wife, a practice ended by the communist Chinese authorities. Men and women were historically allowed sexual freedom before marriage, another tradition stamped out in the mid-20th century. The Va traditions include a polytheistic animist belief system that venerates the spirits of mountains, rivers, and other natural phenomena. The highest of their many gods is Mujij, whose five sons are believed to be the gods in charge of heaven, the creation of the earth, lightning, earthquakes, and the Va people. Frequent religious ceremonies are held to obtain protection from evil spirits, deities, and ghosts. Sacrifices of animals is an important part of the religious rites, mostly chickens, pigs, or oxen, which are very expensive and time consuming. The Va language forms part of the Palaugic branch of the Mon-Khmer or Austroasiatic language family. The Va speak dialects of the Va-Palaung group of languages that are spoken in southwestern Yunnan and adjoining areas of Myanmar and in a small area of Thailand. The language is spoken in six major dialects, and though the Va of China are closely related to their kinsmen across the border, there are few similarities between the dialects spoken in Yunnan

and those in Myanmar and Thailand. Illiteracy remains a major problem in Yunnan, though educational programs have been set up to rectify the lack of schooling in many areas.

In the 1870s, the Wa and other ethnic groups across the Yunnan border renounced their allegiance to the Burmese king. The resulting chaos gave the British colonial administration in India a pretext to intervene. Between 1880 and 1886, the Wa people southwest of Yunnan came under British authority, bringing British rule to the border regions of Yunnan. Chinese alarm resulted in the militarization of the border regions, often with the forced removal of the Va and other indigenous peoples. The Chinese Revolution of 1911 ended the imperial government of China, which was declared a republic. A new administration, often unsympathetic to the ethnic minorities, was put in place in Yunnan by 1922. Many Va joined rebel groups operating in the mountains of Yunnan, many later affiliated with the growing communist party in China. At the end of World War II, the Chinese Civil War resumed between government troops and communist rebels. A communist victory, in 1949, was followed by the declaration of the communist People's Republic of China. Red cadres moved into the Yunnan highlands in 1950 where they quickly eliminated the Kun nobility and the landlord class. Land redistribution allowed many Va to own land for the first time, but collectivization was imposed and the land was confiscated while the Va farmers became employees of the new Chinese government. The outrages and destruction of the Chinese Cultural Revolution,

1967–1977, were followed by the economic and political reforms instituted in the 1980s. Many Va, already involved in cross-border smuggling, turned to trade or even the drug traffic coming across the border from Myanmar. Though advances in education and welfare have helped raise the Va life spans and infant mortality rates, the Va remain among the poorest of the ethnic groups in Yunnan.

Further Reading

McCarthy, Susan K. *Communist Multiculturalism: Ethnic Revival in Southwest China.* Seattle: University of Washington Press, 2009.

Mitchell, Sam. *Ethnic Minority Issues in Yunnan.* Kunming, China: Yunnan Fine Arts Publishing, 2004.

West, Barbara A. *Encyclopedia of the Peoples of Asia and Oceania.* New York: Facts on File, 2008.

Xibe

The Xibe, sometimes known as Sibe, Sibo, or Xibo, are a Tungusic ethnic group living mostly in Xinjiang and northeast China. They form one of the 56 officially recognized ethnic groups of the People's Republic of China. The estimated 193,000 Xibe speak a southern Tungusic language closely related to the Manchu language, which is also spoken in northeast China.

Many scholars believe that the Xibe originated as a southern Tungusic-speaking branch of the ancient Shiwei people as recorded by the ancient archives of the Northern Wei dynasty in the fourth and fifth centuries CE. The Shiwei were the ancestors of the Mongols, a name applied to all of the Shiwei tribes during the rise of Genghis Khan in the early 13th century. The ancestors of the Xibe were partly nomadic and partly settled in small villages and towns. Being part of the southern Shiwei, they adopted agriculture in the third century CE. They were ruled by more powerful neighboring peoples, including the Han Chinese, until the rise of the Turkic Khaganate, which incorporated the Xibe lands between 552 and 744. Under the rule of the Khitan Empire, the Xibe lands reached their maximum extension with new settlements founded and smaller tribes absorbed between the 10th and 12th centuries. After the fall of the Khitans, the Xibe became vassals of the Khorchin Mongols.

The Xibe warriors were routed by Nurhaci, the leader of the Manchu people at the Battle of Gure in 1593, on his way to the conquest of China and the establishment of the Manchu Qing dynasty. Under Manchu rule, the Xibe were incorporated into the Chinese Empire and were sent to garrison cities in northeast China. In 1700, around 20,000 Xibe were resettled in present-day Inner Mongolia and another 36,000 were resettled in Liaoning. Following a serious Xibe uprising in 1764, some 18,000 Xibe were deported to the Ili Valley in the Xinjiang region of northwest China. Although linguistically and ethnically the Xibe are closely related to the Manchu, they were not included in the 17th-century tribal confederation to which the name *Manchu* was later applied. Under the rule of the Manchu Qing dynasty, the Xibe were accepted as a Manchu people and were given high status as first-grade citizens. Over the centuries, with access to the Manchu power structure, many Xibe joined the imperial administration.

The Xibe people are divided with part of the ethnic group in northeast China's Liaoning and Jilin Provinces and part in the far western Xinjiang-Uyghur Autonomous Region. Traditionally, the Xibe were divided into *hala*, clan groupings that consisted of people sharing the same surname. In more conservative areas, the Xibe dwellings house up to three different generations of the same family, since it is believed that while a father is alive, no son should break the family clan by leaving the family home to live elsewhere. In the northeast, the Xibe have adopted many Han Chinese and Manchu traditions and customs, though they retain their own language and script. In Xinjiang, the Xibe settled among the Uyghur and other Turkic peoples and have absorbed many customs from the neighboring peoples. The Xibe have always valued education and have a high literacy rate, which is unusual among the non-Han Chinese peoples of China. Both groups retain a tradition of education and literacy and often work as teachers, administrators, and translators. Their history as imperial administrators and translators earned them the nickname the "translator people." Both groups commemorate Westward Migration Day, which is always celebrated on the 18th day of the fourth lunar month of the year. The Xibe language remains the first language of those living in Xinjiang, but among the Xibe in northeast China, the first language is usually Han Chinese, Manchu, or Mongolian. The language is a Tungusic language closely related to Manch, which is mutually intelligible with Xibe though it has absorbed fewer borrowing from Han Chinese than the Manchu language. The Xibe writing system, which had its origins in the Manchu script, has diverged from Manchu in the position of letters and a different number of syllables. Xibe religious beliefs have changed as a majority, particularly in Xinjiang, has now adopted the Tibetan form of Buddhism; however, vestiges of their former animist religion remain as part of the Xibe culture. The most important deities in the Xibe pantheon are the god of grain and Mother Xili, the goddess of fertility and the protector of the home. Many Xibe combine their Buddhist and animist beliefs, including the veneration of their ancestors to whom they offer fish every March and melons every July. The Xibe still venerate their ancestor's graves, which are cleaned and swept annually.

The Xibe in Xinjiang, after a long and difficult journey from their homes in Manchuria, soon found that the Qing administration stopped supplying provisions to the new garrisons in the hostile region. The Xibe began to reclaim wastelands and to cut irrigation ditches without any government assistance. They quickly repaired an old disused canal to irrigate part of their new homeland. With the increase in their population, this land proved insufficient. Despite such hardships as a lack of grain and seeds and repeated natural disasters, the Xibe remained determined to turn the wastelands on the south bank of the Ili River into farmland to support them and their families. After many setbacks, they succeeded in 1802, after six years of back-breaking work, in cutting a 200-kilometer irrigation canal to draw water from the Ili allowing the settlement of a large region south of the river. In the mid-19th century, they constructed more canals to bring more land under cultivation. In the 1870s, as Qing power waned, the Russians moved into Xinjiang. In 1876, the Chinese government decided to move against the Russian invaders. The Xibe joined the imperial army in defeating the Russians and expelling the Russian colonists. News of the Chinese Revolution in 1911 reached the region with the Xibe staging an uprising in support of the revolutionary ideals. The Xibe in the northeast joined the other peoples of the region to oppose the Japanese incursions into Manchuria. Many joined guerrilla groups after the Japanese conquest of Manchuria in 1931. During World War II, the struggle between the Chinese government and the communist-led rebels was put aside in a joint effort to expel the Japanese invaders. In Xinjiang, in September 1944, a widespread revolt against the Chinese government broke out as the Xibe formed their own armed forces and joined other insurgent groups fighting government troops. The victory of the communists in 1949 brought a series of reforms to the Xibe lands in Manchuria, now known as the northeast China, and Xinjiang. The Qapqal Xibe Autonomous County was established in Xinjiang in 1954 to give the Xibe there a measure of self-government. By the early 21st century, the Xibe in northeast China had mostly assimilated into Han Chinese culture though they mostly retain their animist religious beliefs and many Xibe customs and traditions. In Xinjiang,

the Xibe retain their traditional language and script along with most of their historic culture. Ties between the two parts of the Xibe ethnic group, mostly forbidden during the early years of communist rule and especially during the Chinese Cultural Revolution in the 1960s and 1970s, have been renewed and reinforced with cultural exchanges, family reunions, and official visits.

Further Reading

Janhunen, Juha. *Manchuria: An Ethnic History*. Helsinki, Finland: Finno-Ugrian Society, 1996.

Ma, Xinfu. *Costumes and Festivals of Xinjiang Ethnic Groups*. Beijing: China Travel and Tourism Press, 2008.

People's Daily Online. "The Xibe Ethnic Minority." Last updated August 12, 2011. http://english.people.com.cn/102759/7567650.html

Rhoads, Edward J.M. *Manchus and Han: Ethnic Relations and Political Power in Late Qing and Early Republican China, 1861–1928*. Seattle: University of Washington Press, 2011.

Yagnobi

The Yagnobi, sometimes known as Yagnob, Yagnabi, or Yaghnobi, are a Persian-speaking group concentrated in the Sughd Province of Tajikistan. The Yagnobi are considered the descendants of the ancient Sogdian population that were mostly assimilated by the Tajik and Uzbek peoples. Unlike the Western Iranian language of the Tajik population that surrounds them, the Yagnobi speak an Eastern Iranian language, more closely related to the languages of the Pamiri people of Tajikistan, and the Pashtun of Afghanistan and Pakistan. The estimated 25,000 Yagnobi physically resemble the peoples of the Mediterranean, often with fair skin and hair and blue or green eyes. Most of the Yagnobi are Sunni Muslim, with a minority adhering to the Ismaili Muslim religion. Though they are classified as a subgroup of the Tajik, the Yagnobi are a distinct ethnic group historically, culturally, and linguistically.

The ancient region of Sogdiana, long a frontier region that insulated various Persian empires from the nomadic tribes to the north and east, with the Sogdian defenses centered on the great fortress known as the Sogdian Rock or the Rock of Ariamazes. The fortress was captured by the forces of Alexander the Great in 327 BCE after an extended campaign. United with neighboring Bactria in a single satrapy, the region was garrisoned by Macedonian soldiers. Sogdian military power never recovered from the Greek defeat. A Greek-influenced Bactrian kingdom founded in 248 BCE by Diodotus lasted for about a century though the Sogdians remained under Greek influence until the region was overrun by nomadic Scythians around 150 BCE. The Sogdian peoples formed the Great Sogdian Empire and turned to trade in the second century BCE, establishing a vast trading network across some 1,500 miles (2,415 kilometers) from Sogdiana to China along the trade routes known as the Silk Road that lasted into the 10th century CE. The Sogdian language was the dominant language in the trade and caravan centers along the trade routes and was spoken from eastern China to the borders of India. The sixth century was a golden age of the Sogdian culture with a great flowering of art, music, and literature. Magnificent palaces and public buildings were constructed in the major Sogdian cities such as Samarkand and Bukhara. The Sogdian religion, Zoroastrianism, remained the major religion of the Sogdian heartland and along the trade routes until the Arab invasion of Central Asia between 661 and 750. The invading Arabs defeated the Sogdians at the battle of Mount Mugh in 722, with many of the Sogdians fleeing Arab domination to live in the high mountain valleys. The zealous Muslim Arab warriors destroyed all traces of the Zoroastrian religion and its adherents in the lowlands. The Persian conquest and the Samanid Empire founded in 819 assimilated many of the lowland Sogdian people. Over centuries, many of the Sogdian clans mixed with the Turks to become the ancestors of the modern Uzbek people or were assimilated by the Persian-speaking Tajik in the surrounding districts. The Sogdians in the highland valleys, increasingly known as Yagnobi after the largest population concentration in the Yagnob Valley, remained fairly isolated from outside authority and influences, though a significant number were forced to convert to Islam. Eventually, all of the Yagnobi adopted Islam, though they retained many Zoroastrian rituals and customs that became part of their religious practices. Many scholars believe that the Yagnobi language and culture survived are the relatively late Islamization of the Yagnobi highlands. A Tajik saying "The Yagnobi have been converted to Islam with an axe" illustrates the forced conversions. The Mongol invasion of Central Asia in the 13th century destroyed many of the Yagnobi towns and cities in the lowland oases. In the 17th century, a large number of Yagnobi migrated to the Varzob valley, closer to the lowland Tajik population centers.

The Yagnobi culture is derived from the culture of the ancient Sogdians of Sogdiana, also known as the Great Sogdian Empire, one of the most important states in ancient Central Asia. For thousands of years, the Sogdian refugees in the high, inaccessible mountain valleys managed to maintain their distinct language and culture, while the Sogdians in the lowlands were assimilated into surrounding cultures. Often persecuted by the Tajik, who derisively called them *galcha*, the Yagnobi remained a distinct ethnic group though many were assimilating and few of the lowland Yagnobi were able to speak their traditional language by the early 20th century. Many people in Tajikistan are aware of their Yagnobi heritage but now consider themselves ethnic Tajik. The Yagnobi of the highlands retained the language and the distinct culture to the present due to the isolation and inaccessibility of their home valleys. The Yagnobi language, of the Eastern Persian language group, is spoken in two major geographic eastern and western dialects. Most Yagnobi are bilingual, also speaking Tajik and sometimes Russian. As late as the 17th century, the Yagnobi language was spoken across a large territory, including the densely populated regions between Samarkand and Khujand and in the Fergana Valley. In recent years, the Yagnobi language, written in the Cyrillic script, has been introduced as a subject in the region's primary schools. Religious practices associated with the Yagnobi Muslim ceremonies and rituals often reflect their past Zoroastrianism, including belief in the power of fire.

In the 1820s, Russian expeditions visited the Yagnobi region known as Sogd or Sughd, meaning Sogdiana. The scientists traveling with the expeditions in the early 19th century were the first to discover that the Yagnobi language and culture were quite different from the Tajik language and culture in the lowlands. In 1802, the Sogd region, formerly part of the Uzbek-dominated Bukhara state, became part of the new Khanate of Khokand, which reverted to Bukhara in 1842. During this period, the Yagnobi were often persecuted and were despised as backward mountain

The Yagnob Natural Ethnography Park

In 1991, feasibility studies were begun to establish a special natural and ethnographical part in the isolated Yagnob Valley, the traditional center of the Yagnobi culture. Plans for the park were suspended during the civil war in Tajikistan between 1992 and 1997, but have since been reviewed and initiatives begun both within Tajikistan and in international organizations. In 2007, several governments and organizations prepared an extensive report on the feasibility of the park that would protect the Yagnobi culture, prevent environmentally damaging activities such as overgrazing, and would encourage sustainable and responsible development of tourism. The report concluded that the main task is to improve living conditions for the Yagnobi people.

people. In 1866, the Tsarist Russian military invaded Central Asia, making part of the Yagnobi districts territories of the new Governorate of Turkestan, with the northern districts under the authority of the Russian protectorate of Bukhara. The completion of the Trans-Caspian Railway, running from the Caspian Sea to Samarkand, in 1877 brought the lowland Yagnobi into closer contact with the Russian colonizers, who stressed assimilation of the smaller groups into the Tajik culture. In 1914, the year that World War I broke out in Europe, most of the lowland Yagnobi were considered ethnic Tajik. In 1916, in desperate need of manpower, the tsarist authorities in Central Asia attempted to conscript 250,000 men, including Yagnobi living in the lowland oases towns. A widespread revolt across the Central Asian territories continued until it was overtaken by the Russian Revolution in 1917. Though not directly affected, the turmoil and upheavals often allowed Tajik persecutions, dispossessions, and other abuses with impunity. Between 1909 and 1920, an estimated 10 percent of the Yagnobi population fled the violence and starvation that continually swept through their territories. The Bolshevik victory in 1920 was followed by the occupation of Central Asia by the new Red Army. The consolidation of Soviet power in the lowlands left the Yagnobi isolated until the late 1920s when the first communist cadres entered their highland valleys. During the chaos of the Great Purge, the communist elimination of all cultural, religious, and dissident leaders led to many Yagnobi being exiled or sent to labor camps far from their homeland. In 1924, when the Soviet authorities redrew the borders in Central Asia along ethnic lines, the Yagnobi were counted as a separate group though their territory was included in the new Tajikistan state. The Soviet census placed the Yagnobi portion of the total Tajik population at about 13 percent. The most traumatic events for the Yagnobi were the forced resettlement of much of their population in 1957 and 1970. The Yagnobi populations of the high mountain valleys were forcibly removed, some by helicopter, others by truck or bus, to be resettled in the Zafarobod region in the lowland plains. In their new settlements, they were forced to work on the economically important cotton plantations. Some Yagnobi rebelled, with a few groups escaping back to their mountains, but the majority, punished and working in slave-like conditions, remained in the lowlands. To ensure that escaped Yagnob could not return, the communist authorities destroyed the *kishlaks*, the mountain villages, including mosques, shrines, and the priceless Yagnobi religious books, the oldest of which was 600 years old. The larger towns and villages were erased from maps, and the Yagnobi ethnicity was officially abolished by the Soviet authorities. The radical change in climate and the backbreaking work killed many of the deportees. In 1983, as Soviet control began to slip, Yagnobi families began to return to their highland valleys. The majority remained on the plains and were gradually assimilated, as their children were taught only the Tajik and Russian languages. The collapse of the Soviet Union, in 1991, and the independence of Tajikistan allowed some of the Yagnobi to return to their homeland, but the majority remained in the lowlands as ethnic Tajik. Civil war in Tajikistan, from 1992 to 1997, further decimated the Yagnobi population, with abuse and attacks by both of the warring sides. Attempts to save the Yagnobi language and culture have been launched, with many supporting the idea of a protected region covering the Yagnob Valley to sustain the Yagnobi people, their lifestyle, and their endangered language though the majority of the modern Yagnobi are concentrated around Zafarobod and Dushanbe, the Tajik capital.

Further Reading

Beckwith, Christopher. *Empires of the Silk Road: A History of Central Asia from the Bronze Age to the Present.* Princeton, NJ: Princeton University Press, 2011.

Boulnois, Luce, and Helen Loveday. *Silk Road: Monks, Warriors and Merchants.* Hong Kong: Airphoto International Ltd., 2005.

Krader, Lawrence. *Peoples of Central Asia.* London: Routledge, 1997.

Yao

The Yao people, sometimes known as Mien, Byau Min, Kim Mun, Pai Yao, or Yao Min, number an estimated 2.7 million in China out of the total Yao population of 3.25 million in Asia. In China, the Yao inhabit the mountainous region of Guangxi, where about 60 percent of China's Yao are concentrated, with smaller groups in the neighboring provinces of Hunan, Guangdong, Jiangxi, Guizhou, and Yunnan. The Yao are officially recognized as one of the ethnic groups of the People's Republic of China. Outside China, there is a large Yao population in Southeast Asia and smaller communities in the United States, Canada, France, New Zealand, and Brazil. The Yao speak a number of related dialects belonging to the Hmong-Mien language family. The majority of the Yao adhere to Daoism, with smaller Buddhist and Christian minorities.

The Yao trace their history back some 2,000 years to their origins in the Hunan region of China. Between 206 BCE and 900 CE, the Yao gradually migrated from the middle and lower Yangtze River valleys to the mountainous areas in the south. Often regarded as savages by the Han Chinese, the Yao gradually adopted many Han Chinese linguistic and cultural traditions, including Daoism, which their religious beliefs also influenced. Between the 10th and 13th centuries CE, the Yao arts, crafts, and agriculture advanced rapidly. Iron knives, indigo-dyed textiles, and crossbow weaving looms were recognized as Yao products. Over time, many of the Yao worked as farmers on lands owned by Han Chinese landlords. In the 12th century, most of the Yao came under the authority of hereditary chieftains or headmen. The chieftains were officially recognized by the Chinese court and were responsible for taxes and tribute sent to the Chinese capital. Many of the Mao joined the neighboring Miao (Hmong) in a widespread uprising in the 1370s, when Muslim troops were sent to the region to crush the indigenous groups who refused to pay the high taxes demanded by the government or to accept the power of the chieftains and landlords. In 1449, another rebellion erupted in the region but was again brutally crushed. Sporadic rebellions continued as resistance to Han Chinese colonization continued into the southern homelands of the indigenous peoples. Around the middle of the 17th century, groups of Yao clans moved southward, first into Guangdong, Guangxi, and Yunnan, and from there into Vietnam, Laos, Thailand, and Myanmar. From the 14th to 17th centuries, the use of iron tools allowed the Yao of Guangxi and Guangdong to develop rice paddy fields and different kinds of crops on terraced hillsides. They dug canals and ditches and built strong troughs to bring water from highland springs for daily use and for irrigation.

Modern Yao culture reflects the long relationship between the Yao and the Han Chinese. Yao arts, music, dance, handicrafts, and religious beliefs show continuing Han Chinese influence on the culture. Han Chinese influence is also evident in Yao architecture, with typical houses constructed in a rectangle made of wood and bamboo. Despite their geographic separation, some Yao cultural features are widely shared. They follow principles of patrilineal descent and inheritance, often adopting sons or bringing in a son-in-law when necessary as heirs while providing daughters with a share of the family land as part of her dowry. The Yao usually prefer to marry with the local group with regard to dialect and territory. Yao society is organized in patrilineal clan groups that are further divided into lineages. These clans and subgroups have traditional ritual and legal functions, with members providing mutual assistance. Historically, the clans held property in common, which was ended with the imposition of the communist system when all agricultural and forest lands were owned by the state. With the economic and legal reforms of recent years, many Yao clans again buy and work land in common. The Yao are famous for their oral tradition. The Yao in Guangxi still practice a form of communal cooperation called "singing while digging." Singing forms an indispensable part of their culture, including the courtship rituals. Typically, marriage is a formal affair arranged by go-betweens, marriage brokers who represent the prospective groom's family to the girl's parents. If the groom's proposal is accepted, a bride price or dowry is negotiated. In traditional Yao families, the mother's brothers have a decisive say in family affairs. The mother's brothers are often presented with betrothal gifts as part of the marriage proposal. The marriage customs reflect the ancient matrilineal system the Yao maintained until they adopted the Han Chinese patrilineal model. Historically, the Yao venerated a pantheon of many gods along with their revered ancestors, but most now practice a form of archaic Daoism, which includes many of their ancient religious traditions. The Yao of China speak a number of related dialects that form part of the Mienic or Yao language group that includes the closely related Yao and Hmong dialects, both of which are spoken by different groups officially forming part of the Yao ethnic group in China. The largest of the dialects spoken in China are Iu Mien and Kim Mun, with smaller Yao groups speaking Biao Min, Dzao Min, and the Banu Hmong dialects spoken in some areas. Most Yao also speak and write Mandarin Chinese.

The hereditary headmen and landlords dominated the Yao peasants, with the Qing court ruling the region through the

Yao woman walking in Longsheng, Guangxi Province, China. (Katarzyna Soszka/Dreamstime.com)

Yao headmen in a divide-and-rule system that separated the various Yao groups into territories. Many Yao, to escape the harsh system, followed the rivers south into Laos and Myanmar in the mid-1800s. The Yao migrations were spurred by the continuing migration of Han Chinese farmers into their traditional territories. The Qing government accused the Yao of migrating into Southeast Asia in order to extend the opium trade, but most of the Yao migrants left China in search of arable land and to escape the heavy taxes and abuses of the Chinese system. The imposition of colonial rule, the French in Laos and Vietnam, and the British in Myanmar, greatly curtailed the traditional cross-border trade and communications that had historically tied many of the Yao groups together. In an effort to separate the Yao in China from the Yao under colonial rule, the Qing court sent administrators to the region to ensure continued loyalty to the emperor. The Chinese Revolution of 1911 overthrew the Qing dynasty. A new republican government pursued a system of administration in the Yao areas similar to that of the Qing. Authority was relegated to loyal Yao headmen who wielded almost unlimited power. Abuses and neglect incited numerous conflicts in the Yao regions with most suffering many decades of hardships. Many Yao joined antigovernment groups and societies, many led by communists trained in the Soviet Union. A growing civil war in China was put aside as both the government and the communists fought the Japanese invaders during World War II. The civil war resumed in 1945 and ended with a communist victory in 1949. Communist cadres entered the Yao regions in 1950–1951 where they eliminated the headmen families, the rich peasants, and most religious leaders. Farmlands, at first redistributed to the Yao peasants, were later collectivized along with the forests as state property. The Yao farmers were forced to work on government collectives or cooperatives as employees of the state. The excesses of the early years of communist rule gradually gave way to the horrors of the Chinese Cultural Revolution. From 1967 to 1977, many Yao populations were subjected to the arbitrary rule of Red Guard divisions that summarily executed many leaders, destroyed shrines and temples, and sent many Yao to labor or reeducation camps where many perished. The economic and political reforms introduced in the 1980s ended the chaos of the Cultural Revolution and allowed many capitalist reforms such as small private businesses. Many of the traditional Yao clans regrouped, bought land, or set up small businesses. Their long relationship with the Han Chinese resulted in many Yao prospering as the reforms extended to the mountainous regions in the 1990s and into the 21st century.

Further Reading

Alberts, Eli. *A History of Daoism and the Yao People of South China.* Amherst, NY: Cambria Press, 2007.

Ethnic Groups. "The Yao Ethnic Minority." Accessed July 31, 2013. http://www.china.org.cn/e-groups/shaoshu/shao-2-yao.htm

Hamilton-Merritt, Jane. *Hmong and Yao: Mountain Peoples of Southeast Asia.* London: Survive, 1982.

Litzinger, Ralph A. *Other Chinas: The Yao and the Politics of National Belonging.* Durham, NC: Duke University Press, 2000.

Yi

The Yi, sometimes known as Lolo, Nuosu, Nosu, Butuo, and many other names, are a large ethnic group living primarily in rural areas in Yunnan, Sichuan, Guizhou, and Guangxi in southern China. The Yi are one of the 56 ethnic groups officially recognized by the government of the People's Republic of China. There are smaller Yi communities in Vietnam and Thailand. The estimated 7.8 Yi in China speak the Yi language, which belongs to the Nisoish group of Loloish languages of the Tibeto-Burman language family. Most of the Yi groups retain their traditional animist religious beliefs, often mixed with elements of Daoism, shamanism, and fetishism.

Even though the Yi are divided into a number of cultural and ethnic groups, they are believed to have a common origin as part of the ancient Qiang people, who were also believed to be the ancestors of the Tibetan, Naxi, and Qiang people. The ancestors of the Yi migrated from the Tibetan Plateau region through Sichuan and into Yunnan, where the majority of the Yi people live to the present. Historic Chinese records tell of the Han Chinese conquest of the Anning River valley around 200 BCE, where the Chinese established a county known as Qiongdu, the first Yi region to come under Han Chinese rule. The Shu dynasty that ruled China from 221 to 263 CE fought several wars against the ancestors of the Yi, who had established a tribal confederation ruled by a Yi king. The Han Chinese finally defeated the Yi kingdom and expanded their empire into the conquered territories of the Yi. Successive Chinese dynasties were acknowledged by

the Yi, but Han Chinese control remained weak in many areas, especially in the less accessible mountain regions. The Chinese began to call the inhabitants of the region *Yi*, written in a Chinese character meaning "barbarian." Over the centuries, the different groups linguistically and culturally related to the Yi were known by many different names related to their clans, geographic regions, or the names given to them by the Han Chinese or neighboring peoples. Probably in the second or third century BCE, the Yi people living around Dainchi Lake in Yunnan evolved a stratified class system. The Han dynasty created prefectures in this with the chief of the Dainchi Yi granted the title "King of Dian" by the Chinese emperor. The Yi often took slaves from among the poorer classes or neighboring ethnic groups with part of the Yi economy built on slave labor. In the eighth century CE, the state of Nanzhao was created in the south by the Yi, the Bai, and the Naxi as the dominant peoples. The head of the Nanzhao state took the title "King of Yunnan." In 937, the successor state known as Dali succeeded Nanzhao, which collapsed under the pressure of slave and peasant uprisings. Gradually, the slave system gave way to a landlord system with lands worked by serfs and debt slaves. In the 13th century, the invading Mongols overran Dali and all the Yi territories, which were brought under the rule of the Mongol Yuan dynasty in China. Yuan administrators created civil and military administrations for the Yi regions of Yunnan, Guizhou, and Sichuan, often appointing hereditary chieftains to rule in the name of the emperor. Between the 14th and 17th centuries, large numbers of Han

Chinese immigrants settled in the Yi territories. In the 18th century, the Manchu of the Qing dynasty finally abolished the system of appointing hereditary headmen and confirmed the appointment of officials dispatched to the regions from the Chinese capital. This allowed greater control of the Yi districts and firmly established the feudal landlord system. The majority of the Yi were peasant farmers who worked lands owned by large landowners often paying high rents or suffered other abuses. A policy of cultural assimilation was followed with the Yi often forced to abandon their traditions and customs and to adopt Han Chinese traditions. Numerous uprisings against the excesses of corrupt officials, greedy landlords, and the remnants of the slave system erupted across the Yi regions in southern China in the 18th century.

The Yi people are mostly scattered across the mountainous areas of northern Yunnan, southeastern Sichuan, southwestern Guizhou, and the northern districts of Guangxi Zhuang Autonomous Region. Traditionally, the Yi pride themselves on being a tough, resilient, and aggressive people. The historic manner of construction was to surround the village with stout fences, a sign of the violence that permeates Yi history. The Yi villages are built at different altitudes in their rugged homeland, with many different climates and amounts of precipitation. The striking differences between even nearby villages gave rise to the old Yi saying "the weather is different just a village away." This is the primary reason for the great differences in culture, production, and dialects between the many Yi groups. Historically, the Yi were divided into four different classes—Nuohuo, Qunuo, Ajia, and Xiaxi. The Nuohuo, meaning Black Yi, was the noble class determined by blood lineage and remained permanent, and the other classes could never move up to the Nuohuo class. Qunuo or White Yi was the highest class of commoners and made up about 50 percent of the Yi population. The Qunuo were an appendage of the Nuohuo who enjoyed relative independence and could control or own Ajia or Xiaxi, who were considered inferior. The Qunuo were tied to the regions governed by their Nuohuo lords and were subjected to restrictions on property and movement. The Ajia class, about a third of the population, was rigidly bound to the Nuohuo or Qunuo property owners, mostly as serfs who could be brought and sold. The Xiaxi was the lowest class, making up about 10 percent of the Yi population. They were forbidden to own property, had no personal rights or freedom, and were regarded as "talking tools." In areas where slavery persisted until the mid-20th century, the Xiaxi made up the slave class. Each of the three lower classes worked for the Nuohuo lords with the Qunuo forced to work for the lords for free, using their own draft animals or slaves, between 5 and 10 days a year, and the Ajia were forced to work without pay for up to a third or even a half of all their working hours. Because of the rigid class system, marriage customs stipulated marriage within the same class but outside the immediate clan structure. In many areas, the clan system propagated the class system while safeguarding and supporting the privileges of the Nuohuo nobility. The class system was dismantled by the Chinese government in the 1950s, but traditions such as patriarchal and monogamous families as the basic units of Yi society remain strong. The majority of the Yi retain their historic religious beliefs, which include elements of Daoism, fetishism, and shamanism. Shamans, known as *bimo*, officiate at births, funerals, weddings, and other celebrations. Though some of the Yi groups have adopted Buddhism, most still revere the spirits of fire, trees, rocks, hills, water, earth, sky, wind, and forests. The spirits are believed to play a major role in daily life. A sizable Christian community exists, particularly in Yunnan, as a result of early 20th-century missionary stations in the region. The Yi speak a language, sometimes known as Nuosu, that forms part of the Loloish branch of the Tibeto-Burman languages. There are six Yi languages recognized by the Chinese government, which have between 25 and 50 percent of their vocabulary in common. Many Yi also speak Mandarin Chinese or the languages of neighboring ethnic groups.

The antifeudal resistance among the Yi resulted in numerous uprisings in the 19th century, particularly severe in 1802, 1814, 1838–1839, and from 1875 to 1892. The slave owners of the Liangshan Mountains region of Sichuan and Yunnan were often the targets of unrest. The power of the nobility and the landlords allowed them to repeatedly put down the sporadic uprisings, often brutally. Certain elements of capitalism appeared in the Yi areas along the Yunnan–Vietnam Railway and the new roads constructed in the region. The growth of handicraft industries and modern commerce varied from place to place. The living standard of the Yi living in towns and cities was about equal to that of the Han Chinese but was much lower in the rural mountain communities. After 1860, European missionaries began to visit the Yi

areas, where they established churches and often church schools, particularly in Yunnan, where British and French missionaries were active. Influenced by the Taiping Revolution in northern China in 1851–1864, a revolt broke out among the Yi and some neighboring peoples that kept the region in turmoil for more than a decade. The Chinese Revolution swept away the Qing dynasty in 1911 bringing a new system of government to the Yi, but many of the abusive landlords and nobles retained their traditional powers and prerogatives. The Yi often joined antigovernment groups and societies to fight the worst excesses of the system in the 1920s and early 1930s. In 1935, the rebel communists on their long march north to resist the Japanese invaders passed through the Yi regions leaving a deep and positive impression with their ideals of equality and the liberation of the minority ethnic groups in China. Agents of the communist Red Army, as they passed through, cracked down on local tyrants, cruel nobles, and corrupt government officials. They often opened the barns of the wealthy to feed the starving Yi peasants. Many young Yi joined the new Red Army to fight both the Japanese and the Chinese government. At the Japanese defeat in 1945, the Chinese Civil War erupted again between the Red Army and government troops. A communist victory in 1949 was followed by the overthrow and elimination of the noble class, the landlords, and most traders and private businesses in the Yi areas. In some areas, slavery persisted until the arrival of the communist cadres. Until the 1960s, bandit groups ravaged the more inaccessible regions. The Yi, particularly the former lower classes, advanced rapidly in education and prosperity, though economic advancement remained spotty due to the rugged terrain of the Yi regions. In 1980, a group of Yi scholars decided to promote the contribution of Yi culture to human civilization through the research, saving, collating, translating, and publishing Yi historical records. Though accepted by the central government, the survey of historic records has never been completely carried out. The economic and political reforms begun in the 1980s brought new opportunities for the Yi, particularly in the trade for their mountain and forest products with the increasingly prosperous regions along China's east coast.

Further Reading

Harrell, Stevan. *Perspectives on the Yi in Southwest China.* Berkeley: University of California Press, 2001.

Harrell, Stevan. *Ways of Being Ethnic in Southwest China.* Seattle: University of Washington Press, 2002.

McCarthy, Susan K. *Communist Multiculturalism: Ethnic Revival in Southwest China.* Seattle: University of Washington Press, 2009.

Yugur

The Yugur, sometimes known as Yogir, Ya Lu, Yuku, Yugu, or Yellow Uyghur, are one of the 56 official ethnic groups of the People's Republic of China. The official ethnic group is composed of two distinct groups, the Enger Yugur or Eastern Yugur, who speak a Mongolian dialect, and the Saragh Yugur or Western Yugur, who speak a Turkic language. Both groups live in the Gansu corridor region just south of Inner Mongolia and together have a population of about 15,000. More than half of the Yugur are adherents of Tibetan Buddhism with a large minority that has retained their traditional animist religion.

The Yugur believe that they are descendants of an early nomadic tribe known as the Huiqu or Ouigurs. The Huiqu were first mentioned in the records of the Chinese Tang dynasty, 618–907 CE, as a tribal group dwelling in the grasslands of western Mongolia. The tribe came under the rule of the Uyghur people in the late 700s, forming part of the huge empire known as the Uyghur Empire or the Uyghur Khaganate. The Uyghur state collapsed in 848, leaving the tribal groups of western Mongolia effectively independent. In 860, due to heavier than normal snowfall, combined with attacks by the Kyrgyz people to the north, and squabbling among the Yughur nobility, they were forced to flee their homeland and move south to Gansu. They fell under the authority of the Tibetans briefly before freeing themselves and capturing a large area in the fertile lowlands. They created a kingdom known as Ganzhou in 870. The kingdom, with a population reported in Chinese records of more than 300,000, flourished on the Silk Route caravan trails. They practiced a form of Turkic shamanism known as Tengrism with some adopting the Buddhist religion. Unlike their Uyghur relatives to the west, they were never converted to Islam. Following a bloody war between 1028 and 1036, they were conquered and brought under the rule of the Tangut state. In 1227, the Mongols invaded the region, with one of the Mongol groups settling among the Turkic-speaking Yugur, where they intermarried but without losing their Mongol language. With the passage of time, the two groups merged to form one people, with two languages and significant cultural difference. From the 11th to 16th centuries, many of the Yugur in the western districts assimilated into the larger Uyghur ethnic group. Under the rule of the Han Chinese Ming dynasty, some of the remaining Yugur were forced to move farther east as the frontier region became unsettled. Those moved farther east took their Mongol language with them, which became the language of daily life. Those in the west retained their Turkic language though both groups continued to call themselves Yugur. Those Yugur moved to the east gradually adopted farming like their Han Chinese neighbors, while the western Yugur retained their traditional livestock breeding and hunting. Though they were under loose Chinese rule for many centuries, they were finally incorporated into the Chinese Empire under the Manchu Qing dynasty in 1696. The Qing administration, in an effort to strengthen its authority in the region, divided the Yugur into seven tribes and appointed a headman for each with a superintendent over them all. Tibetan Buddhism, also known as Lamaism, was adopted by many of the Yugur, and each tribe had its own monastery.

Yugur culture, despite the historic, linguistic, and religious differences between the two Yugur groups, retains many elements in common such as their rich oral tradition of legends, folktales, proverbs, and ballads. The Yugur are known as skillful weavers of beautiful patterns on carpets, bags, and horse harnesses. Traditional clothing is also known for the embroidery on collars, sleeves, and cloth boots. The traditional occupations continue to dominate the daily lives of the Yugur, with agriculture mostly among those in the eastern

groups and herding in the west. In the last few decades, their herds have undergone great changes, with wool shearing mechanized, animal stocks improved, and a more progressive use of the grazing lands undertaken. Reservoirs have been constructed, ponds dug, and underground water sources tapped to irrigate large tracts of formerly dry pasture and to provide water for the herds. Another important economic activity, created in 1958, revolved around the creation of large collective farms to domesticate wild deer, valued for their horns and musk. The Yugur speak two distinct languages known as Western Yugur, which belongs to the group of Siberian Turkic languages, and Eastern Yugur, a Shirongolic language of the Mongolic language family. Both languages are not intelligible to speakers of the Turkic Uyghur language. Many Yugur speak Mandarin Chinese, which is often used for communications between the two groups. A small group also speaks Tibetan, the language of their religion. The majority of the Yugur are now Tibetan Buddhist by religion, looking to the Dalai Lama as the head of their religious beliefs. The remainder, though often nominally Buddhist, retain their traditional shamanistic beliefs, a system known as Tengrism or Turkic Shamanism.

In the 19th century, Lamaism was widespread in the Yugur region. The lamas worked closely with the Yugur headmen or chiefs in important tribal matters. In some areas, the Buddhist religion and politics became closely intertwined. The Buddhist monasteries had their own system of feudal rule, including Buddhist courts and prisons. The monasteries often ordered compulsory donations or free forced labor, while

Newly wed couple poses for a photo in a traditional wedding of Yugur ethnic group in Lanzhou, northwest China's Gansu Province, 2013. Many of Yugur ethnic group, living primarily in Sunan Yugur Autonomous County in Gansu Province, still prefer to follow their traditional wedding customs. (Zhang Meng/Corbis)

compelling many children to join the clergy. Donations for religious purposes were a large yearly expense for each family. The excesses of the monasteries and the Yugur headmen left the majority of the Yugur living in poverty, dependent on their meager earnings from farms or herds for survival. At the turn of the 20th century, there were no modern roads or bridges over rivers in the region. The Yugur were among the most isolated of China's many ethnic groups. The Chinese Revolution in 1911 ended loose imperial rule but left the monasteries and headmen to rule as they always had. The communist revolution that ended republican China in 1949 brought rapid changes to the region. In 1954, an autonomous county was established along with an autonomous township for the two separate groups that were then officially recognized as a single ethnic group. The Yugur region remained virtually unknown and cut off for centuries from the outside world until the completion of the Lanzhou–Urumqi railway line that was constructed through their region in 1963. Greater contact with the outside world proved painful during the excesses of the Chinese Cultural Revolution in 1967–1977, but with the economic and political reforms adopted in the 1980s, the Yugur have recovered much of their centuries-old culture and, by 2000, had attained a modest prosperity with their farms, herds, and trade in their traditional products.

Further Reading

Olson, James S. *An Ethnohistorical Dictionary of China.* Westport, CT: Greenwood, 1998.

West, Barbara A. *Encyclopedia of the Peoples of Asia and Oceania.* New York: Facts on File, 2008.

Xiaoming, Xiao. *China's Ethnic Minorities.* Beijing: Foreign Languages Press, 2003.

Yukaghir

The Yukaghir, sometimes known as Jukaghir, Odul, Vadul, Walud, Detkil, Dutke, Dutkil, or Buguch, are a Siberian people living mostly in the Sakha Republic and the Magadan region of northeastern Siberia. The estimated 1,500–2,000 Yukaghir speak two related dialects known as Tundra and Kolyma Yukaghir, though most now speak Russian or Sakha (Yakut). If the Chuvan of the Chukotka region, a closely related people of mixed Yukaghir, Even, Koryak, and Russian background, are counted, the total is close to 4,000. The language's relationship with other known languages is uncertain, though some scholars believe that it is distantly related to the Uralic languages. Most of the Yukaghir are officially Orthodox Christians though they also continue to practice their traditional shamanistic rituals and customs.

Historically, the Yukaghir form part of the Baikal group of Siberian peoples, whose origins are believed to be in southern Siberia. The Yukaghir were formerly much more numerous and inhabited a large territory in northeastern Siberia from the lower reaches of the Lena River in the west to the middle and upper reaches of the Anadyr River in the east. The Yukaghir tribal territories included taiga and tundra lands in the Arctic region south to the Verkhoyansk Mountains east of the Lena River. The Yukaghir clans lived as hunters, fishermen, and reindeer herders. Though culturally and linguistically related, the Yukaghir peoples were spread over a large territory and were divided into various tribes and clans. In the 12th and 13th centuries CE, the Tungus people, the Tungus tribes, the ancestors of the Evenk and Even peoples, invaded northern Siberia from their homeland in the mountains near Lake Baikal. The Tungus invaders clashed with the Yukaghir clans, probably in the regions of the Vilyui and lower Aldan Rivers. Many of the Yukaghir clans fled further north to the basins of the upper Yana, Indigirka, Kolyma, and Anadyr Rivers or took refuge in the forests and the tundra to the north. Some of the Yukaghir clans remained in their traditional territories and gradually intermingled with the Tungus settlers. By the end of the 17th century, the Yukaghir population had declined to some 9,000 though they still controlled a large territory. Their decline continued with the economic competition of other ethnic groups, particularly the Even, and the smallpox epidemics that ravaged the region following its introduction to Siberia by explorers and traders from European Russia. Russian explorers first moved into the Yukaghir territory in the late 17th century, led by Cossack military patrols. The explorers reported on the extensive wealth of region in fur-bearing animals, other game, and fish. At the beginning of the Russian colonization, the Yukaghir tribal groups, the Chuvan, Khodyn, and Anaul, occupied the territory from the Lena River east to the

Anadyr River. Epidemics of smallpox and measles swept through the tribes in 1669 and 1691–1694, destroying many of the Yukaghir clans. Armed conflict with the Even, and later the Russian Cossacks, decimated many Yukaghir clans. Their matrilocal system of marriage, with a tradition of adoption of males into the wife's tribe or clan, resulted in the creation of ethnically mixed groups and eventually to the disappearance of some Yukaghir tribes and the amalgamation of the others. A large number of Yukaghir were assimilated into the Even ethnic group in the western areas, while those in the east adopted the Koryak or Chukchi language and culture in the 18th century. The Yukaghir population continued to decline owing to epidemics of European diseases, internal feuds, conflicts with neighboring peoples, and the brutal Russian colonial policies. Colonization also affected the Yukaghir reindeer with several diseases that killed many herds and the partial blocking of the traditional migration routes of the wild reindeer.

The Yukaghir are one of the smallest ethnic groups in the Russian Federation. Traditionally, the Yukaghir are divided into two regional groups, often known as the Taiga Yukaghir, in the Upper Kolyma District of the Sakha Republic and in the Saimanchansloi District of the neighboring Magadan Oblast to the east. The Tundra Yukaghir inhabit the Lower Kolyma District of the Sakha Republic between the Kolyma and Indigirka Rivers. Both Yukaghir groups live among larger neighboring ethnic groups, particularly the Sakha and Russian population. Even in recent decades, Yukaghir clans such as the Korkodan Yukaghir in the Magadan

region have lost their Yukaghir identity and assimilated into the local population. The three surviving tribes are the Odul of the Nelemnoe region of Sakha, the Vadul of Andryushkino in Magadan, and the Chuvan of the Anadyr River region. Sometimes the Chuvan are considered a separate ethnic group because of the mixed ancestry of the group and the extinction of the Chuvan language. The Yukaghir language, made up of two distinct regional dialects known as Tundra Yukaghir and Kolyma Yukaghir, is severely endangered as many Yukaghir now use Russian or Sakha as their first language. The two dialects are not mutually intelligible. The language is considered an isolated language not clearly related to any of the surrounding language groups. Though the majority of the Yukaghir are nominally Russian Orthodox, they have retained much of their pre-Christian shamanistic beliefs. Their traditional beliefs revere their ancestral spirits, and the spirits of fire, sun, the hunt, the earth, and water. They believe that the spirits are both the protectors and the enemies of the Yukaghir people. The cult of the sun is the most exalted and is considered the highest judge in all disputes. The spirits of the Yukaghir dead go to Aibidzi, where they continue to watch over and help the Yukaghir. Formerly every clan had an *alma*, a shaman who was both the healer and the religious leader.

In the 19th century, the situation of the Yukaghir clans was desperate. Their traditional hunting and fishing lands had been taken by the colonists or neighboring ethnic groups, and official suppression of their shamanistic belief system had ended their ancient cultural practices. Forced conversion to Russian Orthodoxy was official government policy. Famine, diseases, and armed conflicts continued to decimate the declining Yukaghir population. By the early 20th century, many of the Yukaghir clans had disappeared, either died out or assimilated into neighboring peoples. The majority of the Yukaghir clans identified with their local regions not with the idea of a larger ethnic group made up of groups of people with a common culture and dialects of the same language. The beginning of Soviet rule, in 1920, brought great changes to the surviving Yukaghir. The Soviet administrators oversaw the administration of resources, ending the periodic famines in the Yukaghir region, and the wholesale buying of furs, which had exploited the hunting clans, was discontinued. In 1929, when the annual reindeer migrations ended, the Soviet authorities reorganized the Yukaghir for reindeer breeding and fur hunting collectives. In 1931, Yukaghir children attended school for the first time, with illiteracy mostly eliminated over the next decade. During the course of World War II, in the early 1940s, many Russians and whole factories were moved to the region away from the areas of heavy fighting. In the 1950s, most Taiga Yukaghir were settled on collective farms in Russian-style log cabins with vegetable gardens and animal pens. Most of the Tundra Yukaghir were settled on mixed collectives of Russian, Chukchi, Even, and Yukaghir devoted to reindeer herding, hunting, and fishing. Yukaghir hunting and fishing practices, many dating from the Neolithic period, were replaced by modern methods. The Yukaghir religious practices were also banned by the officially atheistic Soviet state. The Russian language, used in education, administration, and publications, became the first language of many Yukaghir. Others adopted the language of the more numerous Sakha people. Cultural Russification, official Soviet policy, further damaged the already fragile Yukaghir culture and language. The collapse of the Soviet regime, in 1991, brought further changes to the surviving Yukaghir. The collectives were converted into clan regions under local administration, though their occupations as hunters, fishermen, and herders remain the same. In 1992, a Yukaghir Council of Elders was established to advise on Yukaghir affairs. In the 21st century, there was a movement to revive the Yukaghir language. Increased contact between the Yukaghir groups reaffirmed the common culture and history that bound them together. For the first time in their history, the Yukaghir began to perceive themselves as one ethnic group with a common past.

Further Reading

Berthier-Folgar, Sheila Collingwood-Whittick, and Sandrine Tolazzi, eds. *Biomapping Indigenous Peoples: Towards an Understanding of the Issues.* Amsterdam: Rodopi, 2012.

Forsyth, James. *A History of the Peoples of Siberia: Russia's North Asian Colony 1581–1990.* Cambridge: Cambridge University Press, 1994.

Vahtre, Lauri and Viikberg, Jüri. The Red Book of the Peoples of the Russian Empire. "The Yukaghirs." Accessed July 31, 2013. http://www.eki.ee/books/redbook/yukaghirs .shtml

Willersley, Rane. *Soul Hunters: Hunting, Animism, and Personhood among the Siberian Yukaghir.* Berkeley: University of California Press, 2007.

Yupik

The Yupik, sometimes known as Yup'ik, Yuit, Yoit, Asiatic Eskimo, or Siberian Yupik, are an Arctic people living on the Chukchi Peninsula in northeastern Siberia and the St. Lawrence Islands, some 40 miles (64 kilometers) east of the peninsula in Alaskan territory. The estimated 1,200–2,000 Yupik in Siberia form the largest part of the Yupik population, which numbers around 1,000 in the United States. The Yupik language, known as Central Siberian Yupik, belongs to the Eskimo-Aleut language group spoken in the Arctic regions of Siberia and North America. The Yupik retain their traditional shamanism and their belief in the spirit world.

The common ancestors of the Inuit, Yupik, and Aleut peoples are believed to have their origin in eastern Siberia, arriving in the Bering Strait region about 10,000 years ago. Around 3,000 years ago, the ancestors of the Yupik evolved a highly effective system of cultural adaptation of the northern maritime type. The territory of the Yupik, below the Arctic Circle, included areas used in the harsh winter months, and summer camping areas along the shores of the Arctic Sea. Long contact with the settled Chukchi to the south had significant influence on their material culture, social organization, and spiritual life. Armed conflict between the Yupik and the reindeer-herding Chukchi often occurred over territory and resources. The nomadic Yupik mostly engaged in hunting marine animals and fishing, gradually moving far up the Vel'mai and other rivers. Occupation of St. Lawrence Island was never permanent, with periods of occupation and abandonment depending on the availability of marine animals and weather conditions. Famine was common, with some bands disappearing due to reduced resources. In the 17th century, contact with first the Russians and later the Americans began as explorers mapped the coasts and the islands of the Bering Strait region. Russian colonization, begun in the 1640s, brought European diseases and demands for taxes in the form of valuable furs. In 1725, Russian Tsar Peter the Great ordered Danish/Russian explorer Vitus Bering to explore the northeastern coasts of Siberia and to subjugate the indigenous peoples. St. Lawrence Island, called Sivuqaq by the Yupik, was visited by Vitus Bering in 1728. Interest in the region by other powers, particularly the United States and the United Kingdom, prompted the Russians to send expeditions to map the Chukchi Peninsula, the islands, and the west coast of Alaska in 1785. The Yupik bands engaged in trade with the Europeans, including Americans, British, Russian, and Norwegian, but mostly rejected European attempts to introduce Christianity or to extend their authority over the Yupik people.

The Yupik culture is based on their traditional way of life as seminomadic hunters and fishermen following the seasonal changes in their environment. Hunting of sea mammals, particularly seals, walrus, and until recent decades, whales, formed the basis of the culture. The gathering of plants and berries added variety to their diet, which is now supplemented by commercial foods purchased in stores. Traditionally, the Yupik spent the spring and summer months in a fish camp, then joined with other bands at permanent villages during the winter. The Yupik used the abundant wood and driftwood to build permanent winter homes, with separate building for men and women. The men's communal dwelling, the *qasgiq*, served as the community center for ceremonies and festivals, and a type of school for boys who were taught how to make tools and kayaks during the winter months. The women's house, the *ena*, was smaller and mostly constructed with sod. It was usually located next to the *qasgiq*, sometimes connected by a tunnel. In the women's house, the girls of the band were taught to sew, cook, and weave. The traditional winter dwelling, the *yaranga*, was round and dome shaped with a framework made of wooden posts. Modern *yaranga* are now covered with canvas rather than skins. Yupik villages usually consisted of as many as 300 people related by blood and marriage. The Yupik believe that no one really dies, but remains in a cycle of life through which the soul of a dead person is transferred to a newborn in the next generation. This cycle of birth, death, and rebirth is also applied to animals. Shamans acted as mediators with the spirit world, contacting the various spirits, souls, and beings of their belief system. Belief in both benign and evil spirits continues, though traditional customs and rituals are often mixed with Christian traditions. The Yupik language, known as Central Siberian Yupik or Bering Strait Yupik, belongs to the Yupik group of the Eskimo-Aleut language family. The language, spoken on the Chukchi Peninsula in Siberian Russia and the St. Lawrence Island of the American state of Alaska, has declined rapidly in Siberia but is spoken by nearly the entire Yupik population in the nearby St. Lawrence Island.

Yupik seal hunter practicing the traditional method of hunting sea mammals. (Edward S. Curtis/Corbis)

In the early 19th century, contacts between the Yupik and the Europeans were sparse and mostly involved trading. Russian attempts to impose a fur tax prompted armed resistance as the Yupik bands refused to pay tribute to a distant monarch. In 1822, Russian Cossacks established several trading posts and fortified centers on the peninsula though contacts between the Yupik and the Europeans were still few. Trade relations increased following the 1867 sale of Alaska, including St. Lawrence Island, to the United States. Competition between Russian and American merchants and traders resulted in Yupik access to boats, guns, folding structures, and other modern tools and implements. Living in the border area between Russian and American territories, the Yupik were not subjected to the sole authority of either side. Yupik life changed rapidly following the Soviet takeover of Russia in 1920. Soviet cadres arrived in the Chukchi Peninsula in 1923. The Yupik tradition of private trading was banned. Hunters and fishermen were forced into Soviet cooperatives. In 1931, as part of the brief Soviet attempt to support ethnic diversity, the Yupik of the region were renamed Yuit or Yuity, and the first Yupik communal village was established. By 1938, the majority of the Yupik had been resettled in collectives dedicated to reindeer herding or fur hunting as state employees. Culturally, the Yupik advanced as the first school was opened in 1925, and centers for political enlightenment were established in 1928. Following the brief period of Soviet support for non-Russian ethnic groups, official policies changed to those of overt colonialism and assimilation into a greater Soviet culture. Contacts between the Yupik of the Chukchi Peninsula and those of St. Lawrence Island were curtailed as relations between the Soviet Union and the United States worsened in the late 1930s. Contacts continued during the years of World War II when the two countries were reluctant allies but were stopped abruptly by the Soviet authorities in 1949. In 1958 and again in 1971, groups of Yupik were deported to the inland regions of the Chukchi Peninsula to ease the work of the frontier forces in the region. The Yupik settlements became part of multiethnic villages, and the language of administration, education, and publishing was Russian. Assimilation into the Russian culture resulted in many old traditions dying out, and young Yupik grew up speaking Russian. Following the collapse of the Soviet Union in 1991, the planned economy ended and a version of capitalism came to the region. Finding themselves without employment, culturally without roots, and often without hope, the Yupik in Russia now mostly subsist on state emergency aid with severe problems with disease, infant mortality, and alcohol abuse.

Further Reading

Burch, Ernest S. Jr. *The Eskimos.* Norman: University of Oklahoma Press, 1988.

Forsyth, James. *A History of the Peoples of Siberia: Russia's North Asian Colony 1581–1990.* Cambridge: Cambridge University Press, 1994.

Slezkine, Yuri. *Arctic Mirrors: Russia and the Small Peoples of the North.* Ithaca, NY: Cornell University Press, 1996.

Z

Zainichi

The Zainichi, sometimes known as Zainichi Korean or Korean Japanese, constitute the largest non-Japanese ethnic group in the country. The name *Zainichi* is used only for the long-term residents of Korean descent who trace their roots to the period of Japanese rule in Korea in the early 20th century. The estimated 800,000 Zainichi include both those who are naturalized Japanese citizens of Korean descent and the larger number of permanent residents of Korean descent. The majority of the Zainichi speak both Korean and Japanese, the language of education and administration. The majority of the Zainichi adhere to various Buddhist sects with a small Christian minority.

The original inhabitants of the Korean Peninsula were probably nomadic migrants from south-central Siberia. They populated the Korean Peninsula in successive waves from the Neolithic to the Bronze ages. Migrants from the Korean Peninsula have been immigrating to Japan since prehistoric times, but only those who came to Japan in the first half of the 20th century are counted as a separate group. In the Stone Age, the Japanese Archipelago was connected to mainland Asia by at least one land bridge and was settled by nomadic peoples from the mainland. The connection between the Korean Peninsula and Japan continued over centuries. Korean migrants settled in the islands and were usually absorbed into the Japanese culture. Early Japanese culture absorbed some Korean influence, but it is uncertain if this was accompanied by migration from the peninsula to the Japanese islands. In the early centuries of the Common Era, several Korean tribal confederations evolved into three rival kingdoms that controlled the peninsula and neighboring parts of mainland Manchuria. The unification of the three kingdoms in 676 CE led to the North and South States era, with the Korean Peninsula divided into the Silla kingdom in the south and Balhae in the north, the division reflecting the modern division of the peninsula. During this period, many Koreans migrated to the nearby Japanese islands to escape the violence and civil wars of the peninsula. The migrants, though at first forced to live in segregated areas, were gradually absorbed into the surrounding Japanese culture. Between 1592 and 1598, the troops of the Japanese Empire invaded the Korean Peninsula. The Japanese were eventually forced to withdraw, taking with them many ethnic Koreans. By the 18th century, Korea was heavily dependent on China for its external affairs and, like China, was isolated from the outside world. This period also saw a number of Korean migrants settling in Japan, and like their predecessors, they too were absorbed into the Japanese culture by the end of the 18th century.

The Japanese name *Zainichi* means "staying in Japan" and implies only temporary residence; however, over time, it has been adopted as the name for the Korean population that migrated or were forced to settle in Japan in the early 20th century. The Zainichi group includes people whose origins are traced back to Joseon, old undivided Korea, along with others who hold North or South Korean nationality. A minority has been able to acquire Japanese nationality, but the Japanese government resists naturalizing the Zainichi even though many have lived in Japan for nearly a century. Though the Zainichi maintain many elements of traditional Korean culture, they have developed a distinct contemporary culture that blends both Korean and Japanese traditions and customs. Traditional Korean art forms are maintained, many still influenced by Buddhism and Confucianism, but distinctly Zainichi art forms have evolved with Korean, Japanese, and even modern American influences. Because of Korea's tumultuous history during the 20th and into the 21st century, the Zainichi are divided into two rival groups, the Chongryon and the Mindan. The Chongryon are pro-North Korea and are more militant in trying to preserve the Korean identity that is being submerged in the Zainichi culture. The Mindan, more pro-South Korean, are more involved in the emerging Zainichi culture, including clubs, restaurants, and other institutions. The Zainichi often speak Korean and Japanese or a dialect that is spoken among themselves that incorporates borrowings from both languages. The religious beliefs of the Zainichi are usually traditional Buddhist and Confucianist beliefs though there is a sizable Christian minority.

During the 19th century, the isolationist policy of the Korean kingdom earned it the name the "Hermit kingdom." The Joseon dynasty attempted to isolate and protect the Korean culture from the outside world. After the first Sino-Japanese War and the Russo-Japanese wars in the late 19th and the early 20th centuries, Japan became the most powerful state in the region. In 1910, the Japanese military occupied the Korean kingdom and deposed the last of the Joseon rulers. Japan placed Korea under the colonial administration of the governor general of Korea. The Japanese adopted a policy of suppressing Korean culture and traditions. Economic and social policies were primarily for the benefit of the Japanese. Anti-Japanese rallies and demonstrations, particularly in 1919, were brutally suppressed with some 7,000 Koreans killed. The confiscation of lands, factories, and properties left many Koreans destitute. The Japanese government forced many Koreans to resettle in Japan, where they were needed as menial workers while others left Korea and moved to Japan in order to survive the devastation of their homeland. The Japanese government claimed that colonization spurred Korea's feudal economy and that the Korean immigrants to Japan were voluntary, but this is disputed by the majority of the Zainichi. Many Koreans were conscripted into the Japanese military as labor battalions or sent to work in Japanese factories and in agriculture. During World War II, a large number of conscripts were moved to Japan to work in war industries. Between 1939 and 1945, an estimated 60,000 ethnic Koreans in Japan died from harsh treatment, inhumane working conditions, and allied bombings. At the end of

World War II in 1945, there were roughly 2.4 million ethnic Koreans in Japan. Most were repatriated by the Allies to the southern half of the Korean Peninsula, leaving only some 650,000 in Japan by the end of 1946. Japan's defeat and the loss of its control of the Korean Peninsula left the nationality status of the Koreans in question. Initially treated as foreign nationals, the Koreans were provisionally registered as nationals of Joseon, the old name for undivided Korea. In 1948, the two Korean states declared independence, with a democratic state in the south and a communist regime in the north. Many Zainichi Koreans were allowed to change their registry to that of nationals of South Korea. Many Zainichi who had obtained Japanese nationality were left stateless. The division of the Korean Peninsula also divided the Zainichi in Japan with pro-democratic and pro-communist factions though younger Zainichi often rejected both as the Korean-Japanese Zainichi culture was embraced.

Another wave of immigration, this time voluntary, started following the division of Korean into two antagonistic states and the beginning of the Korean War in the 1950s. During the years of the Cold War, the Japanese government recognized the government of South Korea as the sole representative of the Korean people, leaving those Zainichi favoring North Korea virtually stateless. During the 1970s and 1980s, nearly 100,000 Zainichi opted to return to the peninsula though the majority, having lived for decades in Japan, rejected the idea of repatriation to a country they didn't feel was theirs. Many Zainichi, since the early 1980s, have gone to South Korea to study or to marry, but most return to Japan where they have family and cultural ties. In the 21st century, the Zainichi have established a stable culture in Japan after years of activism. Most younger Zainichi speak only Japanese, attend Japanese schools, work for Japanese firms, and increasingly intermarry with the Japanese. Though increasingly comfortable in Japan, where attitudes toward non-Japanese residents are changing for the better, many Zainichi choose to retain their Korean or Joseon nationality as part of their unique heritage. In a 2010 survey, over 90 percent of the Zainichi have both a Japanese-sounding name in addition to their Korean names, using one or the other depending on the situation. One of the remaining controversies is the right to vote, which is withheld from residents who have not taken up Japanese nationality no matter how long they or their families have lived in Japan.

Further Reading

Graburn, Nelson, John Erti, and Kenji R. Tierney, eds. *Multiculturalism in the New Japan: Crossing the Boundaries Within.* New York: Berghahn Books, 2010.

Lie, John. *Zainichi (Koreans in Japan): Diasporic Nationalism and Postcolonial Identity.* Berkeley: University of California Press, 2008.

Lie, John. "Zainichi Recognitions: Japan's Korean Residents' Ideology and Its Discontents." *The Asia-Pacific Journal: Japan Focus.* Accessed July 31, 2013. http://japanfocus.org/-John-Lie/2939. Originally published in Chapter 4 of *Zainichi (Koreans in Japan): Diasporic Nationalism and Postcolonial Identity* (Berkeley: University of California Press, 2008).

Weiner, Michael, ed. *Japan's Minorities: The Illusion of Homogeneity.* London: Routledge, 1997.

Zhuang

The Zhuang, sometimes known as Bu-zhuang, Bunong, Butu, Buyang, Buyue, Buman, Chuang, Chwang, Chwan, Tai Zhuang, Rau, or Gaolan, are the largest of the minority nationalities in the People's Republic of China. The estimated 18.9 million Zhuang mostly live in the Guangxi Zhuang Autonomous Region in southern China, with smaller populations in Yunnan, Guizhou, Guangdong, and Hunan Provinces. The Zhuang form the largest of the national minorities recognized by the government of the People's Republic of China. The Zhuang speak a number of mutually unintelligible dialects that belong to the Tai group of Tai-Kadai language family. The majority of the Zhuang adhere to their traditional Mo and Shigong belief systems, with sizable minorities of Buddhists and followers of Daoism.

The Zhuang people are the largest of the indigenous people of southern China, tracing their ancestry back to the Paleolithic era. Rock paintings in the Hua Mountains have been dated at between 475 and 220 BCE. The Tai peoples south of the early Chinese states were usually referred to as "southern barbarians." Around 218 BCE, the Han Chinese invaded the Tai territories to the south, which proved a disaster. But by 214, the western parts of Guangxi have been overrun and way opened to the immigration of hundreds of thousands of Han Chinese. A state known as Panyu was formed by the Tai groups that were alternately free of or under Han Chinese hegemony. The state collapsed in 111 BCE, allowing the Han Chinese to again move south to establish colonies and garrisons in important cities in the south. The Zhuang formed the largest of the Tai peoples that formed the large state known as Nanzhao in Yunnan. The Tai armies of Nanzhao repulsed Chinese imperial armies in 751 and 754 CE but later collapsed due to internal conflicts and peasant uprisings. A successor state, Dali, gained control of much of the region following the downfall of Nanzhao in 902. Under pressure from the Han Chinese to the north and the Annamese in the south, the Zhuang leader Nong Zhigao led a widespread uprising against the encroaching Han Chinese in 1052. He is still remembered as a Zhuang national hero. Around 1070, the Zhuang defeated an Annamese invasion from present-day Vietnam. Despite increasing Han Chinese control, the region remained unsettled. The independence of the Zhuang lasted until the conquest of the region by the Mongols in 1253. The Venetian explorer Marco Polo visited the fallen state soon after the Mongol conquest. Under the loose authority of successive Chinese dynasties, the authorities encouraged Han Chinese migration to the region to dilute the large Tai-speaking populations. An official policy of assimilation into Han Chinese culture was carried out in the region. Officials of the Chinese Ming dynasty, in the 14th and 15th centuries, employed a system of divide and conquer, often pitting one ethnic group against another. Chinese interference and tensions between the Zhuang and the neighboring Yao erupted into open warfare leading to one of the bloodiest battled in Zhuang history; the clash between the two peoples at Big Rattan Gorge in 1465 left more than 20,000 people dead. In the mid-16th century, the Zhuang peoples again united to defeat an invasion from Japan. The Han Chinese took the best and most fertile lands, leaving the less productive and the mountainous regions to the indigenous peoples. The Manchu conquest of China in 1644 was followed by a change in the administration in the southern territories. The Manchu Qing dynasty imposed direct imperial administration on some of the Tai-speaking regions for the first time in 1650. By 1726, the Qing dynasty had brought all of the Zhuang peoples under direct imperial rule.

The Zhuang are historically known as the "water dwellers" as they customarily constructed their settlements close to water with many buildings on stilts or piles over water. The Zhuang are made up of many tribes, clans, and regional groups officially designated as the Zhuang ethnic group in China. Because they are primarily agriculturalists, they are often referred to a *T'u* meaning "people of the soil." The culture retains a wealth of legends, folktales, stories, and ballads that have been handed down from generation to generation. Singing is an important cultural element. Historically, every Zhuang community held regular songfests, allowing youngsters from surrounding villages to use music and song to court a prospective bride or groom. One of the most famous expressions of the Zhuang culture, which combines folk literature, music, dance, and art, is the Zhuang form of opera, which originated as early as the seventh century CE. Also thought to date from the same period is the Zhuang tradition of weaving brocade fabrics. Woven in spectacular designs with natural cotton, the brocade has been prized in China for centuries. Copper drums, sometimes weighing

up to a half ton, still form part of the culture though their original use is not clear. Traditionally, the Zhuang have practiced monogamy, though the ancient marriage traditions have given way to modern forms of courtship and marriage. Respect for the elderly, the source of wisdom, and the common care of children are important cultural traits. The language commonly referred to as the Zhuang language is in reality a group of some 16 mutually unintelligible languages of the Tai language family, often heavily influenced by Southwestern Mandarin Chinese. The Zhuang are an ethnic group but are not a linguistic group. The northern dialect of Zhuang has been adopted as the standard language, but many Zhuang people prefer to use the Chinese Mandarin or Cantonese languages for intergroup communications. The Zhuang script, known as *sawndip*, is still used for writing songs and for daily life. A Latin-based alphabet is used for the official standard Zhuang language, but it is not popular, and most people continue to use *sawndip* or the Chinese alphabet for writing. The Zhuang are polytheists, worshiping a pantheon of various gods and spirits, including the spirits of nature such as huge rocks or boulders, ancient trees, high mountains, various aspects of the landscape, snakes, birds, animals, and their own ancestors. Daoism has had a deep influence on the religious beliefs of the Zhuang peoples. There is a sizable minority that has adopted Buddhism with a small group that adopted the Christianity brought to the region by 19th-century European and American missionaries.

The territories in south China remained under the authority of the Manchu Qing dynasty, but the local rulers appointed by the

Qing court controlled most of the land with the majority of the Zhuang living as share-croppers or tenant farmers. In the mid-19th century, the French, having begun to take control of the Vietnamese territories to the south, attempted to extend their influence into the Zhuang regions of southern China. The French colonial authorities established a sphere of interest in the Zhuang region following the Franco-Chinese War of 1884–1885. In 1898, a weakened Qing dynasty was forced to allow the French wide powers in Guangxi and neighboring regions. Unhindered by the weakening Manchu rulers of China, French missionaries introduced Christianity, modern education, and the Latin alphabet to the Zhuang peoples. The turbulence of the last years of the Qing dynasty and the Chinese Revolution of 1911 gave the Zhuang effective control over their homeland under loose French authority from 1910 to 1916. The weak republic government of China exerted its authority in the region in 1916–1917, but its poor treatment of the Zhuang and other ethnic groups in the region rallied armed resistance to Han Chinese incursions in their homeland. Local Zhuang peasants organized to oppose Han Chinese domination and the abuses of the landowners. From 1926 to 1929, Zhuang militias effectively controlled most of the Tai-speaking regions until they were crushed by government troops. Local warlords took control of South China, which remained only under loose Chinese authority during the growing Chinese Civil War in the 1930s. An agreement between the warlords and the Chinese government allowed central authority to be reestablished in the region in 1936. Communist organizers infiltrated the

region during World War II, quickly taking control following the communist victory in the ongoing civil war in 1949. Greeted as liberators, the communists proved as brutal and unsympathetic to the non-Han Chinese peoples as had the former government. In 1950, the Zhuang rebelled with the covert aid of the French in Vietnam. Dubbed bandits by the new communist government, thousands were killed or executed before the revolt was ended in 1952. The Chinese government erected nominally autonomous regions for the Zhuang and other minority peoples, but collectivization of the land led to renewed conflicts. The Chinese Cultural Revolution from 1967 to 1977 saw Red Guard units rampaging through the region destroying all non-Han Chinese institutions, shrines, religious centers, and cultural sites. Many traditional Zhuang traditions and customs were outlawed as detrimental to progress. Assimilation into Han Chinese culture, considered more advanced among the Zhuang than in the other autonomous regions of the country, began to reverse in the 1990s with the new economic and political laws that provided more protection for minority cultures. In the 21st century, many young Zhuang, though eager to benefit from China's partially capitalist economy, are rediscovering their cultural roots with a new appreciation for the Zhuang dialects and the regional Tai culture.

Further Reading

Huang, Pingwen. "Sinification of the Zhuang People, Culture, and Their Language." Originally published in Ratree Wayland, John Harmann, and Paul Sidwell, eds. *SEALSXII: Papers from the 12th Meeting of the Southeast Asian Linguistics Society* (2002), Canberra, Pacific Linguistics, 2007,

89–100. http://sealang.net/sala/archives/pdf8/huang2002sinification.pdf

Johnson, Eric, and Wang Mingfu. *Zhuang Culture and Linguistic Heritage.* Kunming, China: SIL International and the Nationalities Publishing House, 2008.

Kaup, Kathering Palmer. *Creating the Zhuang: Ethnic Politics in China.* Boulder, CO: Lynne Rienner, 2000.

McCarthy, Susan K. *Communist Multiculturalism: Ethnic Revival in Southwest China.* Seattle: University of Washington, 2009.

Geographical Index

Index

Note: **Bold** page numbers refer to the main entries.

About the Author and Contributors

The Author

James B. Minahan has written a number of reference books on international statehood and identity, including ABC-CLIO's *Ethnic Groups of South Asia and the Pacific: An Encyclopedia* and *The Former Soviet Union's Diverse Peoples: A Reference Sourcebook* and Greenwood's *Encyclopedia of the Stateless Nations, One Europe, Many Nations: A Historical Dictionary of National Groups*, and *Miniature Empires*.

The Contributors

András Boros-Kazai is an adjunct associate professor of political science at Beloit College.

Robert André LaFleur is a professor of anthropology at Beloit College.